2000-2006
Neue Architektur in Südtirol
Architetture recenti in Alto Adige
New Architecture in South Tyrol

Bettina Schlorhaufer
Robert Fleischanderl (photography)
Südtiroler Künstlerbund
kunst Meran / Merano arte

This work is subject to copyright.
All rights are reserved, whether the whole or part of the material is concerned, specifically those of photos, texts, translation, reprinting, re-use of illustrations, broadcasting, reproduction by photocopying machines or similar means, and storage in data banks.

The use of registered names, trademarks, etc. in this publication does not imply, even in the absence of specific statement, that such names are exempt from the relevant protective laws and regulations and therefore free for general use.

© 2006 Springer-Verlag/Wien
Printed in Bolzano (Italy)

SpringerWienNewYork is a part of Springer Science+Business Media
springeronline.com

Layout: Gruppe Gut Gestaltung OHG, Bozen
Photos: Robert Fleischanderl (Innsbruck), Martin Geier (p. 27), Karl Spitaler (p. 105), Bettina Schlorhaufer (p. 29)
Texts: Bettina Schlorhaufer (Innsbruck), Roman Hollenstein (Zurich), Walter Zschokke (Vienna) und Joseph Grima (Milan)
Translation: Luigi Scolari, James Roderick O'Donovan and Norma Keßler
Lectorate: Esther Pirchner, Luigi Scolari, James Roderick O'Donovan und Cristina Vignocchi
Printing and binding: Athesia Druck, Bozen

Printed on acid-free and chlorine-free bleached paper

SPIN: 11774419

ISBN-10   3-211-29954-8 SpringerWienNewYork
ISBN-13   978-3-211-29954-8 SpringerWienNewYork

2000-2006
Neue Architektur in Südtirol
Architetture recenti in Alto Adige
New Architecture in South Tyrol

Bettina Schlorhaufer
Robert Fleischanderl photography
Südtiroler Künstlerbund
kunst Meran / Merano arte

SpringerWienNewYork

Inhaltsverzeichnis   Sommario   Summary

10	Bettina Schlorhaufer	Vorwort	Premessa	Preface
12	Bettina Schlorhaufer	Einmal 60 und einmal 10 – Viel Engagement in Sachen Architektur in Südtirol	60 e 10 anni – grande coinvolgimento per l'architettura in Alto Adige	Celebrating 60 years and 10 years – commitment in the cause of architecture in South Tyrol
18	Bettina Schlorhaufer	„Ich hab' von Südtirol geträumt ... "	"Ho sognato dell'Alto Adige ... "	"I dreamt of South Tyrol ... "
38	Joseph Grima	Ein Blick aus dem Süden	Un punto di vista da sud	My view is from the south
44	Roman Hollenstein	Weingrotten und golden schimmernde Pyramiden – Ein Blick von außen auf die Südtiroler Architektur	Grotte per il vino e sgargianti piramidi dorate. Uno sguardo dall'esterno sull'architettura altoatesina	Wine grottos and golden shimmering pyramids An outsider's view of architecture in South Tyrol
68	Walter Zschokke	Kritischer Blick auf die Bewahrung und Aktualisierung von alter Bausubstanz	Uno sguardo critico sulla conservazione e sull'adattamento agli usi contemporanei degli edifici storici	A critical view of the preservation and modernisation of existing building fabric
	Bettina Schlorhaufer	**Die Projekte**	**I progetti**	**Projects**
76		**Vinschgau**	**Val Venosta**	**Val Venosta**
	Architektur			
78	Arnold Gapp	Messner Mountain Museum „Ortles", Sulden	Messner Mountain Museum "Ortles", Solda	Messner Mountain Museum "Ortles", Solda
82	Arnold Gapp	Kleinsportanlagen und Mehrzweckgebäude, Tschengls, Laas	Impianto sportivo e sala polifunzionale, Cengles, Lasa	Sports facilities and multi-purpose building, Cengles, Lasa
86	ARCHITEKTEN Marx – Ladurner	Aufstockungen von Betriebsgebäuden und Errichtung von zwei Betriebswohnungen, Schlanders	Sopraelevazione di edifici produttivi e realizzazione di due appartamenti di servizio, Silandro	Addition of a storey to two company buildings with the construction of two company apartments, Silandro
90	Werner Tscholl	Haus Schöpf, Vezzan, Schlanders	Casa Schöpf, Vezzano, Silandro	Schöpf House, Vezzano, Silandro
94	Arnold Gapp	Bergstation Seilbahn St. Martin, Latsch	Stazione a monte della funivia di S. Martino, Laces	Ropeway mountain terminal S. Martino, Laces
98	Walter Dietl	Wiederinbetriebnahme der Eisenbahnlinie von Meran nach Mals, Erweiterung Remise Mals und Haltestellen der Vinschgerbahn	Riattivazione della linea ferroviaria Merano-Malles, ampliamento della rimessa di Malles e pensiline della ferrovia della Val Venosta	Revival of the old train line from Merano to Malles extension to Malles train shed and the stations of the Val Venosta railway line
104	Karl Spitaler	Fahrradverleih, Bahnhof Schlanders	Noleggio biciclette, stazione ferroviaria di Silandro	Bicycle hire facility, Silandro railway station
106	Architekturbüro D3	Bahnhof mit Jugendraum, Plaus	Stazione ferroviaria con centro giovanile, Plaus	Railway station and youth space, Plaus
110		**Meran-Bozen**	**Merano-Bolzano**	**Merano-Bolzano**
112	Hanspeter Abler Trojer	Bürogebäude Martin Geier, Algund	Edificio per uffici Martin Geier, Lagundo	Martin Geier office building, Lagundo
116	Matteo Thun	Pergola Residence, Algund	Pergola Residence, Lagundo	Pergola Residence, Lagundo
120	Markus Scherer, Walter Angonese, Klaus Hellweger	Südtiroler Landesmuseum für Kultur- und Landesgeschichte, Schloss Tirol bei Meran	Museo Provinciale di Storia e Cultura Sudtirolese, Castel Tirolo presso Merano	South Tyrol Museum of Cultural and Regional History, Schloss Tirol, near Merano

126	Höller & Klotzner Architekten	„kunst Meran im Haus der Sparkasse", Meran	Merano arte edificio Cassa di Risparmio, Merano	Merano arte in the Cassa di Risparmio building
130	Abram&Schnabl	Kurhauspassage, Meran	Kurhauspassage, Merano	Kurhaus arcade, Merano
134	Holzbox, Baugesellschaft Wolkenstein GmbH., Vorarlberger Ökohaus GmbH.	Wohnanlage Wolkenstein, Meran	Complesso residenziale, Wolkenstein Merano	Wolkenstein housing development, Merano
138	Oswald Zoeggeler	Villa Mozart, Meran	Villa Mozart, Merano	Villa Mozart, Merano
142	PVC – architects, Margit Klammer, Steiner Sarnen Schweiz	Die Gärten von Schloss Trauttmansdorff, Meran	I giardini di Castel Trauttmansdorff, Merano	The Gardens of Schloss Trauttmansdorff, Merano
148	S.O.F.A. architekten mit Georg Mitterhofer	Besucherzentrum „Die Gärten von Schloss Trauttmansdorff", Meran	Centro visite "I giardini del Castello di Trauttmansdorff", Merano	Visitors centre "The Gardens of Schloss Trauttmansdorff", Merano
152	Peter Plattner	Landwirtschaftliches Betriebsgebäude, Ladstätterhof, Sinich bei Meran	Azienda agricola Ladstätterhof, Sinigo presso Merano	Agricultural building, Ladstätterhof, Sinigo near Merano
156	Stefan Hitthaler	Mühlbauerhof, Gargazon	Mühlbauerhof, Gargazzone	Mühlbauer farm, Gargazzone
160	Walter Angonese, Silvia Boday	Personalwohnhaus Goëss-Enzenberg, Siebeneich	Residenza per il personale Goëss-Enzenberg, Settequerce	Goëss-Enzenberg staff residence, Settequerce
162		**Bozen-Tramin-Leifers**	**Bolzano-Termeno-Laives**	**Bolzano-Termeno-Laives**
164	Werner Tscholl	Haus Mumelter, Bozen	Casa Mumelter, Bolzano	Mumelter House, Bolzano
168	Pardeller+Putzer+Scherer	Turnhalle der deutschsprachigen Grundschule „A. Rosmini", Bozen-Gries	Palestra della scuola elementare di lingua tedesca "A. Rosmini", Bolzano-Gries	Gymnasium of the German-language elementary school "A. Rosmini", Bolzano-Gries
172	Christoph Mayr Fingerle	Realgymnasium, Bozen	Liceo scientifico, Bolzano	Secondary school, Bolzano
176	Stanislao Fierro	Tiefgarage und Neugestaltung Gerichtsplatz, Bozen	Autorimessa interrata e nuova configurazione di Piazza del Tribunale, Bolzano	Underground car park and redesign of Piazza del Tribunale, Bolzano
180	Klaus Kada	Europäische Akademie Bozen (EURAC), Bozen	Accademia Europea Bolzano (EURAC), Bolzano	European Academy Bozen (EURAC), Bolzano
186	Höller & Klotzner	Abbruch und Neubau Landesberufsschule, Bozen	Demolizione e nuova edificazione Scuola Professionale Provinciale, Bolzano	Demolition and new building, Regional Vocational School, Bolzano
192	Bischoff Azzola Architekten	Freie Universität Bozen, Bozen	Libera Università di Bolzano, Bolzano	Free University of Bozen, Bolzano
198	Peter Plattner	Sanierung und Erweiterung Haus Amonn, Bozen	Restauro e ampliamento di Casa Amonn, Bolzano	Renovation and extension to the Amonn House, Bolzano
202	Luigi Scolari	Neubau einer Industriehalle mit Bürotrakt, Firma BEL, Bozen	Nuova edificazione di un edificio industriale con uffici, ditta BEL, Bolzano	New industrial building with office wing, BEL Company, Bolzano
206	Lunz & Zöschg Architekten	Kindergarten Maria Rast, St. Michael, Eppan	Scuola materna Maria Rast, S. Michele, Appiano	Maria Rast Kindergarten, S. Michele, Appiano
210	Forer Unterpertinger Architekten	Sanierung und Erweiterung Lanserhaus, St. Michael, Eppan	Restauro ed ampliamento Lanserhaus, S. Michele, Appiano	Renovation and extension of the Lanserhaus, S. Michele, Appiano

214	Walter Angonese, Silvia Boday, Rainer Köberl	Weingut Manincor, Kaltern	Tenuta vinicola Manincor, Caldaro	Manincor vineyard, Caldaro
216	Silvia Boday	Haus an der Weinstraße, Tramin	Casa sulla Strada del Vino, Termeno	House on the Strada del Vino (wine road), Termeno
220	Wolfgang Piller	Oberschule für Landwirtschaft, Ansitz Baumgarten, Auer	Istituto Tecnico Agrario, Castel Baumgarten, Ora	Agricultural school, Baumgarten estate, Ora
224	Höller & Klotzner Architekten	Erweiterung Pfarrkirche, Leifers	Ampliamento della Chiesa Parrocchiale, Laives	Extension to Laives Parish Church, Laives
228		**Eisacktal**	**Val d'Isarco**	**Val d'Isarco**
230	Benno Barth	Haus Kaser, Brixen	Casa Kaser, Bressanone	Kaser House, Bressanone
234	Siegfried Delueg	Landesberufsschule und Studentenhaus, Brixen	Scuola Professionale Provinciale e studentato, Bressanone	Regional vocational school and student residence, Bressanone
242	MODUS architects	Kinder-Tagesbetreuungsstätte im Krankenhaus, Brixen	Centro bambino dell'ospedale di Bressanone	Children's day-care centre in the hospital, Bressanone
246	Gerd Bergmeister	Haus Sachsenklemme, Franzensfeste	Casa Sachsenklemme, Fortezza	Sachsenklemme House, Fortezza
250	Christian Schwienbacher	Wohnhaus in Stilfes, Freienfeld	Casa d'abitazione a Stilves, Campo di Trens	House in Stilfes, Campo di Trens
254		**Pustertal**	**Val Pusteria**	**Pustertal/Val Pusteria**
256	Mutschlechner & Mahlknecht	Neubau Mehrzweckgebäude am Bühel, St. Jakob im Ahrntal	Nuovo edificio polifunzionale a Monte, S. Giacomo in Valle Aurina	New multi-purpose building at Bühel, S. Giacomo in Valle Aurina
260	Mutschlechner & Mahlknecht	Sanierung Stein- und Holzhaus Dr. Tasser, Steinhaus im Ahrntal	Restauro della casa in pietra e legno del Dr. Tasser, Cadipietra in Valle Aurina	Renovation of the stone and timber built Dr. Tasser house, Cadipietra in Valle Aurina
264	Mutschlechner & Mahlknecht	Friedhofserweiterung, Luttach im Ahrntal	Ampliamento del cimitero, Luttago in Valle Aurina	Cemetery extension, Luttago in Valle Aurina
268	Bruno Rubner, dkp_architektur, dreiplus_architektur	Wohnanlage G3D, Bruneck-Stegen	Complesso residenziale G3D, Brunico-Stegona	G3D housing development, Brunico-Stegona
272	Comfort_Architecten	Haus Sonne, St. Lorenzen	Casa Sonne, S. Lorenzo di Sebato	Sonne House, S. Lorenzo di Sebato
276	Architekturbüro D3	Gesundheits- und Sozialsprengel Gadertal, Pikolein, St. Martin in Thurn	Unità socio-sanitaria locale Val Badia, Piccolino, S. Martino in Badia	Gadertal health and social services centre, Piccolino, S. Martino in Badia
280	aichner_seidl ARCHITEKTEN	Haus Huber Schnarf, Olang	Casa Huber Schnarf, Valdaora	Huber Schnarf House, Valdaora
284	Siegfried Delueg	Fernheizwerk, Sexten	Centrale di teleriscaldamento, Sesto	District heating plant, Sesto
288		Baudaten	Dati dei progetti	Construction Data
300		Architekten	Architetti	Architects
308		Autoren, Fotograf	Autori, fotografo	Authors, photographer

Texte   Testi   Texts

Bettina Schlorhaufer
Vorwort

Die vorliegende Publikation „2000–2006 Neue Architektur in Südtirol" entstand in Verbindung mit der gleichnamigen Wanderausstellung und aus Anlass der Jubiläen „60 Jahre Südtiroler Künstlerbund" und „10 Jahre kunst Meran im Haus der Sparkasse". Die beiden bekannten Südtiroler Kultureinrichtungen befassen sich seit ihrer Gründung mit dem Thema Architektur. Es lag nahe, gemeinsam ein groß angelegtes Jubiläums-Ausstellungsprojekt zur neuesten Architektur in Südtirol zu verwirklichen. Diese Ausstellung wurde für die Räume von „kunst Meran" konzipiert, jedoch auch in Hinblick darauf, sie auf Reisen zu schicken.

Der Arbeitsgruppe gehörten von Seiten des Südtiroler Künstlerbundes die Architektin Helga von Aufschnaiter-Straudi (Präsidentin des Südtiroler Künstlerbundes) und der Architekt Wolfgang Piller (Vorstand der Fachgruppe Architektur des Südtiroler Künstlerbundes) an. Für „kunst Meran" engagierten sich die Geschäftsführerin des Ausstellungshauses, Herta Wolf-Torggler, die Architektin Angelika Margesin sowie die Architekten Georg Klotzner (Präsident des Trägervereins von „kunst Meran") und Markus Scherer. Sie stellten sich der schwierigen Aufgabe, ein Konzept für ein möglichst objektives Auswahlverfahren zu entwerfen, durch das die besten Bauvorhaben der letzten Jahre ermittelt werden sollten. Ich möchte in diesem Zusammenhang auch ein persönliches Dankeswort an die Arbeitsgruppe richten, da ich bald nach Beginn des Projekts in dieses Gremium berufen und zur Kuratorin eines Ausstellungs- und Publikationsprojekts bestellt wurde, das zwar äußerst arbeitsintensiv war,

Premessa

La presente pubblicazione "2000 - 2006 Architetture recenti in Alto Adige", nasce in concomitanza con l'omonima mostra itinerante, e in occasione di due anniversari, rispettivamente: i 60 anni del Südtiroler Künstlerbund e i 10 anni di Merano arte edificio Cassa di Risparmio. Le due note istituzioni culturali altoatesine si occupano, fin dalla loro fondazione, di tematiche strettamente collegate all'architettura. La realizzazione di questo progetto è la logica conseguenza della celebrazione degli anniversari e rappresenta la grande opportunità di realizzare una mostra sulla nuova architettura in Alto Adige. Questa mostra è stata concepita per gli spazi di Merano arte, ma anche per essere itinerante.

Il gruppo di lavoro era composto, per il Südtiroler Künstlerbund dall'architetto Helga von Aufschnaiter-Straudi, (presidente del Südtiroler Künstlerbund), e dall'architetto Wolfgang Piller (capogruppo della sezione architettura). Per Merano arte hanno invece collaborato la direttrice del centro espositivo Herta Wolf Torggler e gli architetti Angelica Margesin, Markus Scherer e Georg Klotzner (presidente dell'istituzione meranese). A loro è spettato il difficile compito di definire un metodo di selezione, il più possibile obiettivo, per riconoscere le migliori costruzioni degli ultimi anni. In questo contesto mi sento di dover ringraziare personalmente il gruppo di lavoro, al quale sono stata chiamata a partecipare sin dalle prime fasi, come curatrice del progetto espositivo ed editoriale. Questo ruolo mi ha vista estremamente impegnata, ma allo stesso tempo mi ha offerto la grande e rara opportunità di potermi confrontare con diversi scenari dell'architettura.

Preface

This publication "2000–2006 New Architecture in South Tyrol" was produced in conjunction with a travelling exhibition of the same name on the occasion of two anniversaries: "60 Years of the South Tyrol Artists' Association" and "10 Years of Merano arte in the Sparkasse Building". Since they were founded both these South Tyrol cultural facilities have dealt with the theme of architecture. It therefore seemed sensible for them to join forces in organizing a major anniversary exhibition project on recent architecture in South Tyrol. The exhibition was designed for the rooms of Merano arte, but always taking into account that it would later start to travel.

The members of the working group from the Südtiroler Künstlerbund (South Tyrol Artists Association) were architect Helga von Aufschnaiter-Straudi (President of the Südtiroler Künstlerbund) and architect Wolfgang Piller (head of the specialist group for architecture in the Südtiroler Künstlerbund). For Merano arte the manager of the exhibition building, Herta Wolf-Torggler, architect Angelika Margesin as well as architects Georg Klotzner (president of the central association that operates Merano arte) and Markus Scherer were involved. These people undertook the difficult task of devising a fair selection procedure to choose the best building projects of recent years. In this context I should like to add a personal word of thanks to the working group, as shortly after the start of the project I was invited to sit on this body and was appointed curator of the exhibition and publication project. While this meant a great deal of intensive work it also offered me a rare opportunity to examine in depth an

gleichzeitig aber die Gelegenheit bot, mich in einem selten großen und anspruchsvollen Ausmaß mit einer zugleich interessanten und überaus vielfältigen Architekturlandschaft auseinander zu setzen.

Darüber hinaus betrauten der Südtiroler Künstlerbund und „kunst Meran" auch eine internationale Jury mit der Aufgabe, maximal 50 Bauten aus ganz Südtirol für Buch und Ausstellung zu nominieren. Dieser Jury gehörten Architekt Joseph Grima (Domus, Mailand), Kunsthistoriker Roman Hollenstein (Neue Zürcher Zeitung, Zürich), Architekt Hanno Schlögl (Innsbruck) und ich an. Joseph Grima und Roman Hollenstein standen dem Projekt nicht nur als Juroren zur Verfügung, sondern schrieben auch Texte für diese Publikation, in denen sie ihre persönlichen Eindrücke von der „Neuen Architektur in Südtirol" darlegten. Als weiterer Fachautor war Walter Zschokke aus Wien tätig, der über eines seiner „Spezialgebiete", nämlich die Verbindung von historischer Bausubstanz mit neuer Architektur, einen Beitrag verfasste.

Keine Kuratorin wirkt alleine, ohne Vernetzung mit einem Team. Dieses Team ist letztendlich für die sicht- und lesbare Qualität eines Projekts ausschlaggebend: Fotograf Robert Fleischanderl unternahm für dieses Buch und die Ausstellung den Versuch, neue Bauten nicht nur als Objekte abzulichten, sondern sie auch mit den Menschen zu fotografieren, die sie beleben. Manche von ihnen hat er auch porträtiert und darüber befragt, wie sie der neuen Architektur gegenüberstehen. Die „Gruppe Gut" gestaltete die Grafik und sorgte dafür, dass die Beiträge von uns Autoren, zusammen mit den Plänen der Architekten und den Fotos ein ansprechendes Gesamt-Erscheinungsbild erhielten. Esther Pirchner lektorierte alle deutschsprachigen, Christina Vignocchi die italienischen Texte. Die Übersetzerin Norma Keßler und die Übersetzer James Roderick O'Donovan und Luigi Scolari übertrugen sie ins Deutsche bzw. Englische und Italienische. Allen, die zum Zustandekommen dieses Projektes einen Beitrag geleistet haben, gebührt großer Dank für die kompetente und harmonische Zusammenarbeit.

Innsbruck-Bozen-Meran, Dezember 2005

Il Südtiroler Künstlerbund e Merano arte hanno incaricato una giuria internazionale di selezionare un massimo di 50 edifici provenienti da tutto l' Alto Adige, per la mostra e il catalogo.

Facevano parte della giuria l'architetto Joseph Grima (Domus, Milano), lo storico dell'arte Roman Hollenstein (Neue Zürcher Zeitung, Zurigo), l'architetto Hanno Schlögl (Innsbruck), ed io. Joseph Grima e Roman Hollenstein non facevano solo parte della giuria ma hanno scritto anche i testi per questa pubblicazione nei quali hanno espresso la loro visione personale riguardo le "architetture recenti in Alto Adige". Walter Zschokke architetto e pubblicista di Vienna, ha curato un contributo relativo a uno dei suoi "specifici campi di interesse", ovvero il rapporto di dialogo tra architettura storica e contemporanea

Nessun curatore agisce da solo, senza relazionarsi ad un gruppo di lavoro. Questo gruppo è determinante per dare leggibilità e visibilità alla qualità del progetto: il fotografo Robert Fleischanderl ha intrapreso l'esperimento di mettere in luce i nuovi edifici non solo in quanto oggetti, ma di fotografarli con le persone che li abitano e vivono. Ad alcuni di loro ha fatto dei ritratti e li ha intervistati chiedendo in che rapporto si ponevano con la nuova architettura. "Gruppe Gut", si è occupato della grafica, cercando di rendere i contributi di noi autori, i progetti degli architetti e le foto in una veste accattivante. Esther Pirchner ha supervisionato i testi in lingua tedesca e Cristina Vignocchi quelli in lingua italiana. La traduttrice Norma Keßler e i traduttori James Roderick O'Donovan e Luigi Scolari si sono occupati delle versioni dal tedesco all'inglese e dal tedesco all'italiano. A tutti coloro che hanno contribuito a questo progetto va il mio grande ringraziamento per l' armonia e la competenza con i quali si è svolta la collaborazione.

Innsbruck-Bolzano-Merano, Dicembre 2005

interesting and varied architecture landscape.

The Südtiroler Künstlerbund and Merano arte also entrusted an international jury with the task of nominating a maximum of 50 buildings from throughout South Tyrol for the book and the exhibition. This jury included architect Joseph Grima (Domus, Milan), art historian Roman Hollenstein (Neue Zürcher Zeitung, Zurich), architect Hanno Schlögl (Innsbruck) and myself. Joseph Grima and Roman Hollenstein were not merely jurors but also wrote texts for the book in which they offer their personal impressions of "New Architecture in South Tyrol". Walter Zschokke, who is based in Vienna, was also invited as a guest author and provided a contribution on one of his "specialist" areas, namely the combination of new architecture with historical building substance.

No curator works without the back-up support of a team, which is ultimately responsible for the visual and legible quality of the project: photographer Robert Fleischanderl undertook an experiment for the book and exhibition. Instead of photographing the buildings as objects he sought to include the people who use them and give them life. He also made portraits of a number of these people, and asked them how they like the new architecture. "Gruppe Gut" were responsible for the graphic design and composed the authors' contributions, architects' plans and the photographs into an appropriate overall appearance. Esther Pirchner proofread all the texts written in German, Christina Vignocchi the Italian ones. The translators Norma Keßler, James Roderick O'Donovan and Luigi Scolari translated these texts into German, English and Italian respectively. To all those who contributed to bringing this project to fruition I wish here to express my sincere thanks for their competent and harmonious collaboration.

Innsbruck-Bolzano-Merano, December 2005

Bettina Schlorhaufer

Einmal 60 und einmal 10 – Viel Engagement in Sachen Architektur in Südtirol

Mit dem Ausstellungs- und Publikationsprojekt „2000–2006 Neue Architektur in Südtirol" werden zwei Jubiläen feierlich begangen, der 60. Geburtstag des Südtiroler Künstlerbundes und der zehnte von „kunst Meran im Haus der Sparkasse". Beide Einrichtungen sind aus dem Südtiroler Kulturgeschehen seit langem nicht mehr wegzudenken. Wie sehr sich gerade diese beiden Institutionen um die Vermittlung von zeitgenössischer Architektur bemühen, ist einem überregionalen Leserkreis aber weniger bekannt. Daher soll aus Anlass der runden Geburtstage auch ein kleiner Überblick über die Tätigkeit der beiden Kultureinrichtungen in Sachen Architektur geboten werden.

Südtiroler Künstlerbund, 1946 bis 2006

Der Südtiroler Künstlerbund wurde 1946, also unmittelbar nach Kriegsende, ins Leben gerufen. „Ordentliche Mitglieder können sein", heißt es in der Gründungsschrift der Standesvertretung der Künstler: „Maler, Grafiker, Bildhauer, Architekten, Kunstgewerbler im schöpferischen Sinne, Schriftsteller, Komponisten und Kunstwissenschaftler".[1] Derzeit gehören der Künstlervereinigung im nördlichsten – deutsch,

60 e 10 anni – grande coinvolgimento per l'architettura in Alto Adige

La mostra e il progetto editoriale ad essa collegato "2000-2006 Architetture recenti in Alto Adige", celebrano gli anniversari per i 60 anni del Südtiroler Künstlerbund, e i 10 anni di Merano arte edificio Cassa di Risparmio. Entrambe le istituzioni sono da considerarsi da tempo inscindibili dalla scena culturale altoatesina. Il grande impegno che entrambe le istituzioni hanno investito nella promozione dell'architettura contemporanea, è però poco noto ai lettori di ambito sovraregionale. L'occasione di questi importanti anniversari diventa pretesto per far conoscere le attività legate all'architettura svolte dalle due istituzioni culturali.

Il Südtiroler Künstlerbund, dal 1946 al 2006

Il Südtiroler Künstlerbund è stato fondato nel 1946, alla fine del secondo conflitto mondiale. Come si evince dallo statuto "Possono diventare soci: pittori, grafici, scultori, architetti, creativi in ambito artistico in senso lato, scrittori, compositori e studiosi d'arte".[1] Attualmente fanno parte dell'associazione di artisti più a nord d'Italia, circa 300 rappresentanti di tutte le discipline ed appartenenti ai tre gruppi linguistici, quel-

Celebrating 60 years and 10 years – commitment in the cause of architecture in South Tyrol

The exhibition and publication project "2000–2006 New Architecture in South Tyrol" marks the occasion of two anniversaries: the sixtieth birthday of the Südtiroler Künstlerbund and the tenth birthday of "Merano arte im Haus der Sparkasse". Both associations have long been an integral part of the cultural scene in South Tyrol. But readers from outside the region are possibly unaware of the efforts made by these institutions in the cause of contemporary architecture. Given this fact, these anniversaries offer a fitting occasion to review the activities of both these cultural facilities in the field of architecture.

Südtiroler Künstlerbund (South Tyrol Artists' Association) 1946 to 2006

The "Südtiroler Künstlerbund" was founded in 1946, directly following the end of the war. In the founding charter of this artists' representative body it is stated: "Membership is open to painters, graphic artists, sculptors, architects, creative applied artists, writers, composers and art historians."[1] At present this artists' association in the northernmost region of Italy where German, Italian and Ladin are spoken, has

italienisch- und ladinischsprachigen – Landesteil Italiens rund 300 Personen aus allen genannten Sparten an. Denn im Unterschied z. B. zur Tiroler Künstlerschaft in Österreich, die hauptsächlich bildende Kunstler aufnimmt, ist der Südtiroler Künstlerbund seit seiner Gründung interdisziplinär organisiert. Als Beispiel dafür, dass gerade die spartenübergreifende Tätigkeit des Südtiroler Künstlerbundes direkte Auswirkungen auf die Belebung der Architekturvermittlung nach außen hat, kann der Hinweis dienen, dass sich der Südtiroler Künstlerbund im Jahr 2004 dafür einsetzte, dass neben dem von der Stiftung der Kammer der Architekten[2] im Zwei-Jahres-Rhythmus durchgeführten „Südtiroler Landespreis für Architektur" auch ein „Südtiroler Landespreis für Kunst am Bau" ausgeschrieben wird. Umgesetzt wurde diese Initiative noch im selben Jahr vom Südtiroler Künstlerbund und der Stiftung der Kammer der Architekten gemeinsam. Über die Grundsätze des neuen Südtiroler Landespreises für Kunst am Bau hieß es im ersten Juryprotokoll: „Im besten Fall entsteht ein Kunst am Bau-Vorhaben gemeinsam und in zeitlicher Korrespondenz mit einem architektonischen Projekt. Das Ergebnis einer direkten Zusammenarbeit zwischen einem oder mehreren Künstlern und einem Architekten bzw. einer Architektengemeinschaft sollte sichtbar sein."[3] Das war der Grund, weshalb in dieser Publikation zum Thema neue Architektur in Südtirol der Kunst am Bau Platz eingeräumt wurde. Im Rahmen der detaillierten Vorstellung der 48 ausgewählten Bauten aus allen Landesteilen und ihrer Architekten werden jeweils auch die am Projekt beteiligten Künstler genannt, die das optische Erscheinungsbild eines architektonischen Programms mitbestimmten bzw. akzentuierten.

Als der Südtiroler Künstlerbund ins Leben gerufen wurde, diente er vor allem als Kommunikationsinstrument für die deutschsprachigen Künstler, und die erste Gemeinschaftsausstellung fand im Dezember 1946 im damals noch von Bombentreffern beschädigten Bozner Stadtmuseum statt. Die Fachgruppe Architektur des Südtiroler Künstlerbundes umfasst derzeit 45 Mitglieder, die von einem Fachgruppen-Vor-

lo tedesco, italiano e ladino. A differenza, ad esempio, del Tiroler Künstlerschaft (l'associazione degli artisti austriaci) che si occupa principalmente di arti visive, il Südtiroler Künstlerbund prevede sin dalla sua fondazione un'impostazione interdisciplinare. Il "Premio Arte nell'Architettura", indetto ogni due anni dal Südtiroler Künstlerbund accanto al "Premio Architettura in Alto Adige" promosso dalla Fondazione dell'Ordine degli Architetti[2] è un valido esempio di come l'attività interdisciplinare del Südtiroler Kunstlerbund influisca attivamente nella promozione dell'architettura. Contemporaneamente all'istituzione del premio è nata la collaborazione delle due istituzioni. Riguardo ai principi del nuovo "Premio Arte nell' Architettura in Alto Adige", si legge nel primo protocollo della giuria: "Nel migliore dei casi l'intervento artistico per l'architettura nasce insieme e contemporaneamente al progetto architettonico. Il risultato della collaborazione diretta tra uno o più artisti e un architetto, o un gruppo di architetti deve essere immediatamente percepibile."[3] Questo è il motivo per cui questa pubblicazione sull'architettura in Alto Adige coinvolge l'arte nelle costruzioni. Insieme alla descrizione dettagliata dei 48 progetti selezionati in tutta la provincia, con i loro architetti vengono anche nominati gli artisti che hanno partecipato ai progetti, collaborando a definire e caratterizzare l'aspetto estetico dell'opera edificata.

Quando il Südtiroler Künstlerbund fu fondato, esso era inteso come uno strumento di espressione degli artisti di lingua tedesca, e la prima mostra collettiva si tenne nel 1946, nella sede del Museo Civico allora ancora danneggiato dalle bombe. La sezione di architettura del Künstlerbund conta 45 soci, che si rimettono ad un direttivo. Una volta all'anno questo gruppo di lavoro organizza una mostra di architettura presso il centro espositivo dell'associazione, la Galleria Prisma a Bolzano. Nell'ambito di queste esposizioni vengono presentati architetti locali (Othmar Barth, Werner Tscholl, Karl Spitaler, Wolfgang Piller, Höller & Klotzner Architekten e Walter Dietl), ma anche i colleghi e colleghe internazionali che hanno contatti con l'Alto Adige, tra gli altri i progetti dell'architetto Klaus

around 300 members from all these different branches of the arts. For, in contrast to the Tiroler Künstlerschaft in Austria that is principally made up of visual artists, since its inception the "Südtiroler Künstlerbund" has been organized in an interdisciplinary way. That the activities of this association, which extend across the boundaries between the different categories of art, have a direct effect on the promotion of architecture is shown by the fact that in 2004 the "Südtiroler Künstlerbund" campaigned for the establishment of a South Tyrol Regional Prize for Site-specific Art that would complement the South Tyrol Regional Prize for Architecture, which is awarded every two years by a foundation of the Chamber of Architects.[2]

The "Südtiroler Künstlerbund" implemented this goal in the same year in conjunction with the Chamber of Architects foundation. The principles behind the new award are defined in the jury minutes: "In the best of cases a site-specific art work is made jointly and in a temporal relationship with an architectural project. It should be clearly perceptible that the work is the outcome of direct collaboration between one or more artists and an architect or group of architects."[3] This explains why in this publication on the theme of new architecture in South Tyrol space has been devoted to site-specific art. In the detailed presentation of the 48 selected projects (and their architects) from all parts of the region the artists involved in the project are also named, as they helped to determine or accentuate the appearance of the architectural programme. When founded the "Südtiroler Künstlerbund" served primarily as a means of communication for German-speaking artists in the region. The first exhibition was held in 1946 in the Bolzano Town Museum, which at that time still showed the signs of bomb damage. The specialist group for architecture in the "Südtiroler Künstlerbund" is at present made up of 45 members whose interests are represented by an executive council. This council organizes an annual architecture exhibition that is held in the Gallery Prisma in Bolzano, the association's presentation centre. In these exhibitions the works of local architects (for example Oth-

stand betreut werden. Diese Fachgruppe organisiert im Präsentationszentrum des Südtiroler Künstlerbundes, der Galerie Prisma in Bozen, einmal jährlich eine Architekturausstellung. Im Rahmen dieser Ausstellungen werden sowohl Arbeiten von einheimischen Architekten gezeigt (z. B. Othmar Barth, Werner Tscholl, Karl Spitaler, Wolfgang Piller, Höller & Klotzner Architekten und zuletzt Walter Dietl) als auch die internationaler Kolleginnen und Kollegen mit Südtirolbezug, u. a. Projekte vom in Graz und Aachen wirkenden Klaus Kada, dem Architekten der EURAC, der Europäischen Akademie Bozen, oder von Matteo Thun, der zwar aus Südtirol stammt, aber seit vielen Jahren in Mailand lebt.

Ein weiteres Tätigkeitsfeld der Fachgruppe Architektur des Südtiroler Künstlerbundes ist die Organisation von Exkursionen zu neuen Bauten in Südtirol, aber auch von Informationsfahrten ins Ausland.

„kunst Meran im Haus der Sparkasse", 1996 bis 2006

Das Domizil von „kunst Meran im Haus der Sparkasse" wird im Rahmen von „2000–2006 Neue Architektur in Südtirol" noch an anderer Stelle präsentiert, trotzdem darf hier der Hinweis nicht fehlen, dass zwar die Trägerinstitution einen runden Geburtstag feiert, nicht aber das Kunsthaus, das erst 2001 eröffnet wurde: Zuerst siedelte sich die Kultureinrichtung „artFORUM" in einer Geschäftspassage in der Meraner Altstadt an. Bei ihrer Gründung ging eine Hand voll engagierter Personen daran, ein wenig an Merans verstaubtem Flair einer habsburgischen Kurstadt zu kratzen, deren große Vergangenheit mit dem Ausbruch des Ersten Weltkriegs geendet hatte. Mit der „artFORUM Gallery" wurde ein Ort der Begegnung mit neuen künstlerischen Ausdrucksformen, z. B. Medienkunst, geschaffen, die Betreiber der Galerie entschieden aber bald, ihre Ziele in größerem Umfang zu verwirklichen. 2001 übersiedelte das „artFORUM" in ein neues Haus in den historischen Meraner Lauben und änderte gleichzeitig seinen Namen in „kunst Meran im Haus der Sparkasse". Die Umwandlung der alten Bausubstanz zu einem Kunsthaus geschah ganz im Stil des ehemaligen „art-

Kada attivo a Graz ed Aachen, l'architetto dell'EURAC, l'Accademia Europea di Bolzano, o di Matteo Thun, nativo di Bolzano ma trasferitosi a Milano. Un'altra prerogativa dell'attività del gruppo di architettura del Künstlerbund è l'organizzazione in Alto Adige e viaggi all'estero per informare e aggiornare sulla nuova architettura.

"Merano arte edificio Cassa di Risparmio" dal 1996 al 2006

La sede di Merano arte edificio Cassa di Risparmio verrà presentata anche in altri luoghi grazie alla mostra "2000-2006 Architetture recenti in Alto Adige" verrà presentata anche in altri luoghi, tuttavia non deve mancare la precisazione che è l'istituzione a festeggiare il suo compleanno e non l'edificio che la ospita inaugurato nel 2001.

Inizialmente l'associazione culturale artFORUM era locata in una galleria commerciale del centro storico di Merano. Alla nascita dell'associazione, un gruppo ristretto di persone motivate si è adoprata per togliere a Merano quella vecchia ed impolverata atmosfera di un "centro termale asburgico", il cui fascino si era spento allo scoppiare del primo conflitto mondiale.

artFORUM gallery era divenuto un luogo di incontro caratterizzato da nuove forme di espressione artistica, come ad esempio l'area multimediale. I curatori della decisero ben presto di ampliare maggiormente i loro obiettivi. Nel 2001 artFORUM si è trasferito nella nuova sede, del palazzo storico dei Portici di Merano ed al contempo ha cambiato il suo nome in Merano arte edificio Cassa di Risparmio. La trasformazione

mar Barth, Werner Tscholl, Karl Spitaler, Wolfgang Piller, Höller & Klotzner Architekten and, most recently, Walter Dietl) are presented, as well as work by international architects with a link to South Tyrol including projects by Graz and Aachen-based Klaus Kada, the designer of EURAC (the European Academy Bolzano) or by Matteo Thun, who comes originally from South Tyrol but has lived for many years in Milan..

The special group for architecture within the "Südtiroler Künstlerbund" also organises excursions to new buildings in South Tyrol as well as planning information-gathering trips abroad.

"Merano arte edificio Cassa di Risparmio" from 1996 to 2006

In the context of "2000–2006 New Architecture in South Tyrol" the present home of "Merano arte edificio Cassa di Risparmio" is presented elsewhere, but nevertheless it should be pointed out here that it is the institution which is celebrating a "special" birthday and not the "Kunsthaus", which was only opened in 2001. Initially the cultural association "artFORUM" was set up in a shopping arcade in the city centre of Merano. A handful of committed individuals attempted to offer an alternative to Merano's faded flair as a Habsburg spa town whose heyday had ended with the start of the First World War. The "artFORUM" gallery provided a place to encounter new artistic forms of expression, for example media art, but those who ran the gallery soon decided that their goals could best be met in more spacious surroundings. In 2001 "artFORUM" moved into a new building in the historic Merano Portici (arcades) and changed its name into "Merano arte edificio Cassa di Risparmio". The transformation of the old building substance into a "Kunsthaus" (literally: art house) was carried out very much in the style of the former "artFORUM". Not only does the new premises provide a place

FORUMs", denn dort ist nicht nur die Begegnung mit zeitgenössischer Kunst möglich, mit der Einrichtung eines Cafés wurde auch ein neuer Treffpunkt in Meran geschaffen.

Wie der Südtiroler Künstlerbund ist „kunst Meran" nicht nur auf dem Gebiet der bildenden Kunst, sondern auch auf dem der Literatur, Musik und nicht zuletzt der Architektur tätig. Zu den Schwerpunkten der Meraner Kultureinrichtung gehört die Präsentation der Arbeiten junger Künstler bzw. junger Kunstströmungen. Das jährliche Besucheraufkommen liegt bei 10.000 bis 12.000, was für ein kleinstädtisches Ausstellungszentrum für Gegenwartskunst wirklich beachtlich ist.

Ausschlaggebend für die stete Präsenz von Architektur im Konzept von „artFORUM" und „kunst Meran" war wohl zuerst die engagierte Mitwirkung von Architekten im Trägerverein (dieser umfasst gegenwärtig 29 Personen) und die interessierte Teilnahme lokaler Baukünstler an den Veranstaltungen seiner Ausstellungszentren. Mittlerweile hat sich aber die Präsentation von Architektur zu einem festen Bestandteil des jährlichen Ausstellungsprogramms entwickelt. Ein Blick auf die Architektur-Ausstellungen seit 1996 verrät, dass „artFORUM" und „kunst Meran" ihr Publikum spezifisch mit der Baukunst im Alpenraum, junger Architektur bzw. im Fall von Delugan_Meissl mit dem Schaffen von „Auslands-Meranern" konfrontiert haben: Carlo Baumschlager und Dietmar Eberle (1996); Architekturparallelen – 80 Projekte aus dem Alpen-Adria-Raum (1997); Holz und Architektur – Tradition und Entwicklung der Vorarlberger Holzbauschule (1998); 8 & WILLEM – Junge Architektur aus Frankreich (1999); Architektur.Szene Österreich (2000); Ingenieurdenken – Jürg Conzett aus Chur (2001); State of Flux – Delugan_Meissl – Architects (2002); .scapes (2003/04); Gion A. Caminada – Cul zuffel e l'aura dado (2005).

Die Aktivitäten von „kunst Meran" auf dem Gebiet der Architektur beziehen sich längst nicht mehr auf die Übernahme von Ausstellungen, vielmehr gehören die Produktion von Architekturausstellungen und die Edition von Architekturbüchern genauso zu den Tätigkeiten des Ausstellungshauses

dell'antico edificio in una casa per l'arte è avvenuto nello stile del precedente artFORUM, infatti in questa sede, oltre alla possibilità di confrontarsi con l'arte contemporanea, con l'apertura del caffè si è creato anche un luogo di ritrovo a Merano. Come il Südtiroler Künstlerbund anche Merano arte non si occupa solo di arti visive ma, ma anche di letteratura, musica e non ultima l'architettura. Una delle attività principali del centro culturale meranese è la presentazione del lavoro dei giovani artisti e delle attuali correnti artistiche. Annualmente si contano tra le 10.000 e 12.000 presenze di visitatori, un successo degno di nota per un centro espositivo per l'arte contemporanea di una piccola cittadina.

Decisiva la costante presenza dell'architettura nelle iniziative di artFORUM e Merano arte è stato sin dall'inizio l'inserimento di architetti nel consiglio amministrativo dell'associazione (che consta di 29 persone) e la partecipazione interessata di architetti locali all'attività del suo centro espositivo. Nel frattempo, le mostre di architettura sono divenute parte integrante dell'annuale programma espositivo. Uno sguardo alle mostre di architettura dal 1996 svela che artFORUM e Merano arte hanno confrontato il loro pubblico in modo specifico con l'architettura dell'arco alpino, con la produzione di giovani architetti, e nel caso di Delugan-Meissl con il lavoro degli "altoatesini all'estero", Carlo Baumschlager e Dietmar Eberle (1996); Architettura e paralleli – 80 progetti nella zona dell'Alpe-Adria (1997); Legno e Architettura – tradizione e sviluppo della scuola per la lavorazione del legno nel Vorarlberger (1998); 8 & WILLEM – giovane architettura francese (1999); La scena architettonica austriaca (2000); Il pensiero ingegneristico – Jürg Conzett di Chur (2001); State of Flux – Delugan_Meissl – Architects (2002); .scapes (2003/04); Gion A. Caminada – Cul zuffel e l'aura dado (2005).

Le attività di Merano arte in ambito architettonico, da tempo, non si limitano più ad ospitare mostre di architettura preconfezionate, ma piuttosto realizza proprie esposizioni e progetti editoriali di architettura e organizza attività collaterali pertinenti alle mostre. Obiettivo è quello di richiamare l'attenzione del pubblico sulle relazioni

to view contemporary art but the opening of a café there has provided Merano with a new meeting place.

Like the "Südtiroler Künstlerbund" Merano arte does not restrict its activities to the area of visual art but is also involved in the fields of music, literature and, not least importantly, architecture. The focal points of the Merano culture facility include the presentation of the work of young artists and recent directions in art. The annual number of visitors lies between ten and twelve thousand, which is quite remarkable for an exhibition centre for contemporary art.

The committed involvement of a number of architects in the central association (presently composed of 29 people) along with the participation of local architects in the events held in the exhibition centres was decisive in the ensuring the continued presence of architecture in "artFORUM" and Merano arte. By now the presentation of architecture is a fixed part of the annual exhibition programme. A look at the architecture exhibitions since 1996 reveals that "artFORUM" and Merano arte have confronted their public specifically with architecture in the Alpine area or, as in the case of Delugan_Meissl, with work produced by émigré natives of Merano. Exhibitions in recent years include: Carlo Baumschlager and Dietmar Eberle (1996); "Architecture Parallels – 80 Projects from the Alpine-Adriatic Region" (1997); "Wood and Architecture – Tradition and Development of the Vorarlberg School of Timber Building" (1998); "8 & WILLEM – Young Architecture from France" (1999); "Architecture Scene Austria" (2000); "Engineers Thinking – Jürg Conzett from Chur" (2001); "State of Flux – Delugan_Meissl – Architects" (2002); ".scapes" (2003/04); "Gion A. Caminada – Cul zuffel e l'aura dado" (2005).

For some time the activities of Merano arte in the field of architecture have no longer been confined to showing travelling exhibitions from elsewhere, the production of their own architecture shows and of books on architecture now forms an important part of the activities of the exhibition centre as does the organisation of events specifically tailored to accompany the exhibitions.

wie die Organisation von spezifisch auf die Ausstellungen abgestimmten Begleitveranstaltungen. Ziel dieser Rahmenprogramme ist es, die Besucher auf die Bezugspunkte zwischen der Präsentation eines Themas oder des Schaffens eines Architekten und der eigenen Architekturlandschaft aufmerksam zu machen. Zu den im Jahresrhythmus stattfindenden Architekturausstellungen wurden daher jeweils auch Diskussionen, Vorträge und Exkursionen organisiert, deren Aufgabe es ist, nachhaltige Ergebnisse einer Kulturarbeit in Sachen Architektur für das Land Südtirol und darüber hinaus zu schaffen.

esistenti tra la presentazione del tema di architettura o di attività di un architetto e l'esperienza architettonica individuale e locale.
Nella sequenza annuale di esposizioni di architettura, si inseriscono pertanto anche dibattiti, conferenze ed escursioni, che hanno la funzione di rendere concreto l'impegno culturale rivolto all'architettura della nostra regione ed oltre.

The goal of this supporting programme is to make visitors aware of the links between the presentation of a theme or of an architect's work and the surrounding architectural landscape. Consequently, in addition to the annual architecture exhibitions, discussions, lectures and excursions are organized, cultural activities that aim at achieving a lasting impact in the cause of architecture in both South Tyrol and beyond the borders of the region.

[1] Quelle: Südtiroler Künstlerbund 1946–1960, unveröff. Manuskript.
[2] Stiftung der Kammer der Architekten, Raumplaner, Landschaftsplaner, Denkmalpfleger der Autonomen Provinz Bozen-Südtirol.
[3] Schlorhaufer Bettina, Paul Thuile. Protokoll des ersten „Südtiroler Landespreises für Kunst am Bau", 2004. Juroren und Jurorinnen: Luigi Snozzi (Architekt, Locarno), Ignazio Linazasoro (Architekt, Madrid), Francesco Venezia (Architekt, Neapel), Paul Thuile (Künstler, Gargazon) und Bettina Schlorhaufer (Kunsthistorikerin, Innsbruck). Weiter heißt es im Juryprotokoll: „D. h., dass die nachträgliche ‚Applikation' eines Kunst am Bau-Werks nicht denselben Stellenwert einnehmen kann wie eine künstlerische Intervention, die hinsichtlich Konzept und Umsetzung in Abstimmung mit einer architektonischen Aufgabe gelöst wurde. Für die Jury besteht die Vision von einem schlüssigen Kunst am Bau-Projekt ferner darin, dass es dem klassischen ‚Gesamtkunstwerk-Gedanken' möglichst nahe kommen sollte.

[1] Fonte: Südtiroler Künstlerbund 1946 – 1960 manoscritto non pubblicato.
[2] Ordine degli Architetti Pianificatori Paesaggisti Conservatori, della Provincia Autonoma di Bolzano
[3] Schlorhaufer Bettina, Paul Thuile. Protocollo della prima edizione del „Premio Arte nell'Architettura in Alto Adige" 2006 giurati: Luigi Snozzi (architetto, Locarno), Ignazio Linazasoro (architetto, Madrid), Francesco Venezia (architetto, Napoli), Paul Thuile (artista, Gargazzone), Bettina Schlorhaufer (storica dell'arte, Innsbruck). Successivamente si legge nel protocollo: „un'applicazione artistica successiva non ha lo stesso valore di un intervento artistico concepito in fase di progettazione in concordanza con la realizzazione della costruzione stessa. Per la giuria la visione sensata dell'arte alla costruzione è l'avvicinarsi all'ideale classico del „Gesamtkunstwerk".

[1] Source: Südtiroler Künstlerbund 1946–1960, unpublished manuscript.
[2] Stiftung der Kammer der Architekten, Raumplaner, Landschaftsplaner, Denkmalpfleger der Autonomen Provinz Bozen-Südtirol (Foundation of the Chamber of Architects, Regional Planners, Landscape Planners and Monument Conservationist of the Autonomous Province of Bolzano-South Tyrol).
[3] Schlorhaufer, Bettina, Paul Thuile. Protocol of the first awarding of the "South Tyrol Regional Prize for Site-specific Art", 2004. Jury members: Luigi Snozzi (architect, Locarno), Ignazio Linazasoro (architect, Madrid), Francesco Venezia (architect, Naples), Paul Thuile (artist, Gargazon) and Bettina Schlorhaufer (art historian, Innsbruck). The jury protocol continues: "That is to say that the later ‚application' of an artwork cannot achieve the same value as an artistic intervention that, in terms of concept and implementation, is made in collaboration and harmony with the architectural commission. For the jury the vision of a coherent site-specific artwork involves coming as close as possible to the classic idea of a ‚Gesamtkunstwerk'."

Bettina Schlorhaufer
„Ich hab' von Südtirol geträumt ... "

Ich sah ein Land

„Ich sah ein Land, ein wunderbares/ und Sonnengold lag drüber hin./ Die Wasser rauschten tief im Tale/ und Burgen schauten aus dem Grün./ Ich trank von altem Feuerweine/ im letzten Dolomitenglüh'n./ Ein Falke flog zum Wolkensteine,/ wo Laurins Rosen ewig blüh'n./ Ich hab' von Südtirol geträumt/ und auch vom Rosengarten./ O Land, du wunderbares Land,/ mein Rebland lebe wohl!"[1], heißt es in der charmanten Volksweise „Ich hab' von Südtirol geträumt ... " Die landschaftlichen Reize, die in diesem Lied so farbenprächtig beschrieben werden, sind auf das dort vorhandene, für inneralpine Verhältnisse relativ milde Klima zurückzuführen, dem die Region neben ihrer eindrucksvollen Natur auch ihre reiche (Agri-)Kultur zu verdanken hat. Dennoch gehört dieses folkloristische Stück zu den Kompositionen, in denen romantische Verklärung mehr zählt als eine realistische Beschreibung der tatsächlichen Verhältnisse im nördlichsten Landesteil Italiens.

Aus europäischer Sicht betrachtet, sieht Südtirol in einem komplexen Spannungsverhältnis zwischen seiner Geografie – eines Landes im Gebirge – und dem hier allgemein herrschenden Wohlstand. Die Geografie des Landes bedingt einerseits, dass selbst in Zeiten extremer Mobilität viele Gebiete schwer erreichbar sind und daher den Eindruck erwecken, auf sozioökonomi-

"Ho sognato dell'Alto Adige ..."

Ho visto una terra

"Ho visto una terra stupenda/ e i raggi dorati del sole la irradiavano./ Le acque scrosciavano nel fondovalle/ e i castelli si ergevano dai boschi./ Ho bevuto vini forti, invecchiati allo splendore dei tramonti sulle Dolomiti./ Un falco é volato verso la vetta tra le nuvole,/ dove le rose di Laurino fioriscono per l'eternità./ Ho sognato dell'Alto Adige ed anche del Catinaccio/ O terra, terra meravigliosa,/ terra di vigneti addio!"[1], così risuonano le strofe dell'affascinante lirica popolare "Ho sognato dell'Alto Adige...". Le bellezze del paesaggio, descritte con vivi colori in questo canto, sono da ricondurre al clima relativamente mite di quei luoghi ed al quale la regione deve, oltre alla sua impressionante natura, anche la sua ricca (agri)cultura. E' chiaro che questo pezzo folcloristico appartiene a quel tipo di composizioni in cui la trasfigurazione romantica prevale sulla descrizione della regione più settentrionale d'Italia.

Visto con occhio europeo, l'Alto Adige si gioca in una tensione complessa tra due poli: la sua geografia – un territorio di montagna – ed il benessere che qui è generalmente diffuso.

La geografia territoriale implica che, nonostante l'estrema mobilità della nostra epoca, molte zone sono difficilmente raggiungibili e pertanto danno l'impressione di essere isolate anche sul piano socio-econo-

"I dreamt of South Tyrol ... "

I saw a land

"Ich sah ein Land, ein wunderbares/ und Sonnengold lag drüber hin./ Die Wasser rauschten tief im Tale/ und Burgen schauten aus dem Grün./ Ich trank von altem Feuerweine im letzten Dolomitenglüh'n./ Ein Falke flog zum Wolkensteine,/ wo Laurins Rosen ewig blüh'n./ Ich hab' von Südtirol geträumt/ und auch vom Rosengarten./ O Land, du wunderbares Land,/ mein Rebland lebe wohl!" ("I saw a land, a wondrous land/ the sun lay golden over it./ The waters rushed deep in the valley/ And castles looked from amidst the trees./ I drank old wine in the last evening glow of the Dolomites./ A falcon flew to Wolkensteine,/ Where Laurin's roses eternally blossom./ I dreamt of South Tyrol/ and also of Rosengarten./ O land, wondrous land/My land of vineyards, farewell!")[1]. This is the text of the charming folk song "Ich träumte von Südtirol" (I dreamt of South Tyrol). The beauties of the landscape that are so colourfully described in this song result from a relatively mild climate (for alpine conditions) to which the region owes its impressive natural attractions and its rich agricultural and cultural traditions. Yet this folk song is one of those compositions in which romantic idealism takes precedence over a realistic description of the actual conditions in Italy's northernmost region.

Seen from a European perspective South

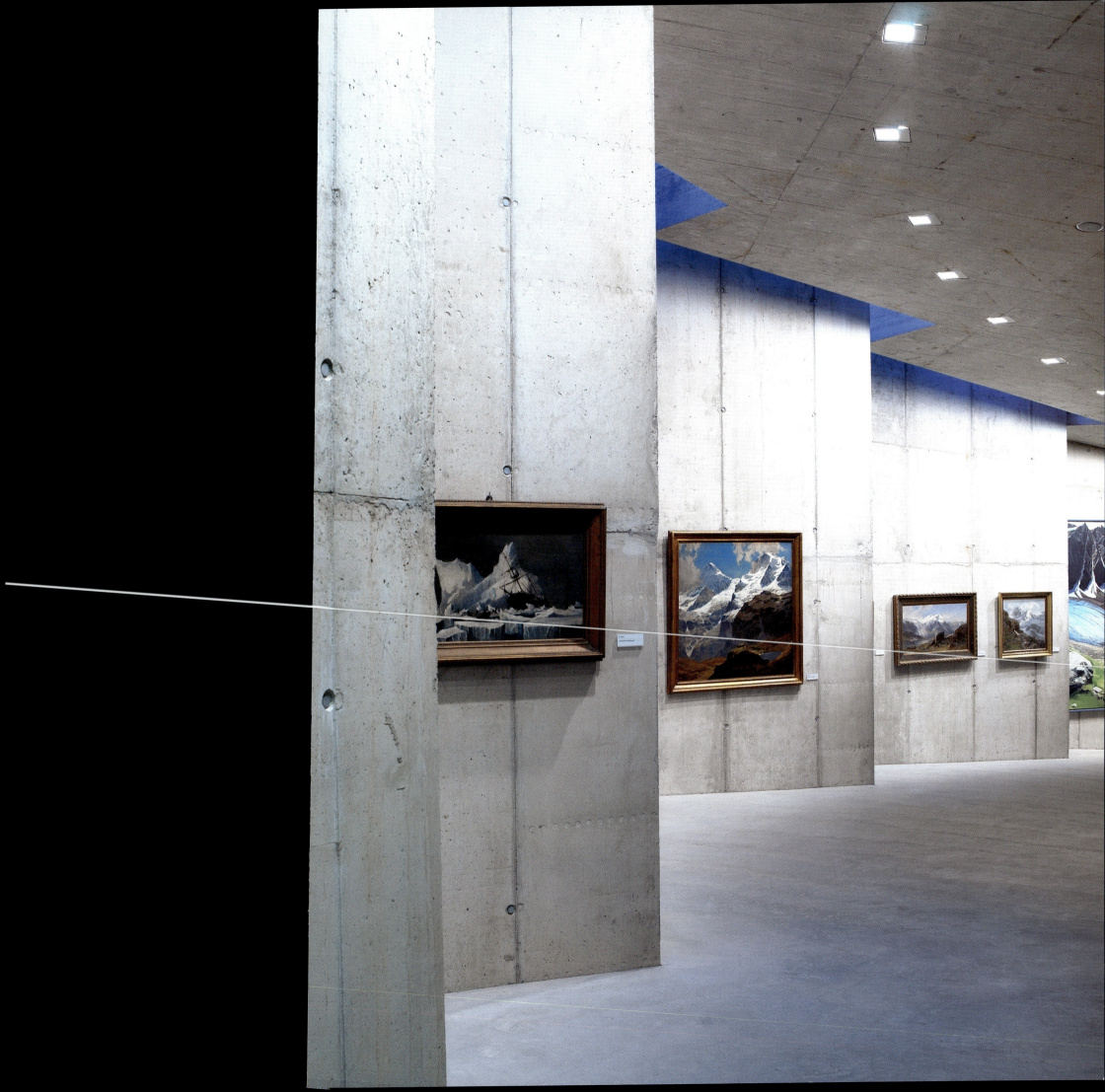

scher Ebene von außen abgeschnitten zu sein. Andererseits ist die Lage Südtirols im Zentrum des europäischen Kontinents Ursache dafür, dass das rege Verkehrsaufkommen von Waren und Menschen dem Land zwar Wohlergehen und wirtschaftliche Prosperität gebracht hat, die dadurch ausgelösten Umweltbelastungen mittlerweile aber ein Ausmaß erreicht haben, das die Entwicklung konkreter Schutzmaßnahmen dringend erforderlich macht. Also ist bei einem Blick auf Südtirol unübersehbar, dass zwischen den Phänomenen „Transport bedingt Wohlstand" und „Transport bedingt Umweltbelastungen" großes Ungleichgewicht herrscht.

Das bisher Gesagte wird von den Bewohnern des Landes noch differenzierter gesehen. Denn sie betrachten ihre Region – sie trägt den offiziellen Namen Autonome Provinz Bozen-Südtirol – auch häufig als eine von der jüngeren Geschichte benachteiligte und als eine, die im Verbund aller Regionen des Staates Italien mit Nachdruck ihr Statut einer autonomen Provinz verteidigen muss. Man ist allzu leicht geneigt, die in Verbindung mit Südtirol immer wiederkehrenden Fragen nach Identität als Koketterie abzutun, ohne dabei zu berücksichtigen, dass ebendiese Fragen berechtigt sind. Bedenkt man, dass das Land Südtirol über Jahrzehnte hinweg Spielball großer, übergeordneter politischer Strömungen war, es besetzt wurde und viele seiner Einwohner verfolgt wurden, dann gelangt man zur Erkenntnis, dass in Südtirol Identitätsfragen nicht vor dem Hintergrund reaktionärer politischer Strömungen der Gegenwart aufgeworfen werden, sondern deshalb, weil sie noch zu klären sind.

Wo Laurins Rosen ewig blüh'n
In diesem Zusammenhang stellt der Tourismus einen problematischen Faktor dar – insbesondere, wenn man über zeitgenössische Architektur sprechen möchte. Für die Zwecke touristischen Marketings werden nämlich Bilder von Landstrichen entworfen, die ähnlich dem eingangs zitierten folkloristischen Musikstück tendenziell vereinfacht sind. Diese Bilder sind ausschlaggebend dafür, dass die das Land besuchenden Gäste vorgefasste Vorstellungen von Südtirol aufbauen, denen die Freizeitindu-

mico. La posizione dell'Alto Adige, al centro del continente europeo, ha consentito al forte traffico di merci e persone di procurare benessere e prosperità economica, ma l'inquinamento ambientale connesso ha raggiunto un livello tale per cui è necessario definire con urgenza concrete misure d'intervento. Rivolgendo lo sguardo all'Alto Adige non si può non percepire che tra i binomi "il trasporto garantisce il benessere" e "il trasporto comporta danni ambientali" esiste una grande disequazione. Quanto esposto, è percepito dalla popolazione residente in modo differente. Gli abitanti considerano spesso la loro terra – dal nome ufficiale di "Provincia Autonoma di Bolzano – Alto Adige" – come penalizzata dalla storia recente, e che nell'insieme delle altre regioni dello Stato italiano deve difendere con vigore il suo statuto di provincia autonoma. Si è portati a liquidare con facilità la ricorrente questione dell'identità come fosse un vezzo, senza considerare che essa è invece ben giustificata. Si deve ricordare che l'Alto Adige è stato trattato per decenni come una palla, passata di mano nei giochi del potere politico internazionale; che è stato occupato; che parte della sua popolazione è stata perseguitata: allora si comprende che per l'Alto Adige la questione identitaria è lecita, non perché sollevata dagli odierni movimenti politici reazionari, ma perché deve essere ancora risolta.

Dove le rose di Laurino fioriscono per sempre.
In relazione a quanto detto, il turismo rappresenta un fattore problematico – soprattutto allorquando si intende parlare di architettura contemporanea. Per soddisfare gli scopi del marketing turistico si progettano a tavolino immagini di paesaggio tendenzialmente semplificate, quanto il brano musicale folcloristico citato all'inizio. Queste immagini sono determinanti, in quanto promuovono negli ospiti che visitano la provincia una rappresentazione predefinita dell'Alto Adige, alla quale poi l'industria dell'intrattenimento potrà dare soddisfazione. Si mette in moto un processo di preconcetti tra clientela ed offerta, che risulta poi difficile interrompere.

Riporto un aneddoto riguardo all'edificio polifunzionale "am Bühel", presentato sul-

Tyrol is positioned in a complex relationship between its geography (as a mountainous region) and the general high level of prosperity that it enjoys. On the one hand the natural geography of the province means that, even in an era of extreme mobility, many areas are difficult to reach and therefore give the impression that they are cut off from the outside at a socio-economic level. On the other hand, thanks to South Tyrol's central position in Europe, the transport of goods and people has brought the region economic prosperity but the environmental damage associated with this wealth has reached such an alarming level that concrete protective measures are now urgently required. So in looking at South Tyrol one cannot avoid seeing great imbalance between the phenomena of "transport that brings prosperity" and "transport that causes environmental damage".

What has been said above is viewed by the inhabitants of the region in a more differentiated way. For they see their region, which bears the official name "Autonomous Province of Bolzano-South Tyrol", as one that has frequently been disadvantaged by recent history and that, in its association with all the regions of the Italian state, must emphatically defend its status as an autonomous province. One is far too easily inclined to dismiss the question about identity that repeatedly arises in connection with South Tyrol as coquetry but to do this ignores the fact that such questions are indeed justified. If one considers that for decades the region of South Tyrol has been tossed like a ball between larger, supra-regional political movements, that the region was occupied and many of its inhabitants persecuted, then one gradually arrives at the awareness that in South Tyrol questions of identity are not raised against a background of reactionary political tendencies but are posed because they have yet to be clarified.

Where Laurin's roses eternally blossom
In this context tourism represents a problematic factor, especially when talking about contemporary architecture. For the purposes of tourism marketing images are created for entire areas that, much like the folksong quoted at the beginning of this

strie dann entsprechen sollte. Das setzt einen Kreislauf von gegenseitigen Vorurteilen zwischen Kunden und Anbietern in Gang, der schwer zu durchbrechen ist.

Dazu eine Anekdote über den Bau auf dem Titelbild dieser Publikation: Das Mehrzweckgebäude am Bühel befindet sich in der Gemeinde St. Jakob im Ahrntal, einem Seitental des Pustertals. Seine architektonische Gestaltung stammt von den Architekten Mutschlechner & Mahlknecht, die für den Bauplatz direkt neben der den Ort optisch dominierenden Kirche ein Bauwerk entwerfen wollten, das sich den bestehenden Bauwerken hierarchisch unterordnet. Dennoch entwickelten sie für ihr Gebäude einen Körper, dessen Stärke seine abstrakte, reduzierte geometrische Form ist. Von den Bewohnern der Gemeinde wurde der Bau gut aufgenommen, als ihn aber die ersten Touristen sahen, brach Verwirrung aus. Das positive Vorurteil, das sich in den Köpfen der Touristen über das Ahrntal bereits gebildet hatte, war angesichts dieses Baues derart erschüttert, dass manche sogar Leserbriefe an eine lokale Zeitung sandten, um ihren Unmut öffentlich kundzutun. Die darin formulierten Vorbehalte gegenüber zeitgemäßer Architektur im entlegenen Dorf entfachten eine Diskussion darüber, ob man so bauen oder doch lieber wieder folkloristische „Lederhosen-Architektur" realisieren sollte. Dabei ist es in ganz Südtirol unübersehbar, dass die „tourismusgerechte Baukultur" die Entwicklung von zeitgemäßen Landschaftsbildern verhindert und auch in Hinblick auf ihre

la copertina di questa pubblicazione, che si trova nel comune di S. Giacomo in Val Aurina, una laterale della Val Pusteria. Gli architetti Mutschlechner & Mahlknecht hanno voluto progettare una costruzione che si ordinasse gerarchicamente agli edifici esistenti, disposta sul lotto accanto alla chiesa che domina visivamente il luogo.

I progettisti hanno ideato un volume la cui forza è proprio la sua forma astratta, e la sua elementare geometria. L'edificio è stato ben accolto dagli abitanti, ma quando lo hanno visto i primi turisti, è scoppiato il pandemonio. L'edificio ha minato a tal punto il positivo preconcetto che i turisti si sono fatti della Val Aurina, che alcuni hanno persino inviato delle lettere ad un giornale locale per comunicare la loro indignazione. Le riserve ivi formulate contro l'architettura contemporanea hanno avviato nel lontano paesino un dibattito, e la popolazione si è tornata a chiedere se si debba costruire ancora così o se piuttosto non sia meglio tornare alla folcloristica architettura in stile tirolese. E' più che evidente peraltro che "l'architettura destinata al turismo" ostacola lo sviluppo di un'immagine contemporanea del paesaggio, e che nell'ottica della durata nel tempo anche i suoi vantaggi economici sono da valutare con estrema criticità.

Tutte queste considerazioni ci riportano alla sempre problematica identità di questa terra, e in rapporto a tale situazione ancora oggi, in tempo di pace, benessere e prosperità economica, è penoso che si giudichi dall'esterno facendo riferimento ad

essay, are, to put it mildly, simplistic in tendency. These images mean that visitors to the region have preconceived ideas that the leisure industry must respond to. This sets up a cycle of preconceived notions and expectations on the part of customers and those who provide services for them that it is very difficult to stop.

Here an anecdote about the building in the illustration on the cover of this publication may be of interest. The multi-functional building "am Bühel" is located in the community of S. Giacomo in the Valle Aurina, a side valley of the Val Pusteria. The design was produced by architects Mutschlechner & Mahlknecht, who were commissioned to create a building for the site directly beside the church that visually dominates the village, with the requirement that the new structure should be hierarchically subordinate to the existing buildings. They designed a volume whose strength lies in its abstract reduced geometric form. The new building was well received by the local residents but when the first tourists saw it consternation broke out. The positive preconceptions about the Valle Aurina that had been formed in the minds of tourists was so shattered by this new building that several of them sent letters to the local newspaper to give public vent to their anger. The reservations about the introduction of contemporary architecture to a remote village expressed in these letters started off a discussion about whether one should build in this manner or instead in a folksy "lederhosen architecture" style.

wirtschaftliche Nachhaltigkeit äußerst kritisch zu betrachten ist.

Das führt uns zurück zur immer noch fehlenden Landesidentität und in diesem Zusammenhang ist es für Südtirol auch heute noch, in Zeiten des Friedens, des Wohlstandes und der wirtschaftlichen Prosperität, fatal, dass es von außen und auf der Basis veralteter Bilder beurteilt wird. Die Anekdote über das Mehrzweckgebäude am Bühel zeigt daher auch auf, dass es in Südtirol wichtig ist, noch mehr auf die Leistungen auf dem Gebiet der Gegenwartsarchitektur zu setzen als auf die Wahrnehmungs-Inszenierungen, die der zukünftigen Entwicklung des Landes mehr schaden als nützen.

Ich hab' von Südtirol geträumt

Bis vor kurzem blieb die Architekturlandschaft Südtirols weitgehend unbeachtet. Nur das Schaffen von Univ.-Prof. em. Architekt Othmar Barth, der viele Jahre Architektur an der Universität Innsbruck lehrte, wurde mit mehr Aufmerksamkeit verfolgt. Das ist wahrscheinlich darauf zurückzuführen, dass Barth als einer der wenigen Architekten des Landes auch außerhalb Südtirols tätig wurde. Zu seinen Hauptwerken zählen das Seehotel Ambach am Kalterer See (1973) und die Schule mit Internat für Schisportler in Stams in Nordtirol (1982).[2]

Um aber der Architekturszene Südtirols den ihr gebührenden Stellenwert zukommen zu lassen, müssen neben den bereits beschriebenen Aktivitäten des Südtiroler Künstlerbundes und von „kunst Meran" noch eine ganze Reihe weiterer Initiativen erwähnt werden, an denen abzulesen ist, welch hohen Stellenwert Architektur in Südtirol genießt und wie viel in dieser Region unternommen wird, um Architektur im eigenen Land bekannt zu machen. Bedauerlich ist in diesem Zusammenhang lediglich, dass die Südtiroler Baukultur bisher viel zu wenig internationale Resonanz hervorrufen konnte und auch das dort zum Teil seit vielen Jahren existierende Engagement in Sachen Architektur-Vermittlung bisher kaum bekannt gemacht wurde – man möge Vergleichbares in anderen Regionen erst einmal finden:

1993 wurde ein „Architekturführer Südtirol" herausgegeben.[3] Für Menschen, die

immagini superate. L'aneddoto dell'edificio polifunzionale "am Bühel" dimostra come in Alto Adige sia importante investire sulle prestazioni dell'architettura del presente, piuttosto che sulla messinscena di un'immagine, che danneggia più che essere funzionale al futuro sviluppo della provincia.

Ho sognato dell'Alto Adige.

Sino a poco tempo fa la scena dell'architettura dell'Alto Adige era poco conosciuta. Solo l'opera dell'architetto Othmar Barth, professore per lunghi anni all'università di Innsbruck, è stata seguita con più attenzione. Forse ciò è da ricondurre al fatto che Barth è stato uno dei pochi architetti locali che hanno lavorato anche fuori dall'Alto Adige. Tra le sue opere principali contano l'albergo Ambach sul lago di Caldaro (1973) e la scuola con studentato per gli sport invernali di Stams nel Tirolo settentrionale (1982).[2]

Per riconoscere allo scenario architettonico dell'Alto Adige il suo dovuto valore, a fianco delle attività del Südtiroler Künstlerbund (Associazione degli artisti sudtirolesi) e di Merano arte sin qui descritte, deve essere menzionata una serie di altre iniziative, dalle quali si può comprendere il valore riconosciuto all'architettura in Alto Adige e quanto qui ci si impegni per promuovere l'architettura nella propria terra. In questo contesto è un peccato che l'architettura altoatesina abbia avuto una eco così limitata a livello internazionale e che l'impegno che da anni esiste a livello locale per la promozione dell'architettura sinora non sia stato che in parte riconosciuto – sarebbe difficile trovare qualcosa di simile in altre regioni.

Nel 1993 è stata pubblicata una guida architettonica dell' Alto Adige[3] che per i lettori interessati alla storia più recente dell'architettura in Alto Adige, costituisce un accompagnamento indispensabile: vi si trovano informazioni sull'architettura della fine Ottocento, della "Gründerzeit", di cui ci sono molti esempi; i progetti dell'Era fascista italiana in Alto Adige e la documentazione dei migliori edifici di tutta la provincia, realizzati sino al 1993. Da lungo tempo si attende una nuova edizione aggiornata. Accanto alla guida "Architettura in Alto Adige" esiste una serie di monografie di architetti, di cui alcune sono com-

Throughout South Tyrol it is impossible to ignore the fact that "architecture suitable for tourism" is preventing the development of contemporary landscape images and, also in terms of its economic sustainability, must be viewed critically.

This brings us back to the region's lack of identity. In this context it remains fatal for South Tyrol that today, in an era of peace and economic prosperity, it is evaluated from outside on the basis of outdated images. The anecdote about the multi-purpose building "am Bühel" shows the importance in South Tyrol of placing emphasis on quality contemporary architecture rather than on creating settings for people's preconceived perceptions, which harm the future development of the region more than they help it.

I dreamt of South Tyrol

Until recently little attentions was paid to the architectural landscape of South Tyrol. Only the work of Univ.-Prof. em. architect Othmar Barth, who taught architecture for many years at the University of Innsbruck, was followed with any interest. This is probably due to the fact that Barth is one of the few architects in the region who was also active outside South Tyrol. Among his main works are the Seehotel Ambach on Lago di Caldero (1973) and the boarding and day school for future skiers in Stams in North Tyrol (1982).[2]

To adequately position the architecture scene in South Tyrol, in addition to the activities of the Südtiroler Künstlerbund and Merano arte already referred to, an entire series of other initiatives should be mentioned that reveal the high esteem in which architecture is held in South Tyrol and how much is being done in the region to make architecture known there. In this context the only regrettable thing is that the culture of building in South Tyrol has not, so far, been able to attract adequate international interest and that the commitment to spreading ideas of modern architecture that has existed there for many years is little known outside the region – even though a comparable situation is rare elsewhere.

In 1993 an "Architekturführer Südtirol" (Guide to the Architecture of South Tyrol) was published[3] which is an indispensable

sich für die jüngere Architekturgeschichte Südtirols interessieren, ist er ein unerlässlicher Begleiter: In ihm findet man Informationen über die in Südtirol überaus reichhaltige Architektur der Gründerzeit, die Projekte aus der faschistischen Ära Italiens in Südtirol und die besten Bauten aus allen Landesteilen, die bis 1993 errichtet wurden. Eine erweiterte Neuauflage dieses Buches ist längst überfällig. Neben dem „Architekturführer Südtirol" existiert eine Reihe von Architekten-Monografien, von denen manche in Verbindung mit Ausstellungen in der Galerie Prisma des Südtiroler Künstlerbundes entstanden sind. In Zusammenhang mit der Edition themenspezifischer bzw. bauhistorischer Bücher darf ferner der Hinweis nicht fehlen, dass die Mehrzahl von ihnen von einheimischen Architekten verfasst wurde – was wiederum Rückschlüsse auf die persönlichen Vorlieben der auf dem Gebiet der Architekturpublizistik tätigen Baukünstler zulässt. Zu den wichtigsten der am Markt (noch) erhältlichen Werke zählen: „Die Architektur für ein italienisches Bozen 1922–1944"[4] über die Architektur in der Epoche des italienischen Faschismus in Bozen, „Dorf und Stadt – Wohngebiete in Südtirol nach 1970"[5] über die Zersiedelung in Südtirol, „Öffentliches Bauen in Südtirol 1993–2003"[6], eine Publikation, die zumindest bei den öffentlichen Bauten an den „Architekturführer Südtirol" anschließt, und der jüngst erschienene Band „Auf Gebautem Bauen"[7] über die Verbindung von historischer Bausubstanz mit zeitgenössischer Architektur, wobei neben öffentlichen Bauten auch Projekte privater Bauherren vorgestellt werden.

Beim Thema Architekturpublizistik in Südtirol darf „turrisbabel"[8] nicht unerwähnt bleiben, die Architekturzeitschrift für die Region. Sie ist aus dem Mitteilungsblatt der Architektenkammer hervorgegangen und erscheint seit März 1985 viermal jährlich in italienischer und deutscher Sprache. Seit 2004 kann die Zeitschrift von allen Interessierten abonniert werden und steht somit nicht mehr ausschließlich den Kammermitgliedern und einigen Interessierten als Informationsquelle zur Verfügung. Die inhaltliche Ausrichtung der Hefte wird von den Architekturwettbewerben

parse in concomitanza delle mostre personali organizzate dalla Galleria Prisma del Südtiroler Künstlerbund. Non può mancare un cenno alla pubblicazione di testi a tema specifico o di storia dell'architettura: che la maggior parte di questi sia stata curata da architetti locali consente di dedurre la passione personale dei progettisti attivi nella pubblicistica di architettura. Tra le opere più importanti e (ancora) reperibili sul mercato si contano: "L'architettura per una Bolzano italiana 1922–1944"[4] sull'architettura all'epoca del fascismo italiano, "Paese e città – Espansioni residenziali in Alto Adige dopo il 1970"[5] sulla dispersione degli insediamenti residenziali in Alto Adige, "Edilizia pubblica in Alto Adige 1993–2003"[6], una pubblicazione che - almeno per gli edifici - pubblici si ricollega alla guida di architettura, e la pubblicazione appena uscita "Costruire sul costruito"[7] sul connubio tra edifici storici ed architettura contemporanea, dove insieme ad edifici pubblici sono presenti anche progetti per committenti privati.

Nella pubblicistica di architettura è doveroso menzionare "turrisbabel"[8], la rivista di architettura dell'Alto Adige. Avviata come bollettino dell'Ordine degli Architetti nel 1985, è una pubblicazione trimestrale in lingua italiana e tedesca. Dal 2004 tutti gli interessati possono abbonarsi alla rivista, che quindi è ora accessibile come fonte di informazione sull'architettura in Alto Adige non solamente agli iscritti all'Ordine o ad un pubblico di lettori selezionati. I quaderni di "turrisbabel" trattano, tra l'altro, degli esiti dei concorsi di architettura in Alto Adige, di cui sono pubblicati i risultati delle gare più importanti; temi d'interesse generale, come ad esempio la documentazione più recente sull'architettura nella Provincia Autonoma di Bolzano. In questo modo "turrisbabel" si è attribuita anche il ruolo di testimoniare la storia dell'architettura in Alto Adige.

Per far conoscere ad un ampio strato di popolazione la nuova architettura altoatesina, l'architetto Helga von Aufschnaiter-Straudi, da anni presidente del Südtiroler Künstlerbund, ha avviato insieme al canale provinciale della RAI- la serie "Ortsgerecht contra ortsüblich – Zeitgenössische Architektur in Südtirol" ("Adatto al luogo"

companion for those interested in the more recent history of architecture in the region. It offers information about the wealth of late 19th century architecture in South Tyrol, the projects from the Italian fascist era and the best buildings from all parts of the province built up to 1993. An expanded new edition of this book is long overdue. In addition to the "Architekturführer Südtirol" there is a series of architects' monographs many of which were produced in conjunction with exhibitions in the Prisma Gallery of the Südtiroler Künstlerbund. In connection with this list of books on specific themes or on the history of architecture it should be said that the majority of them were written by local architects – which suggests something about the personal preferences of the architects involved in the field of architectural journalism. Among the most important works still available on the market are "Die Architektur für ein italienisches Bozen 1922–1944"[4] (Architecture for an Italian Bolzano 1922–1944) about the architecture of the epoch of Italian fascism in Bolzano, "Dorf und Stadt – Wohngebiete in Südtirol nach 1970"[5] (Village and Town – Residential Districts in South Tyrol after 1970) about suburban sprawl in South Tyrol, "Öffentliches Bauen in Südtirol 1993–2003"[6] (Public Building in South Tyrol 1993–2003), a publication that can be seen as a further development of the guide to architecture in South Tyrol, at least in terms of public buildings, and the recently published work "Auf Gebautem Bauen"[7] (Building on an Established Basis) about connecting historical building substance and contemporary architecture in which, in addition to public buildings, projects erected by private clients are also presented.

When dealing with the theme of architecture journalism in South Tyrol mention must also be made of "turrisbabel",[8] the architecture journal of the province of South Tyrol. It is development of the newsletter of the Chamber of Architects and since March 1985 has appeared four times year in both Italian and German. Since 2004 it is possible for all those interested to take out a subscription to this journal, which means that this source of information it is no longer restricted to members of the Chamber

in Südtirol bestimmt. Neben der Präsentation der Ergebnisse der wichtigsten Konkurrenzen werden aber auch allgemeine Themen behandelt, z. B. die jüngere Architekturgeschichte der Autonomen Provinz Bozen-Südtirol. Auf diese Weise kommt „turrisbabel" zusätzlich die Rolle als Baugeschichtsdokumentation zu.

Um breite Bevölkerungsschichten mit neuer Architektur in Südtirol bekannt zu machen, rief die Architektin und langjährige Präsidentin des Südtiroler Künstlerbundes, Helga von Aufschnaiter-Straudi, gemeinsam mit dem Sender RAI-Bozen die Reihe „Ortsgerecht contra ortsüblich – Zeitgenössische Architektur in Südtirol" ins Leben. Im Jahr 2006 wird der bereits 15. Filmbeitrag fertig gestellt und von der lokalen Fernsehstation ausgestrahlt werden. Zu den wichtigsten der jeweils 15-minütigen Beiträge zählen: „Neue Schulbauten in Südtirol", „Mehrfamilienhäuser", „Betriebsgebäude" und „Neue Sakralbauten". Darüber hinaus muss Helga von Aufschnaiter-Straudi auch als Gestalterin von je einem 35-minütigen Filmporträt über die Architekten Univ.-Prof. em. Arch. Othmar Barth und Werner Tscholl erwähnt werden, die ebenfalls für den Sender RAI-Bozen entstanden.

Die wohl bekannteste mit Südtirol in Verbindung zu bringende Initiative ist der internationale Architekturpreis für „Neues Bauen in den Alpen", der 1992 zum ersten Mal verliehen wurde. Die nächste Vergabe erfolgt 2006. Als Mentor dieses Architekturpreises kann Architekt Christoph Mayr Fingerle angesehen werden, der ihn seit seiner Entstehung organisatorisch und inhaltlich betreut. Noch bevor aber diese Konkurrenz über alpines Bauen ins Leben gerufen worden war, engagierte sich Mayr Fingerle bereits für ähnlich gelagerte Themen, veranstaltete – zuerst noch in kleinerem Rahmen – Ausstellungen und verfasste Begleitpublikationen, z. B. „Hotelarchitektur in den Alpen 1920–1940"[9] und „Architektur, Natur und Technik"[10]. Ihre Präsentation erfolgte zum Teil im 1926 von Clemens Holzmeister entworfenen Hotel „Drei Zinnen" im Ort Sexten in einem Seitental des Pustertals.

Im Vorwort zum Katalog des ersten Preises für „Neues Bauen in den Alpen" heißt

contro "tipico del luogo" – Architettura contemporanea in Alto Adige). Nel 2006 si completerà il quindicesimo capitolo della serie. Tra i più importanti della serie da 15 minuti si contano. "Nuovi edifici scolastici in Alto Adige", "Edifici plurifamigliari", "Edifici produttivi" e "Nuovi edifici sacri". Helga von Aufschnaiter-Straudi deve essere menzionata anche per aver curato i ritratti filmici di 35 minuti sul prof. Arch. Barth e Werner Tscholl, realizzati sempre dalla RAI di Bolzano.

L'iniziativa più conosciuta da collegare all'Alto Adige è il Premio internazionale "Neues Bauen in den Alpen", che è stato assegnato per la prima volta nel 1992. La prossima consegna avverrà nel 2006. Come mentore del premio può essere considerato Christoph Mayr Fingerle, che lo ha curato a partire dalle sue origini. Prima di avviare questa competizione riguardante le costruzioni nell'arco alpino, Mayr Fingerle si è impegnato con altri temi analoghi – inizialmente con iniziative di piccola dimensione – mostre e pubblicazioni introduttive, p.es. "Hotelarchitektur in den Alpen 1920-1940" (Architettura alberghiera dell'arco alpino 1920-1940)[9] e "Architektur, Natur und Technik" (Architettura, natura e tecnica)[10].

La sua presentazione è avvenuta in parte all'interno dell'hotel "Drei Zinnen" progettato nel 1926 da Clemens Holzmeister nel paese di Sesto, in una laterale della Val Pusteria.

Nell'introduzione del catalogo del primo premio per "Neues Bauen in den Alpen" si legge: "Il gran numero di esempi negativi rende difficile, soprattutto ai profani, seguire direttive e criteri con i quali riconoscere o dai quali dedurre la qualità nell'architettura ... Ne consegue che la qualità dell'architettura non è riconosciuta ed è respinta"[11]. Dopo il più che decennale impegno investito per questo premio, si può finalmente constatare che costruire nell'arco alpino è divenuto un concetto non solo per gli addetti al mestiere. La premiazione di architetti e progetti non ha mancato il suo obbiettivo: promuovere proponendo dei modelli. Il premio è stato bandito inizialmente solo dall'associazione Sesto Cultura, poi insieme ad altri partner istituzionali (nel 2006 insieme alla Casa dell'Architet-

of Architects. The contents of each issue are determined largely by the architecture competitions held in South Tyrol, but in addition to presenting the results of the major competitions more general themes are also dealt with, for example the more recent history of architecture in the Autonomous Province of Bolzano-South Tyrol. Consequently "turrisbabel" has an additional role as a documentation of building history.

To make broader sectors of the population familiar with more recent architecture in South Tyrol the architect and president of the Südtiroler Künstlerbund for many years, Helga von Aufschnaiter-Straudi, together with the television station RAI-Bolzano established a series called "Ortsgerecht contra ortsüblich – Zeitgenössische Architektur in Südtirol" (Local solutions, suitable as against standard - contemporary architecture in South Tyrol). In 2006 the 15th film in this series will be completed and subsequently broadcast by the local television station. Among the most important of the 15-minute long programmes are: "New Schools in South Tyrol", "Apartment Buildings", "Company Buildings" and vNew Religious Buildings". In addition mention should be made of Helga von Aufschnaiter-Straudi's contribution as the producer of 35-minute film portraits of the architects Univ.-Prof. em. Arch. Othmar Barth and Werner Tscholl that were also made for RAI-Bolzano.

The best-known initiative associated with South Tyrol is probably the international architecture prize for "New Building in the Alps" that was awarded for the first time in 1992. The next presentation will be made in 2006. Architect Christoph Mayr Fingerle can be called the mentor of this award and has monitored it in terms of content and organisation since its creation. But even before this competition was set up Mayr Fingerle was involved with similar themes and organized exhibitions, initially on a small scale, and also wrote the accompanying publications, for example: "Hotelarchitektur in den Alpen 1920–1940"[9] (Hotel Architecture in the Alps 1993–2003) and "Architektur, Natur und Technik"[10] (Architecture, Nature and Technology). Some of these publications were launched in the "Drei Zinnen" hotel designed by Clemens

es: „Die große Mehrzahl negativer Beispiele macht es insbesondere für Laien schwierig, Richtlinien und Kriterien zu verfolgen, wonach Qualität in der Architektur erkennbar und nachvollziehbar wird ... Das führt u. a. dazu, dass Architekturqualität sehr häufig nicht erkannt und abgelehnt wird."[11] Nach der mehr als zehnjährigen Aufbauarbeit, die im Umfeld dieses Preises geleistet wurde, kann aber auf jeden Fall konstatiert werden, dass sich das Bauen in den Alpen nicht nur in Fachkreisen zu einem stehenden Begriff entwickelt hat. Darüber hinaus hat die Auszeichnung von Architekten und Projekten ihr Ziel nicht verfehlt, eine starke Vorbildwirkung auszuüben. Der Preis wurde anfänglich nur von der Vereinigung Sexten Kultur und erst später gemeinsam mit anderen Partner-Institutionen ausgelobt (im Jahr 2006 zusammen mit Kärntens Haus der Architektur „Napoleonstadel"). Die Besetzung der Jury hat sich seit der ersten Vergabe kaum verändert. Friedrich Achleitner, Bruno Reichlin und Manfred Kovatsch begleiten ihn seit seiner Gründung, und vor allem die beiden Erstgenannten haben für die Kataloge zu den bisher vergebenen Preisen Textbeiträge verfasst, die deshalb gewürdigt werden müssen, weil in ihnen der – übrigens nach wie vor nicht unumstrittene – Begriff des „alpinen Bauens" erörtert wird.

Innerhalb Südtirols rief der internationale Architekturpreis für „Neues Bauen in den Alpen" anfänglich kritische Reaktionen hervor. Man bemängelte das Fehlen zahlreicher Auszeichnungen für einheimische Projekte, weil im Verlauf von bisher insgesamt drei ausgeschriebenen Wettbewerben nur ein einziges Bauwerk aus Südtirol erfolgreich war, die Weinkellerei Hofstätter in Tramin von Walter Angonese und Markus Scherer (1998).

Möglicherweise hatten sich die Geldgeber erhofft, dass die Auslobung einer überregionalen Konkurrenz auf dem Gebiet der Architektur automatisch auch dazu führt, dass die Architektur im eigenen Land ausgezeichnet wird – in den deutschsprachigen Alpenregionen bezeichnet man eine derartige Geisteshaltung als „Kirchturmdenken". Nachdem der Preis aber die Architekturszene Südtirols erstmals in ein Verhältnis u. a. zu jener in der Schweiz oder in Österreich

tura della Carinzia il "Napoleonstadel"). La composizione della giuria non è mutata dalla prima premiazione. Friedrich Achleitner, Bruno Reichlin e Manfred Kovatsch accompagnano il premio dagli esordi. Principalmente i primi due hanno curato i testi per i cataloghi dei premi sinora elargiti, e devono pertanto venire apprezzati, perché in essi si dibatte il concetto, non privo di querelles sull'"architettura alpina".

In Alto Adige il premio internazionale di architettura "Neues Bauen in den Alpen" ha procurato inizialmente delle reazioni critiche per la mancanza di un numero maggiore di riconoscimenti a progetti locali: in tutti e tre i concorsi sinora banditi solo un'opera altoatesina aveva avuto successo, la cantina vinicola Hofstätter a Termeno di Walter Angonese e Markus Scherer (1998). Forse i finanziatori del premio avevano sperato che bandire un concorso di architettura a livello sovraregionale portasse automaticamente a segnalare l'architettura della regione ospite – nelle regioni dell'arco alpino tedesco lo si definirebbe un atteggiamento campanilistico. Il premio ha messo per la prima volta a confronto la scena architettonica altoatesina con quella svizzera ed austriaca (tra le altre), evidenziando la necessità di recuperare terreno. Poiché per gli architetti attivi in Alto Adige vale il principio che la concorrenza rende solerti, è evidente che, in tutta la regione, l'iniziativa di confrontare esempi di architettura delle zone alpine e di premiarne i migliori ha portato a mutamenti duraturi. Con l'attività edilizia da anni in continua espansione i progettisti si sono confrontati - in una misura che non ha precedenti - con il tema del costruire nel contesto paesaggistico, ed al contempo con le questioni della coesistenza tra costruzioni storicamente connotate e moderne; con la ricerca di nuove soluzioni per compiti progettuali dotati di requisiti sempre più mutevoli, come per esempio quelli delle attrazioni turistiche e delle residenze agricole. Con molta probabilità si deve ricondurre al premio "Neues Bauen in den Alpen" il fatto che aspetti socioeconomici e legati al genius loci contino più di un decennio fa nell'approccio al progetto di architettura. Aspettiamo quindi con interesse al risultato del prossimo premio, poiché è probabile

Holzmeister in 1926 that stands in the town of Sesto in a side valley of the Val Pusteria.

In the preface to the catalogue produced for the first presentation of the prize for "New Building in the Alps" it is stated: "The great number of negative examples make it particularly difficult for lay people to follow the guidelines and criteria that make quality in architecture recognisable and understandable… This in turn leads to a situation where architectural quality is often not recognised or is rejected."[11] After more than ten years of educational work carried out in connection with this award it can now be confirmed that building in the alps has become a familiar term, not only in specialist circles. Additionally, the awarding of prizes to architects and projects has achieved its goal of becoming a model for others. Initially the prize was awarded by the association "Sexten Kultur" and only later with other partner institutions (in 2006 in conjunction with Carinthia's Haus der Architektur "Napoleonstadel"). Since the awarding of the first prizes the composition of the jury has hardly changed at all. Friedrich Achleitner, Bruno Reichlin and Manfred Kovatsch have accompanied this development since it began and Achleitner and Reichlin in particular have written contributions to the catalogues for the prizes awarded so far. They are mentioned here because in them the term "alpine building" (which, incidentally, remains somewhat controversial) is explored.

Within South Tyrol itself the international architecture prize for "New Building in the Alps" initially met with a critical reaction. People complained about the lack of awards made to local projects, as in the course of the first three competitions only one work from South Tyrol achieved success, the Hofstätter wine cellar in Termeno by Walter Angonese and Markus Scherer (1998).

Possibly those who funded this award had hoped that setting up a supra-regional competition in the area of architecture automatically leads to prizes being awarded to the architecture of one's own region. In German-speaking countries such a parochial way of thinking is known as "Kirchturmdenken" (literally: "church tower thinking").

gesetzt hatte, offenbarte sich, dass in Südtirol in qualitativer Hinsicht noch ein Nachholbedarf besteht. Doch für die in der Region tätigen Architekten gilt im wahrsten Wortsinn „Konkurrenz beflügelt den Eifer" und es ist im ganzen Land unübersehbar, dass die Initiative, Architekturbeispiele aus allen Alpengebieten zu vergleichen und die besten von ihnen auszuzeichnen, in Südtirol sehr wohl zu nachhaltigen Veränderungen geführt hat: In Zusammenhang mit einem seit Jahren anhaltenden Bauboom kam es hier zu einer in diesem Ausmaß noch nicht da gewesenen Beschäftigung mit dem Thema des ländlichen Bauens, wobei man sich auch mit Fragen der Verbindung von historischer Bausubstanz mit neuer Architektur und mit der Suche nach neuen Lösungen für sich verändernde Bauaufgaben, z. B. von Tourismusattraktionen oder landwirtschaftlich genutzten Gutshöfen, auseinander setzte. Mit hoher Wahrscheinlichkeit ist es auf das große Echo des Preises für „Neues Bauen in den Alpen" zurückzuführen, dass topologische und sozioökonomische Aspekte bei Fragen der architektonischen Gestaltung heute in Südtirol eine viel bedeutendere Rolle spielen als etwa noch vor einer Dekade. Man kann also mit Spannung das Ergebnis des nächsten Preises für „Neues Bauen in den Alpen" erwarten, denn es ist anzunehmen, dass sich diesmal noch mehr Architekturprojekte aus Südtirol gegenüber ihren Mitbewerbern aus anderen Alpengebieten durchsetzen werden.

che questa volta possa imporsi un maggior numero di progetti locali rispetto a quelli di altre regioni alpine.

Un falco è volato verso la vetta tra le nuvole.

Quando è stata concepita l'iniziativa per la mostra (e relativo catalogo) "2000-2006 nuova architettura in Alto Adige" era intenzione del Südtiroler Künstlerbund e di Merano arte trovare un criterio di selezione obbiettivo: una priorità era fissata dalla definizione del numero esatto di singoli progetti che concorrono a definire questa iniziativa. La Provincia Autonoma di Bolzano è stata suddivisa in cinque settori e per ognuno di essi è stata nominata una coppia di architetti. In seguito Verena Dander, Dorothea Aichner, Magdalena Schmid, Arnold Gapp, Werner Tscholl, Heinold Gasser, Luigi Scolari, Lukas Abram, Siegfried Delueg und Heinrich Mutschlechner sono stati invitati a stilare una lista dei cinquanta progetti che per loro rappresentavano i migliori per l'area di loro competenza. Questi architetti, con funzione di pre-giuria, dovevano considerare che i progetti da loro nominati fossero realizzati tra il 2000 ed il 2006.

Purtroppo, a causa del limite imposto al periodo di realizzazione degli edifici, non è stato possibile colmare la lacuna temporale rimasta tra l'edizione della prima guida "Architettura in Alto Adige" e questo progetto appena concluso. Sarebbe auspicabile che la Fondazione dell'Ordine degli Architetti si decidesse presto a pubblicare una nuova

But as the prize for the first time drew comparisons between the architecture scene in South Tyrol and those in Austria or Switzerland it revealed that South Tyrol was lagging somewhat behind in terms of quality. But the proverb that "Konkurrenz beflügelt den Eifer" (competition lends diligence wings) is most applicable to architects working in the Autonomous Province of Bolzano-South Tyrol and throughout the region it is impossible to overlook the fact that the idea of comparing examples of architecture from all alpine regions and making awards to the best of them has led to lasting changes in South Tyrol. In conjunction with the boom in the construction business that has lasted several years now the theme of building in the country has been examined at a level previously unknown, whereby questions such as the connection of historical building substance with new architecture and the search for new solutions for commissions such as tourist attractions or country estates used for agricultural purposes have also been looked at. It seems highly likely that the great response to the prize for "New Building in the Alps" is responsible for the fact that in questions of architectural design today topological and socio-economic aspects play a far more significant role in South Tyrol than, say, a decade earlier. And we await with interest the outcome of the next award for "New Building in the Alps" as we can justifiably expect that this time more projects from South Tyrol will emerge successfully from the competition with

Ein Falke flog vom Wolkensteine

Als das Ausstellungs- und Publikationsvorhaben „2000–2006 Neue Architektur in Südtirol" konzipiert wurde, war es dem Südtiroler Künstlerbund und „kunst Meran" ein Anliegen, ein möglichst objektives Auswahlverfahren zu entwerfen: Den Ausgangspunkt bildete die Recherche der genauen Anzahl der Projekte, die dem Gesamtprojekt zugrunde liegen. Die Region wurde in fünf Landstriche unterteilt und in jedem von ihnen wurden zwei Architekten namhaft gemacht. Anschließend wurden Verena Dander, Dorothea Aichner, Magdalena Schmid, Arnold Gapp, Werner Tscholl, Heinold Gasser, Luigi Scolari, Lukas Abram, Siegfried Delueg und Heinrich Mutschlechner gebeten, eine Liste mit den nach ihrer Ansicht 50 besten Bauten ihres geografischen Wirkungskreises zusammenzustellen. Dabei hatten diese als Vor-Jury fungierenden Architekten zu berücksichtigen, dass die von ihnen namhaft gemachten Bauten zwischen 2000 und 2006 errichtet worden waren.

Bedauerlicherweise ist es aufgrund der Eingrenzung der Entstehungsperiode der Bauten nicht gelungen, die zeitliche Lücke zwischen der Herausgabe des Führers „Architektur in Südtirol" und dem nun abgeschlossenen Projekt zu schließen. Es wäre wünschenswert, dass sich die Stiftung der Kammer der Architekten der Autonomen Provinz Bozen-Südtirol doch bald dazu entschließt, einen neuen Architekturführer herauszugeben, denn schon die erste Abfrage unter den Architekten ergab eine Zu-

guida di architettura, perché già solo la prima valutazione tra gli architetti ha annoverato circa 400 progetti. Poiché questi progetti dovevano essere sottoposti ad una giuria internazionale, il Südtiroler Künstlerbund e Merano arte hanno deciso di far fotografare nuovamente tutti gli edifici. Così si è evitato che la giuria fosse fuorviata da belle immagini a scapito della buona architettura. Quindi si è deciso di presentare un massimo di 50 opere costruite, ed ogni architetto o studio di architettura poteva essere presente al massimo tre volte. Contemporaneamente è stata nominata e convocata la giuria, a cui appartengono: l'architetto Joseph Grima della rivista di architettura e design Domus di Milano, lo storico dell'arte Roman Hollenstein del neuen Zürcher Zeitung di Zurigo, l'architetto Hanno Schlögl di Innsbruck ed io.

L'attività della giuria era cosciente che poter visionare e giudicare l'architettura di una intera regione in un sol colpo rappresenta un'occasione rara. Già dopo mezza giornata di seduta di giuria a Merano questa consapevolezza ha portato i giurati a decidere di visitare direttamente sul luogo tutti i progetti presi in considerazione per la mostra e la pubblicazione. In cinque giorni sono stati visitati quasi cento edifici, malgrado il tragitto percorso fosse enorme: i chilometri dovrebbero ammontare a quasi 1.300! Dobbiamo essere riconoscenti che dappertutto si siano resi disponibili degli architetti, che in convoglio hanno condotto i giurati di costruzione in costruzione – senza il loro ausilio la giuria si sarebbe persa in

buildings from other regions of the Alps.

A falcon flew from Wolkensteine

When the exhibition and publication project "2000–2006 New Architecture in South Tyrol" was first conceived both the Südtiroler Künstlerbund and Merano arte were particularly concerned that the selection procedure should be as objective and transparent as possible. The starting point was research into the exact number of projects that would form the basis for the overall project. The Autonomous Province of Bolzano-South Tyrol was divided into five regions in each of which two architects were named. Following this these persons, Verena Dander, Dorothea Aichner, Magdalena Schmid, Arnold Gapp, Werner Tscholl, Heinold Gasser, Luigi Scolari, Lukas Abram, Siegfried Delueg and Heinrich Mutschlechner were asked to make a list of the 50 best buildings in their respective geographic areas. These architects, who formed a kind of preliminary jury, were asked to restrict their selection to buildings that had been erected between 2000 and 2006.

Regrettably, this restriction of the period from which the buildings selected should date made it impossible to fill the gap that exists between the last edition of the guide "Architecture in South Tyrol" and the buildings covered by this recently completed project. If the foundation of the Chamber of Architects of the Autonomous Province of Bolzano-South Tyrol were in the near future to decide to issue a new architec-

sammenstellung von fast 400 Projekten. Da diese 400 Projekte in einheitlicher Form einer international besetzen Jury vorgelegt werden sollten, entschlossen sich der Südtiroler Künstlerbund und „kunst Meran" dazu, von allen Bauten neue Fotos machen zu lassen. So sollte vermieden werden, dass die Preisrichter von guten Fotos und nicht von guten Bauten beeindruckt würden. Darüber hinaus wurde entschieden, dass maximal 50 Bauwerke präsentiert werden sollten, wobei ein Architekt bzw. Architekturbüro insgesamt nur drei Mal vorkommen sollte. Zur selben Zeit wurde die Jury zusammengestellt und einberufen: Ihr gehörten Architekt Joseph Grima von der Architektur- und Designzeitschrift Domus in Mailand, Kunsthistoriker Roman Hollenstein von der neuen Zürcher Zeitung in Zürich, Architekt Hanno Schlögl aus Innsbruck und ich an.

Die Arbeit der Jury war vom Bewusstsein geprägt, dass es eine seltene Gelegenheit darstellt, die Architektur einer ganzen Region geschlossen betrachten und beurteilen zu können. Das führte dazu, dass sich die Preisrichter schon nach einem halben Sitzungstag in Meran dazu entschlossen, alle für die Ausstellung und das Buch in Erwägung zu ziehenden Projekte vor Ort zu besichtigen. Also wurden binnen fünf Tagen fast hundert Bauten besucht, wobei allein die Fahrstrecken enorm waren: Die insgesamt zurückgelegte Kilometerzahl dürfte bei ca. 1.300 liegen. Dankenswerterweise stellten sich in allen Landesteilen Architekten zur Verfügung, die die Juroren qualche valle laterale: si ringraziano quindi Werner Seidl, Wolfgang Piller, Georg Klotzner e Martin Geier, che ci hanno accompagnati con competenza tecnica e conoscenza dei luoghi tra le montagne e le valli dell'Alto Adige.

Purtroppo questa traversata, simile ad una maratona, ha avuto anche un rovescio della medaglia: le leggendarie e rinomate locande dell'Alto Adige non sono state oggetto delle nostre soste: infatti non c'è stato il tempo per godere della gastronomia locale. Dovendo visitare proprio tutti gli edifici che ci eravamo prefissati, alcuni progetti sono stati approvati al calare del buio – praticamente dopo l'ultimo "splendore dei tramonti sulle Dolomiti".

Infine – dopo un ulteriore giro finale della giuria – si è giunti alla decisione: in tutto 48 edifici da tutte le zone della provincia sono stati scelti per la pubblicazione e per essere esposti alla mostra. Due progetti in meno, rispetto a quanto richiesto dalla committenza.

Nuova architettura in Alto Adige
Tra le sorprese più positive emerse dall'insieme dei migliori esempi della nuova architettura in Alto Adige emerge il fatto che in tutte le zone della provincia esiste una cultura architettonica degna di nota, cosa che al contempo ribalta il pregiudizio che nei luoghi distanti da Merano e Bolzano non possa manifestarsi uno scenario di architettura. La giuria ha trovato ovunque, tra Sesto e Solda – i luoghi alle estremità orientale ed occidentale del suo itine- ture guide this would be a very welcome move, as the preliminary selection for this new project alone produced a list of almost 400 projects!

As these 400 projects were to be presented to the international jury in a standardised form the Südtiroler Künstlerbund and Merano arte decided to have new photographs taken of all the buildings. It was hoped that this would avoid the jurors being impressed by good photographs rather than good buildings. It was decided additionally that a maximum of 50 buildings should be finally selected, and that no individual architect or architects practice should be listed more than three times. The jury was chosen and appointed at around the same time: it was made up of architect Joseph Grima from the architecture and design magazine Domus in Milan, art historian Roman Hollenstein from the newspaper, Neue Zürcher Zeitung in Zurich, architect Hanno Schlögl from Innsbruck and myself.

The jury's working method was influenced by the awareness that this was a rare opportunity to view and evaluate the architecture of an entire region as a whole. This in turn led to jurors deciding after the first half-day meeting in Merano to visit all the projects under consideration for the exhibition and the book. Within a period of five days almost one hundred buildings were visited, which involved covering enormous distances: the total number of kilometres travelled was around 1300 (about 810 miles). Thankfully, in all regions of the province there were architects who were willing

im Konvoi von Bau zu Bau führten – ohne ihre Mitwirkung hätte sich die Jury auf ihrer Route wohl in irgendeinem Seitental verirrt, weshalb an dieser Stelle Werner Seidl, Wolfgang Piller, Georg Klotzner und Martin Geier gedankt sei, die uns fach- und ortskundig über die Berge und durch die Täler Südtirols geleitet haben. Bedauerlicherweise hatte dieser marathonähnliche Überflug auch eine Schattenseite: Die der Jury auf den langen Fahrten im Auto da und dort als sagenhaft gut beschriebenen Südtiroler Wirtshäuser mussten auf der Strecke bleiben, denn es blieb für die Einnahme von ortstypischen Mahlzeiten kaum Zeit. Und da auch wirklich alle Bauten besichtigt werden sollten, die man sich vorgemerkt hatte, musste manches Projekt noch nach Einbruch der Dunkelheit begutachtet werden – sozusagen nach dem „letzten Dolomitenglüh'n".

Doch am Ende – und nach einer kleinen Nachjury – stand es fest: Insgesamt 48 Bauten aus allen Landesteilen sollten in die Ausstellung und das Buch aufgenommen werden. D. h. es wurden zwei Projekte weniger ausgesucht, als die Auftraggeber festgesetzt hatten.

Neue Architektur in Südtirol
Zu den positivsten Überraschungen bei der Zusammenstellung der besten Beispiele neuer Architektur in Südtirol zählt die Tatsache, dass es eigentlich in allen Regionen eine beachtliche Baukultur gibt, was zugleich das Vorurteil widerlegt, dass es in von Bozen oder Meran weit entfernten Ge-

rario architettonico – edifici di notevole interesse. Particolarmente degno di nota, sotto questo punto di vista, è il paese di Sesto, situato in una laterale della Val Pusteria. Nel piccolo comune non solo è nato il premio internazionale "Neues Bauen in den Alpen", ma, per la prima volta in Alto Adige, si è deciso di indire un concorso di progettazione per un incarico pubblico a livello municipale. Il progetto vincitore è la centrale di teleriscaldamento di Siegfried Delueg. La costruzione ha un valore esemplare, non solo perché è un'architettura ben risolta, ma perché è particolarmente interessante la storia che precede il bando di concorso. Qui - anche grazie al lavoro di sensibilizzazione del premio "Neues Bauen in den Alpen" - si è riconosciuto che in un paese di alta montagna una zona per insediamenti produttivi che si espande in modo incontrollato sarebbe un intervento tutt'altro che sostenibile per il turismo. Pertanto si è deciso di destinare il terreno per la costruzione della centrale di teleriscaldamento sul limitare del bosco, in modo che risultasse possibile collocare in modo adeguato il volume dell'edificio relativamente grande. Nel progetto, l'attenzione all'inserimento nel contesto del paesaggio, insieme alla scelta dei materiali utilizzati, ha reso possibile evitare un danno all'immagine del paese che vive anche sul turismo. Sarebbe da auspicarsi che altri interventi edilizi comunali di questo tipo, previsti su tutto il territorio provinciale, si ispirassero a questo modello. L'esempio di Sesto dimostra che nel settore dell'archi-

to bring the convoy of jurors from building to building – without their assistance the jury would probably have lost their way in some side valley or other which is why I take this opportunity to thank Werner Seidl, Wolfgang Piller, Georg Klotzner and Martin Geier, who guided us with their expert local knowledge over the mountains and through the valleys of South Tyrol. Regrettably, this marathon outing had a negative side. The South Tyrolean inns described in glowing terms to the jury members during their long car journeys had to be ignored, as there was hardly any time to enjoy the typical local dishes. And, as it was decided to visit all the buildings that had been selected several projects had to be evaluated after nightfall – that is to say after the last legendary "glow of the Dolomites".

But in the end a total of 48 buildings from all parts of the region were selected for inclusion in the book and the exhibition. That is to say two fewer projects than originally envisaged by the commissioning bodies.

New architecture in South Tyrol
Among the positive surprises in compiling the best examples of recent architecture in South Tyrol was the fact that there is a remarkable culture of building in all areas of the province thus refuting the prejudice that there is no architecture scene in the areas remote from Bolzano or Merano. The jury found excellent buildings everywhere between Solda and Sesto in Val Pusteria, the most western and eastern points on their travels. This is particularly worth mention-

bieten keine Architekturszene geben könne. Die Jury fand zwischen Sulden und Sexten – dem westlichsten und dem östlichsten Punkt ihrer Architekturreise – überall hervorragende Bauten vor. Besonders erwähnenswert ist in dieser Hinsicht der Ort Sexten in einem Seitental des Pustertals. In der kleinen Gemeinde wurde nicht nur der internationale Preis für „Neues Bauen in den Alpen" ins Leben gerufen, sondern man entschloss sich dort auch dazu, für eine kommunale Bauaufgabe einen Gestaltungswettbewerb auszuschreiben. Das Projekt, das in dieser Konkurrenz siegreich war und umgesetzt wurde, ist das kleine Fernheizwerk von Siegfried Delueg. Der Bau hat Vorbildcharakter, weil er nicht nur in Bezug auf seine Architektur gut gelöst wurde, sondern weil die Vorgeschichte des ihm zugrunde liegenden Wettbewerbs besonders interessant ist. Man hatte hier – wohl auch aufgrund der langjährigen Aufbauarbeit des Preises für „Neues Bauen in den Alpen" – erkannt, dass in einem Dorf in hochalpiner Lage eine wild wuchernde Gewerbezone wohl alles andere als tourismusverträglich ist. Das führte dazu, dass schon das für den Bau des Fernheizwerks notwendige Bauland an der Waldgrenze ausgewiesen wurde und es somit möglich war, den relativ großen Bau etwas abseits dezent zu platzieren. In Verbindung mit seiner auf die örtliche Situation bezogenen Gestaltung und die verwendeten Materialien konnte so auch eine Störung des Ortsbildes der Tourismusgemeinde vermieden werden. Es wäre ähnlichen kommunalen Bauvorhaben im

tettura ciò che promuove ed è positivo per il turismo non è l'edificazione di alberghi, funivie, ecc., bensì tutti quegli interventi che conservano inalterata l'immagine originaria del paesaggio, ovvero riprendono e sviluppano delicatamente quegli elementi fondamentali del paesaggio che porta l'impronta dell'uomo. Altri esempi di architettura, dove la giuria ha riconosciuto l'intento di perseguire una sorta di rapporto mimetico con il paesaggio, sono l'ampliamento del cimitero di Luttago in Val Aurina, la tenuta vinicola Manincor a Caldaro, l'albergo Pergola residence a Lagundo e il Messner Mountain Museum "Ortles" a Solda. Accanto a questo aspetto, anche il fatto che in Alto Adige sia importante costruire nel paesaggio è stato elevato a criterio di valutazione dalla giuria, che ha pertanto escluso quei progetti di architettura basati solo su considerazioni estetico/artistiche.
Nonostante questo, l'arte gode di un alto riconoscimento per l'architettura in Alto Adige. Probabilmente ciò è dovuto al fatto che il Südtiroler Künstlerbund si è sempre sentito il rappresentante interdisciplinare di ogni espressione artistica e che Merano arte ha inteso se stessa come un'istituzione culturale votata ad un pensiero trasversale. Pertanto in Alto Adige non esiste un solo edificio pubblico in cui l'arte non giochi il suo ruolo. Gli interventi d'arte nell'architettura spaziano dalla consulenza per il colore (tra gli altri, la funivia di S. Martino a Laces, EURAC a Bolzano, il liceo scientifico di lingua tedesca di Bolzano) – sino al coinvolgimento concreto degli artisti nella costruzio-

ing in the case of Sesto in a side valley of the Pustertal. Not only was the international prize for "New Building in the Alps" initially set up in this small community, but a competition for a communal services building in South Tyrol was also held there. The project that won this competition and was later built is the small district heating plant by Siegfried Delueg. The building has a model character not only because it is architecturally well resolved but also because the history of the competition leading up to its construction is particularly interesting. Here, due most likely to the years of work building up the "New Building in the Alps" award, it was recognized that in villages in high-altitude alpine locations the rampant growth of commercial and industrial zones is anything but advantageous for the tourist industry. This realisation led to finding a site for the district heating plant on the edge of the woods, which meant that this relatively large building was placed somewhat outside the village. Thanks to the design that responds to the local situation and uses appropriate materials, it was possible to avoid disturbing the image of this tourist destination. It is to be hoped that similar communal projects throughout the province follow this model, as the example of Sesto shows also what kind of architecture really has a positive effect on tourism. It is not the construction of hotels, ropeways etc. that have a positive impact on this branch of the economy but the contributions to visual design that leave the original appearance of the landscape as

ganzen Land nur zu wünschen, dass sie diesem Vorbild folgen, denn das Beispiel Sexten zeigt auch, was auf dem Gebiet der Architektur in Wahrheit den Tourismus fördert: Nicht der Bau von Hotels, Seilbahnen usw. wirkt sich positiv auf diesen Wirtschaftszweig aus, sondern alle Beiträge der optischen Gestaltung, die das ursprüngliche Bild der Landschaft möglichst unangetastet lassen bzw. tradierte Leitbilder in der von Menschenhand gestalteten Kulturlandschaft aufgreifen und sanft weiterentwickeln. Weitere Architekturbeispiele, die die Jury aufgrund der Tatsache nominieren konnte, dass sie diesen Ansatz einer mimetischen Verbindung von Architektur und Landschaft verfolgen, sind die Friedhofserweiterung in Luttach im Ahrntal, das Weingut Manincor bei Kaltern, das Hotel Pergola Residence in Algund und das Messner Mountain Museum „Ortles" in Sulden. Daneben führte der von der Jury zu einem Bewertungskriterium erhobene Aspekt, dass in Südtirol ein Bauen mit der Landschaft wichtig ist, dazu, dass das eine oder andere aus rein künstlerischen Erwägungen zustande gekommene Architekturprojekt von den Preisrichtern ausgeschieden wurde.

Dennoch genießt Kunst in der Südtiroler Architekturszene einen überaus hohen Stellenwert. Möglicherweise liegt das daran, dass sich z. B. der Südtiroler Künstlerbund immer schon als interdisziplinär angelegte Standesvertretung der Künstler aller Sparten und „kunst Meran" als eine dem Cross-over-Gedanken verpflichtete Kultureinrichtung sahen, dass es wohl ne. "I giardini di Castel Trauttmansdorff" a Merano ed il "Museo Provinciale di Storia e Cultura Sudtirolese" a Castel Tirolo presso Merano sono due strutture per il tempo libero e per la cultura, alla cui realizzazione gli artisti Margit Klammer, Elisabeth Hölzl, Julia Bornefeld, Walter Niedermayr e Gottfried Bechtold, (tra gli altri) hanno partecipato direttamente. Gli artisti hanno partecipato a rendere più attraenti spazi o a differenziare parti di edifici anche in tutte le nuove costruzioni scolastiche provinciali. Per la Libera Università di Bolzano è intervenuto, tra gli altri, Erik Steinbrecher, nell'Istituto tecnico agrario Castel Baumgarten di Ora Margit Klammer, nella scuola professionale di lingua tedesca di Bolzano Heimo Zobernig e nella scuola professionale provinciale di Bressanone la Designer Societät Stuttgart e Josef Rainer (quest'ultimo è stato premiato al primo "Premio per l'arte nell'architettura in Alto Adige").

Anche il ricco patrimonio artistico dell'Alto Adige stimola gli architetti: nella Provincia Autonoma di Bolzano si trovano un folto numero di monumenti di valore che abbisognerebbero di tutela e conservazione, ma anche di accogliere nuove funzioni. In questi casi, sia gli architetti locali sia quelli stranieri devono confrontare i loro progetti con il contesto storico. Gli interventi di restauro e rifunzionalizzazione degli edifici dell'era fascista rappresentano in quest'ambito un compito progettuale particolare e non privo di responsabilità. L'architetto Klaus Kada, attivo a Graz e ad Aachen, si è impegnato ad impostare il suo concetto untouched as possible or that take up traditional images in the cultural landscape shaped by human hand and develop them further. Other examples of architecture nominated by the jury because they pursue this mimetic connection between architecture and landscape are the extension to the cemetery in Luttago in Valle Aurina, the Manincor vineyard near Caldaro, the Pergola Residence Hotel in Lagundo and the Messner Mountain Museum "Ortles" in Solda. In addition the criterion applied by the jury that building with the landscape is an important issue in South Tyrol led to the jurors rejecting a number of projects that were based on artistic considerations alone.

Yet art enjoys a high reputation in the South Tyrol architecture scene. It is possibly because the Südtiroler Künstlerbund has always regarded itself as an interdisciplinary representative body for creative persons from all branches of art and Merano arte is a cultural facility shaped by a "cross-over" mentality that there is probably not a singe public building in South Tyrol in which site-specific art does not play a role. The spectrum of "Kunst am Bau" as site-specific art is called in German (the term literally means "art at the building") extends from colour consultation – an area where artist Manfred Alois Mayr is active (for example the ropeway in S. Martino Laces, EURAC Bolzano, the secondary school in Bolzano) – to the concrete participation of artists in the realisation of a building project. "The Gardens of Schloss Trauttsmansdorff" in

keinen einzigen öffentlichen Bau in Südtirol gibt, in dem Kunst am Bau keine Rolle spielt. Das Spektrum von Kunst am Bau reicht von Farbberatung – ein Arbeitsgebiet, in dem der Künstler Manfred Alois Mayr u. a. tätig ist (u. a. Seilbahn St. Martin bei Latsch, EURAC Bozen, Realgymnasium Bozen) – bis hin zur konkreten Mitwirkung von Künstlern an der Umsetzung eines Bauvorhabens. „Die Gärten von Schloss Trauttmansdorff" in Meran und das „Südtiroler Landesmuseum für Kultur- und Landesgeschichte" in Schloss Tirol bei Meran sind zwei Freizeit- bzw. Kultureinrichtungen, bei deren Realisierung Künstler unmittelbar mitgewirkt haben, u. a. Margit Klammer, Elisabeth Hölzl, Julia Bornefeld, Walter Niedermayr und Gottfried Bechtold. Auch bei allen neu errichteten Bildungsstätten des Landes trugen Künstler dazu bei, die optische Attraktivität von Räumen oder ganzen Gebäudeteilen zu unterstreichen. Bei der Freien Universität Bozen war es u. a. Erik Steinbrecher, bei der Oberschule für Landwirtschaft im Ansitz Baumgarten in Auer Margit Klammer, bei der Landesberufsschule in Bozen Heimo Zobernig und bei der Landesberufsschule in Brixen die Designer Societät Stuttgart und Josef Rainer (der Letztgenannte wurde beim ersten Südtiroler Landespreis für Kunst am Bau ausgezeichnet).

Auch die reiche Kunstgeschichte des Landes fordert die Architekten heraus: In der Autonomen Provinz Bozen-Südtirol befindet sich eine Vielzahl historisch wertvoller Baudenkmäler, die sowohl einer angemessenen Denkmalpflege bedürfen als auch manchmal neue Funktionen übernehmen sollen. In solchen Fällen sehen sich einheimische wie auswärtige Architekten bei der Entwicklung ihrer Gestaltungsvorschläge damit konfrontiert, sich mit dem historischen Kontext auseinander setzen zu müssen. In diesem Zusammenhang stellen Sanierungs- und Revitalisierungsvorhaben an den Bauten aus der faschistischen Ära Italiens besonders verantwortungsvoll zu lösende Bauaufgaben dar. Z. B. unterzog sich der in Graz und Aachen tätige Klaus Kada der Mühe, für die Umwandlung des ehemaligen GIL-Gebäudes aus den 1930er Jahren das originale Planmaterial von Mansutti und Miozzo aus Padua

progettuale per l'odierna EURAC sulla base dei disegni originali della ex Gil, opera degli anni Trenta degli architetti Mansutti e Miozzo di Padova. Rispetto a questo intervento, Stanislao Fierro ha realizzato un "progetto silenzioso": sotto la piazza trapezoidale, compresa tra la Casa Littoria (oggi Uffici Finanziari) ed il tribunale e tra le due vie laterali, si doveva costruire un garage interrato. L'incarico progettuale ha incluso, oltre alla "modernizzazione della piazza", anche l'implementazione di interventi costruttivi, apparentemente meno importanti riguardanti l'autorimessa interrata (ingressi ed uscite carrabili e pedonali); il tutto compreso in uno scenario simile ad un'opera d'arte totale, tipica dell'epoca compresa tra le due guerre. La trasformazione architettonica della piazza dovrebbe essere apprezzata, in quanto si confronta pacatamente ed oggettivamente con edifici risalenti ad un'epoca dello stato italiano politicamente discutibile.

Lungo un itinerario architettonico attraverso l'Alto Adige si incontra una serie di altri progetti che nascono dal confronto con la storia dell'architettura del posto. Molti degli edifici da rivitalizzare devono assumere nuove funzioni, pertanto risulta importante integrare le parti mancanti e procedere con la costruzione sull'esistente. Un vuoto urbano particolarmente poco attraente è stato "chiuso" dalla galleria "Kurhauspassage" nella città vecchia di Merano, dove l'insediamento di negozi ed appartamenti ha rivitalizzato, in senso letterale, una zona precedentemente morta del centro storico. Si è costruito sull'esistente anche in due residenze a sud di Bolzano: il "Lanserhaus" a S. Michele di Appiano che viene utilizzato per manifestazioni culturali, e Castel Baumgarten ad Ora che oggi funge come scuola superiore di agraria. Per soddisfare i requisiti di una moderna costruzione entrambi gli insiemi storici sono stati sottoposti ad interventi sostanziali. Nel caso del "Lanserhaus" tutti gli spazi di distribuzione sono stati disposti principalmente al livello interrato, mentre per Castel Baumgarten si è costruito su più piani proprio a ridosso dell'esistente, per adattarlo all'uso scolastico. Entrambi i progetti dimostrano come si può trarre tanto charme da vecchie pareti in pietra, se non sono completamen-

Merano and the "South Tyrol Museum of Cultural and Regional History" in Schloss Tirol near Merano are two leisure and cultural facilities where artists were directly involved, among them Margit Klammer, Elisabeth Hölzl, Julia Bornefeld, Walter Niedermayr and Gottfried Bechtold. But also in newly erected educational facilities in the province artists have contributed to enhancing the visual attractiveness of rooms or of entire parts of buildings. In the Free University Bolzano the artist involved was Erik Steinbrecher, in the Agriculture School in the Baumgarten estate in Ora it was Margit Klammer, in the Regional Vocational School in Bolzano Heimo Zobernig and in the Bressanone Regional Vocational School the Designer Societät Stuttgart and Josef Rainer were the artists responsible (the latter received a prize at the first South Tyrol award for site-specific art).

The rich art history of the province also presents architects with a challenge. In the Autonomous Province of Bolzano-South Tyrol there are many historically valuable buildings that need appropriate conservation measures as well as, at times, new functions. In such cases local architects and those from outside the region are confronted in their design work with the historic context. In this area the refurbishment and renovation of buildings dating from the Italian fascist era demands a particular sense of responsibility. For example, in restoring the former GIL building from the 1930s Klaus Kada, who works in both Graz and Aachen, went to the trouble of finding the original plans by Mansutti and Miozzo in Padova and using them as a basis for his concept for the present EURAC building. In comparison the project carried out by Stanislao Fierro in Bolzano was relatively "quiet". Underneath the trapezoid-shaped square an underground garage was planned extending between the "Casa Littoria" courthouse building (nowadays the tax office) and the traffic arteries that run along its sides. This commission included the "modernisation" of the square and also the design of the (apparently) subordinate aspects of an underground garage (access and exit ramps, staircases etc.) in a strong setting from the interwar period that has the quality of a "Gesamtkunstwerk". This

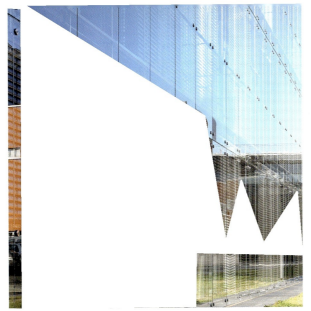

auszuheben und auf seiner Basis das Konzept für die heutige EURAC zu planen. Ein im Verhältnis dazu vergleichsweise „leises Projekt" setzte Stanislao Fierro in Bozen um: Unter dem trapezförmigen Platz zwischen Gerichtsgebäude, „Casa Littoria" (heute Finanzamt) und den an seinen Seiten entlang führenden Verkehrsadern sollte eine Tiefgarage errichtet werden. Die Bauaufgabe umfasste also neben der „Modernisierung des Platzes" auch die Implementierung der scheinbar nebensächlichen baulichen Einrichtungen einer Tiefgarage (Aus- und Einfahrten, Zu- und Abgänge) in eine starke, gesamtkunstwerksähnliche Inszenierung aus der Zwischenkriegszeit. Die architektonische Veränderung des Platzes muss deshalb gewürdigt werden, weil sie den Bauwerken aus einer fragwürdigen politischen Epoche des italienischen Staates mit ebenso viel Zurückhaltung wie Sachbezogenheit begegnet.

Bei einer Architekturreise durch Südtirol stößt man auf eine ganze Reihe weiterer Projekte, die aus einer Auseinandersetzung mit der Baugeschichte des Landes hervorgingen. Viele der zu revitalisierenden Bauten müssen neue Funktionen übernehmen, wobei es wichtig ist, Fehlendes zu ergänzen und Bestehendes weiterzubauen. Eine besonders unattraktive Lücke wurde durch die Kurhauspassage in der Meraner Altstadt geschlossen, wobei der Einbau von Geschäftslokalen und Wohnungen zu einer wörtlich zu verstehenden Revitalisierung einer vorher toten Zone im Stadtzentrum geführt hat. „Weitergebaut" wurden auch

te sacrificate alla nuova costruzione, ma se si riesce invece ad attribuirvi nuove funzioni. A parte queste constatazioni, nel caso di Castel Baumgarten risulta chiaro come anche edifici carichi di memoria storica possano essere affrontati nella loro ulteriore trasformazione architettonica con un approccio giocoso o persino dotato di humor. Proprio questo edificio, che era completamente abbandonato e minacciava di andare in rovina, è stato restituito a nuova vita grazie ad un intervento di questo tipo.

O terra di vigneti, addio!

Un settore in cui la giuria si è trovata in difficoltà nel trovare delle soluzioni degne di nota è stato quello dell'edilizia residenziale. Un solo edificio a Merano ed uno a Brunico, le cui realizzazioni si devono alla passione per l'architettura dei loro committenti, sembrano poco, ma questa situazione si spiega anche con la normativa altoatesina per l'edilizia agevolata. In generale è da constatare che la tipologia residenziale ad alta densità rappresenta una delle pecche della cultura del progetto in Alto Adige, ma essa è da annoverarsi tra uno dei più gravi e irrisolti problemi della regione insieme alla dispersione sempre maggiore dell'edificazione sul territorio. Già nel 1997 Dietmar Steiner sottolineò la questione dell'eccessivo consumo di territorio, ma il suo impegno in questa direzione è rimasto purtroppo inascoltato. Egli ha riassunto il tema in questi termini: " a) la generale tendenza di "sprawl" porta necessariamente ad un fenomeno di dispersione edilizia,

architectural alteration of the square must be praised for the way in which it deals with buildings from a politically dubious era of the Italian state with equal amounts of restraint and objectivity.

Interested visitors making an architecture trip through South Tyrol can view an entire series of further projects that have emerged from an examination of the region's history. Many of the buildings to be revitalised must house new functions, the important aspect here is inserting what was lacking as well as developing the existing substance. A particularly unattractive gap in the urban fabric has been closed by the creation of the "Kurhauspassage" in Merano, where the creation of shops and apartments had led to the literal revival of what had been a dead zone in the city centre. Two country estates to the south of Bolzano have been "further developed": the "Lanserhaus" in S. Michele/Appiano, which is used for cultural functions, and the Baumgarten estate in Ora, today used as an agricultural school. To satisfy contemporary requirements both historic ensembles had to be quite substantially altered. In the Lanserhaus project the necessary circulation spaces could be built for the most part underground, whereas in the Baumgarten estate several storeys had to be added to accommodate the school. Both projects offer proof of how much charm can be extracted from old walls when they are not removed entirely to make room for new buildings but are given new functions. In addition, with regard to the Baumgarten estate it should

zwei ländliche Ansitze südlich von Bozen, das Lanserhaus in St. Michael bei Eppan, das für kulturelle Zwecke genutzt wird, und der Ansitz Baumgarten in Auer, der heute als Oberschule für Landwirtschaft in Funktion steht. Um zeitgemäßen Anforderungen gerecht zu werden, mussten beide historischen Bauensembles relativ stark verändert werden. Im Fall des Lanserhauses wurden die erforderlichen Erschließungsräume hauptsächlich unterirdisch angelegt, wohingegen an den Ansitz Baumgarten gleich mehrstöckig angebaut werden musste, denn in ihm war eine Schule unterzubringen. Beide Projekte stellen unter Beweis, wie viel Charme alten Gemäuern entlockt werden kann, wenn sie Neubauten nicht zur Gänze weichen, sondern ihnen neue Funktionen zugeführt werden können. Darüber hinaus ist in Bezug auf den Ansitz Baumgarten auch festzustellen, dass den geschichtsträchtigen Gebäuden bei ihrer architektonischen Weiterentwicklung durchaus auch mit Verspieltheit oder gar einer Portion Humor begegnet werden darf. Gerade dieses Gebäude, das völlig verwahrlost war und zu verfallen drohte, wurde durch eine derartige Herangehensweise wieder sehr lebendig gestaltet.

Mein Rebland lebe wohl!

Ein Gebiet, in dem es die Jury eher schwer hatte, herausragende architektonische Lösungen zu finden, war der Wohnbau. Nur je ein Wohnbauprojekt in Meran und Bruneck, dessen Realisierung auch wegen des Engagements der Bauherren in Sachen Ar-

con la conseguenza di uno squilibrio nella distribuzione della forza economica – anche quella dei bilanci pubblici – dai vecchi centri urbani verso i loro dintorni, b) la "naturale" identità della cultura e della vita quotidiana di luoghi e regioni, sviluppatasi nei secoli in un'Europa multiforme si perde a favore di un'identità "strutturata" con la giustificazione di voler essere inconfondibili; c) dalla dispersione edilizia e dall'identità "strutturata" deriva logicamente la perdita dello spazio pubblico. Questa tendenza economica e culturale è rafforzata dallo sviluppo tecnologico delle comunicazioni; d) nuovi insediamenti, che nascono in tali condizioni ne rappresentano l'odierno e realistico risultato. Non si intravede una possibile alternativa."[12]

Dietmar Steiner descrive inoltre, come molti dei problemi legati all'architettura di oggi derivino da un fenomeno di mobilità-tempo, che si basa sul fatto che per la società contemporanea la tempistica del trasporto è un valore fondamentale – un fenomeno che risulta evidente quando le strade sono bloccate o si forma una coda, poiché il principio di mobilità – tempo entra in crisi. Sarebbe inappropriato collegare lo stress che ne deriva solamente alle persone, esso ha effetto anche sull'ambiente, e non solo sotto forma di sostanze tossiche invisibili, ma anche in termini di sviluppo errato.

Ne sono testimonianza: la dispersione edilizia, la crescita incontrollata delle zone produttive, ed anche la cacofonia di stimoli audiovisivi che caratterizza certe zone edificate o centri per il tempo libero. Oggigiorno

be said that the architectural development of historic buildings can certainly contain a playful element or even a certain amount of humour. Precisely this building, which was completely neglected and threatened to become a ruin, was redesigned using this kind of approach in a way that has filled it with new life.

My land of vines, farewell!

Housing was one major area where the jury had difficulties in finding excellent architectural solutions. One housing project in Merano and one in Brunico (which were built thanks to the client's commitment to good architecture) seems very few, but the situation can be explained in terms of the legal framework for subsidised housing in South Tyrol. In general it can be said that the construction of dense housing developments not only has a rather shadowy existence but that, together with the rampant suburban sprawl throughout the region, it represents one of the major problems in the province as yet untackled. Although Dietmar Steiner dramatically described the theme of excessive use of land in South Tyrol as early as 1997, his involvement in this area has so far not received any response worth mentioning. Steiner summarised the situation as follows: "a) the general tendency to sprawl leads to disruptive development and a redistribution of economic strength – also of public bodies – from the old core cities to the surrounding areas; b) the so-to-speak ‚natural' identity of culture and everyday life of villages towns and regions that

chitektur zustande kam, erscheint sehr wenig, aber die Situation erklärt sich aus der dem geförderten Wohnbau zugrunde liegenden gesetzlichen Basis in Südtirol. Insgesamt ist festzustellen, dass der verdichtete Wohnbau in der Südtiroler Baukultur nicht nur ein Schattendasein führt, sondern dass er mit der fast überall grassierenden Zersiedelung zu den großen unbewältigten Problemen in der Region zählt. Zwar wurde das Thema der übermäßigen Landnahme in Südtirol von Dietmar Steiner schon 1997 mit Nachdruck dargestellt, sein Einsatz in dieser Sache blieb aber bis heute ohne nennenswerte Resonanz. Er fasste wie folgt zusammen: „a) die generelle Tendenz zum ‚sprawl' führt zwangsläufig zu einer ‚Zersiedelung' mit der Folge einer Umverteilung der ökonomischen Potenz – auch der öffentlichen Haushalte – von den alten Kernstädten zu ihrem Umland; b) die Jahrhunderte lang in einem vielgestaltigen Europa entwickelte, sozusagen ‚natürliche' Identität der Kultur und des Alltagslebens von Orten und Regionen geht zugunsten einer zur Behauptung der Unverwechselbarkeit ‚veranstalteten' Identität verloren; c) aus der Zersiedelung und der veranstalteten Identität ergibt sich mit logischer Konsequenz ein Verlust des öffentlichen Raums. Verstärkt wird dieser ökonomische und kulturelle Trend durch die technologische Entwicklung der Kommunikation; d) neue Siedlungen, die unter den genannten Rahmenbedingungen entstehen, sind die derzeit realistische Reaktion. Eine Alternative dazu ist nicht in Sicht."[12]

Dietmar Steiner beschreibt weiter, dass viele, in der Architektur von heute gegebene Probleme von einem Zeit-Mobilitäts-Phänomen herrühren, das darauf beruht, dass für die Gesellschaft der Gegenwart hauptsächlich die Zeit von Bedeutung ist, die für die Überwindung einer Strecke benötigt wird – ein Phänomen, das z. B. dann besonders sichtbar ist, wenn die Straßen blockiert sind oder ein Stau entstanden ist, weil dann das ins Wanken geratene Zeit-Mobilitäts-Prinzip in Stress gerät. Es wäre völlig unrichtig, die damit in Zusammenhang stehende Anspannung nur auf den Menschen zu beziehen, sie hat durchaus auch auf die Umwelt Auswirkungen. Und zwar nicht nur in Form von zunächst noch

tutte queste problematiche si manifestano con più vigore, quanto più risicata è la superficie edificabile delle strette valli alpine; pertanto nel criterio di selezione per "2000-2006 architetture recenti in Alto Adige" è stato di particolare significato che la giuria potesse nominare anche delle opere infrastrutturali: la ferrovia della Val Venosta, ora riattivata, e le sue nuove pensiline, che sono state progettate da Walter Dietl insieme all'ampliamento della storica rimessa della stazione capolinea di Malles. La ferrovia partecipa a sostenere il traffico lungo la valle, che soprattutto durante il periodo della raccolta delle mele diventa intenso. Nel 1990 la linea ferroviaria esistente era stata dismessa. Oggi essa è stata riattivata e modernizzata come ausilio alla mobilità degli abitanti della valle. Con la ferrovia si è finalmente imposta la visione che un intervento per la tutela dell'ambiente può avere successo solo quando sono conservate e soddisfatte anche le esigenze legate alla qualità di vita della popolazione. La riattivazione della ferrovia ha dimostrato che per la nuova era dei trasporti era necessario, oltre ad un moderno parco macchine, anche il rinnovo delle stazioni. Condizioni favorevoli hanno consentito di non attingere da un programma modulare da catalogo, ma di progettare tutte le nuove stazioni tenendo in considerazione le peculiarità topologiche della Val Venosta.

Sarebbe auspicabile che anche l'architettura di qualità possa diffondersi e che le sue qualità presenti e future possano raggiungere una risonanza sovraregionale. Pertanto speriamo che questa pubblicazione e la mostra omonima possano dare un contributo alla diffusione dell'architettura contemporanea dell'Alto Adige.

developed over centuries in a highly diverse Europe is vanishing and being replaced by an identity that is ‚organized' in order to assert an independent character; c) sprawl and this ‚organized' identity logically result in a loss of public space. This economic and cultural trend is strengthened by the technological development of communication; d) new settlements produced under these circumstances are the realistic reaction. An alternative is not in sight."[12]

Dietmar Steiner continues by explaining that many of the problems existing in architecture today are caused by a phenomenon of time and mobility based on the fact that for present-day society the time needed to cover a certain distance is the time that is most significant – a phenomenon that becomes particularly clear when streets are blocked or a traffic jam builds up because the time-mobility principle starts to totter and this leads to stress. It would be completely mistaken to relate this stress to human beings alone; it also has an effect on the environment. And this stress not only takes the form of initially invisible pollution but is also manifested in the shape of tendencies that are visually inappropriate or simply wrong. These include sprawl, the rampant growth of industrial zones, but also, in a number of residential leisure areas, excessive audio and visual stimulation. The smaller the development areas in the narrow alpine valleys, the more obvious these problems become, which explains why in the selection process for "2000–2006 New Architecture in South Tyrol" it was particularly significant that the jury nominated an infrastructure facility: the Val Venosta railway line which has been reopened, with its new stations planned by Walter Dietl including the extension to the historical train shed in Malles. The railway contributes to maintaining the flow of traffic through the Val Venosta, which is particularly important during harvest time. In 1990 the existing line had been closed down, now it has been revitalised and modernised, to increase the mobility of the people who live in the valley and their guests. Ultimately an awareness has developed that active support for the cause of environmental protection can only be successful when the quality of life of the population is also protected. But the re-

unsichtbaren Schadstoffbelastungen, sondern auch in Form optischer Fehlentwicklungen. Zersiedelung, wild wuchernde Industriezonen, aber auch die in manchen Siedlungsgebieten oder Freizeitstätten vorhandene audiovisuelle Reizüberflutung. Alle diese Probleme treten umso stärker zutage, je kleiner die bebaubaren Flächen in den engen, alpinen Tälern sind, weshalb es in Zusammenhang „2000–2006 Neue Architektur in Südtirol" von besonderer Bedeutung war, dass das Preisgericht auch eine Infrastruktureinrichtung nominieren konnte: die wieder in Betrieb genommene Vinschgerbahn mit ihren neuen Haltestellen, die Walter Dietl einschließlich einer Erweiterung der historischen Remise in Mals gestaltete. Die Bahn trägt dazu bei, den Verkehrsfluss durch den Vinschgau aufrechtzuerhalten, was besonders in der Erntezeit dringend nötig ist. 1990 war eine bestehende Bahnlinie eingestellt worden, nun wurde sie aber zur Unterstützung der Mobilität der Talbewohner und ihrer Gäste wieder revitalisiert und modernisiert. Es hatte sich also die Einsicht durchgesetzt, dass ein aktives Eintreten für den Umweltschutz nur dann erfolgreich sein kann, wenn die an die Aufrechterhaltung von Lebensqualität gebundenen Bedürfnisse der Bevölkerung ebenfalls erhalten bleiben. Doch die Wiederinbetriebnahme des Bahnverkehrs durch den Vinschgau hat auch gezeigt, dass die neue Ära, in welche die Bahn eintreten sollte, nicht nur neue Zuggarnituren und andere neue technische Einrichtungen erforderlich machte, sondern dass auch die Haltestellen zu erneuern waren. Glückliche Umstände führten dazu, dass die Bahnstationen nicht als Modulprogramm aus dem Katalog bestellt wurden, sondern dass unter Rücksichtnahme auf die besonderen topologischen Erfordernisse des Vinschgaues neue Haltestellen entworfen werden konnten.

Es wäre wünschenswert, dass auch weiterhin qualitätvolle Architektur in Südtirol entstehen und umgesetzt werden kann und die bisherigen ebenso wie die zukünftigen Leistungen überregional bekannt gemacht werden können. Daher bleibt nur noch zu hoffen, dass diese Publikation und die gleichnamige Ausstellung einen Beitrag zur Verbreitung der zeitgenössischen Architektur in Südtirol leisten werden.

introduction of train traffic through the Val Venosta also revealed that the new railway era ushered in did not consist only of new trains and other technical facilities but also required the renewal of the stations. Fortunate circumstances finally led to a situation where the railway stations were not ordered as modules from a catalogue, instead new stations were designed that take into account the topological characteristics of the Val Venosta.

It is highly desirable that architecture of quality should continue to be planned and built in South Tyrol and that the existing and future achievements in this field should become known outside the region. And therefore it is hoped that this publication and the exhibition of the same name will make a significant contribution to the spread of contemporary architecture in South Tyrol.

[1] Ich hab' von Südtirol geträumt, Text und Musik: Sepp Weidacher (1911–1989), Tiroler Volksliedarchiv, Sign. IAg (Zusendung von Siegfried Singer, „Mühlauer Sänger", 2005).

[2] Architektenkammer der Provinz Bozen (Hrsg.), Architektur in Südtirol – 1900 bis heute, Bozen 1993, S. 250. Kuz, Zehra, Walter M. Chramosta und Kenneth Frampton, Autochthone Architektur in Tirol, Individuelle Figuren der Tiroler Baukunst im kollektiven Rahmen der alpinen Landschaftsrezeption, Hall in Tirol 1992, S. 22 f.

[3] A. a. O.

[4] Zoeggeler, Oswald und Ippolito Lamberto. Die Architektur für ein italienisches Bozen 1922–1944, Lana 1992.

[5] Architektenkammer der Provinz Bozen (Hrsg.), Dorf und Stadt – Wohngebiete in Südtirol nach 1970, mit Beiträgen von: Christoph Mayr Fingerle (Projektleitung), Paolo Biadene, Peter Constantini und einem Essay von Dietmar Steiner, Bozen 1997.

[6] Autonome Provinz Bozen-Südtirol, Öffentliches Bauen in Südtirol 1993–2003, Bozen 2003.

[7] Waiz, Susanne, Auf Gebautem Bauen – Im Dialog mit historischer Bausubstanz, Wien-Bozen 2005.

[8] turrisbabel, Trimestriales Mitteilungsblatt der Stiftung der Kammer der Architekten, Raumplaner, Landschaftsplaner, Denkmalpfleger der Autonomen Provinz Bozen-Südtirol.

[9] Sexten Kultur (Hrsg.), Christoph Mayr Fingerle, Karin Krummlauf und Joachim Moroder, Hotelarchitektur in den Alpen 1920–1940, Katalog zur gleichnamigen Ausstellung, Sexten 1989.

[10] Sexten Kultur (Hrsg.), Christoph Mayr Fingerle und Walter Niedermayr, Architektur, Natur und Technik. Katalog zur gleichnamigen Ausstellung, Sexten 1989.

[11] Christoph Mayr Fingerle, Neues Bauen in den Alpen, Architekturpreis 1992, Bozen 1992, S. 5.

[12] Steiner, Dietmar, Über neuzeitliches Siedeln und Hausen., in: Architektenkammer der Provinz Bozen (Hrsg.), Dorf und Stadt – Wohngebiete in Südtirol nach 1970, Bozen 1997, S. 206 f.

[1] Ho sognato dell'Alto Adige, testo e musica: Sepp Weidacher (1911–1989), Tiroler Volksliedarchiv, Sign.IAg (Invio di Siegfried Singer, "Mühlauer Sänger", 2005).

[2] Ordine degli Architetti della Provincia di Bolzano (A cura di), Architettura in Alto Adige– dal 1900 ad oggi, Bolzano 1993, pag. 250. Kuz, Zehra, Walter M. Chramosta und Kenneth Frampton, Autochthone Architektur in Tirol, Individuelle Figuren der Tiroler Baukunst im kollektiven Rahmen der alpinen Landschaftsrezeption, Hall in Tirol 1992, pag. 22 e segg..

[3] vedi nota 2

[4] Zoeggeler, Oswald e Ippolito Lamberto. L'architettura per una Bolzano italiana 1922–1944, Lana 1992.

[5] Ordine degli Architetti della Provincia di Bolzano (Editore), Paese e città – Espansioni residenziali in Alto Adige dopo il 1970, con contributi di: Christoph Mayr Fingerle (Coordinamento), Paolo Biadene, Peter Constantini ed un testo di Dietmar Steiner, Bolzano 1997.

[6] Provincia Autonoma di Bolzano, Opere pubbliche in Alto Adige 1993–2003, Bolzano 2003.

[7] Waiz, Susanne, Costruire sul costruito – Interventi sugli edifici storici, Vienna-Bolzano 2005.

[8] turrisbabel, Notiziario trimestrale della Fondazione dell'Ordine degli Architetti, Pianificatori, Paesaggisti, Conservatori della Provincia Autonoma di Bolzano.

[9] Sesto Cultura (Editore), Christoph Mayr Fingerle, Karin Krummlauf und Joachim Moroder, Hotelarchitektur in den Alpen 1920–1940, Catalogo della mostra omonima, Sesto 1989.

[10] Sesto cultura (Editore), Christoph Mayr Fingerle und Walter Niedermayr, Architektur, Natur und Technik (Architettura, natura e tecnica). Catalogo della mostra omonima, Sesto 1989.

[11] Christoph Mayr Fingerle, Neues Bauen in den Alpen (Nuove costruzioni dell'arco alpino), Premio di architettura 1992, Bolzano 1992, pag. 5.

[12] Steiner, Dietmar, Abitare ed insediarsi oggi, in: Ordine degli Architetti (Editore), Paese e città– Espansioni residenziali in Alto Adige dopo il 1970, Bolzano 1997, pag. 206 e segg.

[1] Ich hab' von Südtirol geträumt, text and music: Sepp Weidacher (1911–1989), Tiroler Volksliedarchiv, Sign. IAg (Zusendung von Siegfried Singer, "Mühlauer Sänger", 2005).

[2] Architektenkammer der Provinz Bozen (ed.), Architektur in Südtirol – 1900 bis heute, Bolzano 1993, p. 250. Kuz, Zehra, Walter M. Chramosta and Kenneth Frampton, Autochthone Architektur in Tirol, Individuelle Figuren der Tiroler Baukunst im kollektiven Rahmen der alpinen Landschaftsrezeption, Hall in Tirol 1992, p. 22 f.

[3] See endnote 2.

[4] Zoeggeler, Oswald und Ippolito Lamberto. Die Architektur für ein italienisches Bozen 1922–1944, Lana 1992.

[5] Architektenkammer der Provinz Bozen (ed.), Dorf und Stadt – Wohngebiete in Südtirol nach 1970, mit Beiträgen von: Christoph Mayr Fingerle (Projektleitung), Paolo Biadene, Peter Constantini und einem Essay von Dietmar Steiner, Bolzano1997.

[6] Autonome Provinz Bozen-Südtirol, Öffentliches Bauen in Südtirol 1993–2003, Bolzano 2003.

[7] Waiz, Susanne, Auf Gebautem Bauen – Im Dialog mit historischer Bausubstanz, Vienna-Bolzano 2005.

[8] turrisbabel, Trimestriales Mitteilungsblatt der Stiftung der Kammer der Architekten, Raumplaner, Landschaftsplaner, Denkmalpfleger der Autonomen Provinz Bozen-Südtirol.

[9] Sexten Kultur (ed.), Christoph Mayr Fingerle, Karin Krummlauf und Joachim Moroder, Hotelarchitektur in den Alpen 1920–1940, catalogue to the exhibition of the same name, Sesto 1989.

[10] Sexten Kultur (ed.), Christoph Mayr Fingerle und Walter Niedermayr, Architektur, Natur und Technik. catalogue to the exhibition of the same name, Sesto 1989.

[11] Christoph Mayr Fingerle, Neues Bauen in den Alpen, Architekturpreis 1992, Bolzano 1992, p. 5.

[12] Steiner, Dietmar, Über neuzeitliches Siedeln und Hausen., in: Architektenkammer der Provinz Bozen (ed.), Dorf und Stadt – Wohngebiete in Südtirol nach 1970, Bolzano 1997, p. 206 f.

Joseph Grima
Ein Blick aus dem Süden

Das Leben in Berglandschaften ist unweigerlich mit einer gewissen Isolation verbunden, die von schlichter Abgeschiedenheit bis zu einem Gefühl kultureller Entfremdung reichen kann, wodurch dann schnell der Eindruck des Provinziellen entsteht. Bergregionen sind wie Inseln abgeschlossene Einheiten; im neuen, durch die Telematik „grenzenlos" gewordenen Jahrtausend unterschätzt man leicht die Hartnäckigkeit und Beharrlichkeit einer kulturellen Identität, die sich vor dem Hintergrund der sehr bestimmenden Präsenz einer stets wunderschönen, aber auch rauen Natur aufbaut. Im Fall von Südtirol gibt es eine zusätzliche Barriere, nämlich die der Sprache, die die Region noch stärker von der Gemeinschaft, zu der sie zumindest politisch gehört, entfremdet.

Eher selten jedoch wird bedacht, dass diese abgeschlossenen Einheiten nicht notwendigerweise Brutstätten für provinzielles Denken sind, sondern auch der Nährboden für neue gedankliche Prozesse sein können und es tatsächlich auch häufig sind, Forschungslaboratorien, in denen Lösungen entwickelt werden, die unter den Bedingungen eines „gebildeten Konformismus" niemals hätten angedacht werden können. Der Westen erliegt derzeit dem Drang nach kultureller Grenzenlosigkeit. Eine der damit verbundenen Gefahren ist der Verlust der Fähigkeit, originelle Lösungen durch das Übertragen von lokalem Wissen zu finden,

Un punto di vista da sud

L'ambiente montano comporta inevitabilmente una certa segregazione, che può spaziare dal mero isolamento fino ad un senso di estraneità culturale, sulla quale attecchisce velocemente il provincialismo. Le regioni montane sono unità chiuse in se stesse, come isole, e nel nuovo secolo telematico "globalizzato" si sottovalutano facilmente la caparbietà e l'ostinazione di un'identità culturale formatasi al cospetto di una natura splendida ma al contempo rude, la cui presenza è fortemente caratterizzante. Nel caso dell'Alto Adige/Südtirol si aggiunge un'ulteriore barriera, quella della lingua, che isola ancor più la regione dalla comunità a cui essa almeno politicamente appartiene.

Raramente si considera che queste unità isolate non sono necessariamente dei luoghi d'incubazione per una mentalità provinciale, ma sono invece terreno fertile per nuovi processi di pensiero, effettivi laboratori di ricerca dove si sviluppano soluzioni che mai si sarebbero potute pensare in condizioni di "conformismo intellettuale".

Uno dei pericoli dell'impulso verso una cultura senza confini, a cui oggi è esposto l'Occidente, è la perdita della capacità di trovare soluzioni originali per trasmettere il sapere locale, di farsi ispirare da stimoli che non sottostanno alla tendenza dominante, al mainstream, oppure anche solamente la perdita della capacità di consentire e di promuovere intuizioni non conformistiche.

My view is from the south

Inevitably, mountainous topographies give rise to conditions of isolation varying in intensity from simple logistical "remoteness" to a perception of cultural alienation that could easily be perceived as "provincialism". Mountains, like islands, act as containers; in this new, telematically "borderless" millennium, it is easy to underestimate the tenacious persistence of a cultural identity forged around nature's overbearing presence, unrelentingly beautiful and harsh. In the case of South Tyrol, there is an additional barrier, that of language, that further alienates the region from the body to which, at least politically, it belongs.

What is less frequently considered is that these "containers" are not necessarily hotbeds of provincialism but can, and often do, become incubators of new processes of thought, laboratories of research that generate solutions that would never have arisen from a condition of "informed conformism". One of the dangers implicit in the drive towards cultural borderlessness that the West is currently caught up in is a loss of the ability to derive original solutions from the adaptation of local knowledge, to draw inspiration from approaches different from those offered by the mainstream or even simply cultivate intuitions unstifled by conformism.

Italy has suffered an unprecedented identity crisis in the past 50 years: its awakening to its role as custodian of 70% of the

sich von Ansätzen inspirieren zu lassen, die nicht dem Mainstream unterliegen, oder sogar einfach nur nonkonformistische Intuitionen zuzulassen und zu kultivieren. Italien litt in den vergangenen 50 Jahren an einer noch nie da gewesenen Identitätskrise: Der erwachenden Erkenntnis, dass das Land 70% des Weltkulturerbes im Bereich der Kunst beherbergt und schützen muss, folgte eine Kurzschlussreaktion in Form von unvorstellbaren Einschränkungen für zeitgenössische Arbeiten, woraufhin sehr viele Architekten in ein unfreiwilliges Exil verbannt wurden, das da Innenarchitektur, Restaurierung oder, bei den wenigen, die Glück hatten, Produktion von netten, konservativen und widerlichen öffentlichen Gebäuden heißt.

Als ich die Projekte zur nun vorliegenden Publikation und der gleichnamigen Ausstellung sah, wurde mir zunehmend klar, dass Südtirol zumindest im Bereich der Architektur in den vergangenen Jahrzehnten diese „Laborsituation" für sich kultivieren konnte. Ich schaue von Süden her, kulturell, wenn nicht sogar geografisch, und es ermutigt mich, eine Region in Italien vorzufinden, die zu einem gewissen Grad immun gegen dieses „Kühlschrank-Syndrom" ist, unter dem fast jede andere Region der Halbinsel leidet. Ganz besonders ermutigend finde ich dabei Architekten, die eine engagierte Aussage treffen: zu zeitgenössischen Einstellungen oder zu einer breiten Palette von Typologien, die auch außerhalb Italiens der Verwertung gedankenloser Entwicklungsplaner oder einer kommerziell geprägten Designgestaltung überlassen werden.

Diese Region ist für ihre Tradition einer zurückhaltenden, aber innovativen Architektur bekannt, die eine Brücke zwischen dem Schweizer Minimalismus und der österreichischen Schlichtheit schlägt, indem sie dem Ganzen einen Schuss italienisches Flair beimengt. Bei der Besichtigung vieler Projekte lernte ich diese zwar schätzen, war aber auch nicht überrascht. Einfamilienhäuser wie das Haus Sachsenklemme von Gerd Bergmeister oder die Sanierung von Schloss Tirol von Scherer, Angonese und Hellweger wurden für die Ausstellung ausgewählt, da sie zweifellos von Interesse sind und es anzuerkennen

L'Italia negli ultimi cinquant'anni ha sofferto di una crisi d'identità senza precedenti: alla crescente consapevolezza che la nazione ospita il settanta per cento del patrimonio culturale mondiale artistico, e alla necessità di tutelarlo, è seguita una reazione a corto circuito sotto forma di un'incomprensibile chiusura verso le opere contemporanee. Molti architetti sono stati pertanto confinati in un esilio involontario, che ha comportato la limitazione della produzione architettonica all'architettura d'interni, al restauro o per quei pochi fortunati ad un'edilizia pubblica vezzosa, conservatrice e stucchevole.

Quando ho potuto visionare i progetti di questa pubblicazione e della mostra omonima, mi sono progressivamente reso conto che nei passati decenni l'Alto Adige, almeno in campo architettonico, ha potuto gestire a proprio favore questa "realtà di laboratorio". Il mio è uno sguardo, una percezione culturale ma anche geografica, che parte da sud, e mi incoraggia trovare una regione italiana che in parte è rimasta immune a questa "sindrome da congelamento" della quale soffre quasi ogni distretto della penisola.

Particolarmente confortante in questo caso è stato trovare architetti che sottoscrivono con il loro lavoro una dichiarazione d'impegno verso modi di intendere la contemporaneità o verso un'ampia gamma di tipologie, che anche al di fuori dell'Italia sono abbandonati allo sfruttamento di pianificatori privi di concetti o ad un design meramente commerciale.

Questa regione è conosciuta per la sua tradizione architettonica sobria ed innovativa, che getta un ponte tra il minimalismo svizzero e la sobrietà austriaca, aggiungendo al tutto un tocco italiano. Durante le visite a molti edifici ho imparato sì a stimarli, ma non ne ero sorpreso. Case unifamiliari come quella a Sachsenklemme di Gerd Bergmeister o la ristrutturazione di Castel Tirolo di Scherer, Angonese e Hellweger sono state selezionate perché sono di indubbio interesse e perché si deve riconoscere che la loro qualità progettuale non è una cosa ovvia. Poi c'era ancora una serie di progetti che non saltavano immediatamente all'occhio e dove ho trovato soluzioni innovative e a volte impreviste per numerosi aspetti

world's artistic heritage was followed by a knee-jerk reaction that saw unimaginable constraints imposed on contemporary production, which in turn led to architects being banished en masse to involuntary exile in the realms of interior design, restoration or, for the lucky few, the production of polite, conservative and obnoxious public buildings.

Vising the projects in this exhibition, it became increasingly clear to me that at least in architectural terms Alto Adige has, in recent decades, been capable of nurturing this "laboratory" condition. My view is from the south, culturally if not geographically, and it heartens me to see a region of Italy apparently - to some extent - immune to the "refrigerator syndrome" afflicting just about every other region of the peninsula. It was especially encouraging to see architects engaged in reflecting on contemporary approaches to a broad range of typologies which even outside Italy are often left as fodder to thoughtless developers or commercial design.

This region is, of course, well-known for a tradition of restrained but innovative architecture that bridges the gap between Swiss minimalism and Austrian sobriety by adding a pinch of Italian flair. It was, therefore, with appreciation but without surprise that I visited many of these projects; single-family dwellings such as Haus Sachsenklemme by Gerd Bergmeister or the refurbishment of Schloss Tirol by Scherer, Angonese and Hellweger were chosen for the exhibition due to their indisputable interest and in recognition of the fact that quality in design cannot be taken for granted. But it was in a number of other projects, of less immediate appeal, that I could see new and sometimes unexpected solutions emerging on a variety of problematic themes. Issues of urban densification, a response to the need for low-cost social housing, openness to the use of local materials and a low-impact approach to urban contextualisation were all combined in a successful experiment, Residence Wolkenstein (Holzbox, Baugesellschaft Wolkenstein and Vorarlberger Ökohaus), which in certain other European countries might be taken for granted but which in an Italian context is hardly to be taken for granted.

gilt, dass qualitätvolle Gestaltung nichts Selbstverständliches ist. Aber dann gab es da auch noch eine Reihe anderer Projekte, die nicht sofort ins Auge sprangen und bei denen ich neue und manchmal unerwartete Lösungen für eine Vielzahl von Problemstellungen fand. Themen wie urbane Verdichtung, die Reaktion auf den Bedarf an günstigen Sozialwohnungen, die Offenheit für die Verwendung örtlicher Baumaterialien sowie Bebauungen mit möglichst geringer Auswirkung auf den urbanen Kontext werden alle erfolgreich im Projekt der Wohnanlage Wolkenstein angegangen (Holzbox, Baugesellschaft Wolkenstein und Vorarlberger Ökohaus); in gewissen anderen europäischen Ländern sind solche Projekte wohl bereits eine Selbstverständlichkeit, aber in Italien ist das noch kaum der Fall. Eine Reihe von Projekten zeigte erfrischend zeitgenössische Einstellungen zu traditionellen Bautypologien, die sonst meist gar nicht ernst genommen werden (zum Beispiel Bauernhäuser wie der Ladstätterhof von Peter Plattner oder das Haus Mumelter von Werner Tscholl). Ein Problem, vor dem viele europäische Städte stehen, nämlich die Frage, wie man bestehende und manchmal historisch bedeutende Bausubstanz in neue Bauprogramme oder bauliche Anforderungen einbindet, ging eine Art „Einzigart-Architekten" mutig (wenn auch ein wenig formalistisch) im Entwurf einer parasitären Hauserweiterung an – das Projekt, das Haus Köllensperger in der Vittorio Veneto Straße in Bozen, fand aber letztlich nicht den Weg in die Aus-

progettuali. Temi come la densità urbana, la risposta alle richieste di abitazioni sociali ragionevolmente economiche, la disponibilità ad utilizzare materiali locali e l'edificazione mirata a ridurre il più possibile i suoi effetti sul contesto urbano, sono affrontati con successo nel progetto del complesso residenziale Wolkenstein (Holzbox, impresa di costruzioni Wolkenstein e Vorarlberger Ökohaus). In altri Paesi europei progetti simili sono all'ordine del giorno, ma non ancora in Italia. Altri progetti dimostrano un approccio innovativo e contemporaneo alla tipologia costruttiva tradizionale, che altrimenti non viene quasi mai affrontata seriamente (ne sono un esempio gli edifici rurali come il Ladstätterhof di Peter Plattner o Casa Mumelter di Werner Tscholl). Una delle questioni con le quali si confrontano molte città europee, cioè come si rapporta il patrimonio esistente (a volte di valore storico) con i nuovi programmi di edificazione o con le nuove esigenze delle costruzioni, è stata affrontata in modo singolare dal progetto di "Einzigart-Architekten" per casa Köllensperger in via Vittorio Veneto a Bolzano, che però non ha trovato collocazione nella mostra. Casa Kaser di Benno Barth risolve abilmente la complessità delle norme di pianificazione che gli architetti sono chiamati a rispettare. Altrettanto incoraggiante è stato verificare la progettazione e il design di qualità con cui si presenta la residenza per dipendenti agricoli della tenuta Enzenberg di Walter Angonese e Silvia Boday, che in altre regioni italiane sarebbero impensabili.

A number of projects brought refreshingly contemporary approaches to traditional architectural typologies, to which no second thought is usually given (for example farmhouses such as Ladstätterhof by Peter Plattner or Haus Mumelter by Werner Tscholl). A problem facing many European cities, how to adapt existing and sometimes historically significant buildings to new programmes or exigencies, was courageously (if somewhat formalistically) addressed in "Einzigart Architekten's" parasytical house extension design (Haus Köllensperger in Bolzano), ultimately not included in the exhibition. The complex planning legislation architects must face was ingeniously outmaneuvered in Benno Barth's Wohnhaus Kaser. And it was heartening to see farm labourers offered a design of such quality and thoughtfulness as Walter Angonese's Personal-Wohnhaus Enzenberg, something almost unthinkable in many other Italian regions.

It must be said, however, that the spark of inspiration that lights up the occasional architectural project remains obfuscated by the region's apparent inability to overcome the ills that afflict its urbanism on a wider scale. Driving up the valleys that branch out from Bolzano and Merano, it is impossible to ignore in the landscape the signs of decay brought about by the inability to control sprawl, the disease affecting every Italian city from the Alps to the islands. Clumps of factories and warehouses hug the motorways at irregular intervals, highrise condominiums or single-family bunga-

stellung. Die komplexe Planungsgesetzgebung, die Architekten beachten müssen, wurde in Benno Barths Wohnhaus Kaser geschickt umgangen. Und es war ermutigend zu sehen, welch qualitätvolles Design und welch gute Planung einem Gebäude wie dem Personalwohnhaus Goëss-Enzenberg von Walter Angonese und Silvia Boday für die Mitarbeiter eines landwirtschaftlichen Betriebs zugrunde liegt, was in vielen anderen italienischen Regionen fast undenkbar ist.

Aber, und das muss auch gesagt werden, der Funke der Inspiration, der die Bauprojekte bisweilen erleuchtet, bleibt klein, da die Region nicht fähig zu sein scheint, die Probleme der Verstädterung insgesamt zu überwinden. Fährt man von Bozen und Meran aus in die umliegenden Täler, springen einem unweigerlich die alarmierenden Zeichen in der Landschaft ins Auge, denn man ist hier nicht in der Lage, die unkontrollierte Zersiedelung einzudämmen, eine Krankheit, unter der jede italienische Stadt von den Alpen bis zu den Inseln im Süden leidet. Überall im Land finden sich entlang der Autobahnen Industrieansiedlungen; Wohnblöcke und Einfamilienhäuser verteilen sich wie ein ansteckender Ausschlag über die Agrarlandschaft. Und wo nicht Industrieanlagen oder Wohnbebauungen der Natur und Landschaft einen kaum aufzuhaltenden Schaden zufügen, trügt die oberflächliche Beschaulichkeit des Tourismus in Gestalt von riesigen „Alpen-Chalets" oder auf alt getrimmten Hotels im Stil von Tiroler Burganlagen. Die Region hat sich, wie

Si deve però ammettere che la scintilla per l'ispirazione che ha sinora illuminato questi progetti di architettura rimane piccola, perché la provincia non sembra in grado di superare i problemi legati ai processi di urbanizzazione. Se si sale nelle valli, partendo da Bolzano e da Merano, ci si accorge inevitabilmente degli interventi allarmanti che segnano il paesaggio, infatti qui non si è in grado di arginare la dispersione incontrollata dell'edificazione sul territorio, una "malattia" di cui soffrono tutti i centri urbani italiani, dalle Alpi alle isole del Sud.

Ovunque, lungo le autostrade si trovano insediamenti produttivi; complessi edilizi e casette unifamiliari si diffondono come un'eruzione cutanea contagiosa su tutto il territorio rurale. Dove non sono gli insediamenti produttivi o residenziali a recare danno inarrestabile alla natura ed al paesaggio, è la superficiale quiete turistica ad ingannare con immagini di giganteschi Alpen-Chalets o di finti vecchi alberghi ispirati allo stile dei castelli tirolesi. L'Alto Adige, come altre ampie zone della Penisola, si è lasciato istigare dai facili guadagni del turismo ad avviare uno sviluppo rapido ed irresponsabile e nella maggior parte dei casi, ha ceduto alla tentazione di chiudere coscientemente gli occhi per non vedere quali conseguenze comporta sottoporre il paesaggio ad un tale pericolo.

Ci sono comunque segnali di speranza: in poche altre parti d'Italia e d'Europa è possibile trovare una centrale di teleriscaldamento che è il risultato del progetto vincitore di un concorso di architettura, o

lows scattered throughout the orchards between them like the spots on the skin of an ailing patient. Where it is not industrial or residential development that is wreaking uncontrollable havoc on the natural landscape, tourism's skin-deep picturesque is painted on in the form of massive "alpine chalets" or fake Tyrolese-castle hotels. South Tyrol has, like much of the rest of the peninsula, been lured into unreasonably fast development by the quick money tourism affords, succumbing in most cases to the temptation to turn a blind eye to the all too obvious implications of breeding a diseased landscape.

There are signs of hope: in few other parts of Italy, or even Europe, is one likely to find a district heating plant that is the result of an architectural competition or housing for labourers. So why not take this evident appreciation for quality in one's environment even further? It is a pity that it is only luxury residences like Matteo Thun's Pergola Residence can consider, and therefore minimise, their environmental impact. These are problems facing the whole country, and one can only hope that Alto Adige's privileged position as one of Italy's few "design incubators" will be of benefit, in the coming decades, to the whole country.

weite Teile der Halbinsel ebenfalls, durch das schnelle Geld im Tourismus zu einer unverantwortlich rasanten Entwicklung verleiten lassen. In den meisten Fällen erlag man dabei der Versuchung, die Augen bewusst davor zu verschließen, welche Folgen es hat, wenn man eine solche Not leidende Landschaft heranzüchtet.

Es gibt auch Zeichen der Hoffnung: Nur in wenigen anderen Teilen Italiens oder auch Europas findet man ein Fernheizwerk, das als siegreicher Entwurf aus einem Architekturwettbewerb hervorgegangen ist, oder neu entstandene Arbeiterwohnungen. Warum sollte man diese offensichtliche Wertschätzung einer qualitätvollen Umwelt nicht weiter fördern? Es ist sehr schade, dass man nur bei Luxuswohnungen wie Matteo Thuns Pergola Residence deren Umweltverträglichkeit in die Überlegungen mit einbezieht, um damit negative Umwelteinflüsse zu minimieren. Dies sind Probleme, vor denen das gesamte Land steht, und man kann nur hoffen, dass Italien in den kommenden Jahrzehnten von der herausragenden Stellung Südtirols als einem der wenigen „Nährböden für gutes Design" profitieren kann.

nuove realizzazioni per residenze operaie. Perché non si dovrebbe promuovere ulteriormente questa evidente valorizzazione della qualità ambientale? E' un peccato che per minimizzare gli effetti negativi sul paesaggio si realizzino valutazioni di sostenibilità ambientale solo per appartamenti di lusso come il residence Pergola di Matteo Thun. Si tratta di problemi con cui si confronta tutta la nazione, e si può solo sperare che nei prossimi decenni l'Italia sappia approfittare di questa eccezionale situazione dell'Alto Adige che si presenta come uno dei pochi "terreni di coltura per il buon design".

Roman Hollenstein
Weingrotten und golden schimmernde Pyramiden – Ein Blick von außen auf die Südtiroler Architektur

Wie die meisten Bereiche unseres Lebens bleibt auch die Architektur von der Globalisierung nicht verschont – mit dem Resultat, dass sie immer austauschbarer wird. Gleichwohl konnten sich im zentralen Alpenraum bis heute regionale Positionen behaupten. So folgten auf die Tessiner Tendenza, die vor rund 20 Jahren weltweite Aufmerksamkeit auf sich ziehen konnte, der steirische Neoexpressionismus sowie eine neue Einfachheit in Graubünden und in Vorarlberg. Vor nicht allzu langer Zeit gelang es dann den Nord- und Osttiroler Architekten, sich aus dem Schatten dieser selbstbewussten Szene zu befreien. Nur um Südtirol blieb es lange still, und dies obwohl sich dort schon in den späten 60er Jahren Exponenten wie Othmar Barth und Helmut Maurer für eine Erneuerung der Architektur stark gemacht hatten. So setzte Barth mit einer Wohnsiedlung am Fuß der bewaldeten Porphyrfelsen von Haslach bei Bozen ein Zeichen, das auch nördlich des Brenners und westlich des Ofenpasses wahrgenommen wurde.

Von der Landschaft zur Architektur

Seit dem Inkrafttreten des Autonomiestatuts flossen in Südtirol aufgrund der politischen und wirtschaftlichen Entwicklungen vermehrt öffentliche Gelder in Verwaltungs-

Grotte per il vino e sgargianti piramidi dorate. Uno sguardo dall'esterno sull'architettura altoatesina

Analogamente alla maggior parte degli ambiti della nostra esistenza, la globalizzazione non ha risparmiato l'architettura, che risulta così sempre più indifferente ai luoghi.
Malgrado questo, al centro dell'arco alpino si sono affermate alcune declinazioni regionali. Alla Tendenza ticinese, che vent'anni fa si è attirata l'attenzione internazionale della critica, ha fatto seguito il Neoespressionismo della Stiria e una nuova essenzialità (Einfachheit) nei Grigioni e nel Voralberg. Da non molto tempo, anche gli architetti dell'Austria settentrionale e orientale sono riusciti a liberarsi del peso del vernacolo. Solo in Alto Adige lo scenario architettonico è rimasto a lungo silente, nonostante già negli anni Sessanta figure come Othmar Barth e Helmut Maurer si fossero intensamente impegnate per un rinnovamento dell'architettura. Con la realizzazione di un insediamento residenziale, sorto ai piedi delle boscose rupi di porfido che incombono sul quartiere di Aslago a Bolzano, Othmar Barth ha lasciato un segno che lo ha reso noto anche a nord del Brennero e a ovest del Passo Forno.

Dal paesaggio all'architettura

Dall'entrata in vigore dello Statuto di Autonomia, motore di uno sviluppo sia politico che economico, in Alto Adige sono confluiti

Wine grottos and golden shimmering pyramids
An outsider's view of architecture in South Tyrol

Like most areas of our lives architecture is not immune to the influence of globalisation – with the result that it is increasingly becoming similar everywhere. At the same time however in the central alpine area regional positions have managed to survive until the present. The Tessiner Tendenza that attracted worldwide attention about 20 years ago has been followed by Styrian expressionism as well as the new simplicity in Grisons (Switzerland) and Vorarlberg (Austria). Not all too long ago architects from North and East Tyrol succeeded in liberating themselves from the shadows of these self-confident scenes. But in South Tyrol things remained quiet for a very long time, even though in the late 1960s exponents such as Othmar Barth and Helmut Maurer had campaigned for the renewal of architecture. With a housing development at the foot of the forest-covered porphyry rocks at Aslago near Bolzano Barth for example sent a signal that was received both north of the Passo del Brennero and west of the Passo Forno.

From the landscape to architecture

After the introduction of autonomy status political and economic developments meant that public funds started to flow increasingly into South Tyrol, in particular

und Schulbauten sowie in die Infrastruktur.[1] Schon 1993 konnte der Bozner Architekt Christoph Mayr Fingerle in einer von der Autonomen Provinz Bozen-Südtirol herausgegebenen Publikation die ersten Früchte des öffentlichen Bauens präsentieren. Außerdem wurde „Ende der 80er Jahre auch die Dorfgestaltung zu einem eigenständigen Thema", wie Mayr Fingerle festhielt.[2] Dennoch ließ es sich nicht verhindern, dass vor allem kleinere Orte mit bizarren Tourismusbauten im Pseudo-Südtirolerstil verunstaltet wurden – eine Tendenz, die leider bis heute anhält.

Immerhin konnte die prachtvolle Landschaft weitgehend vor der Zersiedelung bewahrt werden. Wohl findet man an den Sonnenhängen von Bozen und Meran eine Vielzahl von Villen, doch stammen sie vor allem aus der Zeit des Jugendstils und der Moderne. Die jüngsten Wellen der Verhäuselung, die andere Bergregionen heimsuchten, schwappten hingegen nicht über den Alpenhauptkamm. Dies ist nicht zuletzt einem weitsichtigen Planungsgesetz zu verdanken, das seit 1972 mittels strenger Bauleitpläne das Bauen im Landwirtschaftsgebiet und in der Landschaft regelt. Mit dieser für Außenstehende erstaunlichen „Architektur des Territoriums" konnte allerdings die Baukunst lange nicht mithalten. Erst in den vergangenen Jahren sind vermehrt Gebäude entstanden, die mit ihrer oft eigenwilligen Mischung aus lokalen Eigenheiten und internationalem Ausdruck überraschen. Gründe für diesen architektonischen Aufschwung gibt es viele: von der verbesserten Wettbewerbskultur bis hin zum Architektennachwuchs, der in Ermangelung einer regionalen Schule in Innsbruck, Venedig oder Wien studiert und so immer wieder neue, den Architekturdiskurs anregende Ideen mit nach Hause bringt.

Tourismus als Motor
Ist man vom Engadin aus mit dem Bus und der im vergangenen Mai wieder eröffneten Vinschgau-Bahn nach Meran unterwegs, so begegnet man schon bald den ersten Beispielen des architektonischen Aufbruchs. Bei der Fahrt durch das mittelalterliche, seit den 70er Jahren vorbildlich sanierte Städtchen Glurns denkt vermutlich kaum jemand an zeitgenössische

ingenti finanziamenti pubblici per la realizzazione di edifici amministrativi, scolastici ed infrastrutture.[1]

Già nel 1993 l'architetto bolzanino Christoph Mayr Fingerle ha presentato i primi frutti della produzione di edilizia pubblica in una pubblicazione finanziata dalla Provincia Autonoma di Bolzano. Lo stesso ha confermato che "alla fine degli anni '80 anche l'immagine compositiva dei paesi era divenuta un tema autonomo".[2] Tuttavia non si è evitato che soprattutto le piccole località fossero deturpate da bizzarre costruzioni turistiche in stile pseudo-sudtirolese – una tendenza che purtroppo perdura fino ad oggi.

Il magnifico paesaggio naturale è stato comunque in larga parte risparmiato dalla dispersione degli insediamenti.

Le numerose ville che si trovano sulle pendici soleggiate di Bolzano e di Merano risalgono, infatti, agli anni del Liberty e del Modernismo.

Le più recenti ondate di edilizia dispersa sul territorio, che hanno afflitto altre regioni montane, non si sono spinte oltre la barriera delle Alpi. Questa situazione è da far risalire, tra l'altro, ad una lungimirante normativa di pianificazione che dal 1972 regola l'edificazione nelle zone rurali e nel paesaggio con rigidi vincoli urbanistici.

Per lungo tempo l'architettura non ha saputo confrontarsi in maniera adeguata con questa "architettura del paesaggio", che tanto meraviglia il turista.

Solo negli ultimi anni è stato realizzato un numero crescente di edifici, che sorprendono per la loro eccentrica mescolanza tra caratteristiche peculiarità locali ed espressioni internazionali.

Le ragioni di questo balzo in avanti della produzione architettonica sono molteplici, e vanno da una migliore cultura dei concorsi, fino alla nuova generazione di progettisti, che in mancanza di una scuola regionale, ha studiato a Innsbruck, Venezia o Vienna e ha pertanto importato idee stimolanti per il dibattito architettonico.

Il turismo come motore
Usciti dall'Engadina, viaggiando verso Merano in autobus e poi con la nuova ferrovia della Val Venosta, riattivata lo scorso maggio, si incontrano da subito i primi segni di

for administration and school buildings as well as for improvements to the infrastructure.[1] Even back in 1993 architect Christoph Mayr Fingerle from Bolzano was able to present the first fruits of public building activity in a publication produced by the Autonomous Province of Bolzano-South Tyrol. In addition, as Mayr Fingerle recorded[2]: "At the end of the 1980s village design emerged as an independent theme". Nevertheless it was not possible to prevent many places, in particular smaller villages, from being mutilated by bizarre tourism buildings in a pseudo South Tirolean style, a tendency that unfortunately still survives today.

But it has proved possible to preserve the magnificent landscape for the most part from the effects of urban sprawl. Although in the sun-facing slopes around Bolzano and Merano one finds numerous villas, they date largely from the Jugendstil and classic modern periods. The latest wave of house building that afflicted other mountain regions did not sweep over the main ridge of the Alps. This is due to some considerable extent to an important and perspicacious piece of planning legislation introduced in 1972 that has regulated building in agricultural areas and in the landscape by means of strict building guidelines. Architectural design was for a long time not able to keep up with this "architecture of the territory" that is so extraordinary for outsiders. It is only in recent years that increasing numbers of buildings have been erected that often offer positive surprises through individual combinations of local characteristics and international expression. There are many reasons for this architectural revival, ranging from the increase in the number of competitions held to the younger generation of architects who, due to the lack of a local school of architecture, must study in Innsbruck, Venice or Vienna and thus constantly bring new ideas home with them that stimulate the architectural discourse.

Tourism as a motor
If one travels by bus from Engadin and with the Val Venosta railway (that reopened last May) to Merano one soon encounters the first examples of this new architectural upsurge. When travelling through the lit-

Baukunst. Dennoch wurden hier unlängst – wohl angeregt durch Vorbilder in Sils, Pontresina und Zuoz – die Interieurs des Hotels Grüner Baum, eines der prächtigsten Häuser am Hauptplatz, von Christian Kapeller und Andreas Flora ganz zeitgemäß, wenn auch in manchen Details vielleicht allzu modisch umgebaut. In Mals, das mit seinen alten Türmen einen urbanen Akzent ins weite Gebirgstal setzt, erblickt man an der Bahnhofstraße dann ein frühes Hauptwerk der neuen Südtiroler Architektur, das 1970 vollendete Gamperheim des Bozner Altmeisters Helmut Maurer. Die Stärke dieses inzwischen fast schon „historischen" Baus resultiert daraus, dass sich Maurer – im Gegensatz zu den oft zu selbstverliebten jüngeren Südtiroler Architekten – auf einen kritischen Dialog mit der gebauten Umgebung einließ.

Man trifft in Mals aber auch auf präzise Interventionen aus jüngster Zeit, wie man beim Verlassen des Postautos am Bahnhof sogleich feststellt. Es sind dies die für die neuen Zugkompositionen nötig gewordenen Erweiterung der alten Lokremise sowie eine geplante Waschanlage. Wie die meist einfachen, aber formschönen Haltestellen auf der Strecke zwischen Mals und Meran stammen sie von Walter Dietl. Gleichsam den Edelstein in dieser Perlenkette bildet die kleine Bahnstation mit Mehrzweckraum in Plaus, die nach Plänen des Architekturbüros D3 (Kathrin Gruber, Richard Veneri) formal, materiell und farblich auffälliger als die übrigen Haltestellen gestaltet wurde. Kaum eröffnet, ist damit die Vinschgau-Bahn bereits zu einem Aushängeschild der neuen Südtiroler Architektur geworden, die sich immer wieder durch entwerferische Klarheit und Experimentierfreude beim Einsatz von Holz, Stein, Metall oder Glas auszeichnet. Davon zeugen in der sich nach Meran öffnenden Talschaft unter anderem zwei bemerkenswerte Bauten von Arnold Gapp, die hoch über Latsch errichtete Seilbahnstation St. Martin und das Messner Mountain Museum in Sulden, aber auch das Hotel Pergola von Matteo Thun.

Dem aus Bozen stammenden Mailänder Designer ist bei Algund – in leicht erhöhter Aussichtslage über dem Meraner Talkessel – ein für Südtirol wichtiger Ho-

questo nuovo corso dell'architettura.

A nessuno, probabilmente, viene in mente l'architettura contemporanea, attraversando la cittadina medioevale di Glorenza, restaurata in modo esemplare negli anni Settanta. Proprio qui invece, di recente – su esempio degli interventi realizzati a Sils, Pontresina e Zuoz – gli interni dell'albergo Grüner Baum, uno degli edifici più fastosi della piazza principale, sono stati ristrutturati secondo un approccio contemporaneo, anche se in alcuni dettagli forse troppo aderente alle mode, da Christian Kapeller e Andreas Flora.

Nel paese di Malles, le cui torri conferiscono un carattere urbano all'ampia vallata, si scorge su via Stazione una delle prime importanti opere della nuova architettura altoatesina, il Gamperheim, lo studentato del vecchio maestro bolzanino Helmut Maurer, terminato nel 1970. La forza di questa costruzione, ormai quasi "storica", deriva dal fatto che Maurer – a differenza dei giovani architetti altoatesini, troppo spesso vittime di amor proprio – si è confrontato in maniera critica con le costruzioni limitrofe.

A Malles si incontrano però anche interventi puntuali più recenti, come si può immediatamente verificare lasciando l'automobile in stazione. Si tratta dell'ampliamento della rimessa ferroviaria con annesso impianto di lavaggio, resi necessari dalle nuove dimensioni dei vagoni ferroviari. È un'opera di Walter Dietl, come la maggior parte delle fermate della linea tra Merano e Malles, semplice ma rigorosa.

La piccola stazione con annessa sala multifunzionale di Plaus, più appariscente rispetto alle altre per colori, forme e materiali, e progettata dallo studio D3 (Kathrin Gruber, Richard Veneri) si inserisce come una pietra preziosa in questa collana di perle.

Appena inaugurata, la ferrovia della Val Venosta è divenuta un'icona della nuova architettura altoatesina, caratterizzata da chiarezza compositiva e passione per la sperimentazione dell'uso di materiali quali legno, pietra, metallo o vetro. Lo dimostrano altri due progetti degni di nota nella valle che si apre verso Merano: la stazione della funivia di S. Martino, che sale sopra Laces, ed il Messner Mountain Museum, entrambi di Arnold Gapp. A questi si aggiunge l'Hotel Pergola di Matteo Thun.

tle mediaeval town of Glurns that has been restored in an exemplary fashion since the 1970s hardly anyone probably thinks of contemporary architecture. But here, possibly stimulated by examples in Sils, Pontresina and Zuoz, the interior of the Hotel Grüner Baum, one of the finest buildings on the main square, has recently been converted by Christian Kapeller and Andreas Flora in a highly contemporary manner, although perhaps with a number of excessively fashionable details. In Malles, where old towers set an urban accent in a broad mountain valley, you can see on Bahnhofstrasse an early work of recent South Tyrol architecture, the Gamperheim by the old Bolzano master, Helmut Maurer that was completed in 1970. The strength of this by now almost "historic" building is derived from the fact that – in contrast to the often self-absorbed quality of younger South Tyrol architects – Maurer engaged in a critical dialogue with the built environment.

But, as you note on leaving the bus at the railway station, in Malles you can also see precise interventions that were made very recently. These are the adaptation of the old train shed that was required to take the new trains now used on the line and a planned coach washing plant. Like the generally simple but beautiful stops on the line between Malles and Merano these buildings were planned by Walter Dietl. The jewel in this collection so-to-speak is the small railway station with multi-purpose space in Plaus designed by the architects practice D3 (Kathrin Gruber, Richard Veneri) which formally and in terms of material and colours is more striking than the other stations. Although it has only been opened a short time the Val Venosta railway has already become a showpiece of new South Tyrolean architecture that is repeatedly characterised by clarity of design and a delight in experimentation in the use of wood, stone, metal or glass. In the valley area that opens towards Merano evidence of this trend is offered by two remarkable buildings by Arnold Gapp offer the ropeway station S. Martino erected high above Laces and the Messner Mountain Museum in Solda, but also by Matteo Thun's Hotel Pergola.

This Milan-based designer, who comes

tel-bau gelungen, der sich mit seinem Sockelgeschoss aus Naturstein und seinen Aufbauten und Laubenkonstruktionen aus Lärchenholz ganz selbstverständlich in die von alten „Pergln" geprägten Weinberge einfügt. Zu einer ähnlichen Lösung hatten allerdings schon 1983 die Bozner Architekten Abram & Schnabl bei dem aus massiven Porphyrmauern und leichten Vorbauten aus Holz komponierten Haus Sand am Kalterer See gefunden, das zu den besten Privatbauten der ganzen Provinz zählt.

Das Hotel Pergola und das ebenfalls nach Thuns Entwürfen auf dem Vigiljoch bei Lana realisierte Hotel Vigilius beweisen mit aller Deutlichkeit, dass dank Privatinitiativen auch im sonst von biederen Bauten dominierten Tourismusbereich Vorzeigearchitekturen möglich sind. Als Gegenbeispiel muss jedoch der von der Kurbad AG in Meran in Auftrag gegebene Doppelbau genannt werden, der aus einem kubischen Thermengebäude, einem abgewinkelten Stadthotel und einer großen Tiefgarage besteht. Dieser derzeit der Vollendung entgegengehende, städtebaulich und architektonisch gleichermaßen unbefriedigende Gebäudekomplex basiert auf dem erstplatzierten Wettbewerbsentwurf des jungen Berliner Architektenduos Rüdiger Baumann und Julia Zillich. Wegen konzeptioneller Mängel wurde das Projekt anschließend von Matteo Thun überarbeitet und damit möglicherweise noch verschlechtert. Hier hat Meran zweifellos die Chance zu einem großen Auftritt verpasst.

Mehr Glück hatte die Stadt mit einem an-

Il designer milanese, originario di Bolzano, è riuscito a realizzare a Lagundo – in posizione panoramica leggermente sopraelevata sulla vallata meranese – uno degli edifici alberghieri più importanti dell'Alto Adige, una costruzione con basamento in pietra, e parte in elevazione con loggiati in legno di larice, che si inserisce con naturalezza tra le vecchie pergole dei vigneti. Già nel 1983, gli architetti di Bolzano Abram & Schnabl avevano realizzato una soluzione analoga, nella casa Sand sul lago di Caldaro, costruita con murature in pietra di porfido e struttura in legno: una delle più belle residenze private di tutta la provincia.

L'Hotel Pergola e l'Hotel Vigilius a S. Vigilio presso Lana, anch'esso progettato da Thun, dimostrano con chiarezza che anche nel settore turistico, altrimenti pervaso da costruzioni di impronta tradizionale, è possibile realizzare delle architetture esemplari, sia pure su iniziativa privata.

Sul versante opposto è doveroso citare il complesso delle Terme di Merano (promosso dalla società Terme Merano Spa), e composto da un edificio per le cure termali a pianta quadrata, da un edificio a "C" per l'Hotel Città e da una grande autorimessa sotterranea. Questo complesso di edifici ora in via di completamento, insoddisfacente sia dal punto di vista urbanistico che architettonico, si basa sul progetto vincitore di un concorso del giovane duo berlinese Rüdiger Baumann e Julia Zillich. A causa di carenze nell'elaborazione complessiva, il progetto è stato successivamente rimaneggiato da Matteo Thun e, se possibile,

originally from Bolzano, has succeeded in producing in a slightly elevated location near Lagundo, above the valley containing Merano, a hotel building that is important for South Tyrol. Its plinth of natural stone and the pergolas and upper elements made of larch are completely naturally inserted in the vineyards dominated by the old wooden pergolas ("Pergln"). In 1983 The Bolzano architects Abram & Schnabl arrived at a similar solution with their Sand House with its massive porphyry walls and lightweight front elements made of timber that is located at the western lakeside of Lago di Caldaro and is among the best private buildings in the entire province.

The Hotel Pergola and the Hotel Vigilius on the S. Vigilio near Lana also carried out according to a design by Thun clearly prove that, even in the tourist branch that is generally dominated by a very staid kind of architecture, thanks to private initiatives model results are possible. But mention must be made here of the double building commissioned by the Kurbad AG in Merano which is anything but a model. It consists of a cubic spa building, an angular city hotel and a large underground garage. This building complex presently approaching completion is unsatisfactory both in terms of urban planning and architecture. It is based on the competition-winning design by the young Berlin architects Rüdiger Baumann and Julia Zillich. Due to conceptual deficiencies the project had to be reworked by Matteo Thun which perhaps even made it worse. Here Merano has without doubt

deren touristisch wichtigen Projekt: der Umwandlung von Schloss Trauttmansdorff in ein Ausflugsziel mit Tourismus-Museum und botanischem Garten. Dazu musste der an einem Steilhang über dem Villenviertel Obermais gelegene, 1850 im Geist des romantischen Historismus erneuerte Herrensitz, in welchem sich Kaiserin Sisi 1870 und 1889 längere Zeit aufgehalten hatte, restauriert und umgebaut werden. Früh schon mit dabei war neben PVC – architects und Steiner Sarnen aus der Schweiz auch die Künstlerin Margit Klammer. Sie alle schufen im Parkareal mehrere Pavillons und andere Kleinarchitekturen. Später realisierten S.O.F.A. architekten (Rita Pirpamer, Andreas Grasser, Kurt Rauch) gemeinsam mit Georg Mitterhofer unter anderem ein Besucherzentrum außerhalb des Gartengeländes. Dieses wurde nötig, weil Trauttmansdorff inzwischen wegen seiner lieblichen, von Teichen und Terrassen geprägten Landschaftsgestaltung, aber auch als Sisi-Wallfahrtsort pro Jahr fast 300.000 Besucher anlockt.

Der Neubau, der sich elegant inmitten eines abgestuften Parkplatzes erhebt und über eine Brücke mit den Gärten verbunden ist, wirkt mit seinem auf schrägen Mikadostützen aufgestelzten schachtelförmigen Volumen wie ein Verschnitt aus Rem Koolhaas' Villa dall'Ava und Mies van der Rohes Barcelona-Pavillon. Doch die bald fleischig, bald floral anmutende Verkleidung der Eingangsseite mit brasilianischem Granit gibt ihm eine sinnliche Objekthaftigkeit, die sich gut mit den zarten Gelbtönen des Schlosses und dem üppigen Grün der Vegetation verträgt. Im Inneren empfängt der hufeisenartig um einen kleinen Bambus-Hof geführte Bau die Besucher mit Raumsequenzen, die auf das verschlungene Wegsystem des Parks einstimmen.

Noch mit einem anderen Vorzeigeprojekt kann das touristische Meran aufwarten: dem hoch gelegenen, das Burggrafenamt beherrschenden Schloss Tirol. Die Höhenburg, deren strenges Äußeres die Antithese zum touristisch übernutzten Dorf Tirol bildet, wurde aufgrund eines 1998 von Markus Scherer und Walter Angonese mit Klaus Hellweger entwickelten Konzepts bis 2003 zum Landesmuseum für Kultur- und Landesgeschichte umgebaut. Das Haupt-

ancora peggiorato. Merano ha senz'ombra di dubbio perso una grande occasione per profilarsi sulla scena architettonica contemporanea.

La città ha avuto più fortuna con un altro importante progetto legato al turismo: la trasformazione del castello di Trauttmansdorff in luogo di svago con museo del turismo e orto botanico.

Per raggiungere questo obbiettivo è stata recuperata una dimora signorile, situata sul pendio a monte dell'elegante quartiere residenziale di Maia Alta. L'antica dimora, dove l'imperatrice Sisi si intrattenne a lungo tra il 1850 ed il 1870, era già stata rinnovata nel 1850 secondo lo spirito dello storicismo romantico.

Nel progetto per il Museo del Turismo è intervenuta sin dall'origine, a fianco di PVC-architects e dello svizzero Steiner Sarnen, l'artista Margit Klammer, che ha collaborato anche alla realizzazione, nell'area del parco, di numerosi padiglioni ed altre architetture in miniatura.

In seguito, lo studio S.O.F.A.-architekten (Rita Pirpamer, Andreas Grasser, Kurt Rauch) assieme a Georg Mitterhofer ha progettato il centro visite posto all'ingresso del parco, resosi nel frattempo necessario perché Trauttmansdorff attira ogni anno quasi 300.000 visitatori, sia grazie al piacevole inserimento ambientale del laghetto e dei terrazzamenti, ma anche come luogo di pellegrinaggio dedicato a Sisi.

Il nuovo edificio, innalzato al centro di un parcheggio terrazzato e collegato al parco da un ponte pedonale, con i suoi volumi sostenuti da esili colonne oblique, richiama in parte la villa dell'Ava di Rem Koolhaas e il padiglione di Barcellona di Mies van der Rohe. Eppure il rivestimento in granito brasiliano del lato d'ingresso che suggerisce un effetto alternativamente carnoso e floreale, gli attribuisce una sensuale concretezza, che ben si combina ai delicati toni di giallo del castello ed al verde rigoglioso della vegetazione. L'edificio, disposto a ferro di cavallo intorno ad un piccolo cortile di canne di bambù, accoglie i visitatori al suo interno con una sequenza di spazi in sintonia con i percorsi che si snodano nel parco.

La Merano turistica accoglie il visitatore con un altro progetto esemplare, Castel

missed a great opportunity.

The town had more luck with another important tourist project: the transformation of Schloss Trauttmansdorff into a goal for tourist excursions and a botanical garden. The castle building was built in 1850 on a steep slope above the villa district of Maia Alta in the spirit of romantic historicism and Empress Sisi spent longer periods there in 1870 and 1889. It had to be restored and converted. Artist Margit Klammer was part of the design team from an early stage – in addition to PVC architects and Steiner Sarnen from Switzerland. In the park they created together several pavilions and smaller pieces of architecture. Later S.O.F.A.-architekten (Rita Pirpamer, Andreas Grasser, Kurt Rauch) together with Georg Mitterhofer created a visitors centre outside the gardens. This was required as, thanks to its attractive landscape design with ponds and terraces but also due to the number of Sisi "pilgrimages", Trauttsmannsdorff attracts almost 300,000 visitors annually.

The new building that rises elegantly from amidst a terraced car park and is connected by bridge to the gardens has a box-like form carried on tilted "Mikado sticks" and is reminiscent of Rem Koolhaas Villa dall'Ava and Mies van der Rohe's Barcelona Pavilion. But the Brazilian granite cladding of the entrance side that at some places seems fleshy, at others floral gives it the sensual quality of an object that harmonises well with the delicate yellow tones of the castle and the abundant green of the vegetation. Internally this horshoe-shaped building is organised around a small courtyard planted with bamboo and receives visitors with a sequence of spaces that prepares them for the winding routes in the park.

Merano can even boast a further tourist-oriented model project: Schloss Tirol that dominates the Burgraviato from its lofty position. This elevated castle whose severe exterior is the antithesis to the overexposed Tyrolean village concept was converted in the years leading up to 2003 into a museum for cultural and regional history according to a concept by Markus Scherer and Walter Angonese with Klaus Hellweger. The architects focussed their attention on the donjon and designed a suspended con-

augenmerk der Architekten galt dabei dem Bergfried, für dessen völlig ausgehöhltes Inneres sie eine abgehängte Konstruktion aus angerostetem Stahl entwickelten. Diese bildet nun ein ideales Gefäß für die suggestive Präsentation der Geschichte Südtirols. Einen auch von außen sichtbaren Eingriff durften die Architekten im Burggarten mit dem in Lärchenholz gehüllten kleinen Bau des Seminarzentrums ausführen, der – an diesem geschichtsträchtigen Ort nicht ohne Reiz – auf das Thema der Urhütte anspielt.

Nachholbedarf im Wohnungsbau

Setzten sich Scherer, Angonese und Hellweger mit der mittelalterlichen Burg auseinander, so studierten Höller & Klotzner die Typologie der ineinander verschachtelten Meraner Altstadtbauten. Davon profitierte nicht nur ihr subtiler Umbau eines von Laubengängen gegliederten Hofhauses zum Ausstellungszentrum „kunst Meran", sondern auch das 2002 vollendete Wohnhaus Steinach mit Bar und Atelier im ältesten Teil der Meraner Altstadt. Zur Haller- und zur Ortensteingasse hin gibt es sich mit seiner ortstypischen Putzfassade zurückhaltend. Vom Steinachplatz her gesehen überrascht es jedoch mit einem zeitgenössischen, durch große Fensterflächen, Balkone und ein offenes Treppenhaus geprägten Hof.

Schon 1992 hatten Abram & Schnabl mit der Erweiterung der Pfarrplatzpassage eine zeittypische Sanierung im Altstadtgefüge vorgenommen. Weiter gingen die beiden

Tirolo, che dalla sua posizione elevata domina tutto il Burgraviato. L'aspetto severo della fortezza si contrappone al borgo di Tirolo, ipersfruttato a fini turistici. Il castello è stato trasformato nel 2003 in museo storico-culturale della provincia di Bolzano secondo il progetto espositivo elaborato nel 1998 da Markus Scherer, Walter Angonese e Klaus Hellweger. L'attenzione principale degli architetti si è rivolta al mastio, per il cui spazio interno, completamente svuotato, è stata progettata una struttura appesa in acciaio arrugginito. Questa struttura rappresenta ora un contenitore ideale per la spettacolare rappresentazione della storia altoatesina. Nel vallo del castello, è stato consentito agli architetti realizzare un intervento visibile anche dall'esterno: una costruzione rivestita in legno di larice per il centro conferenze, che in questo luogo denso di storia rimanda al tema della capanna primordiale in modo affascinante.

Sulla necessità di recuperare l'edilizia residenziale

Come Scherer, Angonese e Hellweger si sono confrontati con la rocca medioevale, analogamente Höller & Klotzner hanno studiato la tipologia degli edifici inscritti della città storica di Merano. Questa esperienza ha interessato non solo la fine ristrutturazione di una casa a corte articolata da ballatoi, trasformata nel centro espositivo Merano arte, ma anche la ristrutturazione, nella parte più vecchia del centro storico di Merano, dell'edificio residenziale Steinhaus, terminato nel 2002 con l'inse-

struction of rusted steel for its completely hollowed out interior. This now forms an ideal container for presenting the history of South Tyrol. The architects were also permitted to make an intervention that is externally visible: the small seminar centre building clad in larch which plays with the theme of the primitive hut, a concept that has a certain attraction at this historic place.

Deficit in the area of housing

While Scherer, Angonese and Hellweger examined the mediaeval castle, Höller & Klotzner studied the clustered buildings in the old town centre of Merano. This not only benefitted their subtle conversion of a courtyard building with access galleries into the exhibition building Merano arte, but also their Steinach apartment building with bar and atelier in the oldest part of Merano that was completed in 2002. Towards Via Haller and Vicolo Ortenstein it has restrained rendered facades but seen from Piazza Steinach it is more surprising, the contemporary courtyard has large windows, balconies and an open staircase.

As early as 1992 Abram & Schnabl had carried out a renovation of the arcade on Piazza Duomo in the old town that was typical of its time. The two Bolzano architects went somewhat further with their development (involving some new construction) of a site about 95 metres long between the historical Via Portici and Corso Libertà. Their Kurhaus arcade, which is articulated by three internal courtyards, includes

Bozner Architekten nun bei der teilweisen Neubebauung einer rund 95 m langen Parzelle zwischen der historischen Laubengasse und der Freiheitsstrasse. Die durch drei Innenhöfe gegliederte Kurhauspassage, welche neben Ladengeschäften und Büroräumlichkeiten auch 30 durch Laubengänge erschlossene Eigentumswohnungen umfasst, gleicht mit ihren hintereinander gereihten Bauten einer Stadt in der Stadt. Die neue Architektur tritt nur nach innen und an der stilistisch heterogenen Freiheitsstrasse in Erscheinung – hier aber mit einer extravaganten Geste: Neigt sich der Bau doch, abgestützt auf ein kleines spätklassizistisches Bankhaus, dem benachbarten Jugendstilgebäude zu. Dieser spannungsvoll komponierte Baukörper steht in diametralem Gegensatz zur ruhigen historischen Fassade des revitalisierten Altbaus an der Laubengasse.

Abgesehen von diesen Altstadtbauten wurden in Südtirol in jüngster Zeit – anders als etwa in den 70er Jahren – kaum noch architektonisch relevante Wohnhäuser errichtet. Eine Ausnahme bilden zwei Meraner Beispiele – der ökologisch konzipierte vierstöckige Holzbau von Holzbox, Baugesellschaft Wolkenstein und Vorarlberger Ökohaus in der Wolkensteinstraße und der kubistisch verschachtelte Luxuswohnblock Villa Mozart von Oswald Zoeggeler in der St. Markus-Straße – sowie der an Vorarlberger Vorbilder erinnernde soziale Wohnbau von Bruno Rubner, dkp_architektur und dreiplus_architektur in Stegen bei Bruneck.

rimento di bar e atelier. Verso via Haller e vicolo Ortenstein, l'edificio presenta una tipica facciata intonacata dall'aspetto discreto. Osservato da piazza Steinach esso sorprende per l'impatto della corte, caratterizzata in senso contemporaneo da grandi superfici vetrate, balconi e da un corpo scala all'aperto.

Già nel 1992, con l'ampliamento della galleria di piazza Duomo, Abram & Schnabl avevano anticipato un intervento di restauro contemporaneo nel tessuto della città storica. Su queste basi, hanno in seguito realizzato la parziale nuova edificazione di una particella edilizia, profonda novantacinque metri tra la Via dei Portici e Corso Libertà. La galleria Kurhaus-Passage, articolata in tre corti interne, comprende accanto a negozi ed uffici anche trenta appartamenti distribuiti da ballatoi, e assomiglia con i suoi corpi di fabbrica allineati gli uni dietro agli altri, a una città nella città. La nuova architettura si manifesta solo all'interno delle corti e sul fronte di Corso Libertà, contraddistinto da uno stile eterogeneo. Qui, con un gesto stravagante, la costruzione si piega verso il vicino edificio Liberty, separata e sostenuta da una colonna dal piccolo edificio tardoclassico sottostante. La composizione ricca di tensioni di questo corpo edilizio, si pone all'esatto opposto della discreta facciata storica dell'antico edificio su via dei Portici, a cui la ristrutturazione ha conferito una nuova vitalità.

A prescindere da questi edifici storici, e - diversamente da quanto accadde negli anni

shops and office spaces as well as 30 privately owned flats that are accessed from external galleries. The different parts of the design are organised one behind the other forming a kind of city in the city. The new architecture is revealed only internally and on the stylistically heterogeneous Corso Libertà – where it uses an extravagant gesture. The new building inclines toward the neighbouring Jugendstil building, supporting itself on a late classicist bankhouse. This excitingly composed volume forms a complete contrast to the calm historicist facade of the renovated old building in Via Portici.

Apart from these buildings in old city areas, in the situation in the 1970s few architecturally interesting residential buildings have been erected in South Tyrol in recent times. Two examples in Merano provide an exception – a four-storey timber building with an ecological concept in Via Wolkenstein designed by the Innsbruck architects Holzbox, and Villa Mozart, an interlocking cubist g luxury apartment building by Oswald Zoeggeler in Cia San Marco. To these examples one could add the social housing block by Bruno Rubner and Armin Pedevilla in Stegona near Brunico, which is reminiscent of examples in Vorarlberg.

Influenced by the number of commissions architects' interest seems to have recently turned more in the direction of the single family house. In the higher valleys, in addition to the ubiquitous pseudo South Tyrolean architecture, one can now enounter an increasing number of contemporary

Nicht zuletzt durch die Auftragslage bestimmt, scheint das Herzblut der Architekten derzeit eher in Richtung Einfamilienhaus zu fließen. So trifft man gerade in den höher gelegenen Tälern neben der noch immer allgegenwärtigen Pseudo-Südtirolerarchitektur vermehrt auf zeitgenössisch interpretierte Holzhäuser mit Flachdächern und großzügigen Fensterfronten, von denen das Niedrigenergiehaus Huber-Schnarf von aichner_seidl Architekten in Olang bei Bruneck wohl das attraktivste ist. Etwas befremdlich mutet hingegen die Ummantelung eines alten Bauernhauses mit einer aufgeständerten Hülle aus Holz und Glas in St. Jakob im Ahrntal an. Dennoch wurde dieser exaltierte Bau von Stefan Hitthaler 2002 mit dem zweiten Südtiroler Architekturpreis ausgezeichnet. Zeitgemäßer und weltoffener als dieses Zwitterwesen scheint das von Comfort_Architecten in St. Lorenzen im Pustertal errichtete Einfamilienhaus Sonne. Bei diesem Lückenfüller zwischen zwei banalen Neubauten sorgt eine „Split-Level"-Konstruktion für wabenartige Fassadenbilder.

Mindestens so gewagt wie dieser Verbindungsbau ist ein Wohnkubus aus Beton mit rotem Glasabschluss, den eine Wirtefamilie neben ihrem Gasthaus und einem alten Kirchlein direkt am Eisack bei Franzensfeste nach Plänen des sonst eher als Innenarchitekt bekannten Gerd Bergmeister erbaute. Der Gegensatz zwischen dem bunkerartigen Äußeren, dem raffinierten Interieur und der einladenden Gartenterrasse könnte nicht größer sein.

Settanta, – in tempi recenti non sono stati realizzati edifici residenziali di interesse architettonico. Fanno eccezione due esempi meranesi: – l'edificio in legno di quattro piani in via Wolkenstein, concepito secondo principi ecologici da Holzbox, Baugesellschaft Wolkenstein GmbH., Vorarlberger Ökohaus GmbH, e Villa Mozart in via S. Marco di Oswald Zoeggeler, un caseggiato di lusso i cui volumi cubici si incastrano l'uno nell'altro. A questi si aggiunge l'intervento di edilizia sociale a Stegona presso Brunico di Bruno Rubner, dkp_architektur e dreiplus_architektur che rimanda a modelli del Vorarlberg.

Attualmente sembra che l'attenzione degli architetti, si rivolga prevalentemente verso le case unifamiliari, non da ultimo per le richieste della committenza. Proprio nelle valli montane, a fianco della onnipresente architettura pseudo-sudtirolese, capita così sempre più spesso di incappare in case in legno interpretate in chiave contemporanea, con tetti piani e ampi fronti finestrati. La casa a basso consumo energetico Huber- Schnarf di aichner_seidl Architekten di Valdaora presso Brunico, ne è l'esempio più interessante. Sconcertante è invece l'incapsulamento di un vecchio maso con una sovrastruttura in legno e vetro a S. Giacomo in Val Aurina. Eppure, questo celebrato edificio di Stefan Hittaler è stato insignito del Premio di Architettura in Alto Adige alla sua seconda edizione, nel 2002. Più contemporaneo e cosmopolita di questa creatura ermafrodita, appare la casa unifamiliare Sonne, a S. Lorenzo di Sebato

timber houses with flat roofs and large areas of glazing of which the low energy Huber-Schnarf house by aichner_seidl Architekten in Valdaora near Brunico is probably the most attractive. In contrast to this project the encasing of an old farm house with an elevated shell of timber and glass in S. Giacomo in Valle Aurina seems rather strange. Nevertheless this eccentric building by Stefan Hitthaler was awarded the second South Tyrol Architecture Prize in 2002. The single family Sonne house erected by Comfort_Architekten in S. Lorenzo di Sebato in Val Pusteria seems more contemporary and open than Hitthaler's hermaphroditic design. The Sonne house fills a gap between two banal new buildings and uses a split-level organisational system that produces facades reminiscent of a honeycomb.

The residential cube of concrete terminated by red glass that Gerd Bergmeister, better known as an interior designer, erected beside his clients' inn and near a small old church directly on the River Isarco near Fortezza is just as daring as the project by Comfort_Architekten. The contrast between the bunker-like exterior, the refined interior and the inviting garden terraced could hardly be greater.

In contrast the inside and outside of the Kaser House in Bressanone-Milland seem at first glance to harmonize completely. Here civil engineer Benno Barth succeeded in building a house for a young family with a narrow plan on a tight site that is far more generous than it initially seems. This can

Inneres und Äußeres stimmen hingegen auf den ersten Blick beim Haus Kaser in Brixen-Milland überein. Auch gelang hier dem Bauingenieur Benno Barth das Kunststück, auf einer engen Parzelle über schmalem Grundriss für eine junge Familie ein Haus zu bauen, das weit großzügiger ist, als es zunächst erscheinen mag. Das erklärt sich daraus, dass ein ins Erdreich abgesenktes und begrüntes Atrium den Einbau von gut belichteten Räumen unter dem Garten erlaubte. Nutzen diese beiden Bauten geschickt Kleinstparzellen aus, auf denen anderswo gar nicht erst gebaut werden dürfte, so machen sich in Bozen-Gries neue Villen scheinbar ungehindert in den Weingärten breit, darunter zwei Häuser von Werner Tscholl, die man zu den repräsentativsten der letzten Jahre in Südtirol zählen darf.

Städtebauliches Einfühlungsvermögen

Vom vorstädtischen Gries, einem der schönsten Stadteile Bozens, gelangt man schnell ins Zentrum der mit 100.000 Einwohnern größten Stadt Südtirols. Diese verdankt ihr urbanes Flair nicht zuletzt den intelligenten Planungen der Gründerzeit und der Zwischenkriegsjahre. Selbstbewusst gibt sich in jüngster Zeit der Gerichtsplatz, die neben dem Siegesplatz wohl wichtigste Platzanlage der faschistischen Stadterweiterung. Dank dem Bau einer von Stanislao Fierro mit überraschenden Effekten belebten Tiefgarage konnte sie anschließend nach dessen Plänen mit zurückhaltender Grandezza umgebaut werden. Stanislao Fierro

in Val Pusteria. In questa costruzione, che chiude il vuoto edilizio compreso tra due nuove banali edificazioni, un sistema a livelli sfalsati determina la composizione a nido d'ape della facciata.

Audace almeno quanto questo corpo edilizio di collegamento, è la casa-cubo in cemento con coronamento in vetro rosso, che una famiglia di ristoratori ha fatto costruire a fianco del proprio albergo e di una vecchia chiesetta, su progetto di Gerd Bergmeister, conosciuto prevalentemente per le sue architetture d'interni. Il contrasto tra gli esterni, che assomigliano ad un bunker, e la raffinatezza degli interni con la invitante terrazza-giardino, non poteva essere più grande. Esterni ed interni si accordano al primo sguardo in casa Kaser a Bressanone-Milland dell'ingegnere Benno Barth, a cui è riuscito pure un "gioco di prestigio": realizzare su un lotto stretto una casa per una giovane famiglia, con una pianta allungata, che è effettivamente più grande di quello che appare dapprincipio. Questo "trucco" si spiega con la realizzazione di un atrio verde, sprofondato nel terreno, che ha reso possibile l'inserimento di locali ben illuminati sotto il giardino.

Così come entrambi questi edifici hanno sfruttato con sapienza piccoli lotti, dove non era altrimenti possibile costruire, analogamente a Bolzano-Gries nuove ville si fanno ampio spazio tra le vigne, apparentemente senza ostacoli normativi. Tra queste, due case di Werner Tscholl, si possono annoverare tra le più rappresentative degli ultimi anni in Alto Adige.

be explained by the fact that a planted atrium was embedded in the ground allowing well-lit spaces to be made below garden level. Whereas these two buildings cleverly exploit very small sites that perhaps elsewhere it would not be permitted to build upon, in Bolzano-Gries new villas seem to spread unhindered in the vineyards, including two houses by Werner Tscholl, which can be numbered among the most prestigious to be built in South Tyrol in recent years.

Sensitive urban planning

From the suburb of Gries, one of the most attractive districts of Bolzano, one can quickly reach the centre of this city which is the largest town in South Tyrol with 100,000 inhabitants. Bolzano owes its urban flair in part to the intelligent planning of the late 19th century and the interwar period. In recent times Piazza del Tribunale has acquired a self-confident air, together with Piazza della Vittoria it is the most important square created during the expansion of Bolzano carried out under the fascist regime. Following the construction of an underground garage with a surprisingly enlivening effect by Stanislao Fierro Piazza del Tribunale was reconstructed according to his plans with a restrained grandezza. Together with Matteo Scagnol, Luigi Scolari, Paolo de Martin and Paolo Bonatti, who delivered a contemporary interpretation of the ideas of rationalism in a new building for the Environmental Agency in Bolzano, Stanislao Fierro is one of the few

zählt zusammen mit Matteo Scagnol, Luigi Scolari, Paolo de Martin und Paolo Bonatti, der in einem Neubau für das Umweltamt in Bozen Ideen des Rationalismus zeitgemäß uminterpretiert, zu den wenigen italienischsprachigen Architekten Südtirols, die derzeit mit herausragenden Leistungen aufwarten können. Ob sich hierin die allgemeine Krise der italienischen Baukunst spiegelt, die sich von Mailand bis Venedig seit längerem auch lähmend auf die Architektenausbildung auswirkt, oder ob es sich um ein anderes Phänomen handelt, ist schwer zu sagen. Sicher ist nur, dass es bis in die 70er Jahre vor allem Architekten italienischer Herkunft waren, die in Bozen Zeichen setzten.

Der neu gestaltete Gerichtsplatz aber darf sich sehen lassen, bringt er doch die Pfeilerhalle des monumentalen Gerichtsgebäudes und die „Casa Littoria" mit dem 40 m langen Duce-Relief, in der heute das Finanzamt untergebracht ist, mit der nötigen Zurückhaltung zur Geltung. Mit Faschismus-Begeisterung hat das nichts zu tun (obwohl es diese in Bozen durchaus noch gibt). Vielmehr soll hier die städtebauliche Intervention ganz offensichtlich dazu dienen, eine dunkle, von Fremdherrschaft bestimmte Epoche der heute zu knapp drei Vierteln italienisch sprechenden Stadt im kritischen Gedächtnis zu behalten.

Neben Monumentalbauten besitzt Bozen auch mehrere rationalistische Meisterwerke aus der Mussolini-Zeit, darunter die Badeanstalt Lido und das zwischen 1934 und 1936 realisierte ehemalige GIL-Gebäude,

Sensibilità per l'inserimento urbanistico

Dal borgo di Gries, uno dei quartieri più belli di Bolzano, si giunge velocemente al centro del più grande insediamento urbano dell'Alto Adige, con una popolazione di 100.000 abitanti. La città deve la sua piacevole atmosfera, tra l'altro, all'intelligente pianificazione di fine Ottocento e del periodo tra le due guerre.

Piazza del Tribunale, che insieme a Piazza della Vittoria, costituisce il vuoto urbano più importante dell'ampliamento fascista, si propone di recente con rinnovato orgoglio. Dopo aver qualificato con effetti sorprendenti il progetto di un nuovo garage, Stanislao Fierro ha ristrutturato la piazza secondo un principio di silente grandezza. Stanislao Fierro, Matteo Scagnol, Luigi Scolari, Paolo de Martin e Paolo Bonatti, che nella nuova sede dell'Agenzia per l'ambiente a Bolzano hanno interpretato le idee del Razionalismo in chiave contemporanea, sono tra i pochi architetti di madrelingua italiana in Alto Adige che al momento emergono dal panorama locale.

È difficile stabilire se questa condizione sia l'esito di una crisi complessiva dell'architettura italiana, che da Milano a Venezia da molto tempo ha un effetto paralizzante anche sulla formazione professionale, o se si tratti invece di un altro fenomeno. Certo è, che sino agli anni Settanta, sono stati in maggioranza gli architetti di origine italiana a lasciare un segno a Bolzano.

La nuova Piazza del Tribunale merita di essere vista, perché mette in evidenza, senza enfasi, il loggiato a colonne del monumen-

Italian-speaking architects in South Tyrol that today does excellent work. Whether this fact reflects the general crisis in Italian architecture that has had a paralysing effect on the education of architects from Milan to Venice for a number of years, or whether it is due to a different phenomenon is hard to say. But it can be stated with certainty that until the 1970s it was primarily architects of Italian origin who made their mark in Bolzano.

Bu the redesigned Piazza del Tribunale is well worth seeing as, employing the necessary reserve, it accentuates the columnar hall of the monumental courthouse and the "Casa Littoria" (with the 40-metre-long relief of the Duce) that today houses the tax office. This has absolutely nothing to do with a fascination with fascism (although doubtless this exists in Bolzano). Here the urban intervention is clearly intended to preserve a critical memory of a dark era of foreign domination in a town which today is three-quarters Italian speaking.

In addition to these monumental buildings Bolzano also has several rationalist masterpieces from the Mussolini era, including the Lido baths and the GIL Building that was built between 1934 and 1936 and which with its red tower long dominated the square that opens towards the Drusus Bridge. This architecture monument was expanded between 1995 and 2002 by Graz architect Klaus Kada for the European Academy (EURAC) with a restrained, dark coloured glass building, which makes the entire complex into a kind of bridgehead and

das mit seinem roten Turmbau lange den zur Drususbrücke hin offenen Platz beherrschte. Dieses Architekturdenkmal wurde zwischen 1995 und 2002 vom Grazer Architekten Klaus Kada für die Europäische Akademie (EURAC) um einen zurückhaltenden, in dunklen Farben gehaltenen Glasbau erweitert, der nun den Gesamtkomplex zum eigentlichen Brückenkopf macht und so das urbanistische Gewebe an einer sensiblen Stelle geschickt verdichtet.

Von städtebaulichem Einfühlungsvermögen zeugt auch das architektonisch bemerkenswerte, 1977 von Marcello Aquilina realisierte Realgymnasium, welches jüngst von Christoph Mayr Fingerle saniert wurde. Erwähnenswert ist aber auch die Turnhalle, die von den Architekten Pardeller+Putzer+Scherer unweit des Lyzeums als Scharnier zwischen das relativ dicht bebaute Areal im Bereich zwischen Martin Knoller- und Fagenstraße und den Villenhang von Gries gesetzt wurde. Dass der städtebauliche Auftritt eines Projekts durch unvorhergesehene bauliche Fremdeingriffe schlagartig in Frage gestellt werden kann, zeigt sich bei der vor Jahren schon geplanten und nun in der ersten Phase soeben vollendeten Landesberufsschule von Höller & Klotzner an der Romstraße. Der aus zwei rechtwinklig zur Straße gestellten Riegeln bestehende Bau war als Nachbar der architektonisch interessanten, aber renovierungsbedürftigen Messehalle von Guido Pelizzari und Heiner Rössler gedacht.[3] Nachdem aber die Stadt dieses Baudenkmal aus den frühen 50er

tale edificio del tribunale e la Casa Littoria con l'altorilievo dedicato al Duce, lungo 40 metri sulla facciata degli odierni Uffici Finanziari. Nulla a che vedere con una atteggiamento entusiastico verso il Fascismo (nonostante questo persista senz'altro a Bolzano).

In senso urbano, l'intervento è volto invece a marcare in quella parte di cittadinanza che parla italiano – quasi tre quarti della popolazione cittadina – una coscienza critica verso un'epoca buia, caratterizzata dal dominio straniero.

Dell'epoca mussoliniana Bolzano possiede, oltre agli edifici monumentali, anche molti capolavori razionalisti, tra cui l'impianto del Lido e l'edificio ex-GIL, realizzato tra il 1934 e il 1936, che con la sua alta torre rossa ha dominato a lungo sulla piazza prospiciente il Ponte Druso.

Questa notevole architettura è stata ampliata tra il 1995 ed il 2002 dall'architetto di Graz Klaus Kada per conto dell'Accademia Europea (EURAC). La parte nuova, aggiunta con discrezione, è realizzata con uno scuro corpo di fabbrica in vetro, e trasforma il complesso in una vera e propria testa di ponte che con abilità densifica il tessuto urbano in una zona sensibile.

E' testimone di un buon inserimento urbanistico anche l'interessante edificio del liceo scientifico realizzato nel 1977 da Marcello Aquilina, recentemente ristrutturato da Christoph Mayr Fingerle.

Degna di nota anche la palestra a fianco del liceo realizzata dagli architetti Pardeller+Putzer+Scherer, in una posizione di cernie-

thus cleverly condenses the urban fabric at a sensitive place.

A further example of urban sensitivity is the architecturally remarkable Lyceum built by Marcello Aquilina in 1977, which was recently renovated by Christoph Mayr Fingerle. Also worth mentioning is the gymnasium built by architects Pardeller+Putz+Scherer not far from the Lyceum that forms a kind of hinge between the relatively built-up area between Via Martin Koller and Fagenstrasse and the villa-covered slopes of Gries.

The fact that the urban appearance of a project can suddenly be made questionable by unforeseen architectural interventions from outside is shown by the regional vocational school built by Höller and Klotzner on Via Roma that was planned years ago, although the first phase was only recently completed. This building that consists of two blocks at right angles to the street was intended as a neighbour to Guido Pelizzari's architecturally interesting trade fair hall that was in need of renovation[3]. However, as the authorities had this monument from the 1950s demolished at short notice to make an open space surrounded by large housing blocks, the architectural rhetoric of Höller and Klotzner's northern block that stands on tall panel-like piers is no longer appropriate to the current urban situation.

Minimalist school buildings

The complex of buildings making up the Free University of Bolzano designed in the manner of German Swiss minimalism was

Jahren kurzerhand abreißen ließ, um hier einen von großen Wohnblocks gefassten Freiraum zu verwirklichen, entspricht leider die baukünstlerische Rhetorik des auf hohen, scheibenartigen Pfeilern stehenden Nordriegels der heutigen urbanen Situation nicht mehr.

Minimalistische Schulbauten

Passgenau in die Bozner Innenstadt eingefügt ist hingegen der dem Deutschschweizer Minimalismus verpflichtete Gebäudekomplex der Freien Universität Bozen, den die Zürcher Architekten Matthias Bischoff und Roberto Azzola in der Folge eines 1998 europaweit ausgeschriebenen Wettbewerbs umsetzten konnten. Auch wenn der kubisch strenge Auftritt der Anlage zur Sernesistraße hin von vielen Einwohnern als klobig und abweisend beanstandet wird, lassen sich vielfältige Bezüge zur Architektur der Stadt ausmachen: von den barocken Stadtpalästen bis hin zu den Repräsentationsbauten der 30er Jahre. Zudem fügt sich die von nüchterner Sachlichkeit und kontextuellem Rationalismus zeugende Fassade sensibler in die gründerzeitliche Häuserflucht der Sparkassenstraße ein, als es etwa Boris Podreccas kulissenartiger Passagenarchitektur im baulichen Patchwork der Altstadtgassen an der Rückseite des am Waltherplatz gelegenen Hotels Greif gelingt.

Ebenfalls aus einem internationalen Wettbewerb hervorgegangen ist der heute den Bildungswissenschaften dienende Neubau der Freien Universität Bozen in Brixen. Diesen abstrakten Kubus, der aus einem Stahlbetongerippe und abwechselnd transparenten sowie transluzenten Glastafeln besteht, haben die Stuttgarter Architekten Kohlmayer & Oberst unmittelbar an den Ostrand der Brixner Altstadt gesetzt. Selbst wenn er sich möglicherweise auf das Geviert der bischöflichen Hofburg bezieht und in seiner Strenge vielleicht sogar den Dialog mit den klar konzipierten Brixner Schulbauten von Giulio Brunettas Sommerakademie (1955) und Othmar Barths Cusanus-Akademie (1962) sucht, bildet er im kleinteiligen Stadtgefüge doch einen ungelenken Fremdkörper.

Hier zeigt es sich, dass Projekte ausländischer Architekten dann zum Problem

ra tra il fitto tessuto urbano tra le via Fago e via Martin Knoller ed il pendio contrappuntato dalle ville urbane di Gries.

Che il corretto inserimento urbano di un progetto possa essere messo repentinamente in dubbio da interventi edilizi successivi non previsti, è reso esplicito dalla scuola professionale di via Roma degli architetti Höller & Klotzner, progettata anni or sono ed ora terminata nel suo primo lotto.

La costruzione, composta da due corpi di fabbrica a stecca disposti perpendicolarmente alla strada, era concepita per attestarsi vicino all'interessante edificio della fiera di Guido Pellizzari e Heiner Rössler, che si prevedeva di ristrutturare.³ Dopo che la città ha lasciato abbattere senza esitazione questo monumento degli anni '50, per realizzare una piazza delimitata da un complesso residenziale, il gesto retorico della stecca settentrionale sorretta da pilastri a setto non corrisponde più alla situazione attuale.

Edifici scolastici minimalisti

Il complesso di edifici della Libera Università di Bolzano, realizzato dagli architetti Matthias Bischoff e Roberto Azzola di Zurigo a seguito del concorso internazionale del 1998, inserisce con precisione nel centro cittadino di Bolzano un'espressione del minimalismo svizzero-tedesco.

Anche se l'effetto del grande volume quadrato su via Sernesi viene criticato per il suo impatto pesante e respingente, è possibile riconoscervi molti riferimenti all'architettura della città: dai palazzi barocchi agli edifici monumentali degli anni '30. La facciata, segno di una sobria oggettività e di un razionalismo contestualizzato, si inserisce nella cortina edilizia dei primi del Novecento su via Cassa di Risparmio, con maggiore sensibilità rispetto a quella della galleria realizzata da Boris Podrecca sul retro dell'Hotel Grifone di Piazza Walther, sorta di quinta architettonica nel patschwork delle viuzze del vecchio centro storico.

È l'esito di un concorso internazionale anche l'edificio per la Facoltà di Pedagogia della Libera Università di Bolzano a Bressanone. Progettato dagli architetti Kohlmayer & Oberst, questo astratto cubo posto ai margini orientali del centro storico di Bressanone si compone di un'ossatura in

inserted with absolute precision in the old town of Bolzano by Zurich architects Matthias Bischoff and Roberto Azzola, winners of a competition held in 1998 that was open to entries from throughout Europe. Although the severe cubist appearance of the complex on Via Sernesi is criticized by many locals as too blocky and hostile, one can discern a number of references to the architecture of the town, from the Baroque town palaces to the impressive public buildings of the 1930s. In addition the facade that is characterised by a sober functionalism and contextual rationalism is more sensitively inserted in the line of late 19th century houses on Via Cassa di Risparmio than Boris Podrecca's stage-set like passageway architecture in the patchwork of old city lanes behind Hotel Greif on Waltherplatz.

The new building for the Free University of Bolzano in Bressanone that houses the educational sciences faculty is another product of an international competition. This abstract cube made up of a reinforced concrete and alternating transparent and translucent panes of glass was placed directly on the eastern edge of the old city centre of Bressanone by Stuttgart architects Kohlmayer & Ortner. Even though it possibly relates to the area around the episcopal Hofburg and with its severity perhaps seeks to engage in a dialogue with the conceptual clarity of Bressanone school buildings such as Giulio Brunetta's Sommerakademie (1955) and Othmar Barth's Cusanus-Akademie (1962), it nevertheless remains an awkward foreign element in the smallscale mesh of the city.

This reveals that projects by foreign architects can become a problem if they wrongly interpret local characteristics or do not even understand them in the first place. Therefore one can only hope that the cheefully modernist design for the Monguelfo tripartite school centre in Val Pusteria by Daniel Marques from Lucerne and Ursa Rosner, and the double cube by German architects Stefan Burger and Birgit Rudacs in Funse that was carefully adapted to the landscape (and yet attracted hostile reactions) will succeed in enriching regional architecture. In terms of their striking architectural quality we can already compare

werden können, wenn lokale Eigenheiten falsch interpretiert oder gar nicht verstanden werden. Da kann man nur hoffen, dass es dem heiter-modernistischen, von Daniele Marques aus Luzern zusammen mit Ursa Rosner erarbeiteten Entwurf für das dreiteilige Schulzentrum Welsberg im Pustertal und dem Projekt eines sorgfältig auf die Landschaft bezogenen (und trotzdem heftig angefeindeten) Doppelkubus der deutschen Architekten Stefan Burger und Birgit Rudacs in Villnöß gelingen wird, die regionale Architektur zu bereichern. In ihrer baukünstlerischen Prägnanz jedenfalls kann man diese Projekte schon jetzt mit der um einen begrünten, nach Norden offenen Hof angelegten Landesberufsschule in Brixen von Siegfried Delueg und mehr noch mit dem benachbarten, abstrakter und geschlossener erscheinenden Studentenhaus desselben Architekten vergleichen.

Schillerndes privates Engagement

Bis heute erweist sich der Schulbau als eine der schönsten Blüten des öffentlichen Bauens in Südtirol. Herausragende Architekturen, die aus privaten Initiativen hervorgegangen sind, finden sich demgegenüber noch immer eher selten – einmal abgesehen von einigen Privat- und Bürohäusern oder von Bauten wie der Kurhaus-Passage in Meran, den Hotels von Matteo Thun oder den Umbauten der beiden Bozner Stadthotels Figl durch Wolfgang Piller und Greif durch Boris Podrecca. So ist der neue Hauptsitz des Verbands für Kaufleute

cemento armato su cui si alternano vetrate trasparenti ed opache. Nonostante il riferimento al recinto della corte vescovile e il tentativo di dialogo con gli edifici scolastici concepiti con estrema chiarezza da Giulio Brunetta nell'Accademia estiva dell'Università di Padova (1955) e da Othmar Barth nella Cusanus-Akademie (1962), esso introduce nella grana minuta del tessuto urbano un corpo estraneo e maldestro.

Si dimostra così come i progetti di architetti stranieri possano divenire un problema, quando le peculiarità locali sono erroneamente interpretate o addirittura incomprese.

In ragione di questo, si può solo sperare che il progetto per i tre corpi di fabbrica del centro scolastico di Monguelfo in Val Pusteria, elaborato in stile prettamente modernista da Daniele Marques di Lucerna con Ursa Rosner, e il progetto degli architetti tedeschi Stefan Burger e Birgit Rudacs per Funes, i cui due cubi sono inseriti con sensibilità nel paesaggio e ciononostante fortemente osteggiati, possano riuscire ad arricchire l'architettura regionale.

Già oggi, comunque, questi progetti sono paragonabili per la precisione della loro architettura alla scuola professionale provinciale di Bressanone di Siegfried Delueg, impostata intorno ad una corte verde aperta verso nord, e ancora di più con il vicino studentato dello stesso architetto, che appare ancora più astratto e chiuso.

Cangiante impegno privato

Fino ad oggi l'edilizia scolastica ha dato

these projects with Siegfried Delueg's regional vocational school in Bressanone with its planted courtyard open towards the north and even more so with the same architect's neighbouring, more abstract and closed student building.

Dazzling private commitment

Up to the present school building has been the most successful area of public building activity in South Tyrol. In contrast excellent examples of architecture that result from private initiatives are rather rare – apart from a number of private and office buildings or buildings such as the Kurhaus-Passage in Merano, the hotels by Matteo Thun or the renovations of the two city hotels in Bolzano, Figl by Wolfgang Piller and Greif by Boris Podrecca. The new headquarters of the Associazione dei Commercianti (association of retailers) by Demande-Architekten (Lukas Wielander, Jürgen Winkler) in Via Piani di Mezzo in Bolzano uses a somewhat too polished international idiom, its glass facade on the street side is animated by solar blinds but refuses to engage in a dialogue with the heterogeneous suburban surroundings. But the cheeky projecting roof top element and the small pond give it a rather playful quality. The rationalist, cube-shaped architectural sculpture of the office block that Werner Tscholl has placed in the rural industrial zone of Laces also rises out of an artificial pool. This building provides the wholesale fruit company Selimex with an anonymous and yet internationally comprehensible image. In this

von Demande-Architekten (Lukas Wielander, Jürgen Winkler) am Bozner Mitterweg einem allzu geschliffenen internationalen Idiom verpflichtet. Seine durch Sonnenblenden belebte straßenseitige Glasfassade verweigert den Dialog mit der heterogenen vorstädtischen Umgebung. Dafür verleihen ihm der keck vorstehende Dachaufbau und die kleine Wasserfläche etwas Spielerisches. Ebenfalls aus einem künstlichen Teich erhebt sich die rationalistische, würfelförmige Architekturskulptur eines Bürohauses, das der im Vinschgau erfolgreiche Werner Tscholl in die ländliche Industriezone von Latsch gesetzt und so dem im Obstgroßhandel tätigen Unternehmen Selimex zu einem ebenso anonymen wie global verständlichen Auftritt verholfen hat. Mit diesem „grünen Schloss" hat Tscholl ein modisches Formenrepertoire ähnlich unbefangen übernommen, wie dies gewisse jüngere Büros tun, die Kritikern zufolge vor lauter Aufträgen keine Zeit mehr für eigene Recherchen finden.

Zu diesen Mahnern zählt Walter Angonese,[4] ein Hauptexponent der Südtiroler Szene. Seine 2004 zusammen mit Silvia Boday und Rainer Köberl vollendete Kellereianlage für das leicht erhöht über dem Kalterer See gelegene Weingut Manincor wird auch im Ausland viel beachtet. Nur an fünf Stellen tritt die tief in die sanfte Hangneigung eingegrabene „Grottenarchitektur" mit skulpturalen Bauteilen und einem Lichthof aus dem Weinberg an die Oberfläche. Damit ordnet sie sich ebenso sensibel wie raffiniert der lieblichen Landschaft und dem barocken Herrenhaus unter, ohne dabei auf die Ausdruckskraft von Form und Material zu verzichten.

Ein tempelartiges, aus Holzpfeilern, Glaswänden und einem Betondach gebildetes Verkaufsgebäude empfängt die Besucher. Rechts von dieser formschönen Kleinarchitektur neigt sich der Zugang zur Kellerei rampenartig in die Tiefe. Die aus rostroten Stahltoren, grünschimmernden Vitrinen und einem weißen Screen gebildete Eingangsfront lässt bald an einen riesigen Schlund, bald an die zeitgenössisch interpretierte Szenenwand eines antiken Theaters denken. Im Inneren des im Tagbau in den Fels gehauenen Bauwerks, über dem der alte Weinberg wiederhergestellt wurde,

i frutti più maturi dell'edilizia pubblica in Alto Adige. Architetture degne di nota dovute all'iniziativa privata, sono al confronto piuttosto una rarità, fatta eccezione per alcune residenze private, palazzi per uffici, oppure per edifici come il Kurhaus-Passage a Merano, l'albergo di Matteo Thun o entrambe le ristrutturazioni degli alberghi cittadini, il Figl di Wolfgang Piller e il Grifone di Boris Podrecca.

Così la nuova sede dell'associazione commercianti di Demande-Architekten (Lukas Wielander, Jürgen Winkler) ai Piani di Bolzano, è vincolata ad un idioma internazionale eccessivamente raffinato. La facciata vetrata su strada, vivacizzata dalle lamelle parasole, nega qualsiasi dialogo con i dintorni di una periferia eterogenea. D'altra parte l'aggetto ardito della costruzione sul tetto e la piccola superficie d'acqua antistante attribuiscono all'edificio qualcosa di giocoso.

Similmente, nel paesaggio rurale della zona artigianale di Laces, da un laghetto artificiale si erge il volume cubico e razionalista di un'architettura-scultura, un edificio per uffici realizzato da Werner Tscholl, affermato architetto della Val Venosta. L'intervento ha garantito all'azienda Selimex, attiva nel commercio della frutta, di acquisire un'immagine tanto impersonale quanto genericamente comprensibile.

Con questo "castello verde", Tscholl ha ripreso un repertorio formale alla moda come già fanno in modo spregiudicato certi giovani studi, che al seguito del successo di critica davanti all'incalzare di grandi incarichi, non hanno più tempo per impostare una ricerca personale.

Tra i critici si conta Walter Angonese,[4] un esponente di spicco della scena altoatesina. Il complesso della cantina vinicola della tenuta Manincor, sulle colline circostanti il lago di Caldaro, terminato nel 2004 sulla base del progetto realizzato con Silvia Boday e Rainer Köberl, è stato oggetto di molta attenzione all'estero.

L'architettura ipogea scavata nel lieve pendio, emerge dalla superficie del vigneto solo in cinque punti con corpi scultorei ed una corte illuminata dall'alto.

L'intervento si sottomette così, in modo parimenti sensibile e raffinato, sia al dolce paesaggio che alla residenza signorile

"green palace" Tscholl has employed in a relaxed manner a fashionable repertoire of forms often used by certain younger practices that, according to the critics, have no longer any time to carry out research as they have so much work.

Among these people is Walter Angonese[4], one of the main exponents of the South Tyrol scene. His wine cellar complex for the Manincor vineyard on a slightly elevated site above Lago di Caldaro, which he completed in 2004 with Silvia Boday and Rainer Köberl, has received considerable acclaim abroad. The "grotto architecture" embedded in the gentle slope emerges on the surface of the vine covered slopes at only five places in the form of sculptural building elements and a light well. It subordinates itself to the delightful landscape and the Baroque estate house in a manner that is both sensitive and sophisticated, without neglecting the expressive power of form and materials.

A temple-like sales building with wooden columns, glass walls and a concrete roof receives visitors. To the right of this delightful smallscale architecture the access to the cellar slopoes downwards. The entrance front made of rust-red steel doors, green shimmering display cases and a white screen suggests a gigantic maw, or a contemporary interpretation of the stage screen in an antique theatre. The interior of the building that was hewn into the rock and above which the vineyards were laid out again after the completion of the construction work contains the following functional areas: the delivery complex, the wine presses, and the cellars for the barriques, wood barrels and steel tanks. The architectural highpoint of the tour is reached in the tasting room that emerges out of the hill almost like a submarine, offering views across the lake and the hilly landscape through a panorama window and from a wisteria-covered terrace.

As already mentioned the young native of Merano Silvia Boday was involved in this project, the most important private building commission to be built in South Tyrol for many years. At present in the neighbouring village of Termeno she is building on a tiny site a vaguely deconstructivist pitched roof house of concrete that has a roof light on

sind – den funktionalen Abläufen gehorchend – unter anderem die Anlieferungsanlage, die Weinpressen und die Keller für die Barriques, Holzfässer und Stahltanks untergebracht. Den architektonischen Höhepunkt des Rundgangs erreichen die Besucher im Degustationsraum, der fast wie ein Unterseeboot aus dem Erdreich in den Weinberg vorstößt, wo er mittels eines Panoramafensters und einer Glyzinienterrasse einen weiten Blick über den See und die Hügellandschaft freigibt.

An diesem seit langem wichtigsten privat realisierten Bauwerk Südtirols war wie erwähnt auch die junge Meranerin Silvia Boday beteiligt. Derzeit errichtet sie auf einem winzigen Grundstück im benachbarten Ort Tramin ein leicht dekonstruktivistisch verzogenes Giebelhaus aus Beton, das mit seinem straßenseitig übereck gestellten Dachfenster nicht ohne Ironie auf ein Lebkuchenhaus anspielt. Dass das Bozner Unterland und die von der Natur verwöhnte Gegend rund um den Kalterer See heute zu den architektonisch abwechslungsreichsten Gebieten Südtirols zählt, beweisen auch der aus farbigen Kuben zusammengesetzte Kindergarten Maria Rast der Bozner Lunz & Zöschg in St. Michael bei Eppan, der Umbau des Ensembles Lanserhaus in Eppan zu einem Kulturzentrum durch Gerhard Forer und Ursula Unterpertinger aus Bruneck sowie die zurzeit im Bau befindliche Erweiterung des Strandbades am Kalterer See durch die Architekten des Wiener Büros nextENTERprise (Marie-Therese Harnoncourt, Ernst Fuchs). Ebenfalls im

barocca, senza al contempo rinunciare alla forza espressiva di forme e materiali. I visitatori sono accolti nell'edificio vendite, una sorta di tempio realizzato su colonne in legno con pareti vetrate ed una copertura in cemento. A destra di questa piccola architettura dalle forme delicate, l'ingresso alla cantina piega come una rampa verso le profondità del terreno. Il fronte d'ingresso, composto da rossi portoni metallici arrugginiti, vetrine cangianti di verde e da uno schermo bianco, rimanda all'immaginario di un'enorme gola o piuttosto alla parete di scena di un antico teatro interpretato in chiave contemporanea.

All'interno della costruzione, scavata a cielo aperto nella roccia, e sulla quale è stata ripristinata la vecchia vigna, trovano posto - secondo quanto richiesto dalla sequenza funzionale - tra gli altri la zona di consegna, le presse per il vino, le cantine per le barriques, le botti in legno e i serbatoi in acciaio.

L'apice del percorso si raggiunge nella sala degustazione, che dal suolo emerge sulla vigna quasi come un sommergibile, e dove attraverso una vetrata panoramica e una terrazza di glicini è possibile liberare lo sguardo sull'orizzonte del lago e delle colline.

Come già menzionato, nella realizzazione di questa opera privata, da lungo tempo la più importante in Alto Adige, era coinvolta anche la giovane meranese Silvia Boday. Nel vicino paese di Termeno l'architetto sta costruendo su un piccolo lotto una casa in cemento con tetto a due falde, leggermente

the street side that goes around the corner making an ironic reference to a gingerbread house. There are further indications that the Bassa Atesina around Bolzano and above all the area around Lago di Caldaro, which has been particularly blessed with natural beauty, belongs to the architecturally most varied regions of South Tyrol. These include the kindergarten Maria Rast by Bolzano designers Lunz & Zöschg in S. Michele/Appiano which is made up of coloured cubes, the conversion of the Lanserhaus ensemble in Appiano into a culture centre by Gerhard Forer and Ursula Unterpertinger from Brunico as well as the extension to the lakeside baths on Lago di Caldaro currently under construction and designed by the young Viennese practice nextENTERprise (Marie-Therese Harnoncourt, Ernst Fuchs).

Also commissioned by the client of Manincor, Count Michael Goëss-Enzenberg, Walter Angonese together with Silvia Boday has built a remarkable apartment building for farm workers in Settequerce near Terlano in the Val d'Adige, which rises from the ground by means of a bridge structure resting on two concrete plinths and thanks to a red metal facade with industrial connotations fits perfectly into its surroundings that are partly agricultural and partly commercial. One of the few farmhouses of architectural importance to be built in recent years is more picturesquely situated than this building: the Ladstätterhof in Sinigo, south of Merano planned by Peter Plattner and commissioned by the Autono-

Auftrag des Bauherrn von Manincor, des Grafen Michael Goëss-Enzenberg, realisierte Walter Angonese in Zusammenarbeit mit Silvia Boday ein bemerkenswertes Landarbeiterwohnhaus in Siebeneich bei Terlan im Etschtal, das sich mittels einer auf zwei Betonsockeln ruhenden Brückenkonstruktion vom Erdboden absetzt und dank seiner roten, industriell anmutenden Blechfassaden perfekt in das teils landwirtschaftlich, teils gewerblich genutzte Gebiet einfügt. Malerischer gelegen als dieses Bauwerk ist eines der wenigen in jüngster Zeit entstandenen Bauernhäuser von architektonischem Belang: der von der Autonomen Provinz Bozen-Südtirol in Auftrag gegebene und von Peter Plattner geplante Ladstätterhof in Sinich südlich von Meran. Am Fuß der östlichen Talflanke inmitten von Apfelkulturen errichtet, bildet er ein abgewinkeltes Konglomerat aus holzverkleideten und betongrauen Bauteilen, in dem ein Wohn- und Verwaltungsbau, ein Landarbeiterwohnhaus und eine offene Lagerhalle zu einer Art modernem Weiler gruppiert sind. Wie wichtig in Südtirol die Landwirtschaft noch heute ist, zeigt neben diesem Neubau auch das in Auer im Bozner Unterland gelegene Schloss Baumgarten. Ausgehend von einer zeitgenössischen Neuinterpretation alter Typologien wurde dieser Ansitz jüngst von Wolfgang Piller mit viel Sinn für die historische Bausubstanz zur Landwirtschaftsschule erweitert.

deformata alla maniera decostruttivista, che con una finestra in copertura prolungata oltre l'angolo sul lato della strada, non senza ironia rimanda ad una casa di panpepato.
Che la bassa atesina ai piedi di Bolzano e la zona naturalistica intorno al lago di Caldaro siano le zone dell'Alto Adige dove l'architettura è più eterogenea, lo dimostrano alcune realizzazioni: la scuola materna Maria Rast a S. Michele di Appiano degli architetti bolzanini Lunz & Zöschg, composta da cubi colorati, la trasformazione in centro culturale del complesso Lanserhaus ad Appiano di Gerhard Forer ed Ursula Unterpertinger di Brunico, così come l'ampliamento del lido di Caldaro, ora in costruzione, dei giovani architetti viennesi nextENTERprise (Marie-Therese Harnoncourt, Ernst Fuchs).
Ancora su incarico del committente di Manincor, il conte Michael Goëss-Enzenberg, Walter Angonese ha realizzato in collaborazione con Silvia Boday una notevole residenza per agricoltori a Settequerce presso Terlano in Val d'Adige: una costruzione che grazie a due zoccoli di cemento si erge dal suolo come un ponte, e che si inserisce perfettamente nel paesaggio a destinazione parzialmente agricola e produttiva grazie alla sua rossa facciata in lamiera, ispirata ad un'estetica industriale.
Inserita nel paesaggio ancora più pittorescamente di questa costruzione, è una delle poche architetture a destinazione agricola degne di nota, affidata per incarico dalla Provincia Autonoma di Bolzano e progettata dall'architetto Peter Plattner:

mous Province of Bolzano South Tyrol. Built amidst apple trees at the foot of the east side of the valley it forms an L-shaped conglomerate of timber-clad and grey concrete elements in which a residential and administration building, an apartment building for agricultural workers and an open storage building are grouped to form a modern interpretation of a hamlet. How important agriculture still remains in South Tyrol is shown also by Schloss Baumgarten in Ora in the Bassa Atesina near Bolzano. Starting from a contemporary interpretation of old typologies this estate was recently converted into an agriculture school by Wolfgang Piller showing considerable sensitivity for the historical building fabric.

Mysterious religious buildings

Whereas in Ora Piller cultivated a restrained dialogue with the existing architectural substance, when commissioned to enlarge the Roman Catholic parish church in the rapidly growing neighbouring town of Laives Höller & Klotzner decided on a spectacular addition in the form of a golden shimmering, slightly asymmetrical pyramid. This building sculpture that at first glance appears as trendy as it is subjective, in fact results from a precise architectural and urban analysis of the place, as these two architects from Merano wanted to avoid detracting from the effect made by the Romanesque church tower or impairing the urban integrity of the neo-Gothic nave that now used as a hall and for weekday services. Therefore they moved the annex

Geheimnisvolle Sakralbauten

Pflegte Piller in Auer einen verhaltenen Dialog mit dem Bestand, so entschieden sich Höller & Klotzner im schnell gewachsenen Nachbarstädtchen Leifers bei der Erweiterung der katholischen Pfarrkirche für einen spektakulären Anbau in Form einer leicht asymmetrischen Pyramide. Diese auf den ersten Blick ebenso modisch wie subjektiv erscheinende Bauplastik resultiert aus einer architektonischen und städtebaulichen Analyse des Ortes, denn die beiden Meraner Architekten wollten die Fernwirkung des romanischen Kirchturms und die Integrität des neugotischen Kirchenschiffes, das heute als Vorraum und Werktagskirche genutzt wird, nicht beeinträchtigen. Deshalb rückten sie den mit Buntmetallschindeln geschuppten Annex, dessen leicht durchhängendes Dach im Längsschnitt entfernt an Le Corbusiers Wallfahrtskirche in Ronchamp erinnert, ein wenig von der bestehenden Kirche nach Norden ab und bildeten die Verbindungsstelle in Glas aus. Tritt man nun durch das nördliche Seitenportal des alten Gotteshauses hindurch in den neuen, mit warmem Ahornholz ausgekleideten Kirchenraum, so erfasst einen kurz ein Schwindelgefühl. Denn die Schrägen der leicht nach innen geneigten Stirnwand und der Decke sowie die perspektivische Weitung der Seitenwände erzeugen eine Atmosphäre des Schwebens und Schwankens, die von der sakralen Lichtregie des nur von Westen und oben erhellten Altarbereichs noch verstärkt wird. Dieses aufgrund seiner überzeugenden funktiona-

il Ladstätterhof di Sinigo a sud di Merano. Questo insediamento, costruito in mezzo alle monocolture di mele ai piedi del fianco orientale della valle, forma un articolato conglomerato di corpi di fabbrica, realizzati in grigio cemento e rivestiti in legno, nel quale si raggruppano, come in un moderno borgo, un corpo residenziale e uno per l'amministrazione, una casa per agricoltori e un capannone per il magazzino all'aperto.

Quanto, ancor oggi, l'agricoltura sia importante in Alto Adige lo dimostra, accanto a questa nuova edificazione, anche Castel Baumgarten adagiato nella Bassa Atesina presso Ora.

Partendo da una nuova interpretazione contemporanea di vecchie tipologie, questa residenza è stata da poco ampliata e trasformata in sede di un istituto tecnico agrario da Wolfgang Piller con molto rispetto per la preesistenza storica.

Edifici sacri carichi di mistero

Se Piller ha curato un rapporto di dialogo con l'esistente, diversamente hanno agito Höller & Klotzner nel vicino paese di Laives, che ha goduto di una rapida crescita. Qui con l'ampliamento della parrocchiale essi hanno deciso di optare per la realizzazione di un corpo annesso di forma spettacolare: una piramide leggermente asimmetrica riluciente d'oro.

La plasticità del volume edilizio, che dal primo sguardo appare decisamente alla moda e arbitraria, è invece il risultato di un'attenta analisi architettonica ed urbanistica del luogo. I due architetti meranesi

clad with coloured metal shingles and with a slightly hanging roof that in longitudinal section is slightly reminiscent of Le Corbusier's pilgrimage church in Ronchamp towards the north slightly away from the old church, and made a connecting element of glass.

If you enter through the northern side entrance of the old church into the new church space lined with warm maple wood you briefly experience a feeling of dizzyness. The incline of the slightly inwardly sloping end wall and the roof, as well as the perspective effect of the side walls creates a feeling of hovering and swaying, that is strengthened by the religious handling of light in the altar space which comes from the west and from above. Thanks to its convincing realisation in terms of function, form and materials this masterpiece was rightly awarded the third South Tyrol architecture prize in 2004.[5] Together with the Manincor vineyard complex and the transformation of Schloss Tirol this building gives current architecture in South Tyrol a new and individual face. Other building works commissioned by the Catholic Church have also led in recent years to architecturally remarkable solutions. These are extensions to existing cemeteries with integrated chapels of rest. How the walled graveyards that have traditionally accentuated the mountain landscape of South Tyrol can be architecturally reinterpreted and expanded in a compact way was demonstrated by Merano architect Willy Gutweniger back in 1980 in the mountain cem-

len, formalen und materiellen Umsetzung zu Recht mit dem 2004 zum dritten Mal vergebenen Südtiroler Architekturpreis[5] geehrte Meisterwerk verleiht zusammen mit der Kellerei von Manincor und der Transformation von Schloss Tirol der heutigen Südtiroler Architektur ein neues, eigenständiges Gesicht.

Aber auch andere Aufträge der katholischen Kirche führten in den vergangenen Jahren zu architektonisch bemerkenswerten Lösungen. Es handelt sich dabei um Friedhofserweiterungen mit integrierten Aufbahrungskapellen. Wie die ummauerten Grabstätten, die von alters her die Südtiroler Berglandschaft akzentuieren, architektonisch neu interpretiert und kompakt erweitert werden können, machte der Meraner Willy Gutweniger schon 1980 mit dem Bergfriedhof von St. Pankraz bei Lana vor, von dem aufgrund der hohen Trockenmauern und des Glockenturms eine geradezu archaische Ausstrahlung ausgeht. Elf Jahre später gelang Christoph Mayr Fingerle in Feldthurns südlich von Brixen erneut eine beachtenswerte Friedhofserweiterung, der jüngst Robert Veneri mit einer weiteren Anlage im nördlich von Brixen gelegenen Bergdorf Vals antwortete.

Übertroffen werden diese Eingriffe durch die präzise architektonische und landschaftsgestalterische Lösung von Mutschlechner & Mahlknecht in Luttach im Ahrntal. An der Gelenkstelle zwischen der Zugangsrampe, die den Nordabhang des Kirchhügels entlang führt, und dem westlich des Gotteshauses terrassenartig ab-

non hanno voluto pregiudicare l'effetto prospettico della torre romanica e l'unitarietà della navata neogotica, che oggi viene utilizzata come cappella feriale.

Per questo motivo il corpo annesso, rivestito di scaglie di metallo iridescente, con una copertura a vela che ricorda vagamente la cappella di Ronchamp di Le Corbusier, è stato scostato verso nord rispetto alla chiesa esistente, e il collegamento tra l'una e l'altra è stato realizzato in vetro. Passando a nord dal portale laterale della chiesa esistente, verso il nuovo spazio sacro, rivestito in caldo legno di acero, si è presi da una vertigine. Le inclinazioni verso l'interno della parete di fondo e della copertura, così come l' amplificazione prospettica delle pareti laterali, provocano un'atmosfera di sospensione e galleggiamento, rafforzata dall'effetto sacrale della regia luminosa che, solo da ovest e dall'alto, rischiara l'ambito dell'altare.

Questo capolavoro, meritoriamente premiato nel 2004 alla terza edizione del Premio di Architettura in Alto Adige[5] per la sua convincente esecuzione funzionale, formale e materica, insieme alla cantina vinicola Manincor e al recupero/conversione di Castel Tirolo, restituisce un'immagine indipendente all'architettura altoatesina di oggi.

Anche altri incarichi ecclesiastici hanno portato a soluzioni di architettura notevoli: si tratta di ampliamenti di cimiteri con annesse cappelle funebri.

Come i luoghi di sepoltura recintati, che sin dal passato hanno segnato il paesaggio montano, possano essere interpretati in

etery of S. Pancrazio near Lana that has an almost archaic feeling thanks to its high dry stone walls and the bell tower. Eleven years later in Velturno to the south of Bressanone Christoph Mayr Fingerle succeeded in making a further remarkable cemetery extension, recently a response has been made by Robert Veneri with his cemetery in the mountain village of Vals to the north of Bressanone.

These interventions are even surpassed by the architecture and landscaping of the solution by Mutschlechner & Mahlknecht in Luttago in Val Aurina. They placed a chapel of rest made of light-coloured fairfaced concrete that gives the complex as a whole a greater spatial clarity at the joint between the access ramp leading along the northern slope of the church hill and the new terraced graveyard to the west of the church. The new building that is visually extended by the wall with the urn graves offers a slightly veiled look into the chapel space through an opening that is continued around the corner and has a steel door and a large area of glazing thus giving this volume that is otherwise hermetically sealed a rather Japanese feeling.

Simple wooden facades

In the case of the church in the neighbouring village of S. Giacomo in Valle Aurina the same architects placed a polygonal multi-purpose building with an events space against the cemetery wall that they added urn graves to. Here, too, urban planning and architectural precision are combined

fallenden neuen Gräberfeld platzierten sie eine Aufbahrungskapelle aus hellem Sichtbeton, die der Gesamtanlage größere räumliche Klarheit verschafft. Der durch die Wand der Urnengräber optisch markant verlängerte Bau gewährt dank der übereck geführten, mit großen Glasflächen und einer Stahltüre versehenen Öffnung einen leicht verschleierten Einblick in den Andachtsraum und verleiht so dem sonst hermetisch geschlossenen Volumen etwas geradezu Japanisches.

Schlichte Holzfassaden

Bei der Kirche des Nachbardorfs St. Jakob im Ahrntal haben dieselben Architekten ein polygonales Mehrzweckgebäude mit Veranstaltungssaal an die von ihnen neu mit Urnengräbern versehene Friedhofsmauer gerückt. Auch hier vereint sich städtebauliche mit baukünstlerischer Präzision zu einem neuen Ganzen, welches doch eigentlich die architektonisch konservativen Kreise davon überzeugen müsste, dass sich Bergdörfer mit zeitgenössischen Interventionen harmonisch erweitern lassen. Während Mutschlechner & Mahlknecht in St. Jakob das grau verputzte Gebäude in den Fensterbereichen durch den Einsatz von Holz ganz diskret belebten, gingen sie im Nachbarort Steinhaus beim Umbau eines kleinen Schobers in ein Ferienhaus einen Schritt weiter, indem sie dem dunklen Holzhaus durch die Verwendung von angerostetem Stahl einen an Carlo Scarpa gemahnenden Hauch des Preziösen verliehen.

chiave architettonica ed ampliati in modo compatto, è stato anticipato già nel 1980 da Willy Gutweniger con il cimitero di montagna di S. Pancrazio presso Lana, dove l'alto muro a secco e la torre campanaria eretti ex novo emanano una dimensione arcaica. Undici anni più tardi Christoph Mayr Fingerle realizza un ampliamento degno di nota a Velturno a sud di Bressanone, al quale da poco Robert Veneri ha risposto con un'altra edificazione nel paesino di montagna di Vals a nord di Bressanone.

Questi interventi sono stati surclassati dalla precisa soluzione architettonica e paesaggistica di Mutschlechner & Mahlknecht a Luttago in Val Aurina.

Gli architetti hanno collocato nel punto di snodo tra la rampa di accesso, che corre a nord lungo il pendio della collina della chiesa ed il nuovo campo santo, che degrada a terrazze ad ovest della chiesa, una cappella funebre di cemento a vista in tinta chiara, da cui deriva a tutto l'impianto una maggior chiarezza spaziale.

La costruzione, prospetticamente allungata dalla parete dei loculi, consente uno sguardo appena velato nel locale destinato alla preghiera attraverso un'apertura prolungata oltre l'angolo e dotata di grandi superfici in vetro e di una porta metallica. L'apertura conferisce un tocco giapponese ad un volume altrimenti ermeticamente chiuso.

Essenziali facciate in legno

Nei pressi della chiesa del vicino paese di S. Giacomo, gli stessi architetti hanno accostato al nuovo muro del cimitero, dotato

to create a new entity that must surely persuade architecturally conservative circles that it is possible to harmoniously expand mountain using contemporary interventions. Whereas in S. Giacomo Mutschlechner & Mahlknecht discretely enlived the grey rendered building with the use of wood around the windows, in the neighbouring village of Steinhaus in Val Aurina they went a step further in their conversion of a small shack into a holiday home by using rusted steel to give the dark wooden building a hint of something precious in a way that recalls the work of Carlo Scarpa. Christoph Mayr Fingerle acted in a similarly self-confident way in renovating the town hell in Sesto and when inserting a sauna into the hotel Drei Zinnen built by Clemens Holzmeister in 1926 in the form of a monumental farm house. Siegfried Delueg decided on a different kind of large form for his district heating plant in Sesto. The double building defined by irregular areas of wall that he erected in the commercial area of the village is among the finest timber buildings produced to date in South Tyrol. Perhaps comparable with it are the two timber buildings for the health and social services centre connected by a glazed entrance and circulation hall built by the Bolzano practice D3 (Robert and Richard Veneri, Kathrin Gruber, Armin Kienzl) in Piccolino, S. Martino in Badia. Although perhaps not successful in all details, this comparatively large building is more convincing than many other new buildings in the mountains thanks to the harmonious

Ähnlich selbstbewusst gab sich Christoph Mayr Fingerle bei der Sanierung des Rathauses von Sexten und beim Einbau einer Sauna im Hotel Drei Zinnen, das 1926 von Clemens Holzmeister in der Form eines monumentalen Bauernhauses errichtet wurde. Für Großformen anderer Art entschied sich Siegfried Delueg beim Fernheizwerk Sexten. Der von ihm in der Handwerkerzone des Dorfes errichtete, von unregelmäßigen Wandflächen begrenzte Doppelbau zählt zum Besten, was die zeitgenössische Holzarchitektur bisher in Südtirol hervorgebracht hat. Mit ihm vergleichen lassen sich allenfalls die beiden durch eine verglaste Eingangs- und Erschließungshalle verbundenen Holzbauten des Sprengelsitzes, welchen das Bozner Büro D3 (Robert und Richard Veneri, Kathrin Gruber, Armin Kienzl) in Picolin/St. Martin in Thurn im Gadertal verwirklicht hat. Obwohl nicht in allen Einzelheiten gelungen, vermag dieses vergleichsweise große Gebäude wie wenige andere Neubauten im Gebirge durch die harmonische Einfügung in die Topographie und in den baulichen Kontext des kleinen Dorfes zu überzeugen.

Unausgeschöpftes baukünstlerisches Potenzial

Bis hinauf in die entlegenen Bergtäler trifft man heute in Südtirol auf interessante Neubauten. Von vielen dieser Schätze ahnt man als Auswärtiger kaum etwas, wenn man nur die Veröffentlichungen des Architekturpreises Südtirol in der Architekturzeitschrift „turrisbabel" oder die Publi-

da loro di nicchie per le urne funerarie, un edificio multifunzionale poligonale con sala per rappresentazioni. Anche qui la precisione dell'architettura e dell'inserimento urbanistico si completano in modo efficace, e questo dovrebbe convincere anche i settori più conservatori della critica architettonica, che i paesi di montagna si possono ampliare con interventi contemporanei. Mentre Mutschlechner & Mahlknecht vivacizzano con discrezione l'edificio intonacato di grigio con l'inserimento di elementi in legno vicino alle finestre, nella vicina località di Cadipietra gli stessi architetti hanno fatto un passo avanti con la ristrutturazione di un piccolo fienile in residenza per le vacanze, conferendo alla scura casa in legno, tramite l'uso di acciaio arrugginito, un tocco di precisione che ricorda Carlo Scarpa. Con la stessa consapevolezza, Christoph Mayr Fingerle si è accinto al restauro del Municipio di Sesto e all'inserimento di una sauna nell'albergo Drei Zinnen, realizzato nel 1926 da Clemens Holzmeister all'insegna di una monumentale casa contadina. Siegfried Delueg si è dedicato ad altre tipologie di grande scala con la centrale di teleriscaldamento di Sesto. I due corpi di fabbrica realizzati nella zona artigianale del paese e delimitati da facciate non uniformi, sono da annoverare tra le migliori realizzazioni di architettura contemporanea in legno in Alto Adige. A quest'opera si possono paragonare le due costruzioni in legno collegate da un atrio d'ingresso e distribuzione in vetro della sede dell'unità sanitaria locale, realizzate dallo studio bolzanino D3

way it is inserted into the topography and the built structure of the small village.

Architectural potential not yet exhausted

Even in remote mountain valleys one can find interesting new buildings in South Tyrol. As an outsider one is hardly aware of many of these treasures if one is only familiar with the details of the South Tyrol architecture award as published in the architecture magazine "turrisbabel" or the publications about the public buildings of the Autonomous Province of Bolzano-South Tyrol. These initiatives accompanied by the international architecture prize "New Building in the Alps" set up in the early 1990s by Sexten Kultur have without doubt led to a remarkable improvement in the standard of architectural production. One finds these good new buildings primarily where the architects have been challenged by the urban and cultural context or where an existing building has encouraged them to engage in a creative dialogue.

The architectural potential has not yet been exhausted. Standards can be raised further if in addition to public funding that, thanks to competitions, often buildings of real quality, increasing numbers of private clients emerge as open-minded commissioners of new buildings. However many of them must overcome their conservative fundamental approach that tends towards architectural traditionalism. But we can hope that those indications of a sensitivity towards good new architecture (that is also effective for tourism) that can already be

kationen über die öffentlichen Bauten der Autonomen Provinz Bozen-Südtirol kennt. Diese Initiativen, zu denen sich noch der in den frühen 90er Jahren von Sexten Kultur ins Leben gerufene internationale Architekturpreis „Neues Bauen in den Alpen" gesellt, haben zweifellos zu einer erstaunlichen Steigerung der baukünstlerischen Leistungen beigetragen. Man findet diese Bauwerke vor allem dort, wo die Architekten durch den städtebaulichen und kulturellen Kontext oder aber durch ein bestehendes Gebäude zu einem kreativen Dialog herausgefordert wurden.

Noch ist das baukünstlerische Potenzial nicht ausgeschöpft. So ließe sich das Niveau weiter heben, wenn neben der öffentlichen Hand, die dank Wettbewerben oft qualitätvolle Bauten realisiert, vermehrt private Bauherren als weltoffene Auftraggeber in Erscheinung träten. Viele von ihnen müssten dazu allerdings ihre konservative, zum architektonischen Traditionalismus neigende Grundhaltung überwinden. Doch darf man hoffen, dass die heute schon auszumachenden Vorzeigebauten den Sinn für gute (und auch touristisch wirksame) neue Architektur weiter fördern werden. Wohl nur auf diese Weise kann verhindert werden, dass die Bergregionen zu einem alpinen Disneyland verkommen.

(Robert und Richard Veneri, Kathrin Gruber, Armin Kienzl) a Piccolino, S. Martino in Badia. Anche se non riuscito in ogni sua parte, questo edificio di grandi dimensioni riesce a convincere come poche altre nuove costruzioni di montagna per il suo inserimento armonico nella topografia e nel contesto edificato del piccolo paese.

Un potenziale inespresso dell'arte di edificare

Sino nelle più lontane valli di montagna si incontrano oggi interessanti nuove costruzioni. Di molti di questi tesori non ci si immagina nemmeno, venendo dall'esterno, se si conoscono unicamente le pubblicazioni del Premio di Architettura in Alto Adige sulla rivista di architettura "turrisbabel" o le pubblicazioni sull'edilizia pubblica della Provincia Autonoma di Bolzano. Queste iniziative editoriali, alle quali si è unito il premio internazionale di architettura "Neues Bauen in den Alpen", nato grazie a Sesto Cultura nei primi anni '90, hanno senza dubbio contribuito ad una crescita incredibile della qualità dell'arte delle costruzioni. Si incontrano queste opere soprattutto laddove gli architetti sono costretti ad un dialogo creativo con il contesto urbano e culturale o con l'esistente. Il potenziale dell'architettura però non è ancora sfruttato fino in fondo. Il livello potrebbe ancora migliorare, se a fianco della committenza pubblica, che grazie ai concorsi realizza spesso costruzioni di qualità, il settore privato intervenisse maggiormente con una committenza più cosmopolita e di più

discerned will continue to encourage new architecture. This is most probably the only way that it is possible to prevent mountain regions from degenerating into a kind of Alpine Disneyland.

ampi orizzonti. Pertanto molti di questi committenti dovrebbero superare il loro atteggiamento conservativo più propenso ad un'architettura tradizionalista. D'altra parte è lecito sperare che gli edifici che già oggi sono indicati come modelli esemplari, possano promuovere la sensibilità per la buona (e turisticamente attrattiva) nuova architettura. Solo in questo modo si può impedire che le regioni montane diventino una Disneyland alpina.

[1] Eine gültige Einführung in das Südtiroler Architekturgeschehen und dessen historische und soziale Aspekte gibt: Architektur Südtirol. 1900 bis heute. Hrsg. Architektenkammer der Autonomen Provinz Bozen-Südtirol. Edition Raetia, Bozen 1993.

[2] Mayr Fingerle, Christoph. Öffentliches Bauen in Südtirol. Hrsg. Autonome Provinz Bozen-Südtirol, Bozen 1993, S. 6.

[3] Architektur in Südtirol. A. a. O., S. 190, Nr. 152.

[4] Eine kritische Würdigung der aktuellen Südtiroler Architekturszene gibt Walter Angoneses Aufsatz „Südtirol. Ein Hauch von Optimismus", erschienen in: Architektur Aktuell, Nr. 12/2004, S. 78–91.

[5] 3. Südtiroler Architekturpreis. In: turrisbabel. Trimestrales Mitteilungsblatt der Stiftung der Architektenkammer der Autonomen Provinz Bozen-Südtirol, Nr. 65, 12/2004, S. 2–4 und 14–21.

[1] Una valida introduzione agli aspetti storico-sociali dello scenario dell'Architettura in Alto Adige è contenuta in: Architettura in Alto Adige dal 1900 ad oggi. A cura dell'Ordine degli Architetti della Provincia Autonoma di Bolzano. Editore Raetia, Bolzano 1993.

[2] Mayr Fingerle, Christoph. Edifici pubblici in Alto Adige. A cura della Provincia Autonoma dell'Alto Adige, Bolzano 1993, Pag.6.

[3] Architettura in Alto Adige. A. a. O., Pag. 190, N. 152.

[4] Un apprezzamento critico dell'attuale scenario architettonico altoatesino è espresso nell'articolo „Südtirol. Ein Hauch von Optimismus" apparso in: Architektur Aktuell, N. 12/2004, pagg.78–91.

[5] 3. Premio di Architettura in Alto Adige. In: turrisbabel. Bollettino trimestrale della Fondazione dell'Ordine degli Architetti della Provincia Autonoma di Bolzano – Alto Adige, N. 65, 12/2004, pagg. 2–4 e 14–21.

[1] A good introduction to architecture in South Tyrol and its historical and social aspects can be found in: Architektur in Südtirol. 1900 bis heute. ed. Architektenkammer der Autonomen Provinz Bozen-Südtirol. Edition Raetia, Bolzano 1993.

[2] Mayr Fingerle, Christoph. Öffentliches Bauen in Südtirol. ed. Autonome Provinz Bozen-Südtirol, Bolzano 1993, p. 6.

[3] Architektur in Südtirol. See note 1, p. 190, no. 152.

[4] Walter Angonese's essay „Südtirol. Ein Hauch von Optimismus" (South Tyrol. A Hint of Optimism) offers a critical appreciation of the current South Tyrol architecture scene. It appeared in: architektur.aktuell, no. 12/2004, pp. 78–91.

[5] Third South Tyrol Architecture Prize. In: turrisbabel. Trimestrales Mitteilungsblatt der Stiftung der Architektenkammer der Autonomen Provinz Bozen-Südtirol, no. 65, 12/2004, pp. 2–4 und 14–21.

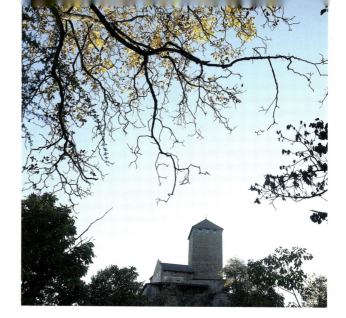

Walter Zschokke
Kritischer Blick auf die Bewahrung und Aktualisierung von alter Bausubstanz

Südtirol verfügt über eine dichte Kulturlandschaft mit zahlreichen baulichen Zeugnissen aus nahezu jeder Epoche der Geschichte seit der Römerzeit. Lange Zeit wurde mit diesem Erbe – nicht nur in Südtirol – auf unterschiedliche Arten umgegangen. Mal wurde gehegt und gepflegt, mal überformt, nicht selten abgebrochen und neu gebaut. Neben architektonischen Qualitäten, die zu allen Zeiten – allerdings nicht zwingend – die Argumente zur Bewahrung lieferten, war es in vielen Fällen trockenes ökonomisches Kalkül, dass einzelne Gebäudeteile oder der Rohbaukern eines Bauwerks weiterverwendet wurden, im aktualisierten Bau aufgingen und uns so überliefert wurden. Denn der wechselnde Zeitgeschmack hätte mit vielem, das uns heute lieb und teuer ist, ohne viel Aufhebens aufgeräumt. Im 19. Jahrhundert nahmen die Verluste von historischer Bausubstanz als Folge der beschleunigten industriell-technischen Entwicklung europaweit dramatisch zu, was wiederum zu Bestrebungen führte, alte Bauwerke unter Schutz zu stellen, zu pflegen und nicht selten mehr oder weniger phantasievoll zu restaurieren. Die anerkannten historisch-kulturellen Werte wurden ebenso zur Selbstdarstellung genutzt wie historisierende Neubauten, und für den aufkommenden Tourismus kamen zuerst

Uno sguardo critico sulla conservazione e sull'adattamento agli usi contemporanei degli edifici storici

L'Alto Adige possiede un denso territorio antropizzato ricco di testimonianze architettoniche di quasi tutte le epoche, a partire da quella romana. Per lungo tempo, non solo in Alto Adige, ci si è confrontati con questo patrimonio secondo approcci diversi: a volte si è salvaguardato e tutelato, altre volte si è intervenuti con costruzioni sull'esistente e spesso si è demolito ed edificato ex novo. Insieme alla qualità architettonica dell'edificio che è sempre stata un motivo - anche se non vincolante - per la conservazione, è stato in molti casi il freddo calcolo economico a far sì che singole parti d'edifici, o la loro nuda struttura interna, fossero riutilizzate, integrandosi nella costruzione adattata agli usi contemporanei e che ci fossero infine tramandate così come oggi le troviamo. Fosse per i gusti mutevoli di ogni epoca, la maggior parte di quanto oggi stimiamo degno di valore culturale ed affettivo sarebbe stato demolito senza tante discussioni.
In seguito al rapido sviluppo tecnico-industriale del 19. secolo, le perdite al patrimonio storico costruito aumentarono drammaticamente in tutta Europa. Ciò comportò una crescita dell'impegno per la tutela e la salvagurdia dei vecchi edifici, che frequentemente venivano restaurati in modo più o meno fantasioso.

A critical view of the preservation and modernisation of existing building fabric

South Tyrol has a rich cultural landscape with numerous buildings offering testimony of almost every epoch in its history since Roman times. Over the years legacies of this kind have been dealt with in a number of different ways – not only in South Tyrol. At certain times they have been cared for and cultivated, at others transformed, and, not infrequently, demolished and rebuilt. In addition to the architectural qualities that have always provided arguments (albeit not decisive ones) for preservation, in many cases it was simply dry economic considerations that led to the decision to continue using individual parts or the core of a building, or to incorporate them in a modernised building and thus hand them down to us in this form. Had it been regarded necessary the different taste prevailing in earlier eras would have, without much reflection, led to the demolition of much of what we so highly admire today. One consequence of the accelerated pace of industrial and technological development in the 19th century was that throughout Europe the loss of historic building substance increased dramatically. This in turn led to efforts to protect old buildings and, not infrequently, to attempts to restore them, often inspired by fantasy, that was employed to a greater or lesser degree. Recognised historic and

die einen, und – nach einigen Jahrzehnten Wartefrist sowie ihrer Historisierung – auch die anderen als Objekte der Anschauung infrage. Vor ihnen geruhte man in bildungsbürgerlicher Ergriffenheit niederzusinken.

Die neu gewonnene Rolle der Denkmäler als touristische Anziehungspunkte öffnete einen weiteren ökonomischen Aspekt, der vorerst ihre Erhaltung sichern mochte – sich aber durchaus auch zu einer Bedrohung auswachsen konnte, was heute für manche Bauwerke immer mehr zum Problem wird. Denn eine zu intensive touristische Nutzung zerstört sukzessive das, dessentwegen die Gäste anreisen. Im Gegensatz dazu erleichtert eine geringer werdende historische Bildung den Verzicht auf originale Substanz und historisch kritische Erneuerung. Dennoch bleibt – wie sich an der Diskussion um das „Weltkulturerbe" zeigt – in breiten Bevölkerungskreisen das Bestreben aufrecht, das gewohnte Erscheinungsbild einer Stadt oder Landschaft zu wahren und einschneidende Veränderungen zu verhindern. Die schleichenden kleinen Veränderungen, die ein ganzes Ensemble unerwartet zum Kippen bringen können, werden jedoch oft übersehen. Daher rührt das Bestreben der Denkmalpfleger, den Umgang mit wertvoller alter Bausubstanz zu regeln, Listen und Dokumentationen zu erstellen und die Störung durch Neubauten oder Neubauteile so gering wie möglich zu halten.

Immer wiederkehrende Probleme und der Wunsch nach „Berechenbarkeit" denkmalschützerischer Absichten, der von Eigentümern, Betreibern und Nutzern vorgetragen wird, lassen die Aufstellung allgemein gültiger und fester Regeln sinnvoll scheinen. Dem ist jedoch entgegenzuhalten, dass ein genereller Ansatz nur in einem ersten Schritt der Annäherung dienlich ist. Denn bei genauerem Hinsehen wird nahezu jede denkmalpflegerische Aufgabe zum Einzelfall.

Mögliche Antworten, wie mit dem Alten umzugehen sei, ergeben sich zudem auch aus dem Wesen des zu planenden Neuen; es können sich daher die Schwerpunkte im Verlauf der Projektarbeit verschieben. Der ursprüngliche Ansatz verändert sich und wirkt sich auf die Bewertung des Vorhandenen aus, was wiederum Konsequenzen für die Überlegungen bezüglich des Entwurfs und für das abschließende Resultat hat.

Per promuovere la propria immagine pubblica, da una parte si riconosceva il valore del patrimonio storico-culturale, dall'altra si utilizzavano anche le nuove costruzioni storicizzanti, e per attirare il turismo nascente si faceva riferimento al primo e solo dopo alcuni decenni di attesa, quando avevano acquisito valore storico anche le altre costruzioni. Al loro cospetto ci si compiaceva di sprofondare in un sentimentalismo di stampo borghese.

Il nuovo ruolo che i monumenti acquisiscono come attrazione turistica svela una valenza economica, che se in prima istanza intende garantirne la conservazione, può poi evolvere in una minaccia, aspetto che oggi risulta sempre più problematico per alcune opere.

Infatti, con il tempo, l'intenso sfruttamento turistico distrugge proprio le opere che lo hanno promosso. All'opposto, con il crescente impoverimento dell'educazione storica, risulta più facile rinunciare alla sostanza costruttiva originaria e ad interventi di rinnovo impostati su un metodo storicocritico. Eppure tra ampi strati di popolazione, come dimostra il dibattito intorno al "patrimonio culturale mondiale", rimane la preoccupazione sincera di conservare l'immagine abituale di una città o del paesaggio e di evitare mutamenti incisivi. Nonostante tutto, spesso vengono ignorate tutte quelle piccole, striscianti alterazioni che possono rovinare inaspettatamente un intero insieme di valore storico e paesaggistico.

Per questo colpisce la volontà dei conservatori di voler regolare il modo di rapportarsi con la sostanza storica di pregio, di voler redigere liste e documenti, e di voler limitare il più possibile le incongruenze provocate dalle nuove costruzioni o anche solo da nuove parti costruttive.

Il riproporsi continuo di determinate problematiche, il desiderio di rendere "quantificabili" gli interventi di conservazione, espressi dai proprietari, dai gestori e dagli utenti, sembrano dare senso alla definizione di regole fisse e valide per tutte le situazioni. Occorre però tenere conto che un approccio generale è utile solo per un primo approccio, perché, ad un'osservazione più attenta, ogni intervento di restauro dei monumenti è un caso a sè stante.

cultural values were used for the purpose of self-representation, in much the same way as historicist new buildings. For the developing tourist industry the old buildings became suitable objects of admiration and later, after a waiting period of several decades during which they too became part of history, the second group of historicist renovations also achieved this status. In a display of deep emotion the educated bourgeoisie genuflected in respect before such buildings.

Monuments' newly acquired role as tourist attractions has opened up a further economic aspect that, while initially making it possible to preserve them, can easily develop into a threat and could become an increasing problem for many historic buildings today. For excessive tourist use gradually and inexorably destroys what tourists travel to see. In contrast, the decline in the general level of education in history makes it easier to discard original substance and historically critical renewal. Nevertheless, as the discussion on world cultural heritage shows, in broad sectors of the population preserving the familiar appearance of a city or a landscape and preventing disruptive changes still remains an important goal. In contrast the gradual, smaller changes that can suddenly transform an entire ensemble are often overlooked. Therefore the efforts of the conservationists are based on regulating the way in which valuable old building fabric is dealt with, compiling lists and documentation and keeping the damage or disruption caused by new buildings or building elements to a minimum.

Reoccurring problems and a desire for "predictable" recommendations from conservationists that is regularly expressed by property owners, operators and users may make it seem sensible to draw up universally valid and fixed rules. However, it can be safely said that a common starting point is useful only for the first step in approaching a building, on looking closer almost every conservation job in fact turns out to be a special case.

Possible solutions to the question of how to deal with the old substance arise from the nature of the new project to be planned; therefore the focus can shift considerably in the course of working on the project. The

Diese dynamische Interpretation ist einerseits richtig, andererseits birgt sie auch die Gefahr, dass gewiefte Planer und Investoren mit einem taktisch angelegten Projekt oder – indem sie einen so genannten Stararchitekten vorschieben – versuchen, Schutzbestimmungen oder Teile davon zu umgehen. Das wissen die Fachleute in den Denkmalämtern und argumentieren zu Beginn entsprechend vorsichtig.

Um sich über prinzipielle denkmalpflegerische Haltungen und Erkenntnisse zu verständigen, formulierten und beschlossen sie am „II. Internationalen Kongress der Architekten und Techniker der Denkmalpflege" (Venedig, 1964) ein Dokument, das in 16 Artikeln die Grundlagen denkmalpflegerischen Arbeitens festlegt. Als „Charta von Venedig"[1] gilt es bis heute als Richtlinie für den Umgang mit historischen Bauwerken.

Wegen schlechter Erfahrungen mit im Übereifer gemachten Restaurierungen wurden „originalgetreue" Rekonstruktionen daher besonders für die Bereiche der Hypothese ausgeschlossen, siehe Artikel 9: „Wenn es aus ästhetischen und technischen Gründen notwendig ist, etwas wiederherzustellen, von dem man nicht weiß, wie es ausgesehen hat, wird sich das ergänzende Werk von der bestehenden Komposition abheben und den Stempel unserer Zeit tragen."[2] Das Wort „Stempel" erscheint allerdings etwas hart. In einer anderen Übersetzung findet sich dafür der moderatere Begriff „Charakter". Unabhängig von diesem kleinen Unterschied dürfte dennoch hierin eine Grundlage für die Theorie vom notwendigen gestalterischen Gegensatz liegen, die Architekten im Umgang mit bestehender Bausubstanz gern vorbringen und anwenden: Sie berufen sich dabei – wohl aus einem Missverständnis heraus – auf den Artikel 9, um bedenkenlos ihren persönlichen oder einen gerade modischen Stil zu exekutieren. Es ist zwar schon über 20 Jahre her, aber ich erinnere mich an die Antwort eines heute nicht ganz unbekannten Architekten auf meine zurückhaltend vorgebrachte städtebauliche Kritik an seinem autistischen Projekt: „Das mit dem Bauen im Kontext ist heute vorbei!" Möglicherweise sieht er es heute anders, trotzdem steht die Aussage für eine Position, die sich um bestehende

Le risposte possibili a come si debba affrontare un edificio storico dipendono anche dalla tipologia del nuovo intervento che si deve progettare, e pertanto i princìpi d'intervento stabiliti all'inizio del progetto possono modificarsi nel corso dello stesso. L'approccio iniziale muta e ha effetto sulla valutazione dell'esistente, ripercuotendosi in modo nuovo sulle definizioni del progetto e sul risultato finale. Questa interpretazione dinamica dell'approccio alla materia storica, se da una parte è corretta, dall'altra nasconde il pericolo che scaltri progettisti o imprenditori cerchino di aggirare le normative di tutela o una parte di esse con progetti ad hoc o promuovendo l'intervento di architetti di fama. I tecnici delle soprintendenze conoscono questi stratagemmi e pertanto, almeno inizialmente, argomentano con circospezione. Per rendere comprensibili le conoscenze e i princìpi basilari della conservazione nel 1964, a Venezia durante il "II Congresso Internazionale di Architettura e Tecnica della Conservazione"[1], essi hanno formulato e definito un documento, che enuncia in 16 articoli i princìpi della conservazione. Con la denominazione di "Carta di Venezia" esso è ancora valido come direttiva per intervenire sulle opere storiche.

In seguito ad esperienze negative con interventi di restauro portati all'estremo, le ricostruzioni "aderenti all'originale" sono state bandite, soprattutto laddove la ricostruzione si fonda su basi ipotetiche. Secondo l'articolo 9: "Se si dovesse rendere necessaria per motivi estetici e tecnici la ricostruzione di parti, di cui non si conosce l'immagine originale, allora l'integrazione dovrà discostarsi dalla composizione esistente e riconoscersi perché porta il marchio del nostro tempo".[2] Il termine "marchio" sembra piuttosto duro; in un'altra traduzione (dall'italiano al tedesco) si è utilizzato un vocabolo più moderato "carattere". Indipendentemente da questa piccola differenza, il testo contiene il fondamento teorico, che prevede il necessario contrasto tra vecchio e nuovo, e che gli architetti riprendono ed utilizzano volentieri quando si confrontano con la materia storica. Gli architetti fanno riferimento all'articolo 9, sebbene secondo un'interpretazione scorretta, per adottare, senza tante riflessioni,

original starting point changes and this has an effect on the evaluation of the existing building, which in turn has consequences for the design and the final result.

While this dynamic kind of interpretation is a correct one, it does involve the danger that smart planners and developers may attempt to use a tactically conceived project (perhaps headed by a so-called star architect) to find a way around the preservation legislation or at least a part of it. The experts in the conservation authorities are aware of this fact and in the early phase their line of argument is accordingly cautious. To provide a basis for discussion about the principles of conservation and to increase the awareness of the subject, at the Second International Congress of Architects and Technicians in Monument Conservation[1] (Venice, 1964) they formulated and passed a document that lays down in 16 articles a basis for conservation work. Known as the "Charter of Venice" this document is regarded up to the present day as the guideline for dealing with historical buildings.

Due to negative experiences with restoration work carried out with excessive zeal, restorations that recreate "the original state" were rejected, particularly where they involve hypotheses, see article 9: "It must stop at the point where conjecture begins, and in this case moreover any extra work which is indispensable must be distinct from the architectural composition and must bear a contemporary stamp.[2]" The word "stamp" may sound somewhat too harsh to modern ears, and perhaps the more moderate term "character" now seems more appropriate. But ignoring this slight difference we can possibly find here the basis for the theory of the "design contrast" that architects often like to use in dealing with existing building substance. Here, in what is surely a misunderstanding of the original text, they quote article 9 to justify carrying out something in their own style or in whatever style is currently fashionable, without any further considerations. Although it is over 20 years ago I still remember the answer to my discretely phrased urban criticism of his autonomous project that I was given by an architect who had achieved a certain measure of fame:

Bausubstanz nicht schert. Diesem Ansatz ist entgegenzuhalten, dass fast jede Bauaufgabe in einem Beziehungsgeflecht steht und diesbezüglich fast immer ein Einzelfall ist. Der Satz, dass Hinzugefügtes jedenfalls erkennbar aus unserer Zeit stammen werde, enthebt nicht einer der Planung vorausgehenden genauen Analyse, was übrigens im Artikel 9 ebenso festgehalten ist.

Am Anfang steht wohl die Frage danach, was vorliegt. Sind es amorphe und rudimentäre Reste oder ein ideomorphes Werk aus einem Guss; ist es historisch mehrschichtig und architektonisch komplex; ist es künstlerisch hochwertig, vielleicht auch fremdartig, oder traditional und von bestechender Einfachheit; oder aber ist es zwar historisch bedeutend, aber architektonisch banal?

Die Frage der Größenordnung, das proportionale Verhältnis des Neuen zum Alten wird sich aus der Aufgabenstellung ergeben: Ist es bloß eine kleine Anfügung, handelt es sich um eine ungefähre Verdoppelung des Volumens oder steht einem winzigen Altbau ein riesiges Neubauvolumen gegenüber?

Als Nächstes wird sich die Frage nach der grundsätzlichen Haltung stellen: Soll sich das Neue unterordnen, einordnen, selbstbewusst auftreten, ja gar dominant wirken oder womöglich arrogant darüber hinaus schießen? Dies ist inhaltlich zu klären und darf nicht der subjektiven Befindlichkeit des Architekten – oder der Architektin – überlassen werden, denn je nach Problemstellung und späterer Nutzung wird sich die eine oder andere Haltung als richtig erweisen.

Im Zuge der Bearbeitung kann es sich erweisen, dass nicht auf jeder Interventionsebene gleich stark vorgegangen werden sollte. Es gibt die Ebene der Baukörper, die Strukturebene, jene der Formen und Stilmerkmale, die Detailebene, die Materialien und Farben. Hier geht es darum, Abstände festzulegen sowie Nähe und Distanz zwischen Alt und Neu abzuwägen. Eine ungeschickte Annäherung, ein falscher Abstand können jede architektonische Spannung lähmen. Ein grobes Angleichen oder peinliches Amalgamieren hingegen führt meist zu unkontrollierten Interferenzen, etwa bei Farben, bei Materialien, aber auch bei der Detailgestaltung.

Das numerische Alter allein sagt noch nichts aus, kommt es doch darauf an, welcher Epoche ein Gebäude zuzurechnen ist:

un loro stile personale oppure uno di moda in quel momento. Sono passati venti anni ma ricordo ancora la risposta di un architetto, che oggi possiede una certa fama, quando avanzai una modesta critica di natura urbanistica al suo progetto artistico: "Oggigiorno progettare nel rispetto del contesto è un approccio superato".

Probabilmente egli oggi si esprimerebbe diversamente, ma la sua dichiarazione corrisponde ad una posizione che dimostra poco interesse per la materia edilizia esistente.

A questo approccio si deve contrapporre quello per cui quasi ogni intervento edilizio consta di un complesso intreccio di relazioni, e pertanto è quasi sempre da trattare come un singolo caso. La frase secondo la quale ogni aggiunta alla struttura esistente debba essere riconoscibile e pertanto ricondotto al nostro tempo, non esime da una precisa analisi che parta dalla progettazione, cosa che peraltro è definita anche nell'articolo 19.

Dapprincipio ci si pone sempre la domanda su cosa esiste a priori. Si tratta di resti amorfi e rudimentali, o di un'opera ideomorfa fatta in un sol getto? Si tratta di una stratificazione storica e di un'architettura complessa, possiede un alto valore artistico, forse anche non comune, oppure di stampo tradizionale e di affascinante semplicità, oppure è sì di rilevanza storica, ma architettonicamente banale? La domanda riguardo all'ordine di grandezza, al rapporto di proporzione tra vecchio e nuovo si definisce in base all'obbiettivo progettuale. Si tratta di una piccola costruzione annessa, o del raddoppio della volumetria, oppure si contrappone ad un piccolissimo edificio storico un gigante moderno? Quindi ci si deve porre la questione di fondo sull'atteggiamento da tenere. La nuova edificazione deve soggiacere, integrarsi, apparire consapevole, possedere un effetto dominante, o dove possibile emergere arrogantemente? Si devono definire i contenuti di questo atteggiamento e non si può lasciarlo alla percezione soggettiva dell'architetto, perché in funzione del compito progettuale posto e dell'utilizzazione seguente si dimostrerà valida l'una piuttosto che l'altra posizione.

Durante la lavorazione ci si può rendere conto che non si deve intervenire con la

"This idea of building in the context is over and done with". Perhaps he sees things differently today but his statement typifies a position that does not bother much with the existing building substance. Faced with such an approach one could object that almost every building commission stands in some kind of mesh of relationships and in this sense is almost always a special case! The assertion that something new added will, in any case, clearly date from our time does not remove the need for a precise analysis to be made before the planning begins, a requirement that, incidentally, is also expressed in article 9.

The first question is, surely, what are we confronted with, whether these are just amorphous and rudimentary remnants or an ideomorphous work made in one piece: is it historically and architecturally complex, is it of significant architectural value, perhaps somewhat foreign, is it traditional and strikingly simple, or is it perhaps historically important but architecturally banal?

The question of scale, the proportional relationship of the new to the old will result from an examination of the task at hand. Is it merely a small addition, does it represent a doubling of the existing volume or will a tiny old building be confronted with a gigantic new volume?

The next question is that of the fundamental approach: should the new building be modestly retiring, should it integrate itself, should it make a self-confident statement or have a dominant appearance or, should it even go further than this, possibly in an arrogant way? This aspect must be clarified in terms of content and should not be left up to the subjective sensitivity of the architect. According to the problem and the subsequent use of the building one approach or another will turn out to be the correct one.

In course of the work it may turn out that not all interventions should be made on the same level. There is the level of the building volume, the structural level, the levels of form and stylistic characteristics, the detail level and the levels of material and colours. The issue is here to determine both the distance and the proximity that should exist between new and old. An un-

Bauwerke aus der einen Phase halten oft mehr aus als Bauten aus einer anderen. Eine mittelalterliche Bruchsteinmauer ist etwas anderes als ein exakter Steinschnitt, ein Barockbau nicht zu vergleichen mit einem neobarocken aus der Zeit des Historismus, und nicht zuletzt sind Bauten der Moderne des 20. Jahrhunderts extrem empfindlich gegenüber gut gemeinten, aber schlecht gemachten Interventionen.

Ebenso unsinnig ist es, die ideologischen Kämpfe der Urgroßväter auf dem Rücken von Bauwerken nachzuspielen. Es ist beispielsweise keine besondere Heldentat, als nachgeborener Architekt, ein halbes Jahrhundert danach, einem Bauwerk, das in der Zeit des Faschismus entstanden ist, pathetisch eins auszuwischen. Etwas anderes ist sicher die inhaltliche Auseinandersetzung mit verdrängten Fakten, eine bildhafte Umsetzung wird jedoch nur im Ausnahmefall auch Jahrzehnte später noch verstanden.

Diese recht allgemeine Auffächerung zeigt, wie rasch sich bei genauerem Hinsehen eine Aufgabe zum Einzelfall entwickelt, sodass man sich als Architekt eine breite Palette möglicher Maßnahmen offen halten muss. Man kann nicht einfach Glas, Stahl, Beton oder beliebige andere Materialien verwenden, einfach weil sie den Stempel unserer Zeit tragen.

Wenn man nun die oben dargelegten Kriterien auf ein kürzlich erneuertes, nicht ganz unwesentliches Baudenkmal wie das Schloss Tirol anwendet, wird man zunächst feststellen, dass die ehemalige Ruine schon im 19. Jahrhundert romantisierend

stessa misura ad ogni livello. Esiste il livello dell'edificio, quello della struttura, quelli delle forme e dei caratteri stilistici, quello del dettaglio, i materiali ed i colori. In questo caso si tratta di stabilire le distanze, così come di valutare la vicinanza e la lontananza tra vecchio e nuovo. Un avvicinamento maldestro, una distanza sbagliata possono rovinare qualsiasi emozione architettonica. Un intervento che proponga una grezza similitudine, o una penosa combinazione, porta ad interferenze incontrollate riguardo all'uso dei colori, dei materiali ma anche nella definizione dei dettagli. La definizione cronologica non comunica informazioni sufficienti, tutto dipende invece dall'epoca a cui riferire un edificio: costruzioni appartenenti ad un'epoca sopportano di più di quelle di un'altra. Un muro di sassi a spacco di epoca medievale è diverso da quello realizzato con pietre tagliate con precisione, un edificio barocco non è confrontabile con un edificio neobarocco dell'epoca dello storicismo, e non da ultimo gli edifici del Ventesimo secolo del movimento Moderno sono estremamente sensibili ad interventi ben pensati ma male eseguiti.

Allo stesso modo non ha senso riproporre negli edifici le battaglie ideologiche dei bisnonni. Per esempio non è un particolare atto di coraggio, da parte di un architetto della nuova generazione, criticare pateticamente mezzo secolo più tardi un edificio sorto durante il fascismo. Tutt'altra cosa è il confrontarsi con i fatti storici rimossi: solo in casi eccezionali una realizzazione esemplare è compresa anche decenni dopo.

suitable approach, the wrong distance can paralyse any form of architectural excitement. On the other hand crude imitation or embarrassing amalgamation generally leads to uncontrolled interference, for example in the area of colour and materials but also in the area of detailing.

The age in years alone does not tell us much, far more important is what epoch the building belongs to: buildings from one phase can often tolerate far more than buildings from another. A mediaeval rubble stone wall is very different to precisely cut stone, a Baroque building is not comparable with a baroque edifice from the historicist period, and 20th century modernist buildings are particularly sensitive to well meaning but poorly executed interventions. It is equally senseless to wage the ideological battles of our forefathers over old buildings. For example: for an architect born in more recent times it should not be regarded as particularly heroic to strike, half a century later, a destructive blow against a building that was erected in the Fascist era. The investigation of hidden or obscured facts is something very different, but it is only very rarely that a visual interpretation remains comprehensible decades later.

This very general review shows how quickly, once we examine it more closely, a conservation task becomes a specific and highly individual case. This means that as an architect one must keep a wide range of options open. One cannot use glass, steel concrete or whatever other materials one wants simply because they bear the stamp

überhöht wurde, indem man den Turm um einige Geschosse aufstockte. Neben der beherrschenden Lage, der historischen Bedeutung und einer komplexen Baugeschichte ist es vor allem das Material, der roh gemauerte Naturstein, der den Charakter der mittelalterlichen Burganlage prägt. Mit dem Einbau der Stahlstruktur für das Museum wurde dem verwitterten Naturmaterial mit rostenden Stahlblechen ein ebenso ausdrucksstarkes, von Menschen gemachtes Material zur Seite gestellt. Die Reduktion auf zwei Hauptmaterialien und deren je individuell verwitterter Charakter erzeugen eine strukturelle Verwandtschaft, die Alt und Neu gut ausbalanciert. Unterstützt wird dies dadurch, dass die Anteile der beiden Materialien als etwa gleich groß wahrgenommen werden. Das rührt daher, dass mit den rostenden Einbauten auf einer sehr primären Ebene äußerst kontextuell auf die vorhandenen Natursteinmauern eingegangen wurde: Das Alte wurde in seiner Einfachheit und Rohheit nicht von gestylten und polierten Oberflächen konkurrenziert, sondern auf einer strukturellen Ebene, aber mit einem anderen Material weitergebaut. Diese Klarheit macht von nahe besehen die besondere Stärke des erneuerten Bauwerks aus. Zwar wird rostendes Stahlblech heute oft und gerne verwendet, ist also ein gestalterisches Element unserer Zeit, aber nicht immer ist der Einsatz dieses Materials in mehrfacher Hinsicht so angemessen und sinnlich wirksam wie bei der Erneuerung von Schloss Tirol. Womit wir wieder beim – hier gut gelösten – Einzelfall wären.

Questa classificazione generica dimostra come l'approccio al compito del progetto diventi rapidamente, dopo una valutazione più attenta, quello del caso singolo, per cui l'architetto deve lasciarsi aperta tutta una serie di possibili soluzioni. Non si possono utilizzare semplicemente solo vetro, metallo, calcestruzzo o altri materiali a scelta, perché portano il marchio del nostro tempo.
Se si applicano i criteri sopra esposti a Castel Tirolo, un monumento di non indifferente valore e da poco ristrutturato, si riconoscerà innanzitutto che già nel 19. secolo il preesistente rudere era stato interpretato in senso romantico, rialzando la torre di alcuni piani. Insieme alla posizione dominante, al significato storico e ad una complessa vicenda costruttiva, è soprattutto il materiale, la pietra grezza con cui si sono realizzate le murature a dare carattere all'impianto fortificato medievale. Inserendo la struttura metallica destinata al museo, con le lamiere arrugginite, si è abbinato al materiale segnato dagli agenti atmosferici un elemento che esprime altrettanto chiaramente i segni del lavoro dell'uomo. La riduzione a due materiali principali ed il loro carattere individuale consumato dagli agenti atmosferici, creano una affinità strutturale che bilancia bene il vecchio con il nuovo. L'effetto è rafforzato dalla percezione che i due materiali sono presenti in eguale proporzione. Ciò dipende dal fatto che gli inserti in metallo arrugginito si confrontano su un piano primario ed elementare con la struttura muraria esistente: la vecchia materia con la sua semplicità e rudezza non è confrontata con superfici lavorate e lucidate, ma su un piano strutturale e materico, però si è proceduto a costruire con un materiale differente. Questa chiara distinzione è quella che, vista da vicino, realizza il carattere particolare dell'opera ristrutturata. Il metallo arrugginito oggi viene sì impiegato frequentemente, e pertanto è percepito come un elemento compositivo del nostro tempo, ma non sempre il suo impiego è sotto molti punti di vista così coerente ed percettivamente efficace come nella ristrutturazione di Castel Tirolo. Con questo esempio siamo tornati al caso singolo, che qui è stato appropriatamente risolto.

of our times.
If we apply the criteria presented here to a recently renovated and not unimportant building monument such as Schloss Tirol the first thing we note is that the former ruin was expanded in the 19th century in a romantic fashion by adding several storeys to the tower. In addition to its dominant position, historical significance and complex building history it is above all the material used, the roughly laid rubble stone that determines the character of the mediaeval castle complex. Through the insertion of a steel structure for the museum the weathered natural material has now been joined by rusted sheet steel, a man-made material that has a similar expressive strength. The reduction to two main materials, each with its own weathered character, creates a structural relationship that balances old and new. This is supported by the fact we perceive the amount of both materials used to be approximately the same. This is due to the fact that the rusting insertions represent an extremely contextual response to the existing rubble walls that is made on a very primary level. The old substance with its simplicity and roughness is not exposed to competition from styled and polished surfaces but is simply continued on another structural level, albeit using a different material. Seen close up this clarity is what constitutes the particular strength of the renovated building. Although rusted steel is today widely employed, and is therefore a design element of our time, this material is not always used in such an appropriate and sensuously effective way as in the renovation of Schloss Tirol: which leads us back again to the principle of treating each project as an individual case that demands an appropriately individual solution.

¹ Das 1964 verabschiedete Dokument bildet die einzige verbindliche Grundlage für den Umgang mit historischer Bausubstanz auf internationaler Ebene und ist auch in der Einzelaussage noch aktuell, Download: www.bda.at/download/charta-von-venedig/Charta_von_Venedig_dt.doc

² Charta von Venedig, Art. 9: Der Restaurierung kommt immer der Charakter einer ausnahmsweisen Maßnahme zu. Ihr Ziel ist es, die ästhetischen und historischen Werte zu erhalten und aufzudecken. Sie gründet sich auf die Respektierung des alten Originalbestands und auf authentische Urkunden. Sie findet dort ihre Grenze, wo die Hypothese beginnt: Dort, wo es sich um hypothetische Rekonstruktionen handelt, wird jedes Ergänzungswerk, das aus ästhetischen oder technischen Gründen unumgänglich notwendig wurde, zu den architektonischen Kompositionen zu zählen sein und den Charakter unserer Zeit aufzuweisen haben. Vor Inangriffnahme und während der Restaurierung werden stets kunstwissenschaftliche und historische Untersuchungen anzustellen sein.

¹ Il documento sancito nel 1964 definisce l'unica base vincolante a livello internazionale per il rapporto con la materia storica ed è tuttora attuale. Download: www.bda.at/download/charta/venedig/Carta_di_Venezia-ital.doc

² Carta di Venezia, art. 9: Il restauro è un processo che deve mantenere un carattere eccezionale. Il suo scopo è di conservare e di rivelare i valori formali e storici del monumento e si fonda sul rispetto della sostanza antica e delle documentazioni autentiche. Il restauro deve fermarsi dove ha inizio l'ipotesi: sul piano della ricostruzione congetturale qualsiasi lavoro di completamento, riconosciuto indispensabile per ragioni estetiche e tecniche, deve distinguersi dalla progettazione architettonica e dovrà recare il segno della nostra epoca. Il restauro sarà sempre preceduto e accompagnato da uno studio storico e archeologico del monumento.

¹ This document produced in 1964 provides the only binding basis on an international level for dealing with historical building fabric, and the individual statements contained in it are still relevant, Download: www.icomos.org/docs/venice_charter.html.

² Charter of Venice, Article 9: The process of restoration is a highly specialized operation. Its aim is to preserve and reveal the aesthetic and historic value of the monument and is based on respect for original material and authentic documents. It must stop at the point where conjecture begins, and in this case moreover any extra work which is indispensable must be distinct from the architectural composition and must bear a contemporary stamp. The restoration in any case must be preceded and followed by an archaeological and historical study of the monument.

Vinschgau   Val Venosta

Kirchturm in Graun, Reschenstausee
Campanile della Chiesa a Curon, Lago Resia, bacino artifciale
The church tower in Curon, Resia reservoir

Arnold Gapp
Messner Mountain Museum „Ortles", Sulden
2004

Der Lebenstraum von Bergsteiger Reinhold Messner, seine Privatsammlung in mehreren Themenmuseen zu präsentieren, geht Schritt für Schritt in Erfüllung. Von insgesamt fünf der Messner Mountain Museen sind drei bereits realisiert (Schloss Juval bei Meran, Monte Rite bei Cortina und das Museum „Ortles" in Sulden), das vierte wird 2006 eröffnet (Schloss Sigmundskron bei Bozen). Das Ausstellungszentrum in Sulden ist dem bedeutendsten Gletscher Südtirols, dem Ortler, gewidmet und bezieht sich auf das Thema Eis. Teil der Bauaufgabe war es, den in der Nähe liegenden Ortler genauso im Museum „auszustellen" wie Kunstwerke von Rang, z. B. Bilder von E. T. Compton.

Den Ausgangspunkt für den Entwurf des Museums bildete ein bestehendes Gebäude im Besitz Messners, dessen Keller schon seit langem umgebaut werden sollte. So wurde das gesamte Museum unterirdisch angelegt, um dieses ungenützte Untergeschoß in die Ausstellungsfläche mit einzubeziehen. Nur an einer Stelle ist die reale Ortlerspitze zu sehen. Eingerahmt von einem Fenster wurde sie effektvoll in die Ausstellung „gehängt".

Die Besucher überqueren eine kleine Wiese vor dem Eingang und treffen im Inneren des Museums auf eine Art Empfangsplattform. Von dort zieht sich eine Rampe durch

Arnold Gapp
Messner Mountain Museum "Ortles", Solda
2004

Il sogno di una vita dello scalatore Reinhold Messner, quella di presentare la sua collezione privata in diversi musei a tema, si sta un po' alla volta realizzando. Fino ad ora dei cinque musei previsti, ne sono stati realizzati tre (Castel Juval nei pressi di Merano, Monte Rite a Cortina, ed il Museo "Ortles" a Solda), il quarto sarà aperto nel 2006 (Castel Firmiano a Bolzano). La sede espositiva di Solda è dedicata al più importante ghiacciaio dell'Alto Adige, l'Ortles, e presenta il tema del ghiaccio. L'obbiettivo del progetto è quello di "esporre" nel museo il ghiacciaio che si erge lì vicino, ma anche opere d'arte importanti come quelle di E.T. Compton.

Spunto per la realizzazione del progetto del museo è stato un edificio esistente, già in possesso di Messner, il cui piano interrato da tempo doveva essere ristrutturato. Per integrare nell'area espositiva questo spazio sotterraneo inutilizzato, si è disposto tutto il museo al livello interrato. La cima dell'Ortles è visibile dal vero solo in un punto. Inquadrata da una finestra, essa risulta "appesa" come un quadro dell'esposizione, con notevole effetto scenico.

I visitatori attraversano un piccolo prato davanti all'ingresso e sono accolti all'interno del museo da una specie di piattaforma. Dall'ingresso una rampa conduce attraverso l'esposizione fino a terminare nella can-

Arnold Gapp
Messner Mountain Museum "Ortles", Solda
2004

Mountaineer Reinhold Messner has a life-long dream to present his private collection in several theme museums. He is gradually approaching the fulfilment of this dream step-by-step. Three of a total of five planned Messner Mountain Museums have already been completed (Schloss Juval near Merano, Monte Rite near Cortina and the Museum "Ortles" in Solda), a fourth (Castel Firiano near Bolzano) is planned to open in 2006. The exhibition centre in Solda is devoted to the most important glacier in South Tyrol, the Ortler glacier and deals with the theme of ice in general. Part of the brief was to "exhibit" the nearby Ortler in the museum, along with important art works such as paintings by E. T. Compton. An existing building owned by Messner, where it had long been planned to convert the basement, formed the starting point for the museum design. To incorporate this converted basement in the exhibition area the entire museum was laid out underground. There is only one place in the museum where the real peak of the Ortler can be seen: it has been effectively "hung" in the exhibition by framing it with a window. Visitors cross a small meadow to reach the entrance, inside the museum they meet on a kind of reception platform. From there a ramp leads through the exhibition and ends in the basement of the old building.

die Ausstellung, die im Keller des Altbaues endet. Die Präsentation erfolgt vor einem gefalteten Wandhintergrund aus Sichtbeton. Durch ein gezacktes Fensterband mit integrierter künstlicher Beleuchtung, das wie eine Gletscherspalte in die Wiese geschnitten wurde, wird von oben Licht auf die Exponate geführt.

tina del vecchio edificio. La presentazione avviene davanti ad una quinta in cemento a vista, costituita da facce diversamente orientate. Una finestra a nastro con un sistema d'illuminazione integrato taglia a zig-zag il prato come un crepaccio e consente dall'alto l'illuminazione naturale ed artificiale degli oggetti esposti.

The exhibits are presented against a folded wall made of exposed concrete. A jagged band of glazing with integrated artificial lighting, cut into the meadow like a glacier crevasse, allows light to fall on the exhibits from above.

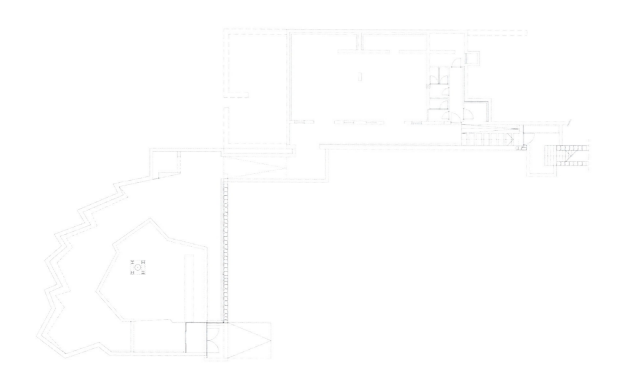

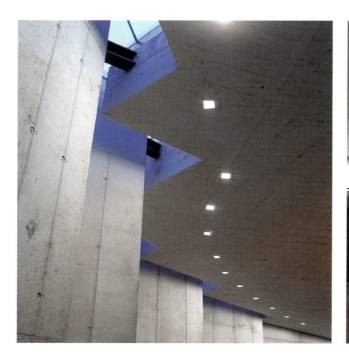

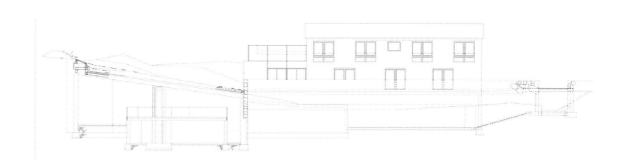

Reinhold Messner, Bauherr

„Arnold Gapp hat zur Idee ‚Das Eis am Beispiel Ortler' eine geniale und praktische Lösung gefunden. ‚Im Ende der Welt' ist ein Kristall, in dem sich Kunst und Licht vielfach brechen, ein Erlebnisraum, wo sich Kunst und Unendlichkeit zur Heimat des Eises verdichten."

Reinhold Messner, Committente

"Per il tema - Il ghiaccio e l'Ortles - Arnold Gapp ha trovato una soluzione pratica e geniale. In capo al mondo c'è un cristallo su cui si rifrangono la luce e l'arte, uno spazio dove provare sensazioni, dove l'arte e l'infinito si identificano nella patria dei ghiacci"

Reinhold Messner, client

"Arnold Gapp found a clever and practical solution for the idea of 'Das Eis am Beispiel Ortler' (Ice using the Ortler as an example). 'Im Ende der Welt' (In the end of the world) is a crystal in which art and light are fractured, an adventure space where art and infinity are condensed to create the homeland of ice."

Arnold Gapp
Kleinsportanlagen und Mehrzweckgebäude, Tschengls, Laas
2005

Arnold Gapp
Impianto sportivo e sala polifunzionale, Cengles, Lasa
2005

Arnold Gapp
Sports facilities and multi-purpose building, Cengles, Lasa
2005

Aufgrund ihrer Hanglage ist es in vielen Orten Südtirols schwierig, große ebene Plätze anzulegen, weil für ihren Bau massive Stützmauern notwendig sind. Daher entschied man in Tschengls, wo die Grundschule ein Fußballfeld benötigte, nur eine kleine Sportarena von 40 x 60 m zu realisieren. Gleichzeitig nahm man aber die Gelegenheit wahr, im Gebäude mit den Nebenräumen des Sportplatzes auch noch andere Einrichtungen unterzubringen. So kam es zu einer umfassenden Erweiterung des Bauprogramms, die ein Probelokal für die Blasmusik, einen Schießstand, eine Kegelbahn, ein Jugendzentrum und Zimmer für die medizinische Nahversorgung mit allen dazugehörigen Erschließungszonen und Nebenräumen mit einschließt. Alle diese Räumlichkeiten sollten am Rand des Fußballfeldes Platz finden.
Der Entwurf des Areals folgte der Idee, dass jede der hier zukünftig angesiedelten Einrichtungen autark sein, d. h. mit einem eigenen Eingang ins Gebäude ausgestattet sein sollte. Das führte dazu, dass in Verbindung mit der sensiblen Hanglage des Bauplatzes ein Konzept entwickelt wurde, das

In molti luoghi dell'Alto Adige, a causa delle condizioni del territorio prevalentemente in pendio, risulta difficile realizzare grandi spianate, poichè sono necessari massicci muri di sostegno.
A Cengles la scuola elementare necessitava di un campo da calcio e si era deciso di realizzare unicamente una piccola arena sportiva delle dimensioni di quaranta per sessanta metri. Al contempo si è riconosciuta l'occasione per predisporre anche altre attrezzature nei locali di servizio del campo sportivo.
Il programma di costruzione è stato ampliato di molto, comprendendo un locale di prova per gli strumenti a fiato, un poligono, un bocciodromo, un centro giovanile, locali per l'assistenza medica e tutti gli spazi di servizio e distribuzione. Tutti questi locali dovevano trovare spazio a bordo campo. Il progetto dell'areale doveva consentire a tutti gli impianti di futura attivazione, di essere gestiti in modo autonomo e di essere quindi dotati di un ingresso indipendente nell'edificio. Rispettando la delicata situazione orografica è stato elaborato un progetto composto da corpi di fabbrica di

In many areas of South Tyrol the mountainous terrain makes it difficult to lay out areas of level ground, as this requires massive retaining walls. Therefore in Cengles, where the primary school needed a soccer pitch, it was decided to build only a small sports arena measuring 40 x 60 metres. At the same time this was seen as an opportunity to accommodate other facilities in the building containing the service spaces for the sports field. Consequently, the brief was expanded to include a rehearsal room for the local brass band, a shooting gallery, a skittles alley, a youth centre and a room for local medical services plus all the necessary circulation and service spaces. Room had to be provided for all these facilities at the edge of the soccer pitch.
The design is based on the idea that each of the facilities established here should be autonomous, that is to say should have its own separate entrance. In combination with the sensitive nature of the sloping site this aim led to a concept based on a number of differently dimensioned volumes that were

aus mehreren, unterschiedlich dimensionierten Baukörpern besteht, die auf dem Niveau des Fußballfeldes teilweise in den Hang geschoben wurden. Die Architektur der Sport- und Freizeitanlage passt sich den Bedürfnissen der Dorfbewohner und der landschaftlichen Situation gut an und wurde daher von der Bevölkerung sofort bereitwillig angenommen.

differenti dimensioni, che in parte sono stati incassati nel pendio al livello del campo di calcio.
Avendo soddisfatto le esigenze degli abitanti del paese, il progetto per l'impianto sportivo e per le attività di svago è stato accettato subito e di buon grado dalla popolazione.

partly slid into the slope at the level of the football field. The architecture of this sport and leisure complex is adapted to the needs of the local villagers and excellently suited to its position in the landscape, which led to its immediate acceptance by the local population.

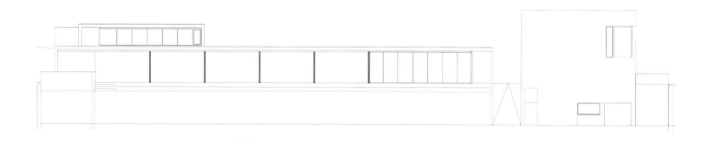

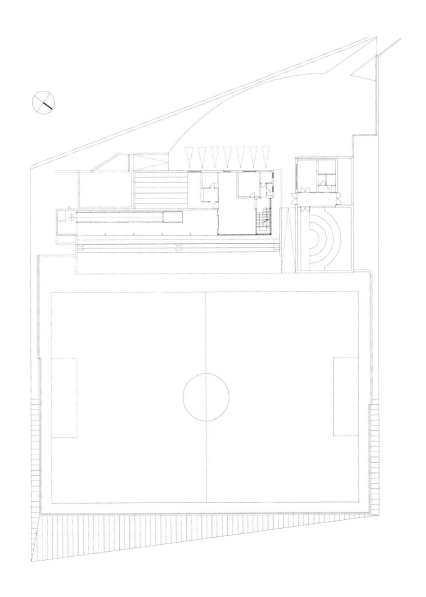

85

Architekten Marx – Ladurner

Aufstockungen von Betriebsgebäuden und Errichtung von zwei Betriebswohnungen, Schlanders
2004

In Schlanders ansässige Textilhandels- bzw. Raumausstattungs-Unternehmen ließen sich auf bestehenden Gebäuden aus den 70er Jahren zwei Betriebswohnungen errichten. Dabei erwies es sich als günstig, dass jeder der beiden Teile des Unternehmens über je einen Bauteil verfügt, denn so war es möglich, eine außen dunkel gehaltene Betriebswohnung über dem einen und eine außen hell gehaltene über dem anderen zu errichten.

Der an der rückwärtigen Seite des Unternehmens liegende Baukörper für Lager und Textilverarbeitung hat ein rein sachbezogenes Äußeres, weshalb ihm die Architekten eine Wohnung auf das Dach setzten, deren Grundriss ebenso pragmatische Züge hat. Im östlichen Teil wurden drei Schlafzimmer eingerichtet, westlich davon schließen Wohnraum, Essplatz und Küche an, eine Terrasse grenzt die Wohnung nach Westen ab.

Die zweite Betriebswohnung befindet sich am Dach des Verkaufsgebäudes und kann über dessen Innentreppe erreicht werden. Von der Straße aus ist der neue Bauteil mit seiner über die westliche Gebäudeseite hinausragenden, überdachten Terrasse nicht zuletzt deshalb gut erkennbar, weil alle Brüstungen mit hellem Markisenstoff ummantelt wurden. Kochen, Essen und

Architetti Marx – Ladurner

Sopraelevazione di edifici produttivi e realizzazione di due appartamenti di servizio, Silandro
2004

A Silandro due ditte specializzate nel commercio di tessuti e nell'arredamento d'interni hanno fatto realizzare due appartamenti di servizio sopra agli esistenti edifici degli anni Settanta.

Di rilevante importanza per il progetto la disponibilità da parte delle aziende di due parti distinte della costruzione originale. È stato così possibile realizzare due appartamenti di servizio, la cui immagine esteriore è stata poi trattata diversamente attraverso una contrapposizione tra chiaro e scuro.

Il corpo di fabbrica destinato a deposito e lavorazione dei tessuti sul retro dell'azienda, possiede un'immagine estremamente oggettiva e pertanto gli architetti vi hanno posto sul tetto un appartamento, la cui pianta ha un'impostazione altrettanto pragmatica. Nella parte ad est sono state disposte tre stanze da letto, ad ovest si aggiungono il soggiorno, lo spazio pranzo e la cucina, una terrazza delimita l'appartamento ad ovest.

Il secondo appartamento di servizio si trova sul tetto dell'edificio destinato alle vendite, ed è raggiungibile grazie ad una scala interna. Dalla strada la nuova costruzione è ben riconoscibile non solo per la terrazza coperta, che aggetta sul lato ovest dell'edificio, ma anche perché tutti i parapetti

ARCHITEKTEN Marx – Ladurner

Addition of a storey to two company buildings with the construction of two company apartments, Silandro
2004

A textile and interior furnishing company based in Silandro had two so-called "company apartments" erected on existing buildings dating from the 1970s. It turned out to be particularly opportune that each of the two sections of the company is housed in a separate building, allowing a dark apartment to be erected on one and a light-coloured flat on the other.

The building housing the storerooms and textile processing section is at the rear of the premises and has a plainly functional exterior, consequently the apartment that the architect placed on the roof has an equally pragmatic floor plan. Three bedrooms in the eastern part of the flat are adjoined to the west by the living room, dining area and kitchen; a terrace forms the western termination of this apartment.

The other company flat is on the roof of the sales building and can be accessed from an internal staircase. From the street the new element with its covered terrace projecting beyond the western edge of the building is easily recognisable, not least of all because all the railings were wrapped in a light-

Wohnen wurden auch hier zu einem Raum zusammengefasst, wobei die Küche in Form einer Nische auf die Terrasse hinausragt. Auf der östlichen Seite der Wohnebene befinden sich die Schlafzimmer.

sono stati rivestiti con tessuti per tendoni di colore chiaro. Le funzioni dell'abitare, cucinare e mangiare sono raccolte anche qui in un unico ambiente, ma la cucina sporge come una nicchia sul terrazzo. Sul lato est del piano dell'abitazione si trovano le stanze da letto.

coloured awning fabric. In this apartment cooking, eating and living are combined in a single space, the kitchen projecting into the terrace as a niche. The bedrooms are to the east of the living area.

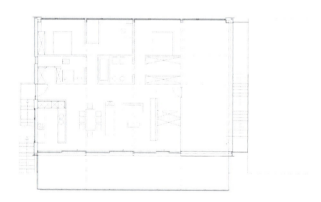

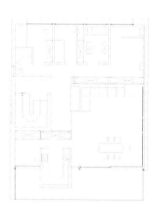

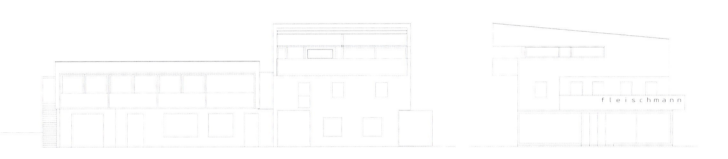

Werner Tscholl
Haus Schöpf, Vezzan, Schlanders
2004

Werner Tscholl
Casa Schöpf, Vezzano, Silandro
2004

Werner Tscholl
Schöpf House, Vezzano, Silandro
2004

Das Haus für die Besitzer einer Gärtnerei wurde an der Stelle ihres ehemaligen Wohnhauses errichtet. Es befindet sich am Rand des Betriebsgeländes in bester Aussichtslage auf die südliche Talseite des Vinschgaues. Um für seine Bewohner das vielfältige Panorama einzufangen, wurde die Architektur des Hauses auf der Basis von zwei C-förmigen, durch ein Atrium verbundenen Riegeln gelöst. Diese länglichen Baukörper wurden gespiegelt und im spitzen Winkel zueinander stehend auf einen zweigeschossigen Betonsockel gesetzt, in den auch ein Badeteich integriert wurde. In den Untergeschossen befinden sich u. a. Nebenräume der Gärtnerei. Der Baukörper des darüber liegenden Wohnhauses besteht aus massivem Holz. Die Holzbauteile wurden teilweise vorgefertigt zur Baustelle geliefert.
Der äußere Rand der „Cs" ragt an drei Seiten über die Riegel hinaus. Im westlichen befinden sich die Küche und der Wohnbereich, darüber das Elternschlafzimmer. Im östlichen Riegel wurden eine Einliegerwohnung, ein Büro, Wirtschaftsräume, eine Bibliothek und weitere Schlafzimmer untergebracht. Die Räume dieses Riegels sind auch über eine außen liegende Wendeltreppe erreichbar. Die Atmosphäre im Inneren dieses Hauses ist von einem Spiel mit verschiedenen Formen der Transparenz geprägt: Beste Aus- und Durchblicke

La casa, i cui proprietari possiedono una floricoltura, è stata costruita al posto della casa precedente. La casa con la migliore esposizione panoramica si situa al limitare del terreno dell'azienda sul versante meridionale della Val Venosta. Per carpire la vista sul panorama variegato, a favore della condizione abitativa, l'edificio è stato risolto con due elementi a "C" collegati da un atrio. I due lunghi corpi di fabbrica sono speculari e giacciono reciprocamente ad angolo acuto. Essi sono posati su di una base a due piani in cemento armato, in cui è inserito anche uno stagno balneabile. Nei piani inferiori sono collocati, tra gli altri, i locali di servizio per la giardineria. Il corpo di fabbrica della parte abitativa è realizzato in legno massiccio. Parti della struttura sono state fornite già prefabbricate in cantiere.
Il bordo esterno delle "C" sporge su tre lati. In quello ad ovest si trovano la cucina e lo spazio soggiorno, al piano superiore la stanza da letto dei genitori. In quello ad est si trovano un appartamento indipendente, un ufficio, spazi di servizio, una biblioteca ed altre stanze da letto. I locali di questo corpo di fabbrica sono collegati dall'esterno da una scala a chiocciola. L'atmosfera degli interni si gioca tutta su diversi gradi di trasparenza: i parapetti vetrati dei balconi e delle terrazze, le pareti dotate di generose

This new house for the owners of a market garden was erected on the site of their former house. It is located at the edge of their company premises, with excellent views of the southern side of the Val Venosta valley. To capture this rich panorama for the inhabitants of the house the design is based on two C-shaped blocks connected by an atrium. These long, roughly similar, building volumes are placed at an acute angle to each other and stand on a two-storey concrete plinth in which a (natural) swimming pool was also integrated. The lower levels contain service rooms for the market garden and other spaces. The dwelling house above is made of solid timber. Some of the timber elements were delivered prefabricated to the site.
On three sides the outer edge of the "C" projects beyond the block below. The western element contains the kitchen and living area, with the parents' bedroom above, while the eastern one houses a self-contained apartment, an office, service spaces, a library and further bedrooms. The rooms in this block can also be reached directly by an external spiral staircase. The atmosphere in the interior of this house is created by a game played with different forms of transparency: Generous amounts of glazing allow excellent views through the building and of the landscape, as do

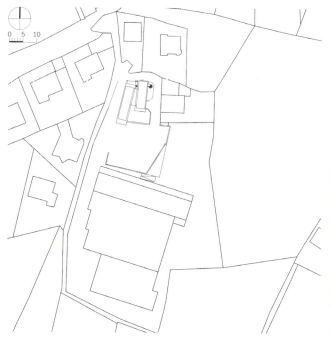

auf die Landschaft ermöglichen großzügig durchfensterte Wandabschlüsse sowie die gläsernen Geländer von Balkonen und Terrassen, während der Einsatz von satiniertem Glas für die angenehme Lichtwirkung in den hinteren Räumen ausschlaggebend ist.

aperture garantiscono la vista migliore verso l'esterno, mentre l'uso di vetro satinato è decisivo per consentire una piacevole diffusione della luce negli spazi sul retro.

glazed parapets to the balconies and terraces, while the use of satin-finished glass provides a pleasant light in the rooms at the rear.

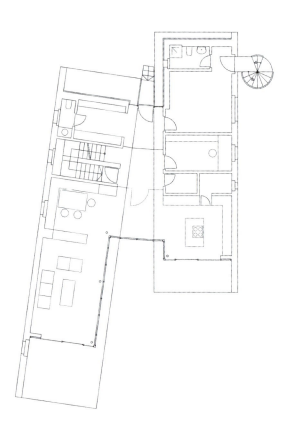
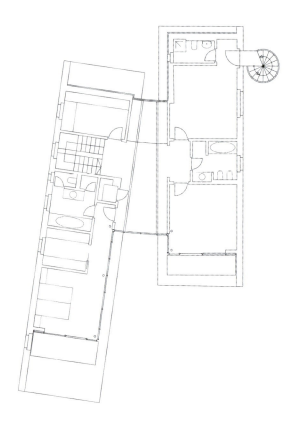

Arnold Gapp
**Bergstation Seilbahn
St. Martin, Latsch**
2002
Kunst am Bau: Manfred Alois Mayr (u. a. Farbkonzept Gondeln)

Arnold Gapp
Stazione a monte della funivia di S. Martino, Laces
2002
Intervento artistico: Manfred Alois Mayr (compreso il concetto cromatico per le cabine)

Arnold Gapp
Ropeway mountain terminal S. Martino, Laces
2002
Site-specific artwork: Manfred Alois Mayr (including the colour concept for the gondolas)

Den Weiler St. Martin am Kofel und seine Wallfahrtskirche erreicht man von Latsch mit der Seilbahn. In wenigen Minuten steigt man von 630 auf 1.740 m Seehöhe auf. Da der Weiler bewohnt ist, dient die Seilbahn aber nicht nur touristischen Zwecken, sondern sie ist auch ein wichtiges Verkehrs- und Transportmittel. Im Zuge einer Erneuerung der Bahn und einer Vergrößerung ihres Beförderungsvolumens musste auch die Bergstation den neuen Anforderungen angepasst werden. Glückliche Umstände führten dazu, dass das Stationsgebäude von einem Architekten gestaltet wurde, der seine Entwürfe an der Wallfahrtskirche orientierte. Von der Kirche geht eine hohe optische Präsenz aus, weshalb die Seilbahnstation hinter eine hohe Bruchsteinmauer gesetzt wurde. Diese dient dazu, das technische Bauwerk von der reizvollen Landschaft ihrer Umgebung optisch zu trennen. Der dahinter liegende Wagenbahnhof wurde aber nicht überbaut: Alle technischen Bestandteile der Seilbahn – die Kupplungen, Seile und Rollen – befinden sich auf dem Dach eines als Bahnsteig dienenden Glaskubus, während die Abspannungen an seiner Unterseite angebracht sind. Während die Fahrgäste im

Il borgo di S. Martino al Monte e il suo santuario si raggiungono in funivia. In pochi minuti si sale da seicentotrenta a millesettecentoquaranta metri sul livello del mare. Il borgo è abitato, pertanto la funivia non serve solo ai turisti, ma è un importante mezzo di trasporto e di traffico per la comunità. In seguito alla ristrutturazione della funivia e all'ampliamento della sua capacità di portata, anche la stazione a monte è stata adattata alle nuove esigenze. Fortunatamente l'incarico progettuale è stato affidato ad un architetto, che ha impostato il progetto confrontandosi con il santuario. La presenza della chiesa è fortemente percepibile, pertanto la stazione è collocata dietro un'alta parete in pietra a spacco. La parete serve a separare visivamente l'opera tecnica dallo splendido paesaggio circostante. La stazione macchine retrostante non è stata sopraelevata: tutte le attrezzature tecniche della funivia, i giunti, i cavi, i rulli, si trovano sul tetto di un cubo di vetro che serve come pensilina, mentre gli ancoraggi si trovano nella parte inferiore. I viaggiatori possono salire nelle cabine, coperti e all'asciutto, mentre l'impianto della funi-

The hamlet San Martino al Monte and its pilgrimage church are reached from Laces by aerial ropeway. In just a few minutes you can ascend from 630 to 1740 metres above sea level. As the hamlet is still inhabited, the ropeway does not only serve to convey tourists but is an important means of local transport. In the course of renovating the line and increasing its transport capacity the mountain terminal had also to be adapted to suit new requirements. It was most fortunate that the new terminal building was designed by an architect whose proposal takes the pilgrimage church into consideration. This church has a strong visual presence, which explains why the new terminal was set behind a high random rubble wall. This visually separates the technical building from the marvellous landscape of its surroundings. But a roof or machinery building was not erected over the station: all the technical apparatus of the aerial tramway, the couplings, ropes and pulleys, are placed on the roof of a glass cube that serves as a platform, while the guy wires are fixed to its underside. Whereas passengers are protected from

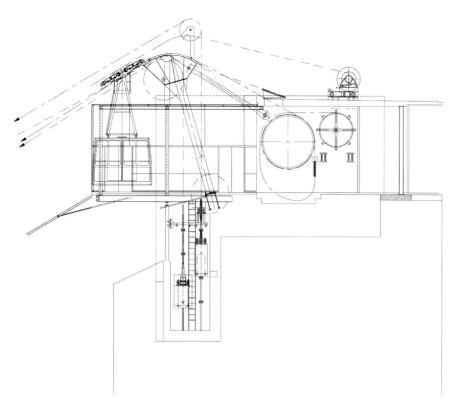

Trockenen in die roten Gondeln eintreten können, liegt die Seilbahntechnik im Freien. Auf diese Weise wurde das Gebäudevolumen der Seilbahn drastisch verringert und alle ihre faszinierenden technischen Komponenten können endlich einmal bei der „Arbeit" beobachtet werden.

via è all'esterno. In questo modo si sono notevolmente ridotte le dimensioni dell'edificio della stazione, e tutte le componenti tecniche dell'impianto possono finalmente essere osservate in funzione.

the rain when boarding the red gondolas, the ropeway technology remains exposed. This drastically reduces the volume of the ropeway building, while also allowing people to watch all its fascinating components "at work".

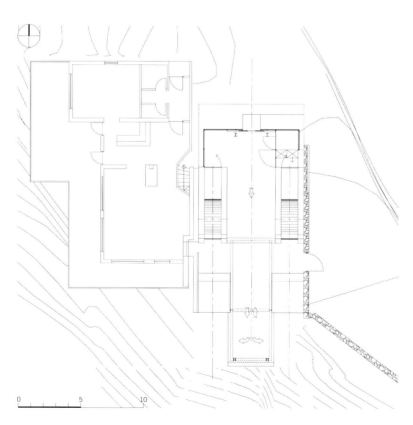

Walter Dietl
Revival of the old train line from Merano to Malles, extension to Malles train shed and the stations of the Val Venosta railway line
2005

The old Val Venosta railway line was first opened in 1906. Following the end of the First World War in 1918 it was handed over to the Italian State Railways and in 1990 it was closed down due to lack of demand. More recently the closure was revealed as a step in the wrong direction as motorised traffic threatened to choke the Val Venosta. Therefore the Autonomous Province of Bolzano-South Tyrol promoted the revival of this local railway line with considerable verve.

The service facilities required for the diesel-powered trains were not built in Merano (the station there is owned by the Italian State) but at the final station on the line in Malles. The historic train shed there was adapted for use by modern trains about 80 metres long by extending it like an accordion. The light fittings are attached to a metal track that projects beyond the building. They illuminate an open space flanked by a building with an L-shaped roof, which contains the fuelling station.

Ein- und Ausstiegszeiten verkürzt werden. Aus diesem Grund gleichen die neuen Haltestellen auch eher solchen von Straßenbahnen als von Bahnhöfen. Ihre Entwürfe basieren auf einem Modulprogramm, das auch einen direkten Bezug zur lokalen Topografie aufweist: In eine Tragekonstruktion aus verzinktem Stahl wurden das Dach und eine Wandausfachung aus unbehandelten Lärchenbrettern ebenso eingehängt wie Sitzbänke, Anschlagtafeln etc. Die Entwässerung erfolgt über in die Trägerkonstruktion integrierte Fallrohre. Der Entwurf des Baukastensystems wurde auf die Bedürfnisse der Lokalbahn abgestimmt. Aus ihm können robuste, zeitlose und ortsverbundene Bahnstationen höchst unterschiedlicher Dimensionen generiert werden.

I treni sostano solo brevemente alle stazioni e i tempi di salita e discesa dai vagoni sono stati ridotti. Per questo motivo le fermate assomigliano più a pensiline tranviarie piuttosto che ferroviarie. Il loro progetto si basa su un programma modulare che corrisponde anche alla locale topografia: una struttura portante in acciaio zincato sorregge le tettoie e contiene e sostiene delle pareti realizzate con assi di larice non trattato, così come panchine e bacheche. I pluviali per l'allontanamento delle acque meteoriche sono integrati nella struttura. Il sistema modulare è stato concepito per le precise esigenze di questa linea locale e se ne possono ricavare robuste pensiline ferroviarie di dimensioni differenti, la cui forma senza tempo rimane legata all'immagine del luogo.

As the trains make only brief stops at the stations it was necessary to reduce the time taken to board and alight to a minimum. Consequently, the stations are more like tram stops than traditional railway stations. The design is based on a modular programme that includes a direct reference to the local topography. The roof and the wall infill panels made of untreated larch boarding, as well as the benches, notice boards etc., were hung from a galvanised steel structure. The roof is drained by downpipes incorporated in the structure. The design of this building block system was adapted to meet the needs of the local railway. It facilitated the construction of robust, locally integrated stations of several different sizes.

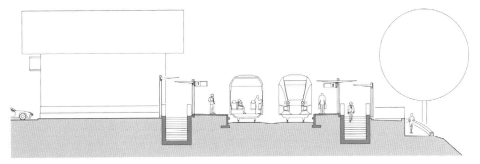

Latsch/Laces

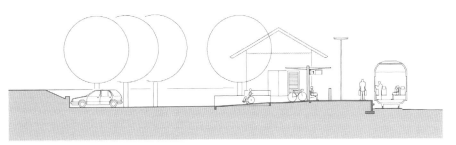

Goldrain/Coldrano

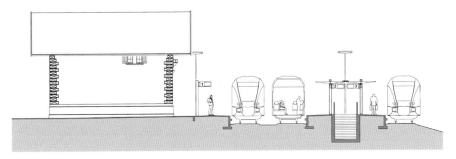

Schlanders/Silandro
(Schnitt/sezione/section)

Schlanders/Silandro
(Ansicht/veduta/view)

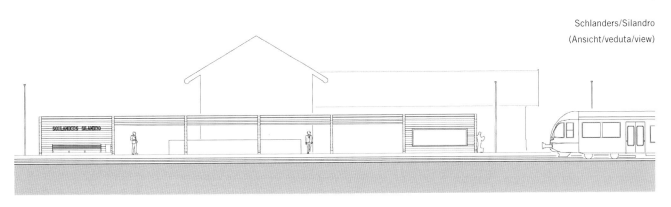

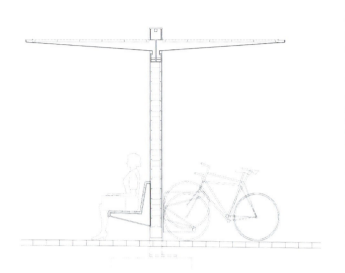

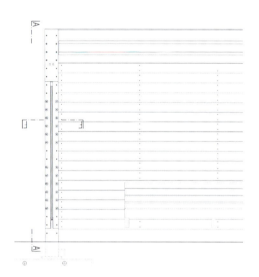
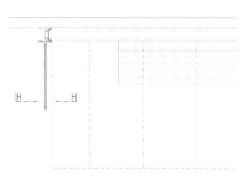
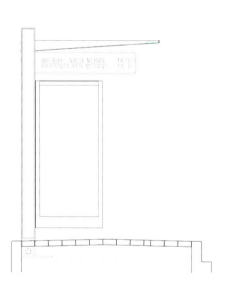

Haltestelle (Detail)
Fermata (dettaglio)
Station (detail)

Erweiterung Remise in Mals
Ampliamento della rimessa di Malles
Extension to Malles train shed

Remise
Rimessa
Train shed

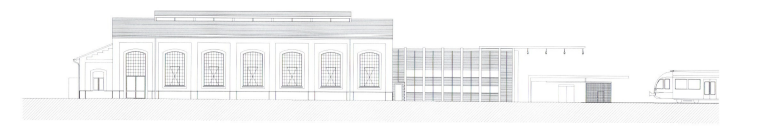

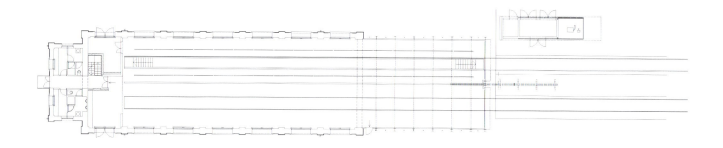

Karl Spitaler
Fahrradverleih, Bahnhof Schlanders
2005

An allen Stationen der Lokalbahn sollen zukünftig Fahrradverleih-Stellen errichtet werden, damit Touristen bestimmte Strecken durch den Vinschgau per Fahrrad, andere mit dem Zug zurücklegen können, ohne dabei auf die Mitnahme eines eigenen Rades angewiesen zu sein. Der Prototyp eines solchen Fahrradverleihs entstand beim Bahnhof Schlanders, wo eine Sichtbetonscheibe so in das Bahnhofsareal hineingesetzt wurde, dass dieses in Richtung zum Ort abgegrenzt wird. Beide Seiten der Betonwand stehen ganz im Dienste des Fahrrades: Auf der einen, quasi öffentlichen, können alle Fahrgäste ihre Räder abstellen, auf der anderen wird in geschlossenen Räumen das Leihgeschäft abgewickelt. Zu diesem Zweck wurde entlang der Längsseite der Wand ein schlichtes Gebäude errichtet, das zum Bahndamm hin von einer Glasfassade abgeschlossen wird, die aus vertikal montierten, matten und transparenten Scheiben zusammengesetzt ist.

Karl Spitaler
Noleggio biciclette, stazione ferroviaria di Silandro
2005

In tutte le stazioni della ferrovia della Val Venosta saranno aperti dei servizi di noleggio biciclette in modo che i turisti possano percorrere alcune tratte con la bicicletta, altre con il treno senza dover portare il proprio veicolo.
Il prototipo di questi centri di noleggio è stato realizzato alla stazione di Silandro, dove una lastra di cemento faccia a vista è stata innestata sul piazzale della stazione in modo tale da realizzare una barriera verso il paese. Entrambi i lati della parete sono destinati alle biciclette: su quello semi-pubblico tutti i viaggiatori possono lasciare la propria bicicletta, sull'altro in un locale chiuso si effettua il servizio di noleggio. Per ospitare questo servizio, sul lato lungo della parete è stata eretta una sobria costruzione, chiusa verso il terrapieno della ferrovia con una facciata in vetro costituita da lastre verticali opache e trasparenti.

Karl Spitaler
Bicycle hire facility, Silandro railway station
2005

In the future it is planned to provide bicycle hire facilities at all the stations of the local railway line so that tourists can travel through certain stretches of the Val Venosta by bike and others with the train, without having to take their bicycles with them. The prototype of such a facility was created at Schlanders railway station where an exposed concrete wall was placed in the station grounds in such a way that it screens the station from the town. Both sides of this wall are placed at the service of bicycles, as it were: passengers can leave their bikes on the more public side, while on the other the business of hiring bicycles is conducted in enclosed spaces. For this purpose a simple building was erected on the long side of the wall, with a glass façade facing towards the railway embankment. The glass front is composed of vertically fixed matt and transparent panes.

Architekturbüro D3
(Richard Veneri, Kathrin Gruber)
Bahnhof mit Jugendraum, Plaus
2005

Nach der Stilllegung der Vinschgerbahn wurden die in Staatsbesitz befindlichen Bahnhöfe an die jeweiligen Gemeinden übergeben und von diesen nicht selten neuen Nutzungsformen zugeführt. Als sich nun die Pläne zur Revitalisierung der Bahnstrecke konkretisierten, wurden die Gemeinden aufgefordert, in ihren alten Bahnhöfen neuerlich Räume für den Bahnbetrieb zur Verfügung zu stellen. In der Gemeinde Plaus bestand ein nicht erhaltenswerter Bahnhof, der nun bis auf die Grundmauern abgerissen wurde, damit in einem Neubau die Haltestelle für die Vinschgerbahn, ein Jugendzentrum und Vereinsräume untergebracht werden konnten. Im zweigeschossigen, in den Bahndamm gesetzten Gebäude befinden sich unten Garagen und die Räume der örtlichen Jäger und Fischer, oben das Jugendzentrum mit einer an den Bahnsteig grenzenden Terrasse. Die Fassaden des Zentrums wurden mit roten und weißen kunststoffbeschichteten Platten beplankt, um es von der mit Stahl und Holz verkleideten Haltestelle farblich abzusetzen.

Ein Ziel der Neugestaltung der Haltestelle war es, die Aufmerksamkeit der Bahnreisenden auf den Ort zu lenken. Diese Bauaufgabe wurde mit einer Stahlkonstruktion gelöst, die den Wartebereich schützend ab-

Studio di architettura D3
(Richard Veneri, Kathrin Gruber)
Stazione ferroviaria con centro giovanile, Plaus
2005

Dopo lo smantellamento della ferrovia della Val Venosta, le stazioni di proprietà statale passarono ai comuni che le destinarono in più casi ad altre funzioni. Quando il progetto della riattivazione della linea ferroviaria divenne un fatto concreto, fu richiesto alle amministrazioni comunali di mettere a disposizione dell'azienda ferroviaria gli spazi delle loro vecchie stazioni. Nel comune di Plaus la stazione non meritava d'essere ristrutturata ed è stata demolita sino ai muri di fondazione, in modo che il nuovo edificio potesse ospitare la fermata ferroviaria, un centro giovanile e per altre associazioni. Nella costruzione a due piani incassata nel terrapieno si trovano, a piano terra l'autorimessa e la locale associazione di caccia e pesca, al piano superiore il centro giovanile con una terrazza che guarda sui binari. Le facciate del centro sono state rivestite con lastre polimeriche di colore rosso e bianco, per distinguerle chiaramente dal rivestimento in legno ed acciaio della fermata ferroviaria. Uno degli obbiettivi del nuovo progetto è stato quello di dover attirare l'attenzione dei viaggiato-

Architekturbüro D3
(Richard Veneri, Kathrin Gruber)
Railway station and youth space, Plaus
2005

After the Val Venosta railway line was closed down the railway stations in state ownership were handed over to the respective local communities, and in many cases given a new use. When plans to revive this train line became more concrete the communities were asked to prove space in the old railway stations for the new train service. In Plaus the old station was not worth preserving and was demolished down to its foundations so that the station for the new Val Venosta railway line, a youth centre and various associations could be accommodated in a new building. The two-storey building set into the railway embankment contains garages and rooms for the local fishermen and hunters at ground floor level, while the youth centre and a terrace adjoining the platform are on the first floor. The façade of the centre was clad with red and white laminated panels to distinguish it in terms of colour from station that is clad with steel and timber.

One goal of the new station design was to attract travellers' attention to the town. This aim was met by using a steel struc-

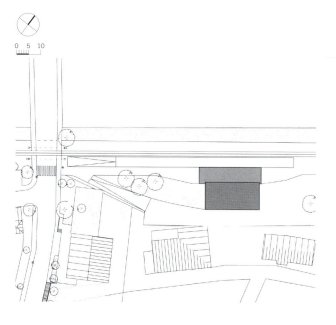

grenzt und in 2 m hohen Lettern den Ortsnamen bildet – ein ungewöhnlicher Entwurf, der nur möglich war, weil der Name Plaus nicht ins Italienische übersetzt wird.

ri sul luogo. La fermata è stata realizzata con una struttura in acciaio che delimita e protegge la zona d'attesa e compone con lettere di due metri di altezza il nome della località: un progetto inusuale che si è reso possibile perché il toponimo di Plaus non si può tradurre in italiano.

ture that shelters and defines the waiting area and forms the name of the town in letters 2 metres high – an unusual design that was possible because the name Plaus is not translated into Italian.

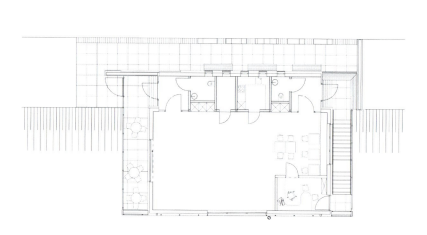

Melanie Folie (l.) und Jacqueline Tappeiner, Fahrgäste

„Es wird auch einen neuen Jugendtreff geben, und wenn der offen ist, sind wir sicher immer dort."

Melanie Folie (sin.) e Jacqueline Tappeiner, utenti della ferrovia.

"Ci sarà anche un nuovo centro giovanile, e quando aprirà, saremmo sicuramente sempre lì."

Melanie Folie (left) and Jacqueline Tappeiner, passengers

"This will be a new meeting place for young people, and once it has opened we'll certainly be there!"

Meran - Bozen   Merano - Bolzano

Promenadenkonzert vor dem Kurhaus in Meran
Concerto sulla passeggiata del Passirio, davanti al Kurhaus a Merano
Promenade concert in front of the Kurhaus in Meran

Hanspeter Abler Trojer
Bürogebäude Martin Geier, Algund
2000

Hanspeter Abler Trojer
Edificio per uffici Martin Geier, Lagundo
2000

Hanspeter Abler Trojer
Martin Geier office building, Lagundo
2000

Geometer Martin Geier verwaltet das Vermächtnis seines Freundes Hanspeter Abler Trojer, der für sich auf dem Grundstück seiner Familie ein kleines Bürohaus geplant hatte. Abler Trojer, u. a. zeitweilig im Büro von Günther Domenig beschäftigt, wollte sich mit dem schlichten Sichtbetonbau einen Lebenstraum erfüllen, er verstarb aber während der Bauphase. Sein Freund und Kompagnon im gemeinsamen Architekturbüro führte das Bauwerk zu Ende und mietet es seitdem an.

Das Gebäude befindet sich an einer strategisch wichtigen Stelle am Dorfrand von Algund, weshalb ihm trotz seines schlichten Äußeren ein hoher Bekanntheitsgrad zukommt. Einfahrtsweg und Parkplätze sind bereits Teil des architektonischen Konzepts. Das Gebäude besteht aus Beton und Glas. Bei seiner Errichtung wurden raue Schalbretter waagrecht verlegt, um ihm einen archaischen Zug zu verleihen. Dieses Schalungsbild des Sichtbetons steht für die Metapher des Bretterverschlags bzw. des Architekturbüros als Dauer-Baustelle.

Über eine Rampe erreicht man eine Eingangszone und den Hauptraum des Büros. Von dort führt eine Treppe in den Keller, wo sich ein zentraler Raum, Nebenräume und ein Lichthof befinden. Hinter dem verglasten Innenhof wurde ein weiterer Raum angelegt, der als Besprechungszimmer

Hanspeter Abler Trojer avrebbe voluto realizzare per sè una casa-ufficio sul terreno di famiglia. E' spettato invece all'amico, il geometra Martin Geier, amministrare il suo testamento e compiere la sua volontà. Abler Trojer, che tra l'altro lavorò per un certo tempo nello studio dell'architetto Günther Domenig, avrebbe voluto realizzare il sogno di una vita con questo sobrio edificio in cemento faccia a vista, ma è morto durante la costruzione.

E' stato il suo amico e compagno di lavoro a completare l'opera e da allora l'ha anche avuta in affitto.

L'edificio è collocato all'estremità del paese di Lagundo su un'area strategica e pertanto, nonostante l'aspetto dimesso, gode di un forte effetto pubblicitario. La strada d'accesso ed i parcheggi sono parte integrante del concetto architettonico. L'edificio è realizzato in cemento e vetro. Nel costruirlo, le tavole grezze per il getto del calcestruzzo sono state disposte in orizzontale per investire l'edificio di un carattere arcaico. L'effetto del cassero grezzo per il cemento faccia a vista è una metafora del tavolato in legno o, se vogliamo, dello studio di architettura inteso come un cantiere sempre aperto.

Lungo una rampa si raggiunge il locale principale dell'ufficio. Da qui una scala porta nell'interrato, dove si trovano uno

Surveyor Martin Geier administers the legacy of his late friend Hanspeter Abler Trojer, who wanted to erect a small office building on a site belonging to his family. Abler Trojer, who worked for some time in the office of Günther Domenig among others, had wanted to fulfill the dream of a lifetime by erecting a plain fair-faced concrete building, but died during the construction phase. Geier, his friend and partner in their joint architecture practice, finished the building and has rented it since its completion.

The office building is located at a strategically important position on the edge of the village of Lagundo, which explains why it is wellknown despite its plain exterior. The entrance route and car parking spaces are part of the architectural concept. The building is made of concrete and glass. To lend the building an archaic touch unplaned boards were used as horizontal shuttering for the concrete. The marks of the shuttering on the concrete stand for the metaphor of the wooden shack or the architect's office as a permanent building site.

The entrance zone and the main office space are reached via a ramp. From there a staircase leads to the basement where there is a central room, ancillary spaces and a light-well. A further space laid out behind the glazed courtyard is used as a

genützt wird. Gemäß dem ursprünglichen Plan sollten in der unteren Etage Wettbewerbe bearbeitet und ausgestellt werden. Zwar hat der Mieter diesen Gedanken nicht umgesetzt, er nützt den Raum aber als Veranstaltungsort für Wechselausstellungen.

spazio centrale, locali secondari e una corte illuminata dall'alto. Dietro il cortile interno e vetrato c'è un altro locale, che viene utilizzato come sala riunioni. Secondo il progetto iniziale, il piano inferiore doveva essere utilizzato per svolgere i concorsi ed esporne gli elaborati. Il locatario non ha attuato questi propositi ma usa lo spazio per esposizioni temporanee.

conference room. According to the original plans the lower level was to be reserved for working on and exhibiting competition entries. Although the tenant has not implemented this idea he does use the space to show travelling exhibitions.

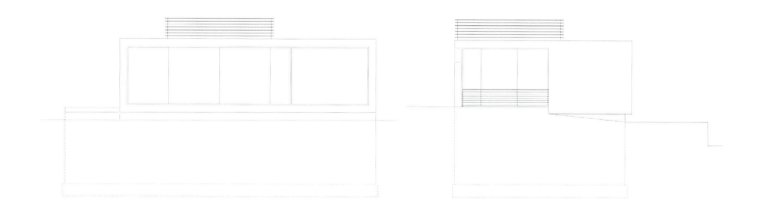

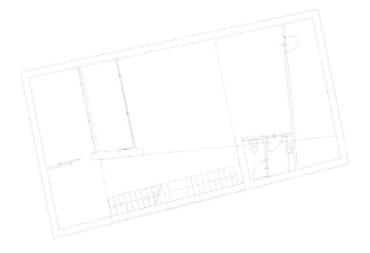

Matteo Thun
Pergola Residence, Algund
2004

Bei einer Reise durch Südtirol stellt man fest, dass beim Bauen für den Tourismus mehr neue Architektur gefragt wäre, zumal dieser Bausektor hier eine überaus beachtliche Geschichte hat. Einer der wenigen Lichtblicke befindet sich in Algund, einer Gemeinde, die nun davon profitiert, dass in Meran vor kurzem eine große Therme (Projekt: Baumann Zillich Architekten, Berlin; Gestaltung: Matteo Thun, Mailand) eröffnet worden ist.

Die Pergola Residence umfasst 14 Suiten, Frühstücksraum und Spa und hebt sich durch dieses ungewöhnliche Raumprogramm vom Bautyp üblicher Hotels ab, weil auf die Einrichtung einer Lobby, eines Restaurants mit Bar etc. verzichtet wurde. Mit Ausnahme des Spas gibt es hier keine Gesellschaftsräume, womit man der Entwicklung Rechnung trägt, dass unter den Gästen von heute immer weniger Kontakt gepflegt wird.

Das Appartementhaus wurde in einen von Weinbergen umgebenen Sonnenhang mimetisch hineingesetzt. Der Baukörper besteht aus vier Terrassen, die sich in den halbmondförmigen Verlauf des Baugrundes einfügen und in Bezug auf ihr äußeres Erscheinungsbild so gestaltet wurden, dass zwischen ihnen und den „Pergln" (Konstruktionen, auf denen die Weinstöcke

Matteo Thun
Pergola Residence, Lagundo
2004

Attraversando l'Alto Adige ci si rende conto che l'edilizia turistica necessita molto di nuova architettura e che inoltre questo specifico settore delle costruzioni possiede una storia estremamente interessante. Uno dei pochi sprazzi di luce si trova a Lagundo, un comune vicino a Merano che gode dei benefici della recente attivazione delle terme meranesi (progetto architettonico: Baumann Zillich Architetti, Berlino; progetto artistico: Matteo Thun, Milano).

Il residence Pergola comprende quattordici suites, sala colazioni e un ambito dedicato alla cura del corpo e si differenzia dalla tipologia dei soliti alberghi per il suo particolare programma spaziale che ha rinunciato alla realizzazione di una zona di accettazione, del ristorante con il bar, ecc.

Tenendo conto della tendenza per cui oggi gli ospiti sono portati a stringere sempre meno relazioni reciproche, ad eccezione della zona dedicata alla cura del corpo, non ci sono altri spazi per la socializzazione.

L'edificio per appartamenti si inserisce mimeticamente nel pendio soleggiato dei vigneti. Il corpo di fabbrica si compone di quattro terrazze disposte sul terreno a mezzaluna, e risolte esteticamente in modo tale che si possa riconoscere un rapporto diretto con le pergole dei vigneti. Diversamente da questo tentativo di adattamento

Matteo Thun
Pergola Residence, Lagundo
2004

On travelling through South Tyrol it is noticeable that, particularly in the area of buildings for tourism, more contemporary architecture is desirable, all the more so as this sector of building has a remarkable history here. One of the few bright spots in this area is in Lagundo, a community that profits from the fact that a large thermal spa has recently been opened in Merano (project: Baumann Zillich Architekten, Berlin; design: Matteo Thun, Milan).

The Pergola Residence consists of 14 suites, a breakfast room and a spa. This unusual programme means that this building differs considerably from a standard hotel, as there was no need for a lobby, a restaurant and bar etc. With the exception of the spa there are no reception rooms, an acknowledgement of the fact that guests nowadays tend increasingly to want less contact with each other.

This apartment building was placed mimetically on a sunny slope amidst the surrounding vineyards. The building consists of four terraces inserted in the half-moon of the site that were designed in such a way that their external appearance establishes a direct visual association with the local "pergln" (a kind of pergola to which the vines are tied). In contrast to this visual adaptation to the surroundings the interior

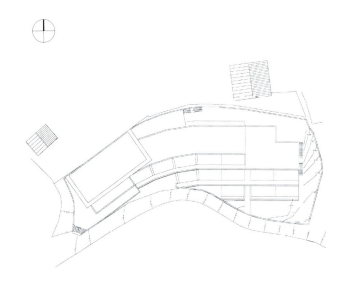

aufgebunden werden) ein direkter Zusammenhang hergestellt werden kann. Im Unterschied zu dieser optischen Angleichung an das Umfeld wurden die Innenräume in Form einer fröhlichen und dennoch sachlich-zeitgemäßen Interpretation des Tirolerhauses gestaltet. Das Projekt begegnet den landschaftlichen Reizen seiner Umgebung mit vorbildlichem Respekt.

al paesaggio, gli interni sono arredati interpretando la casa tirolese in modo allegro, ma al contempo rigoroso e contemporaneo. Il progetto si confronta con esemplare rispetto con la bellezza del paesaggio circostante.

was designed as a cheerful and yet functional and contemporary interpretation of a Tyrolean house. This project pays exemplary respect to the attractive landscape in which it is situated.

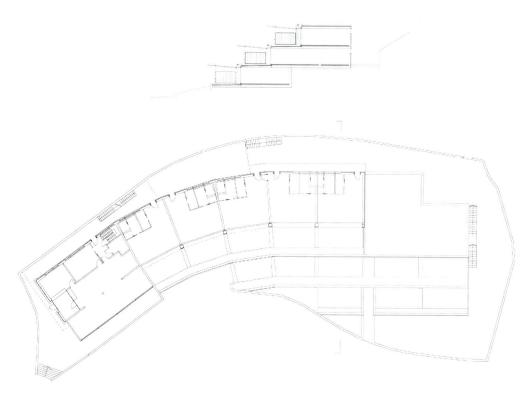

Christoph Hilfert, Weinbauer und Nachbar

„Zumindest ist es keine Jodlerarchitektur! Und es ist sicher eine traditionellere Bauweise als die üblichen Bauten."

Pergola Residence, Christoph Hilfert, Viticoltore e confinante

"Almeno non è un'architettura in stile pseudo tirolese! E presenta una tecnica di costruzione più tradizionale di tanti altri edifici convenzionali."

Pergola Residence, Christoph Hilfert, wine grower and neighbour

"At least it isn't that yodelling kind of architecture! And it's certainly built in a more traditional way than most buildings."

Markus Scherer, Walter Angonese, Klaus Hellweger

Südtiroler Landesmuseum für Kultur- und Landesgeschichte, Schloss Tirol bei Meran

2004

Kunst am/im Bau: Elisabeth Hölzl, Carmen Tartarotti, Kurt Lanthaler, Jörg Müller, Walter Niedermayr mit Hannes Obermair; Kunstprojekte Vorburg: Gottfried Bechtold, Julia Bornefeld (Konzept, Koordination: Marion Piffer-Damiani)

Schloss Tirol bei Meran steht seit Jahrhunderten im Rang eines National-Denkmals, seit seiner Umgestaltung zu einem Landesmuseum ist es auch ein gefragtes Ausflugsziel. Die Sanierung und Einrichtung der Präsentationen waren konsequent mit dem Denkmalamt abzustimmen. Um den historischen Baubestand so wenig wie möglich anzutasten, wurden Vitrinen und andere präsentationstechnisch notwendige „Möbel" in die Räume hineingehängt oder -gestellt, aber nicht eingebaut. Größere Umbauten blieben dem Bergfried, dem Küchenhof und Sonderausstellungsräumen mit Cafeteria und Shop vorbehalten. Neubauten finden sich nur außerhalb der Burganlage. Auf der Vorburg wurde ein Seminarzentrum errichtet und eine frühchristliche Kirchenruine überbaut. Hier ist das vorwiegend verwendete Material rohes Lärchenholz, im Schloss dagegen gerosteter Stahl.

Im Zuge der Umwidmung des Schlosses zum Museum wurde in logistischer Hin-

Markus Scherer, Walter Angonese, Klaus Hellweger

Museo Provinciale di Storia e Cultura Sudtirolese, Castel Tirolo presso Merano

2004

Intervento artistico: Elisabeth Hölzl, Carmen Tartarotti, Kurt Lanthaler, Jörg Müller, Walter Niedermayr mit Hannes Obermair; Interventi artistici nel vallo: Gottfried Bechtold, Julia Bornefeld (concetto e coordinazione: Marion Piffer-Damiani)

A Castel Tirolo è riconosciuto da secoli il rango di monumento nazionale, ma da quando è stato trasformato in museo provinciale è divenuto anche ambita meta di escursioni. Il restauro e l'allestimento sono stati concordati coerentemente con la Soprintendenza ai monumenti. In modo da intervenire il meno possibile sul manufatto storico esistente, le vetrine e gli altri "mobili" tecnicamente indispensabili all'esposizione sono stati appesi o appoggiati, mai inseriti nella struttura dell'edificio. Le opere di ristrutturazione più ingenti hanno interessato il mastio, la corte delle cucine e gli ambienti destinati alle esposizioni itineranti con la caffetteria ed il negozio. Nuove costruzioni sono state erette solo al di fuori del complesso fortificato.

Nel vallo è stato realizzato un centro per seminari e nei pressi si trova la rovina di una chiesa paleocristiana. Qui si è utilizzato prevalentemente il legno di larice non trattato, all'interno del castello invece,

Markus Scherer, Walter Angonese, Klaus Hellweger

South Tyrol Museum of Cultural and Regional History, Schloss Tirol, near Merano

2004

Site-specific artwork: Elisabeth Hölzl, Carmen Tartarotti, Kurt Lanthaler, Jörg Müller, Walter Niedermayr with Hannes Obermair; art projects Vorburg: Gottfried Bechtold, Julia Bornefeld (concept, coordination: Marion Piffer-Damiani)

For centuries Schloss Tirol near Merano has enjoyed the status of a national monument, since its conversion into a regional museum it has also become a popular destination for excursions. Each step in the renovation and the design of the presentation had to be discussed and agreed with the conservation authorities. To reduce interventions in the historic fabric to a minimum the display cases and the other pieces of "furniture" required by the presentation were either suspended or positioned in the space rather than being built in. Larger conversion works were confined to the Bergfried (donjon, keep), the kitchen courtyard and the special exhibition rooms with the cafeteria and shop. The only new buildings are outside the castle complex. On the Vorburg (bailey) a seminar centre was established and the ruins of an early Christian church were built over. Here the predominant material is untreated larch, whereas in the castle itself rusted steel dominates.

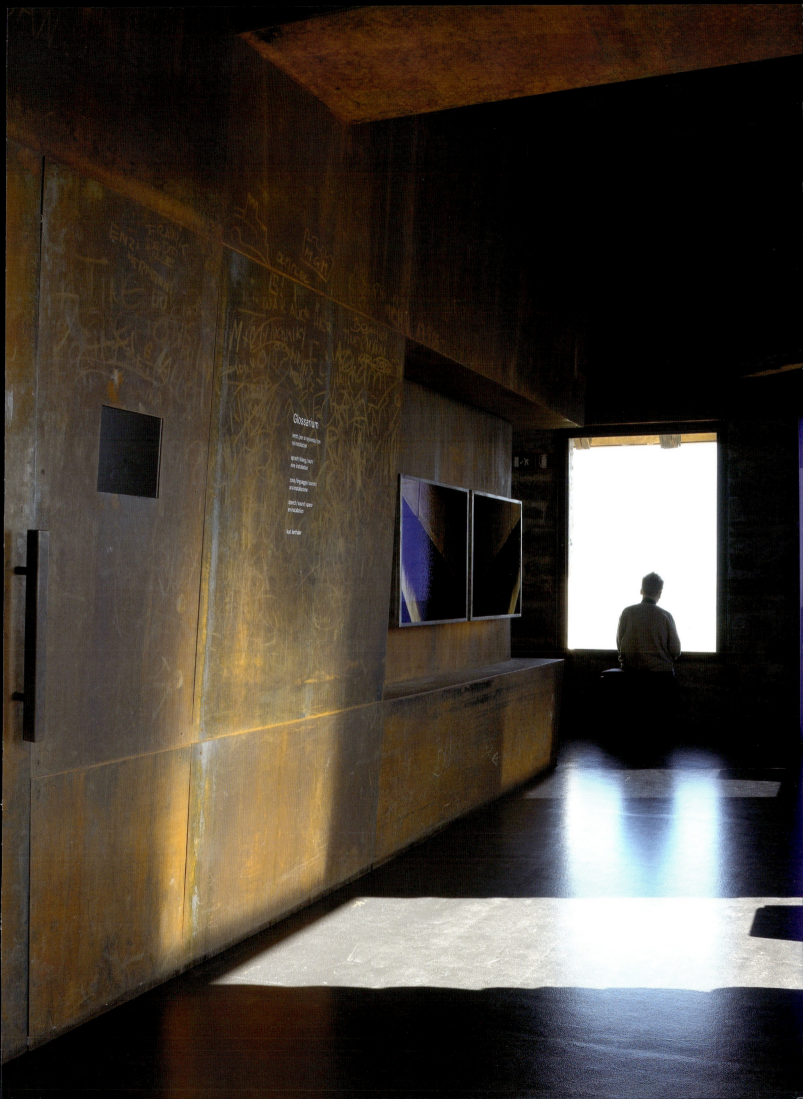

sicht ein Rundgang realisiert – aber diese Lösung einer schwierigen Bauaufgabe fällt wohl den wenigsten Besuchern auf. Im Herzstück der Anlage, dem Bergfried, wurden vier konisch auskragende, frei stehende Pylonen aus 170 t Stahl installiert. Die geometrisch komplexe Figur trägt 22 Schauzonen und erstreckt sich über eine Höhe von ca. 30 m. Um dem symbolischen Stellenwert des Schlosses Rechnung zu tragen, integrierten die Architekten mit viel Feingefühl Beiträge zeitgenössischer Künstler in ihre Arbeit.

l'acciaio arrugginito. Con gli interventi per la trasformazione in museo è stato realizzato un percorso circolare, ma solo pochi visitatori percepiscono la soluzione di questo difficile compito logistico.
All'interno dell'elemento centrale della costruzione, il mastio, sono stati installati quattro piloni conici d'acciaio, svincolati dalla struttura e pesanti 170 tonnellate. La complessa struttura porta 22 piattaforme espositive e si sviluppa per un'altezza di 30 metri.
Con molta sensibilità gli architetti hanno riconosciuto il valore simbolico del castello e completato la loro opera con quella di artisti contemporanei.

In the course of converting the castle into a museum a logically laid out tour was devised – but only few visitors probably notice this solution of a difficult building commission. Four freestanding pylons made of 170 tons of steel that move further apart from each other as they rise were installed in the very core of the complex, the Bergfried. This geometrically complex figure carries 22 display zones and extends through a height of around 30 metres. To adequately express the historic value of the castle the architects integrated contributions by contemporary artists in their work, in the process displaying a remarkable degree of sensitivity.

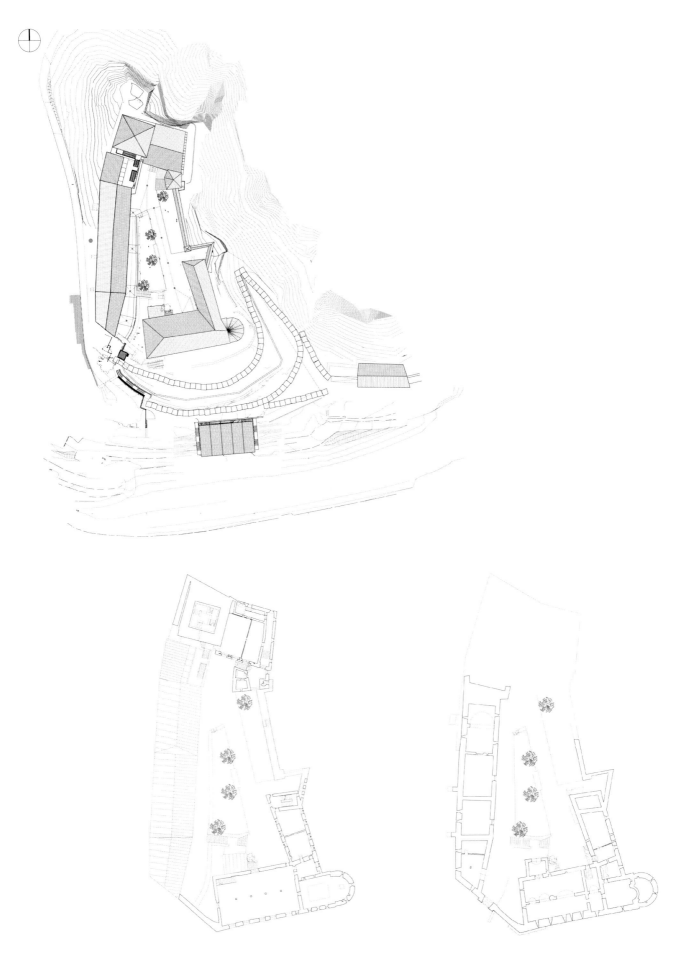

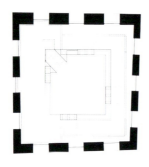
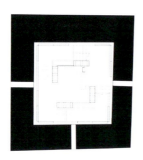
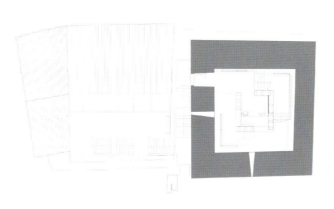
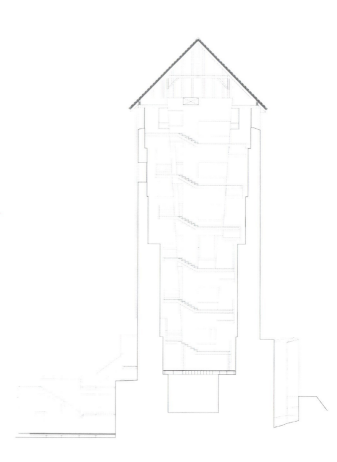

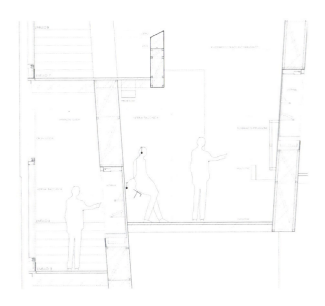

Antonella Gambacorta, Besucherin

„Ich finde das sehr passend, das rostige Metall mit dem Stein – man sieht es ist neu, gehört zu einer anderen Zeit."

Antonella Gambacorta, visitatrice.

"Trovo che sia tutto molto coerente - il metallo arrugginito con la pietra – si vede che è un nuovo intervento, appartiene ad un'epoca differente."

Antonella Gambacorta, visitor

"I find the rusted metal with the stone very appropriate – you see that it is new, that it belongs to a different era."

Höller & Klotzner Architekten
„kunst Meran" im Haus der Sparkasse, Meran
2001

Ein altes Meraner Wohn- und Geschäftshaus wurde zum „Kunsthaus" umgebaut. Der Haupteingang befindet sich unter den historischen Meraner Lauben. Über einen Vorraum gelangt man in die Eingangshalle mit Empfang und Museumsshop. Durchquert man das lange, aber sehr schmale ebenerdige Geschoss, erreicht man das Café des Ausstellungszentrums. Die Ausstellungsräume in den oberen Stockwerken sind um einen überdachten Innenhof geführt. „kunst Meran" verfügt neben seinen Ausstellungsflächen über einen Veranstaltungssaal mit einem kunsthistorisch vielleicht nicht so wertvollen, aber umso charmanteren Freskenbestand, ferner über Büroräumlichkeiten, eine Dachterrasse und eine kleine Atelierwohnung für Gastkünstler.

Im Zuge der Umwidmung des Altstadthauses in einen Präsentationsort für moderne Kunst wurde darauf Bedacht genommen, neue Architektur bzw. Infrastruktur möglichst zurückhaltend einzufügen, damit die Betrachter nichts vom Wesentlichen – der Kunst – ablenkt. Neben einfachen Renovierungsarbeiten am Altbestand zählt die Etablierung eines (behindertengerechten) Rundganges durch die Schauräume, was den Einbau eines Lifts und eines Treppenaufganges in den dritten Stock erforderlich machte, zu den wichtigsten Baumaßnah-

Höller & Klotzner Architetti
Merano arte edificio Cassa di Risparmio, Merano
2001

Un vecchio edificio a destinazione commerciale e residenziale è stato trasformato in una "casa dell'arte". L'ingresso principale si trova sotto gli storici portici di Merano. Attraverso un antivano si raggiunge la sala d'ingresso che ospita l'accettazione e la rivendita del museo. Se si attraversa tutto il piano terra, lungo ma molto stretto, si raggiunge il cafè del centro espositivo. I locali espositivi, situati ai piani superiori, ruotano attorno ad una corte coperta. Merano arte dispone anche di una sala per manifestazioni con pareti affrescate, che seppur non siano di rilevante valore storico-artistico, creano un'atmosfera ancora più affascinante ed inoltre di spazi per uffici, di una terrazza pensile ed un piccolo appartamento-atelier per ospitare gli artisti.

Con la trasformazione del vecchio edificio cittadino in un luogo dove esporre arte moderna, si è ritenuto di dover inserire la nuova architettura e le necessarie infrastrutture in modo garbato, così che nulla distragga l'osservatore dalla percezione dell'essenziale, dall'arte. A fronte delle normali opere di restauro sull'esistente, la sistemazione di un percorso (adatto ai disabili) tra i locali espositivi è stato uno dei più importanti interventi costruttivi. Questo ha reso necessario l'inserimento di un ascensore, e di una scala per il collegamento con il terzo piano, mentre le vie di

Höller & Klotzner Architekten
Merano arte in the Cassa di Risparmio building, Merano
2001

An old residential and commercial building in Merano was converted into the "Kunsthaus" (literally Art Building). The main entrance is from the historic Merano Portici (arcades). An entrance lobby leads into a hall containing the reception area and museum shop. By crossing the long but extremely narrow ground floor you reach the exhibition centre café. The exhibition spaces on the upper floors are grouped around a roofed courtyard. In addition to the exhibition areas Merano arte has an events hall with frescoes, which, while perhaps not of great art historical importance, are nevertheless particularly charming. In addition there are office spaces, a roof terrace and a small studio apartment for visiting artists.

In the course of converting this old town building into a space for the presentation of modern art considerable care was taken to introduce new architecture or infrastructure elements in as restrained a way as possible so as not to distract viewers from the most important thing – the art. In addition to simple renovation work to the existing fabric, one of the most important construction measures was the creation of a tour (accessible to disabled persons) through the exhibition spaces. This made it necessary to insert a lift and staircase leading to the third floor. Some of the escape routes are through the neighbouring building. To allow

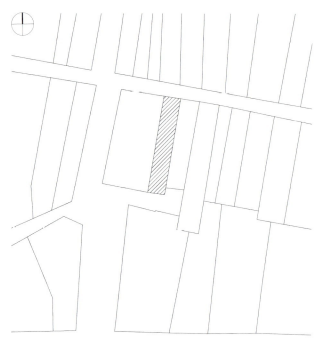

men. Fluchtwege führen zum Teil durch das Nachbargebäude. Damit viel Tageslicht von der Dachzone bis ins Erdgeschoss des Innenhofes fällt, wurde das alte Dach entfernt. Der Dachstuhl wurde angehoben und fast vollständig verglast.

fuga corrono in parte attraverso l'edificio vicino. Per garantire che la luce penetrasse dall'alto fino al piano terra, la vecchia copertura è stata rimossa e la struttura del tetto è stata di poco rialzata e quasi completamente vetrata.

as much daylight as possible to penetrate from the roof zone to the ground floor of the internal courtyard the old roofing was removed, and the roof trusses were raised somewhat and almost completely glazed.

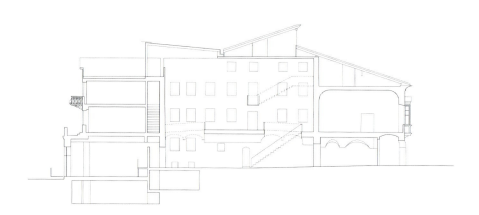

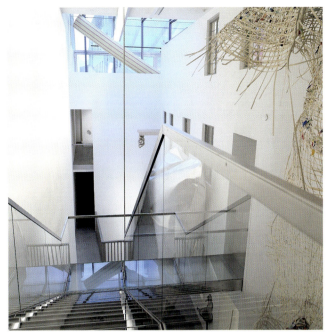

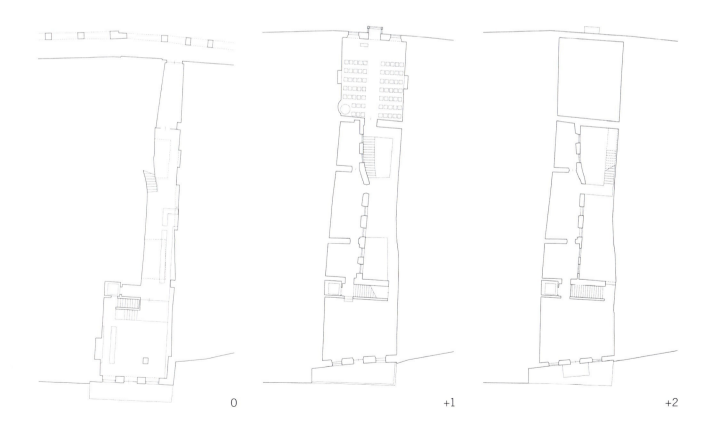

0   +1   +2

Abram&Schnabl
Kurhauspassage, Meran
2004

In Meran lebt das Flair des Fin de Siècle noch gut erkennbar in der Freiheitsstraße fort, wo man in der Glanzzeit der Stadt nahe der Passer eine Flaniermeile anlegte und entlang dieser das Kurhaus und andere elegante Gebäude errichtete. Die Freiheitsstraße verläuft parallel zu den mittelalterlichen Lauben, was zur Folge hatte, dass der dazwischen liegende Stadtraum mit einer Reihe von improvisierten Bauwerken gefüllt wurde, mit Baracken für Dienstboten und Gasthauspersonal, mit Ställen und Lagern. Durch das halböffentliche Gewirr an ärmlichen Bauten und Gassen in den Hinterhöfen führten die kürzesten Wege durch die Innenstadt. Nur eine Lücke zwischen Lauben und Freiheitsstraße wurde nie ausgefüllt und sollte nun durch die Errichtung von Wohnhäusern und Geschäftsräumen über einer öffentlichen Passage geschlossen werden. Zunächst benötigte es viel Geschick bei der Klärung der Besitzverhältnisse, bis drei Höfe mit 16 Geschäften, einer Bar, neun Büros und 30 Wohnungen geplant werden konnten. Der Niveauunterschied zwischen Freiheitsstraße und Lauben beträgt 6 m und wurde in Anlehnung an die historisch gewachsenen Straßenverläufe durch eine ansteigende Passagen-Gasse ausgeglichen. Während die Fassade des Gebäudes in den Lauben bestehen bleiben musste, konnte die Front des Hauses an der Freiheitsstraße zeitgemäß gestaltet

Abram&Schnabl
Kurhauspassage, Merano
2004

A Merano, in Corso Libertà, l'atmosfera fin de siècle è ancora viva e riconoscibile. Proprio qui, ai tempi d'oro della città, fu realizzata la passeggiata lungo il Passirio e costruiti il Kurhaus ed altre eleganti palazzine. Il corso corre parallelo ai portici medievali e lo spazio urbano compreso tra i due assi è stato nel tempo occupato da baracche per gli alloggi dei domestici e del personale delle locande, da stalle e magazzini. Attraversando questi spazi semipubblici e labirintici, fatti di povere costruzioni, e i vicoli dei cortili interni, si raggiungeva per la via più breve il centro cittadino. Tra i portici ed il corso, solo un unico vuoto edilizio non era mai stato occupato, mentre ora una galleria pubblica doveva chiuderlo con degli edifici residenziali e degli spazi commerciali. All'inizio ci è voluta molta abilità per risolvere i rapporti di proprietà e poter progettare un intervento che comprendesse tre corti interne con sedici negozi, un bar, nove uffici e trenta appartamenti.
Il dislivello tra i portici ed il corso è di sei metri, e lo si supera con una galleria in salita che riprende il tracciato dei percorsi stratificatisi nel tempo.
Mentre la facciata sui portici doveva essere conservata, quella sul corso è stata proget-

Abram&Schnabl
Kurhaus arcade, Merano
2004

The flair of the fin-de-siècle is still alive in Corso Libertà in Merano where, during the heyday of this town, a kind of promenade was laid out near the River Passirio along which the Kurhaus and other elegant buildings were erected. Corso Libertà runs parallel to the mediaeval "Portici" (arcades) and the urban space in between was filled with a series of improvised buildings such as shacks for servants and restaurant staff, stables and storehouses
The semi-public muddle of humble buildings and lanes in the back yards offered the shortest routes through the old town. Only one gap between the Portici and Corso Libertà was never filled completely. It was planned to remedy this situation by erecting apartments and commercial spaces above a public arcade. First of all considerable skill had to be exercised in clarifying the ownership of the properties before starting to plan three courtyards with 16 shops, a bar, 9 offices and 30 apartments. The difference in level between Corso Libertà and Portici amounts to 6 metres. Utilizing the example of the historically developed street structure, this difference was handled by making an inclined arcade lane. While the facade of the building on Portici had to be preserved unchanged, the front of the building on Corso Libertà could be

werden. Ihr wurde – nach dem Vorbild der vor- und zurückweichenden Dekorationen der Fassaden der Nachbargebäude – ebenfalls Tiefe verliehen. Diese bewirkt eine durch das Tageslicht erzeugte, plastische Modulation des Fassadenbildes ähnlich der an den Gründerzeithäusern.

tata in modo contemporaneo. Gli architetti hanno dato profondità alla sua composizione, ispirandosi alla decorazione in rilievo dell'edificio vicino. I giochi di luce incidenti sulla facciata generano un effetto plastico che ricorda quelli delle facciate degli edifici fine Ottocento.

designed in a contemporary manner. In response to the projecting and recessed decoration of the neighbouring buildings this façade was given a certain depth, which by daylight creates a sculptural modulation not dissimilar to that of the nearby late 19th century buildings.

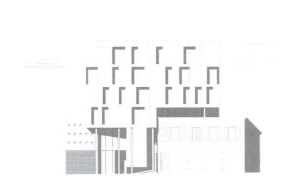

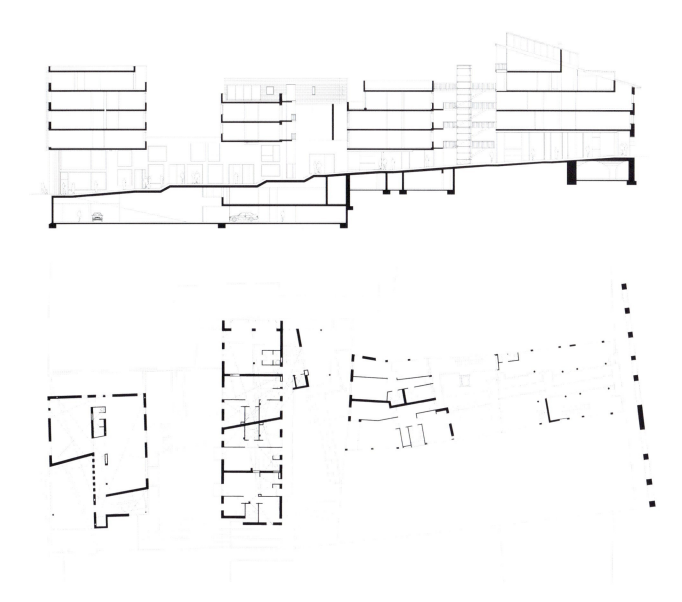

133

Holzbox, Baugesellschaft Wolkenstein GmbH., Vorarlberger Ökohaus GmbH.

Wohnanlage Wolkenstein, Meran
2003

Bei diesem Wohnbau-Projekt handelt es sich um einen „Import" aus Österreich. Das Team von Holzbox aus Innsbruck, das vielfach mit dem Unternehmen Vorarlberger Ökohaus zusammenarbeitet, realisierte in Meran einen massiven Holzbau mit zwölf Wohneinheiten. Die Architekten wollten das Projekt vom Bautyp eines Laubenganghauses auch mit einer mediterranen Note ausstatten und konzipierten einen Palmengarten am Dach. Bei der Umsetzung dieser Idee stießen sie aber an die Belastungsgrenzen des Baustoffes Holz: Es ist schon ungewöhnlich genug, nur Holz als Material für die Errichtung eines viergeschossigen Bauwerks zu verwenden, die wahre Herausforderung bei der Errichtung dieses Wohnbaus lag aber darin, ihn mit dem relativ hohen Gewicht am Dach (Palmentröge und Sonnenkollektoren) zu realisieren. Aus diesem Grund ist der massive Holzbau in Schottenbauweise über einem Betonsockel konstruiert worden. Alle Holzbauteile wurden vorgefertigt zur Baustelle gebracht und konnten in kurzer Zeit montiert werden. Darin offenbart sich einer der großen Vorteile des Holzbaues, denn er ist nicht nur umweltfreundlich, sondern in Hinblick auf

Holzbox, Baugesellschaft Wolkenstein GmbH., Vorarlberger Ökohaus GmbH.

Complesso residenziale Wolkenstein, Merano
2003

Questo edificio residenziale è un progetto "d'importazione" austriaca. Il team Holzbox di Innsbruck, che spesso collabora con l'impresa Vorarlberger Ökohaus (Casa ecologica del Vorarlberg), ha realizzato a Merano una costruzione massiccia in legno per 12 appartamenti. Il progetto dalla tipologia a ballatoio è stato arricchito dagli architetti con una nota mediterranea: un giardino pensile di palme. Per concretizzare questa idea, i progettisti si sono dovuti scontrare con i limiti di portata del legno; è già inconsueto l'impiego esclusivo del legno per la costruzione di un edificio di 4 piani, ma la vera sfida consisteva nel carico sul tetto (i vasi delle palme ed i collettori solari). La costruzione massiccia in legno a setti portanti è stata pertanto posta su uno zoccolo in cemento armato. Tutti gli elementi in legno sono giunti prefabbricati al cantiere e montati in poco tempo; oltre ad essere eco-compatibili, uno dei grandi vantaggi delle costruzioni in legno è infatti la semplicità della gestione logistica del

Holzbox, Baugesellschaft Wolkenstein GmbH., Vorarlberger Ökohaus GmbH.

Wolkenstein housing development, Merano
2003

This housing project is, in fact, an "import" from Austria. The Holzbox team from Innsbruck, which often works with the Vorarlberger Ökohaus Company, carried out a solid timber building in Merano comprising twelve housing units. The architects wanted to use a deck access building type with a Mediterranean note and also designed a palm garden on the roof. In applying their ideas idea they approached the structural limits of timber as a material.

It is unusual enough to erect a four-storey building in timber, but the real challenge in this housing project lay in dealing with the relatively high loads on the roof (solar collectors and the containers with the palm trees). In response the architects chose a solid timber cross-wall system on a concrete plinth. All the timber construction elements were delivered pre-fabricated to the site and could be erected in a short period of time. This reveals one of the major advantages of building in timber; it is not only environmentally friendly but also

die Baustellenlogistik auch wirtschaftlich. Dem hölzernen Gebäude ist eine Stahlkonstruktion vorgelagert, die zur Aufnahme aller Erschließungseinheiten dient. Auch die drei Wohneinheiten pro Ebene sind über diesen äußeren Laubengang erreichbar. In wenigen Jahren wird dieser „Metallraster" von Pflanzen überwuchert sein.

cantiere. Davanti alla costruzione in legno è stata montata una struttura in acciaio che serve ad integrare tutte le unità di distribuzione. I tre appartamenti per piano sono raggiungibili utilizzando questo ballatoio esterno. In pochi anni questo reticolo metallico sarà ricoperto di piante.

economical in terms of building site logistics. A steel structure placed in front of the timber building carries the access decks. Three dwelling units per floor are served by these external decks. In a few years this "metal grid" will be covered by the rampant growth of planting.

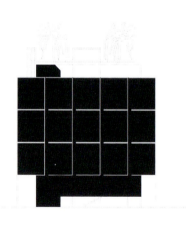

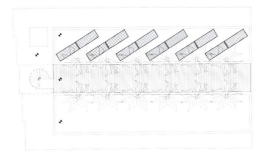

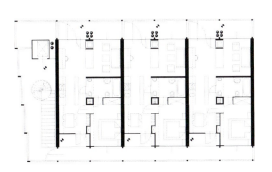 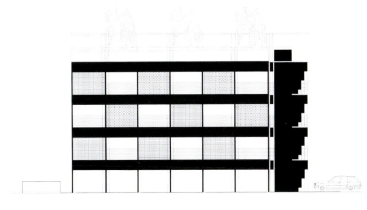

Oswald Zoeggeler
Villa Mozart, Meran
2005

Das Wohnhaus wurde im Villenviertel Merans, einem Stadtteil im Dreieck zwischen der Romstraße und der Straße nach Schenna, errichtet. Dort entstanden um 1900 etliche gründerzeitliche Wohn- und Beherbergungsbauten, die gemeinsam mit den sie umgebenden Parks unter Schutz stehen.
Auch die Villa Mozart wurde auf einem solchen Grundstück mit exotischem Pflanzenbestand geplant. Das hier bestehende Gebäude – ehemals ein bekanntes Luxusrestaurant – musste aufgrund seines mangelhaften Bauzustandes abgerissen werden, wohingegen der ebenfalls hier befindliche Bestand an alten Nadelbäumen bewahrt werden konnte. An der Stelle des Vorgängerbaues entstand ein Mehrfamilienhaus mit einer Wohnung, einem Büro und zwei weiteren Wohneinheiten für die Kinder des Besitzers. Der Baukörper besteht aus zwei würfelförmigen Teilen, die durch ein trapezförmiges Stiegenhaus in ihrem Zentrum miteinander verbunden sind. Die Kuben wurden in schrägem Winkel zueinander unter den Bäumen platziert. Am Grundriss ist erkennbar, dass die quadratischen Grundflächen aufgelöst wurden. Diese „Sprengung" hatte zur Folge, dass ebenfalls schräg zueinander stehende Raumzellen erzeugt werden konnten, in die

Oswald Zoeggeler
Villa Mozart, Merano
2005

L'edificio residenziale è stato realizzato a Merano in un quartiere di ville, in una zona cittadina di forma triangolare compresa tra via Roma e la strada verso Scena.
Qui intorno agli inizi del Millenovecento sorsero parecchi edifici residenziali o destinati all'ospitalità, tipici del periodo, e che ora insieme ai parchi che li circondano sono sottoposti a tutela. Anche Villa Mozart è stata progettata su uno di questi lotti caratterizzato da vecchie piante esotiche. L'edificio esistente, allora un rinomato ristorante di lusso, è stato demolito a causa delle sue condizioni pericolanti, mentre si sono potute salvaguardare le piante conifere esistenti. Al posto dell'edificio precedente è stata edificata una casa plurifamigliare composta da un appartamento, un ufficio e due altre unità abitative per i figli del proprietario. Il corpo di fabbrica consta di due volumi cubici, collegati al centro da un corpo scala trapezoidale. I cubi sono collocati tra gli alberi e si dispongono obliquamente l'uno rispetto all'altro. Dalla pianta si evince come la forma del quadrato sia stata decostruita e che questa "esplosione" ha consentito allo stesso modo di realizzare delle cellule spaziali inclinate le une rispetto alle altre per ospitare il programma spaziale previsto. Nel piano più basso si

Oswald Zoeggeler
Villa Mozart, Merano
2005

This house was erected in the villa district of Merano, an area occupying a triangle between Via Roma and the road leading to Scena. A number of houses and other residential buildings were erected there around 1900; together with the parks surrounding them they are now under a preservation order.
The Villa Mozart was planned on one such site planted with exotic vegetation. The building that previously stood here – once a well-known luxurious restaurant – had to be demolished as it was in a poor condition, but the existing coniferous trees could be saved. The building that was erected in its place contains an apartment, an office and two further dwelling units for the owner's children. It consists of two cube-shaped parts connected at the centre by a trapezoidal staircase. The cubes were placed beneath the trees at an angle to each other. A look at the floor plan reveals how the design "explodes" quadratic areas. This generates spatial cells, also standing at an angle to each other, that easily accommodate the various spaces required

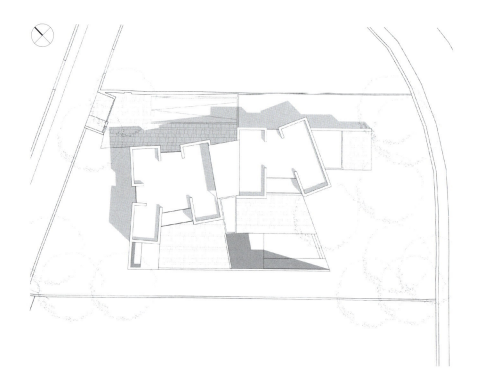

das Raumprogramm eingefügt wurde. Im Tiefgeschoss befindet sich ein großzügiger Saunabereich, in dessen angrenzender Außenzone ein fernöstlicher Garten gestaltet werden soll. In Wiederholung dieses landschaftsarchitektonischen Themas wird ein zweiter solcher Garten am Dach der Villa angelegt.

trova un grande spazio dedicato alla sauna; i suoi spazi esterni saranno allestiti con un giardino ispirato all'estremo oriente. Il tema di questa architettura del paesaggio si ripete sul tetto dove viene allestito un secondo giardino simile al primo.

by the brief. There is a generously sized sauna in the basement, the outdoor area adjoining it will be designed as an oriental garden. As a repetition of this landscaping theme a second, similar garden will be created on the roof of the villa.

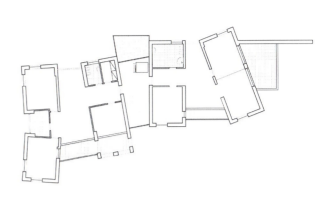
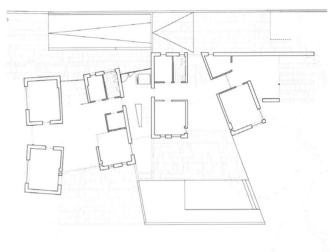
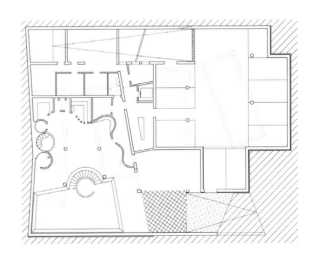

PVC – architects, Margit Klammer,
Steiner Sarnen Schweiz
Die Gärten von Schloss Trauttmansdorff, Meran
2001

Dem Trend zur Schaffung touristischer Erlebniswelten entsprechend, griff man in Meran auf das vorhandene Generalthema des Blumenparadieses zurück und widmete Schloss Trauttmansdorff, einen aus dem 19. Jahrhundert stammenden Ansitz mit Park, in einen botanischen Garten um. Seit seiner Eröffnung entwickelte sich dieser Garten zu einem Publikumsmagneten, denn in ihm vereinen sich ästhetische Ansprüche, Bildungsziele und Wirtschaftlichkeit auf höchst fruchtbare Weise: Der Park umfasst auf 120.000 m^2 Wälder, Teiche, Glashäuser und ein „Touriseum" (Museum für Tourismusgeschichte), das tägliche Besucheraufkommen liegt bei ca. 1.200.

Da diese Gärten nicht im Dienst der Wissenschaft stehen, wurde vor allem auf ihre optische Gestaltung Wert gelegt. Seit Beginn der Planung waren hier Künstler und Architekten Seite an Seite mit Landschaftsgestaltern und Gärtnern tätig. Bisher sind elf Pavillons realisiert. Manche dienen als Informationszentren oder Rastplätze, andere wurden wie Gesamtkunstwerke pittoresk zwischen die Pflanzen eingefügt. Damit erinnert die Gartenanlage an historische Vorbilder, in denen es ebenfalls fantasieanregende Attraktionen – meist mit

PVC – architects, Margit Klammer,
Steiner Sarnen Svizzera
I giardini di Castel Trauttmansdorff, Merano
2001

In conformità alla tendenza che vede sempre più diffondersi i parchi a tema, Merano ha attinto alla locale tradizione del giardino delle meraviglie, ed il Castello di Trauttmansdorff con il suo parco risalenti al 19. secolo sono stati trasformati in orto botanico. Da quando il parco è stato inaugurato, riunendo con il massimo effetto ambizioni estetiche, obbiettivi pedagogici e ritorno economico, esso è diventato una forte attrattiva per il pubblico. I 120.000 mq del parco ospitano boschi, stagni, serre e il „Touriseum" (Museo Provinciale del Turismo), l'afflusso giornaliero è di circa 1.200 visitatori.

Non essendo i giardini un'istituzione scientifica, si è potuto puntare tutto sulla loro definizione estetico-compositiva. Sin dall'inizio artisti ed architetti hanno collaborato fianco a fianco con paesaggisti e giardinieri. Sino ad oggi sono stati realizzati undici padiglioni. Alcuni sono utilizzati come punti informativi o luoghi di sosta, altri sono delle opere d'arte inserite in modo pittoresco nel verde. L'impianto dei giardini rimanda ad esempi storici in cui erano presenti attrazioni fantastiche intitolate per lo

PVC – architects, Margit Klammer,
Steiner Sarnen Switzerland
The Gardens of Schloss Trauttmansdorff, Merano
2001

Reflecting a general trend toward the creation of tourist-oriented "experiences", in Merano the existing theme of a floral paradise was taken up again and Schloss Trauttmansdorff, a 19th century country house and park, was rezoned as a botanical garden. Since its opening this garden has developed into a major public attraction as it combines aesthetic qualities, educational goals and profitability in a highly fruitful manner. The park, which measures 120,000 square metres in area, includes woods, ponds glasshouses and a "Touriseum" (museum of the history of tourism). The daily number of visitors is around 1,200.

As these gardens do not serve scientific research, the primary emphasis was laid on visual design. From the very start of planning artists and architects worked side-by-side with landscape designers and gardeners. To date eleven pavilions have been completed. Some serve as information centres or places to rest, whereas others are like "Gesamtkuntswerke" picturesquely placed between the plants. In this sense the garden recalls some of its historical

französischen Namen wie „Mon Repos" – gab. Dieser Tradition folgend, errichtete man in Meran an einem erhöhten Standort eine Volière, die zugleich als „Belvedere" die Funktion erfüllt, wunderschöne Ausblicke auf den Garten und seine Umgebung freizugeben.

più con nomi francesi, come „Mon Repos". Seguendo questa tradizione in posizione elevata è stata realizzata una voliera che soddisfa al contempo la funzione di belvedere e offre una splendida vista sui giardini e dintorni.

predecessors that were often dotted with attractions to stimulate the fantasy, generally given French names such as "Mon Repos". In accordance with this tradition an aviary was erected here at an elevated location. It also functions as a belvedere offering wonderful views of the gardens and the surroundings.

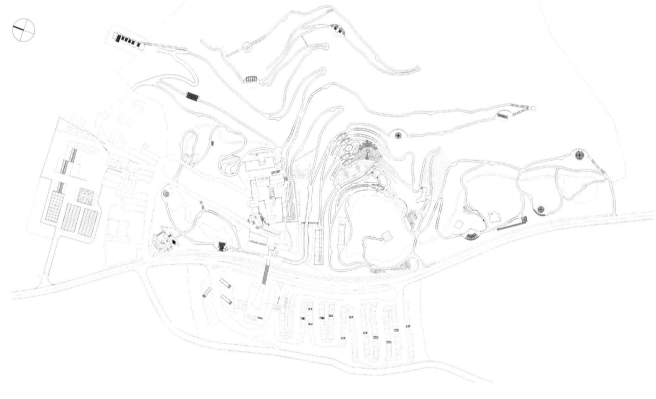

Herbstpavillon
Padiglione d'autunno
Autumn pavilion

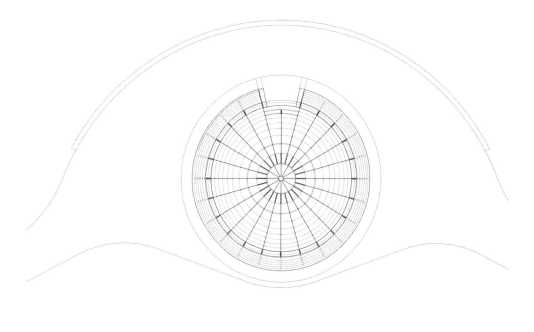
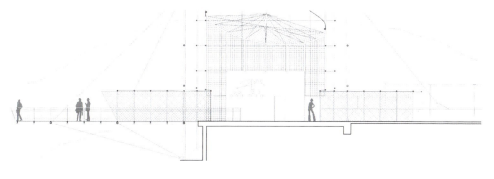

145

Voliere
Voliera
Aviary

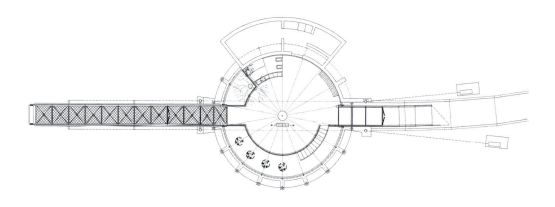
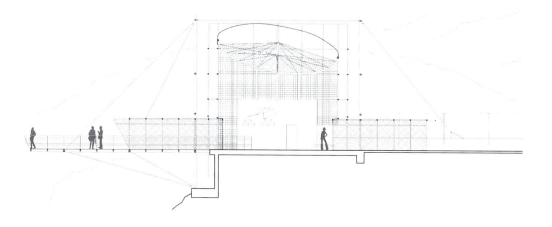

Flaumeichenwald-Pavillon
Padiglione del bosco di roverelle
Pavilion in the Downy Oak wood

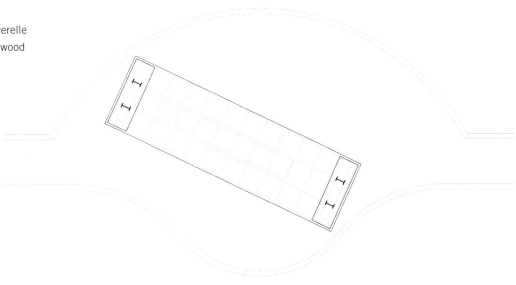

Herbert Jerabek, Besucher

„Die Symbiose mit moderner Architektur, die Durchgängigkeit der Elemente gefällt mir sehr gut. Es verbindet sich sehr gut mit dem Alten."

Herbert Jerabek, visitatore.

"La simbiosi con l'architettura moderna, la continuità tra gli elementi mi piace molto.
Si abbina alla perfezione con il passato."

Herbert Jerabek, visitor

"The symbiosis with modern architecture and the permeable, open quality of the individual elements are what I especially like. It's combined very successfully with the old substance."

S.O.F.A. architekten mit Georg Mitterhofer
Besucherzentrum „Die Gärten von Schloss Trauttmansdorff", Meran
2004
Kunst am Bau: Doris Krüger

S.O.F.A. architetti con Georg Mitterhofer
Centro visite "I giardini di Castel Trauttmansdorff", Merano
2004
Intervento artistico: Doris Krüger

S.O.F.A. architekten with Georg Mitterhofer
Visitors centre "The Gardens of Schloss Trauttmansdorff", Merano
2004
Site-specific artwork: Doris Krüger

S.O.F.A. architekten waren schon mit Pius Pircher in die Sanierung von Schloss Trauttmansdorff und den Neubau eines Restaurants eingebunden, später wirkten sie gemeinsam mit Georg Mitterhofer beim geladenen Wettbewerb für das Besucherzentrum mit.

Eine neue Zufahrtsstraße trennt den Botanischen Garten von den Parkplätzen und dem Besucherzentrum. Die Zonen für das Parken befinden sich auf Terrassen, die sich in einer Schlangenlinie zum Fuß des Eingangsgebäudes hinziehen. Ein Teil des Besucherzentrums ragt über die oberste Terrassenkante hinaus, wo es auf schrägen Stützen aufliegt, die an Baumstämme erinnern. Dieser schattige Platz wird von einem an der Gebäudeunterkante entspringenden Wasservorhang abgeschlossen.

Der Baukörper hat U-Form und mäandriert ebenfalls leicht um einen kleinen Lichthof mit Bambuswäldchen. Das Gebäude besteht aus zwei Betonplatten, die von schräg durch das Besucherzentrum laufenden Stützen wie von überdimensionalen Zahnstochern zusammengehalten werden. Für die Außenverkleidung wurde stark gemusterter, roter brasilianischer Granit verwendet. Im Inneren wurden Räume wie frei

S.O.F.A. architetti erano coinvolti assieme a Pius Pircher nella ristrutturazione di Castel Trauttmansdorff e nella nuova edificazione di un ristorante. In seguito insieme a Georg Mitterhofer hanno partecipato al concorso a invito per il centro visite.

Una nuova strada di accesso divide il parco botanico dai parcheggi e dal centro visite. Le zone destinate a parcheggio si trovano su terrazze che si svolgono come una serpentina fino ai piedi dell'edificio d'ingresso. Il centro visite aggetta sulla terrazza più in alto, sorretto da colonne oblique che ricordano tronchi d'albero. Questo spazio all'ombra è delimitato da un velo d'acqua che scaturisce dal profilo inferiore dell'edificio. Il corpo di fabbrica con pianta ad "U" si snoda intorno ad una piccola corte con un boschetto di bambù. L'edificio è composto da due solai in cemento tenuti insieme e sorretti da colonne oblique che attraversano gli spazi del centro visite come degli stuzzicadenti sovradimensionati. Il rivestimento esterno in granito rosso brasiliano decora vivacemente gli esterni. All'interno i locali sono stati strutturati come fossero dei mobili liberamente spostabili. Dei box impiallacciati in legno di noce contengono i bagni e gli spazi per la pausa delle guide

S.O.F.A. architekten had been involved with Pius Pircher in the renovation of Schloss Trauttmansdorff and the construction of a new restaurant there, they subsequently worked together with Georg Mitterhofer on a design for an invited entry competition for the visitors centre.

A new approach road separates the botanical gardens from the car park and the visitors centre. The parking zones are arranged in a series of terraces extending in a serpentine line down to the foot of the entrance building. Part of the visitors centre that projects beyond the edge of the uppermost terrace is supported by inclined struts reminiscent of tree trunks. This shady area is defined by a curtain of water falling from the underside of the building

The volume is U-shaped in plan and meanders somewhat around a small courtyard with a little bamboo grove. The building consists of two concrete slabs held together by piers resembling giant toothpicks that penetrate the visitors centre at an angle. A strongly patterned red Brazilian granite was used for the external cladding. Inside the building the rooms are placed like flexible pieces of furniture: "boxes" veneered in nut wood contain the sanitary facilities

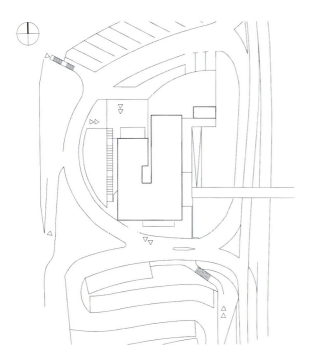 

bewegliche Möbel platziert: Mit Nussholz furnierte Boxen beinhalten die Sanitäreinrichtungen und die Pausenräume der Gartenführer, große Kästen aus Birkensperrholz die Kassen. Silbergrau beschichtete Platten grenzen den Shop ab.

del giardino, grandi armadi in truciolare di betulla contengono le casse. Pannelli rivestiti di grigio argento delimitano lo spazio di vendita.

and relaxation rooms for the guides and large "chests" of birch plywood house the cash desks. Panels with a silver-grey finish define the shop area.

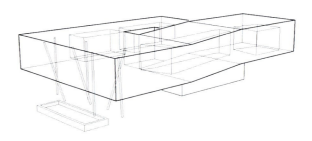

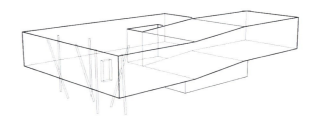

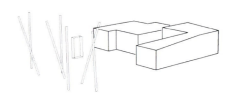

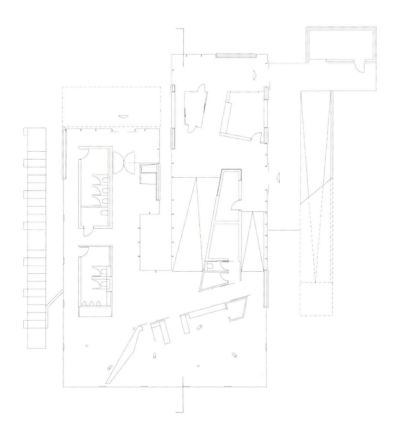
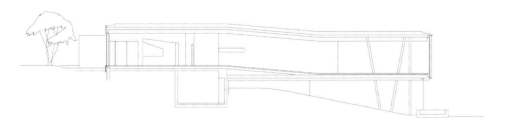

Peter Plattner
Landwirtschaftliches Betriebsgebäude, Ladstätterhof, Sinich bei Meran
2003

Peter Plattner
Azienda agricola Ladstätterhof, Sinigo presso Merano
2003

Peter Plattner
Agricultural building, Ladstätterhof, Sinigo near Merano
2003

Das land- und forstwirtschaftliche Versuchszentrum Laimburg in Auer verwaltet die Güter der Autonomen Provinz Bozen-Südtirol. Zu diesen Gütern gehört auch der Ladstätterhof bei Meran, wo auf ca. 18 ha Agrarland vor allem Äpfel angebaut werden. Der hier entstandene Gutshof konnte sich nicht am Bautyp des Bauernhofs orientieren, denn moderne Landwirtschaftsbetriebe werden als Industrieunternehmen geführt, was großen Einfluss auf ihre Gestaltung hat: In optischer Hinsicht müssen große Bauvolumen in die Landschaft integriert werden, außerdem muss das architektonische Programm auch agrar-ökonomischen Ansprüchen gerecht werden, v. a. in Bezug auf die Optimierung von Arbeitsabläufen.
Das Hofgebäude wurde am Fuß eines Osthanges an der Stelle errichtet, wo der Hang in die Ebene übergeht. Ein Teil der Betriebsflächen wurde unter die Erde verlegt, um ihre relativ großen Volumen unsichtbar zu machen. In den holzverkleideten Boxen über den Lagerräumen und Garagen befinden sich zwei Wohnungen bzw. die Zimmer der Saisonarbeiter. An der Nordseite des Komplexes wurde ein großer Unterstand angebaut. Er wird für die kurzfristige Lagerung der gefüllten Obstkisten während der Ernte benötigt. Neben den Garagentoren

Il centro per la sperimentazione agraria e forestale Laimburg amministra le proprietà terriere della Provincia Autonoma di Bolzano. Il Ladstätterhof vicino Merano fa parte di queste proprietà, con una superficie agricola di circa 18 ettari destinati prevalentemente alla coltivazione delle mele. La tenuta che qui si è avviata, non poteva ispirarsi alla tipologia edilizia del maso contadino, perché le moderne aziende agricole sono gestite come imprese industriali, la qual cosa ha un notevole effetto sulla loro definizione formale: visivamente i volumi edilizi devono integrarsi nel paesaggio, ma il programma architettonico e funzionale deve soddisfare anche i requisiti di economicità di un'azienda agricola, soprattutto per quanto riguarda l'ottimizzazione dei processi produttivi. L'edificio agricolo è stato collocato ai piedi di un pendio orientato ad est, dove inizia la pianura. Una parte delle superfici aziendali è stata interrata per nascondere il loro volume relativamente ingombrante. Sopra i depositi e le rimesse, nei box rivestiti in legno, si collocano gli appartamenti e le stanze dei lavoratori stagionali. Sul lato nord del complesso è stato eretto un capannone, che è utilizzato per lo stoccaggio temporaneo delle casse di frutta riempite durante la raccolta. Accan-

The Laimburg agriculture- and forestry-testing centre in Ora administers the farms owned by the autonomous province of Bolzano-South Tyrol. These include the Ladstätterhof near Merano which has around 18 hectares of agricultural land devoted primarily to the cultivation of apples. The new building erected here could not be based on a traditional farmhouse type, as modern agricultural businesses are run like industries, which of course has a major influence on their design. In visual terms this involves integrating large volumes in the landscape and, additionally, the architectural programme must also meet the agricultural and economic requirements, above all as regards optimisation of the work process.
The building was erected at the point where an east-facing slope meets level ground. Part of the building was put underground to disguise its relatively large volume. There are two apartments and rooms for seasonal workers in the timber clad boxes above the storerooms and garages. A large shelter added to the north side of the complex is

sind mit Holzlamellen verkleidete Konstruktionen zu sehen, hinter denen sich ein Teil der Landwirtschaftsmaschinen verbirgt. Sie wurden an dieser Stelle untergebracht, weil es hier besonders einfach ist, Maschinen zu wechseln.

to ai portoni delle rimesse si vedono delle costruzioni rivestite con lamelle di legno, dietro alle quali si nascondono una parte delle macchine agricole, che vi sono ospitate, perchè sono un luogo particolarmente agevole per cambiare i macchinari.

used during the harvest for the short-term storage of packed fruit crates. Structures clad with timber louvers beside the garage doors conceal some of the farm machinery. They were located here because it is a particularly suitable place to change machines

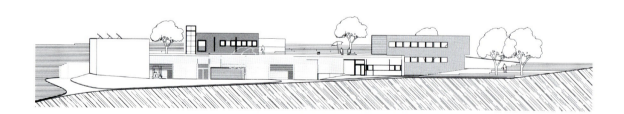

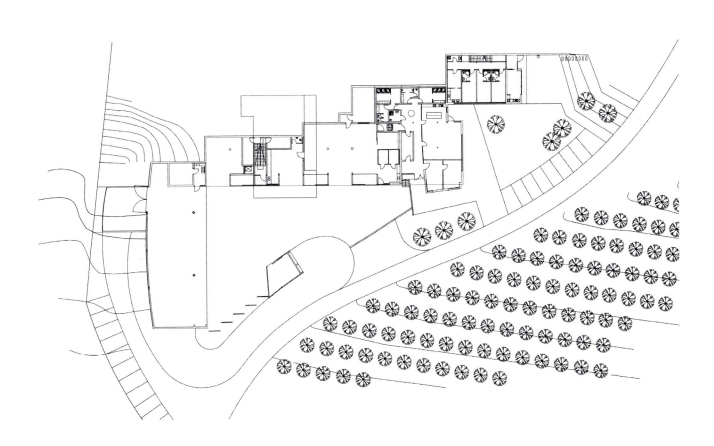

155

Stefan Hitthaler
Mühlbauerhof, Gargazon
2004

Das Ehepaar Kiem plante einen kleinen, privaten Wettbewerb auszuschreiben, um aus mehreren Entwürfen ihr ideales Wohnhaus auswählen zu können, und stieß im Zuge der Vorbereitungen auf die Konkurrenz auf den Architekten, der ihren Bauernhof schließlich als Direktauftrag planen und umsetzen sollte. Die Bauaufgabe umfasste ein Wohnhaus und eine Einliegerwohnung für den Vater der Bauherrin. Beim Entwurf spielte diese Einliegerwohnung eine bedeutende Rolle, da dem Vater der Hoferbin, dem „Mühlbauer", eine besonders schöne Wohngelegenheit geschaffen werden sollte. Der Baukörper wurde über einem im Verhältnis zu den Wohnebenen mindestens dreimal so großen Keller errichtet. In diesem Untergeschoss befinden sich Räume für Landwirtschaftsmaschinen, Lager, Garagen und ein Degustationsbereich mit Weinkeller für den Bauherrn, einen ausgewiesenen Wein-Fachmann. In den übrigen Bereichen des Hauses leben mehrere Generationen von Menschen sowohl miteinander als auch in einer für jeden von ihnen geschützten Privatsphäre, denn im Grunde wurden zwei Häuser errichtet: ein größeres für die junge Familie, ein kleineres für den Altbauern. Im Erdgeschoss wurden die Wohnbereiche durch einen überdachten Durchgang voneinander getrennt, wohinge-

Stefan Hitthaler
Mühlbauerhof, Gargazzone
2004

I signori Kiem hanno avuto l'idea di bandire un piccolo concorso privato per poter così scegliere tra più progetti, quello ideale per la loro casa. Durante la preparazione della gara hanno conosciuto l'architetto a cui infine affidare l'incarico diretto per progettare e realizzare il loro maso. Il progetto comprende una casa d'abitazione con un appartamento autonomo per il padre della committente. Questo appartamento ha giocato un ruolo importante nella fase progettuale, perché per l'abitazione del padre dell'erede del maso, il signor Mühlbauer, era richiesta una soluzione estetica particolare. Il corpo di fabbrica si sviluppa su di una cantina di dimensioni tre volte maggiori della superficie abitabile. Al piano inferiore trovano spazio i locali per le macchine agricole, i depositi, le rimesse ed una zona degustazione con cantina per il committente, un esperto di vini. Nella parte restante dell'edificio convivono diverse generazioni di persone e per ognuna è riservato anche un ambito privato. In realtà sono state realizzate due case, una più grande per la giovane famiglia, ed una più piccola per l'anziano contadino. Al piano terra gli spazi abitativi sono separati da un passaggio coperto, mentre al primo piano quasi tutte le stanze da letto sono collegate da un grande balcone. I committen-

Stefan Hitthaler
Mühlbauer farm, Gargazzone
2004

The Kiems are a married couple that originally planned to set up a small private competition that would enable them to select their ideal home from a number of different projects. In the course of the preparatory work for the competition they met the architect who was finally to plan and build their farmhouse as a direct commission. The brief comprised a dwelling house with a separate flat for Mrs Kiem's father. This "grandfather" flat played an important role in the design, as the couple wanted to provide a particularly pleasant home for the "Mühlbauer" (literally mill farmer) from whom Mrs Kiem will inherit the farm.
The building was erected above a basement that is at least three times as large as the living level. This basement contains space for agricultural machinery, storerooms, garages and a degustation area with a wine cellar for Mr Kiem, who is a wine expert. In the remaining areas of the house the different generations live together, but each has a protected private zone, as essentially two houses were built: one for the young family, and a smaller one for the retired farmer. At ground floor level a roofed passageway separates the living areas from each other, whereas at first floor level a generously dimensioned balcony connects almost all the bedrooms. The clients wanted to have

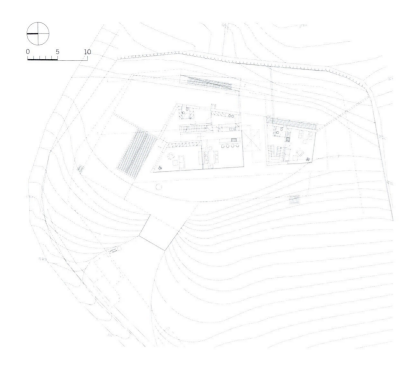

gen fast alle Schlafräume im ersten Stock durch einen großzügigen Balkon miteinander in Verbindung stehen. Die Auftraggeber wünschten sich ein geerdetes Haus, weshalb es in massiver Bauweise errichtet und an seiner Rückseite in einen künstlich geschaffenen Erdwall hineingesetzt wurde.

ti desideravano una casa ben radicata al suolo, pertanto l'edificio è una costruzione massiccia interrata sul retro in un cuneo di terra riportata artificialmente.

a truly "grounded" house, which explains why it was built using a solid construction system and is inserted at the rear into an artificially created earth embankment.

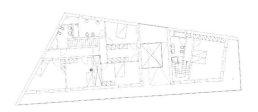

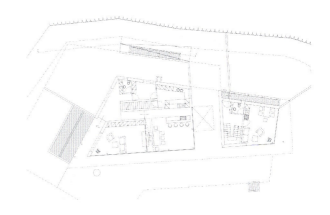

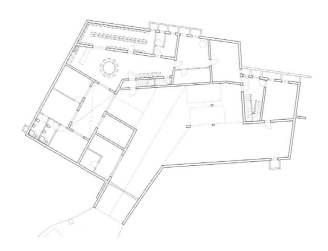

Walter Angonese, Silvia Boday

Personalwohnhaus Goëss-Enzenberg, Siebeneich
2003

In Siebeneich, einer kleinen Ortschaft zwischen Bozen und Meran, liegen die Goëss-Enzenberg'schen Obstanlagen. Sie werden genauso wie die Weinberge des Goëss-Enzenberg'schen Guts „Manincor" teils von Saisoniers, teils von Arbeitern in Dauerstellung bewirtschaftet.

Für die Unterbringung der langjährigen Mitarbeiter im Obstbau entstand ein Personalwohnhaus, das in Bezug auf seine Errichtung preisgünstig und sein Aussehen schlicht und funktional sein sollte. Es besteht aus einem längs ausgerichteten, rechteckigen Baukörper, der auf zwei kubischen Bauteilen aufliegt. Die ebenerdigen Kuben beinhalten Lager, Keller und Heizraum, dazwischen wurde eine aus der „Brücke" herunterführende Stiege frei abgehängt. Über die Treppe gelangt man in den Bauteil darüber, wo sich in einem die zwei kubischen Stützen mit den Nebenräumen waagrecht überbrückenden Riegel die Wohnungen befinden. Blickt man von der Durchzugsstraße auf das Wohnhaus, präsentiert es sich als ein mit weinrotem Wellblech verschaltes, an drei Seiten relativ geschlossenes Gebäude, dessen Dach von einer großen Gaube überhöht wird. Durch den Dachaufbau wird Tageslicht in das Stiegenhaus geführt. Während die drei tragenden Wandscheiben den Riegel zur Straße hin wie ein beliebig in die Landschaft gesetztes Lagerhaus erscheinen lassen, bedingt das Metallfachwerk an der gegenüberliegenden Seite der Fassade, dass die Wohnungen in Südrichtung mit großen Fenstern und einem behaglichen Balkon ausgestattet werden konnten.

Walter Angonese, Silvia Boday

Residenza per il personale Goëss-Enzenberg, Settequerce
2004

A Settequerce, una piccola località tra Bolzano e Merano, si trovano le coltivazioni di frutta di Goëss-Enzenberg.

Come i vigneti della tenuta di Manincor, i terreni sono curati in parte da avventizi, in parte da personale dell'azienda. Per dare ospitalità ai vecchi dipendenti è stata realizzata una residenza per il personale, che doveva avere un arredo economico, possedere un'immagine sobria ed essere al contempo funzionale. L'edificio si compone di un corpo parallelepipedo che poggia alle estremità su due cubi. A piano terra questi contengono un deposito, cantina e locale termico. Dal ponte sospeso scende una scala appesa, dalla quale si raggiungono gli appartamenti del piano superiore, dove le due strutture portanti con locali accessori realizzano la stecca orizzontale. Guardando dalla strada di transito, l'edificio rivestito in lamiera rosso vinaccia si presenta parzialmente chiuso su tre lati mentre il tetto si innalza con un grande abbaino. Il corpo scala è illuminato dalla luce diurna grazie alla costruzione sulla copertura. Se i tre setti portanti, privi di finestre, caratterizzano l'immagine dell'edificio verso la strada come un deposito piazzato a caso nel paesaggio, la struttura reticolare sul lato meridionale consente di dotare gli appartamenti di grandi finestre ed un piacevole balcone.

Walter Angonese, Silvia Boday

Goëss-Enzenberg staff residence, Settequerce
2004

The Goëss-Enzeberg orchards lie in Settequerce, a small community between Bolzano and Merano. Just like at the "Manincor" vineyard owned by the same family the orchards are cultivated and harvested jointly by seasonal staff and full time employees.

To provide living accommodation for the long-term orchard workers a staff residential building was erected that was intended to be economic in terms of construction costs and simple and functional in appearance. It consists of an elongated rectangular volume resting on two cubic elements. The cubes at ground level contain storerooms, cellars and boiler room, between them a staircase is freely suspended from the connecting "bridge". This stairs leads to the part of the building above where the apartments are located in the horizontal wing bridging the two cubic supports containing the service spaces. Seen from the main road the residential building, clad with wine-red corrugated metal, is relatively closed on three sides and the roof is crowned by a large dormer. Through this rooftop element daylight enters the staircase space. Whereas the three load-bearing wall panels facing the road give the block the appearance of a warehouse set in the landscape, the metal frame on the opposite (south-facing) façade allowed the apartments to be provided with large windows and a pleasant balcony.

Bozen-Tramin-Leifers   Bolzano-Termeno-Laives

Città di Bolzano – Questo monumento fu eretto durante il regime fascista per celebrare la vittoria dell'Italia nella Prima Guerra Mondiale. Essa comportò anche la divisione del Tirolo e la separazione della popolazione di questa terra dalla madrepatria austriaca.
La Città di Bolzano, libera e democratica, condanna le divisioni e le discriminazioni del passato e ogni forma di nazionalismo, e si impegna con spirito europeo a promuovere la cultura della pace e della fratellanza.
2004

City of Bolzano – Italy's fascist regime erected this monument to celebrate victory in First World War, an event which brought with it the division of Tyrol and the separation of the population of South Tyrol from Austria, their mother country.
The City of Bolzano, a free, modern and democratic town, condemns the discrimination and divisions of the past, as well as all forms of nationalism and pledges its commitment to promoting a culture of fraternity and peace in the true European spirit.
2004

Gedenktafeln am Siegesplatz in Bozen
Tavole commemorative in Piazza della Vittoria a Bolzano
Memorial plaque on Piazza della Vittoria (Victory Square) in Bolzano

Werner Tscholl
Haus Mumelter, Bozen
2000

Der Baugrund des Wohnhauses liegt am Stadtrand von Bozen, wo sich das besiedelte Gebiet allmählich mit landwirtschaftlich genutztem mischt. Hier im Zentrum des Talkessels ist es möglich, herrliche Ausblicke auf die Berge in der Umgebung zu genießen. Das animierte den Architekten, das Gebäude im übertragenen Sinn wie einen Fern-Seher in die Landschaft zu setzen. Allerdings brachte er diesen für die weitere Gestaltung des Hauses wichtigen Ansatz in eine abstrakte architektonische Form, die zudem davon geprägt ist, dass der Hausherr sich auch als Weinbauer betätigt. Auf der weiten Ebene vor dem Haus wachsen die Reben, aus deren Trauben ein besonders edler Wein namens „Taber" gekeltert wird.

Aus der Ferne betrachtet, scheint das Haus in einem grünen, aus den Blättern der Reben bestehenden See zu ruhen. Dieser optische Effekt des Hauses auf dem grünen Teppich wird dadurch verursacht, dass das ebenerdige Geschoss des Gebäudes auf einer erhöhten Plattform bzw. der Unterseite eines weißen Rahmens, der um die Südseite des Hauses herumgezogen worden ist, zu liegen kommt. Der eigentliche Baukörper der Wohnräume wurde von der Außenkante zurückversetzt in den Rahmen hineingebaut, was sich positiv auf die Beschattung der Südfassade und der ebenfalls im Inneren des Rahmens liegenden Terrasse auswirkt. Das äußere Erschei-

Werner Tscholl
Casa Mumelter, Bolzano
2000

Il terreno su cui sorge la casa si trova al limite della città di Bolzano, dove il territorio urbano si confonde con quello a destinazione agricola. Qui, dal centro della vallata, si gode di una splendida vista sulle montagne del circondario. Queste condizioni hanno convinto l'architetto a disporre l'edificio come fosse un schermo attraverso il quale si osserva il paesaggio. Questo approccio, importante per la definizione complessiva dell'edificio, si è tradotto in forme astratte influenzate dal fatto che il committente si occupa anche di viticoltura. Nella piana antistante l'edificio crescono le vigne, dalle quali si ottiene un vino d'eccezione, denominato "Taber". Da lontano la casa sembra riposare su un lago verde, formato dal fogliame del vigneto. Quest'effetto ottico si genera, poichè il pian terreno dell'edificio poggia su di una piattaforma rialzata, ovvero sulla base della cornice bianca che delimita la facciata sud. Il vero contenitore dell'abitazione è arretrato rispetto al bordo esterno della cornice. L'arretramento consente un migliore ombreggiamento della facciata meridionale e della terrazza.

Werner Tscholl
Mumelter House, Bolzano
2000

The site of this house is on the edge of the town of Bolzano where the built-up area gradually blends with land still used for agricultural purposes. Here, at the centre of the enclosed valley, there are marvellous views of the surrounding mountain. This fact stimulated the architect to interpret the building as a kind of viewing apparatus placed in the landscape. However, he gave his original starting point for the design of the house an abstract architectural form that is additionally influenced by the fact the client is also a winegrower.

Vines grow on the broad plain in front of the house, a particularly fine wine called "Taber" is made from their grapes.

Seen from a distance the house appears to lie in a green sea of vine leaves. This visual effect of a building on a green carpet is achieved by the fact the ground floor of the building sits on an elevated platform, on the underside of a white frame that has been constructed around the south side of the building. The volume containing the living spaces is recessed in this frame, which provides shade for the south facade and for

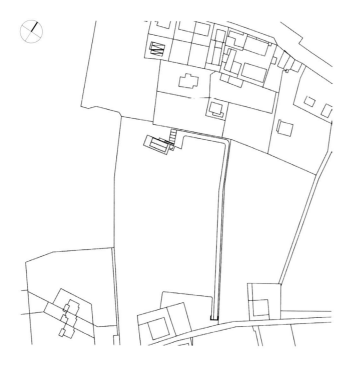

nungsbild des mit Ausnahme des Kellers aus massivem Holz bestehenden Hauses wird vom Weiß des verputzten Rahmens und der dunklen Beize des Baukörpers mit den Wohnräumen dominiert.

L'aspetto esterno del corpo di fabbrica che, ad esclusione della cantina, è costruito completamente in legno, è caratterizzato dal colore bianco dell'intonaco della cornice e dal mordente scuro del volume abitativo.

the terrace that lies within the frame. Apart from the basement the external appearance of this solid timber house is dominated by the white of the rendered frame and the dark stain used on the volume containing the living spaces.

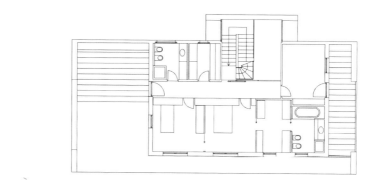

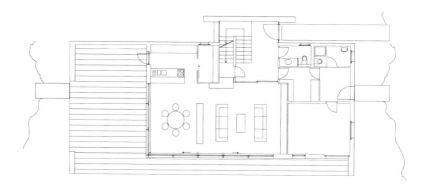

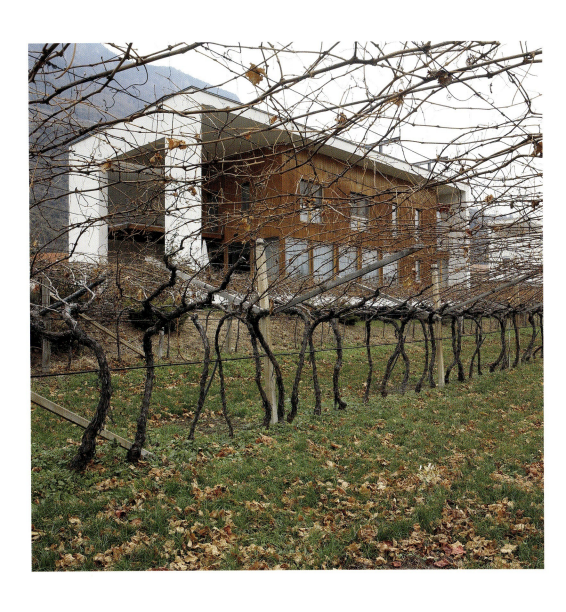

Pardeller+Putzer+Scherer

Turnhalle der deutschsprachigen Grundschule „A. Rosmini", Bozen-Gries
2003

Noch um 1900 wurden „Bozner Agrumen" (Südfrüchte) bis nach München, Prag und Wien geliefert. Das war der Grund, warum sich am Standort der „Rosmini-Schule" in Bozen-Gries früher eine Gärtnerei mit Gewächshäusern für Zitrusfrüchte befand, die später dem mittlerweile denkmalgeschützten Ensemble mit Kirche, Schule und Kindergarten wich. In der schönen Wohngegend Bozens hat sich viel vom mediterranen Flair des Fin de Siècle erhalten, was die Architekten dazu animierte, sich beim Turnsaalbau am Thema der Orangerie zu orientieren und die typische Flora der Umgebung in ihre Ideen einzubeziehen. Die Halle wurde entlang dem Gehsteig wie eine Wanne in die Erde versenkt und an allen Seiten verglast. Auf diese Weise gewinnen die Benutzer des Turnsaales den Eindruck, sie befänden sich im Freien. Von der Straße kann man durch den gläsernen Saal auf die Schule sehen – in der Dämmerung ist ein Blick von hier aus besonders reizvoll.
Bei der Konstruktion der Halle wurde eine Lösung für folgendes Problem gesucht: Tragwerk und Verglasung sollten möglichst leicht und trotzdem ballwurfsicher sein. Das führte dazu, dass Stützen und Glas nicht zu einer Fassade verbunden, sondern voneinander getrennt wurden. So konnte den Stahlträgern eine dünne Glasmembran

Pardeller, Putzer e Scherer

Palestra della scuola elementare di lingua tedesca "A. Rosmini", Bolzano-Gries
2003

Ancora intorno al volgere del secolo scorso gli "agrumi di Bolzano" erano esportati sino a Monaco, Praga e Vienna. Per questo motivo nel quartiere di Gries al posto della scuola Rosmini una volta c'era una giardineria con serre per la coltivazione degli agrumi. In seguito vi sorse l'insieme, comprendente la chiesa, la scuola e l'asilo, che ora è sottoposto a vincolo di tutela. In questa bella zona residenziale si respira ancora l'atmosfera mediterranea di fine secolo, e questo ha convinto gli architetti ad orientarsi sul tema dell'orangerie per la costruzione di una palestra ed a confrontarsi con la tipica flora del luogo. Incassato come una vasca nel terreno, il padiglione della palestra è provvisto di pareti vetrate su tutti i lati e dall'interno i suoi utenti possono percepire la sensazione di trovarsi all'aperto. Dalla strada attraverso la sala vetrata si può vedere la scuola – al tramonto questo punto di osservazione è particolarmente interessante.
Il progetto della palestra ha risolto il seguente quesito: realizzare una struttura portante ed una facciata vetrata possibilmente leggere ma resistenti alle pallonate. Colonne e vetrata non sono integrate per comporre una facciata, ma separate. In questo modo si è potuto anteporre alle colonne d'acciaio una membrana di vetro

Pardeller+Putzer+Scherer

Gymnasium of the German-language elementary school "A. Rosmini", Bolzano-Gries
2003

Around 1900 the so-called "agrumi di Bolzano" (citrus fruits) were still being exported to Munich, Prague and Vienna. This explains why on the site of the "Rosmini School" in Bolzano-Gries there was once a market garden with glasshouses for citrus fruits, which later made way for an ensemble consisting of a church, school and kindergarten that is now under a protection order. In this lovely residential area of Bolzano a considerable amount of the Mediterranean fin-de-siècle air has been preserved, which animated the architects to use the theme of the orangery for the design of the gymnasium and to integrate the typical flora of the surroundings in their ideas. Flanking the footpath the hall was embedded into the ground like a tub and glazed above on all sides. Thus users of the sports hall almost have the impression that they are outdoors. From the road one can see the school through the glazed hall – at dusk the view here is particularly attractive.
The architects sought a solution to the following problem in constructing of the hall: the structure and the glazing were to be as light as possible but yet able to resist the impact of energetically hurled balls. Hence the struts and the glass are not connected to form a single façade but are separated

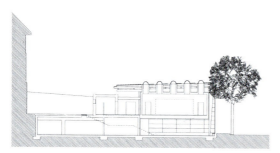 

von nur 40 mm Stärke vorgesetzt werden. Zur Befestigung der Gläser wurde eine elastisch schwingende Hängekonstruktion entwickelt, deren senkrecht verlaufende Spannseile in den Fugen zwischen den Scheiben verlegt sind.

dello spessore di soli quaranta millimetri. Per il fissaggio delle lastre di vetro è stata sviluppata una tensostruttura elastica i cui cavi verticali scorrono nascosti tra le fughe del vetro.

from each other. It was therefore possible to place a glass membrane only 40 mm thick in front of the steel structure. To fix the glazing a flexible suspended system was used in which vertical tension cables were laid in the joints between the glass panes.

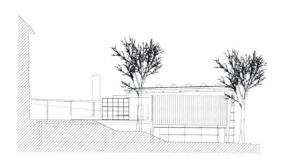 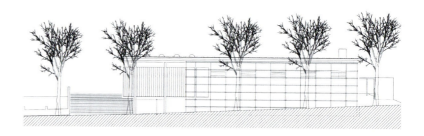

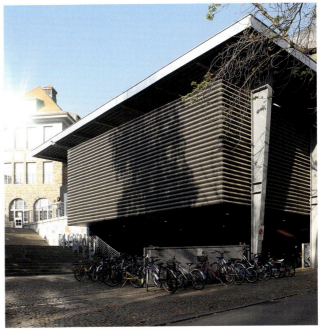
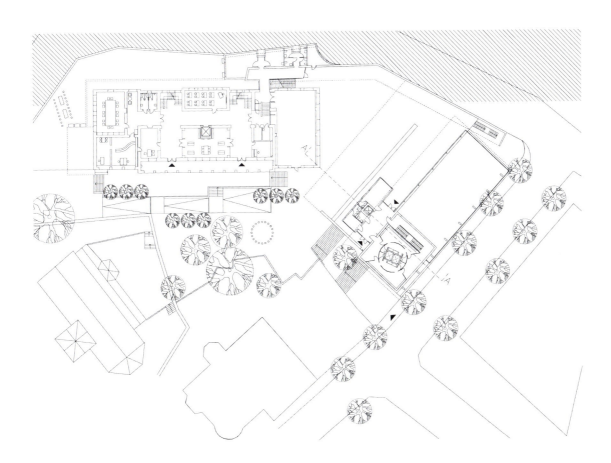

Christoph Mayr Fingerle
Realgymnasium, Bozen
2001
Kunst am Bau: Manfred Alois Mayr

Das Gymnasium war von Marcello Aquilina geplant, nach dessen Tod von seinen Mitarbeitern 1977 vollendet, später aber stark verändert worden. Dieser Schulbau war schon immer bemerkenswert: Er ging von der Frage aus, was Architektur dazu beitragen kann, dass eine Schule auch als Lebensraum begriffen und angenommen wird. Die jüngste Renovierung und Erweiterung des Gebäudes lehnt sich an diese Ausgangslage an und unternimmt den Versuch, diesem Leitmotiv zu neuer Lesbarkeit zu verhelfen: Das Gymnasium befindet sich vor einem Hang und die ansteigende Lage des Bauplatzes wurde dafür genützt, um am hinteren, erhöht liegenden Teil des Baukörpers Nebeneingänge, Pausenplätze usw. zu errichten. Nun wurden dort auch neue Klassen angelegt. Das Gebäude wurde so zwischen die zwei unterschiedlichen Niveaus in Längsrichtung zur Straße hineingesetzt, dass die Klassen im „Split-Level"-System angeordnet werden konnten. Auf diese Weise war es möglich, den direkten Zusammenhang zwischen Topographie und Architektur auch in Bezug auf die innere, dreischiffige Raumaufteilung weiterzuverfolgen. Bereits in der Planungsphase kam es zur Zusammenarbeit zwischen Architekt und Künstler, und vielleicht ist das der Grund für die große Stärke von Umbau und Erweiterung: Im respektvollen Umgang mit

Christoph Mayr Fingerle
Liceo scientifico, Bolzano
2001
Intervento artistico: Manfred Alois Mayr

Il liceo ginnasio fu progettato da Marcello Aquilina e completato dai suoi collaboratori nel 1977 dopo la sua morte, ma poi profondamente modificato. Questo edificio scolastico è sempre stato degno di nota perchè il suo progetto è nato dalla volontà di soddisfare questa domanda: può l'architettura contribuire affinché anche una scuola sia concepita ed accettata come uno spazio vivo? L'ampliamento e la ristrutturazione più recenti dell'edificio condividono questo concetto ed intraprendono il tentativo di dare a questa visione del progetto una maggior leggibilità. Il liceo si trova davanti ad un pendio, e la posizione in salita del terreno è stata sfruttata per realizzare nel corpo di fabbrica sul retro, posto ad un livello superiore, gli ingressi secondari, le piazzole per gli intervalli e quant'altro. Ora vi sono state collocate anche le nuove classi. L'edificio è stato situato tra i due diversi livelli, parallelamente alla strada, in modo che le classi potessero essere disposte secondo un sistema a "split-level". In questo modo è stato possibile riproporre la relazione diretta tra topografia ed architettura anche per la tripartizione interna a navate. La collaborazione tra architetto ed artista è nata già nella fase di progettazione. Probabilmente è questo il motivo del successo della ristrutturazione e dell'ampliamento. Il confronto rispettoso con l'idea fondante

Christoph Mayr Fingerle
Secondary school, Bolzano
2001
Site-specific art work: Manfred Alois Mayr

This gymnasium was planned by Marcello Aquilina, following his death it was completed by his assistants in 1977, but was later altered considerably. This building was always remarkable. It began with an analysis of how architecture can enable a school to be understood and accepted as part of the space we live in. The recent renovation and expansion of this building is based on the same approach and attempts to give this leitmotif a new legibility. The school is situated in front of a slope and the rising terrain was used to place the side entrances, recess yards etc. at the rear part of the building, which lies at a higher level. The new classrooms were also added there. The building was placed between the two different levels with its long axis parallel to the street, allowing the classrooms to be laid out in a split-level system. This means that the direct relationship between the architecture and topography can be traced in the internal tripartite organization of the spaces. Collaboration between the architect and artist developed at an early planning stage, which perhaps explains the remarkable strength of the conversion and extension. The respectful treatment of the fundamental idea behind the original

der Grundidee des Ursprungsbaues konnte dessen „innere Stimmung" positiv verändert werden. Heute wird sie von klaren architektonische Aussagen, viel kommunikativer Transparenz und besonderer Eleganz geprägt.

l'edificio originale ha consentito di mutarne positivamente il "carattere interiore". Questa idea è oggi comunicata con una chiara espressione architettonica, grande trasparenza comunicativa e particolare eleganza.

building allowed the "internal mood" to be altered in a positive way. Today it is characterized by clear architectural statements, considerable communicative transparency and a particular elegance.

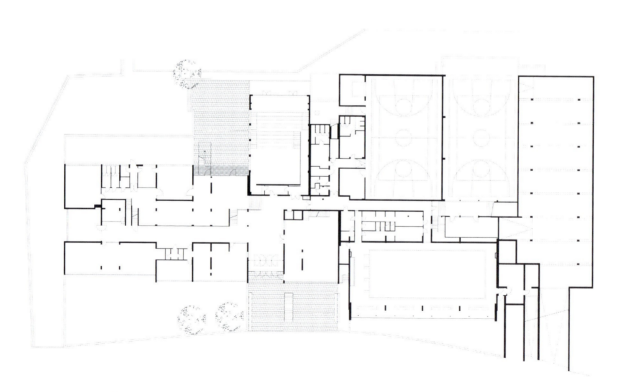

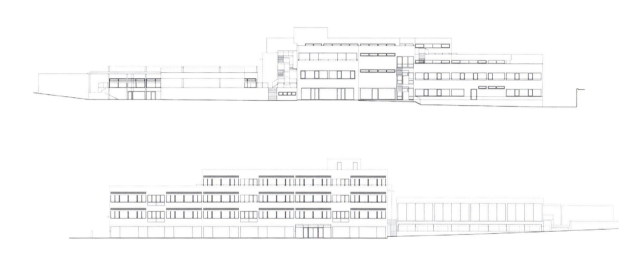

Clemens Waldhart, Schüler

„Man fühlt sich schon wohler, wenn das Umfeld passt und auch die Architektur gut ist, in einem schönen Gebäude, das einen anspricht. Aber wenn man ein paar neue Bänke will, muss es der Architekt extra genehmigen."

Clemens Waldhart, studente.

"In un bel edificio che ti piace, se l'ambiente è soddisfacente e l'architettura è piacevole, ci si sente già meglio. Se però vuoi un paio di banchi nuovi, allora devi chiedere il permesso all'architetto!"

Clemens Waldhart, pupil

"One certainly feels better in the right environment, with good architecture, in a beautiful building that appeals to one. But when we need a few new benches they have to be especially approved by the architect."

Stanislao Fierro
Tiefgarage und Neugestaltung Gerichtsplatz, Bozen
2003

Stanislao Fierro
Autorimessa interrata e nuova configurazione di Piazza del Tribunale, Bolzano
2003

Stanislao Fierro
Underground car park and redesign of Piazza del Tribunale, Bolzano
2003

In der faschistischen Ära Italiens sollte das Stadtbild Bozens radikal verändert werden. Es waren Prachtstraßen, Plätzen und eine Reihe monumentaler Bauten geplant, deren revolutionäre Architektur den ideologischen Geist des Faschismus ausdrücken sollte. Aber nur ein Teil der Projekte wurde umgesetzt, so z. B. das Gericht (Rossi de' Paoli, Busiri Vici, 1939) und die „Casa Littoria" (Pelizzari, Plattner und Rossi, 1942, heute Finanzamt). Beide Gebäude sind zusammen mit dem Platz in ihrer Mitte denkmalgeschützt, weil man ihre architektonische Qualität heute höher bewertet als ihren einstigen Zweck, Erfüllungsgehilfen für eine zweifelhafte politische Propaganda zu sein. Damit sich die denkmalgeschützten Bauten nicht zu Sehenswürdigkeiten des Faschismus entwickeln, hat man ihnen Funktionen zugeteilt, die den jeweils zeitgemäßen Bedürfnissen angepasst werden müssen. 2003 wurde der Bau einer Tiefgarage beendet, was eine Neugestaltung des Gerichtsplatzes nach sich zog: Die Abgänge in die Tiefgarage, die Regenwasser-Kanäle, der nun von der Mitte des Platzes weggerückte Springbrunnen aus den 30er Jahren und die Entlüftungsgitter fügen sich auf eine Weise in das Gesamtkonzept des Ensembles ein, die die einstige Inszenierung behutsam unterstreicht, aber nicht

Nell'era fascista l'immagine urbana di Bolzano doveva essere fortemente caratterizzata. Erano previsti viali fastosi, piazze ed una serie di edifici monumentali, la cui architettura rivoluzionaria aveva il compito di esprimere lo spirito dell'ideologia fascista. Solo una parte dei progetti è stato realizzato: ne sono un esempio il Tribunale (Rossi de' Paoli, Busiri Vici, 1939) e la Casa Littoria (Pelizzari, Plattner e Rossi, 1942, oggi Uffici Finanziari). Entrambi gli edifici e la piazza ivi compresa sono sottoposti a vincolo monumentale, perché se ne riconosce la qualità architettonica piuttosto che l'obbiettivo di un tempo, che doveva essere d'ausilio per la propaganda politica. Per evitare che gli edifici tutelati richiamassero il culto del fascismo, sono state attribuite loro nuove funzioni adatte alle necessità contemporanee. Nel 2003 è stata portata a termine la realizzazione di un'autorimessa interrata che ha coinvolto la piazza in un intervento di nuova configurazione. Le uscite dalla rimessa, i canali per lo scolo delle acque, la fontana degli anni Trenta spostata dal centro su un lato della piazza, le griglie di aereazione inserite nel concetto d'insieme in modo da sottolineare con

During Italy's fascist era plans were made to radically alter the face of Bolzano. Monumental streets, squares and a series of buildings were planned in a revolutionary style of architecture intended to express the ideological spirit of fascism. But only a few of these projects were eventually carried out, for example the courthouse by Rossi de' Paoli and Busiri Vici, 1939 and the "Casa Littoria" by Pelizzari, Plattner and Rossi, 1942, nowadays the income tax office. Both these buildings and the square between them are under a preservation order, as today their architectural quality is seen as more important than their former use as instruments of a dubious political propagandas. To avoid these listed buildings becoming fascist "sights" as it were, they have been allotted functions that suit contemporary requirements. In 2003 the construction of an underground car park was completed, which then naturally involved the redesign of Piazza del Tribunale: the access points to the underground garage, the rainwater drains, the fountain from the 1930s now moved away from the centre of the square and the ventilation grilles are integrated in the overall concept of the ensemble in a way that carefully underlines the former presentation without

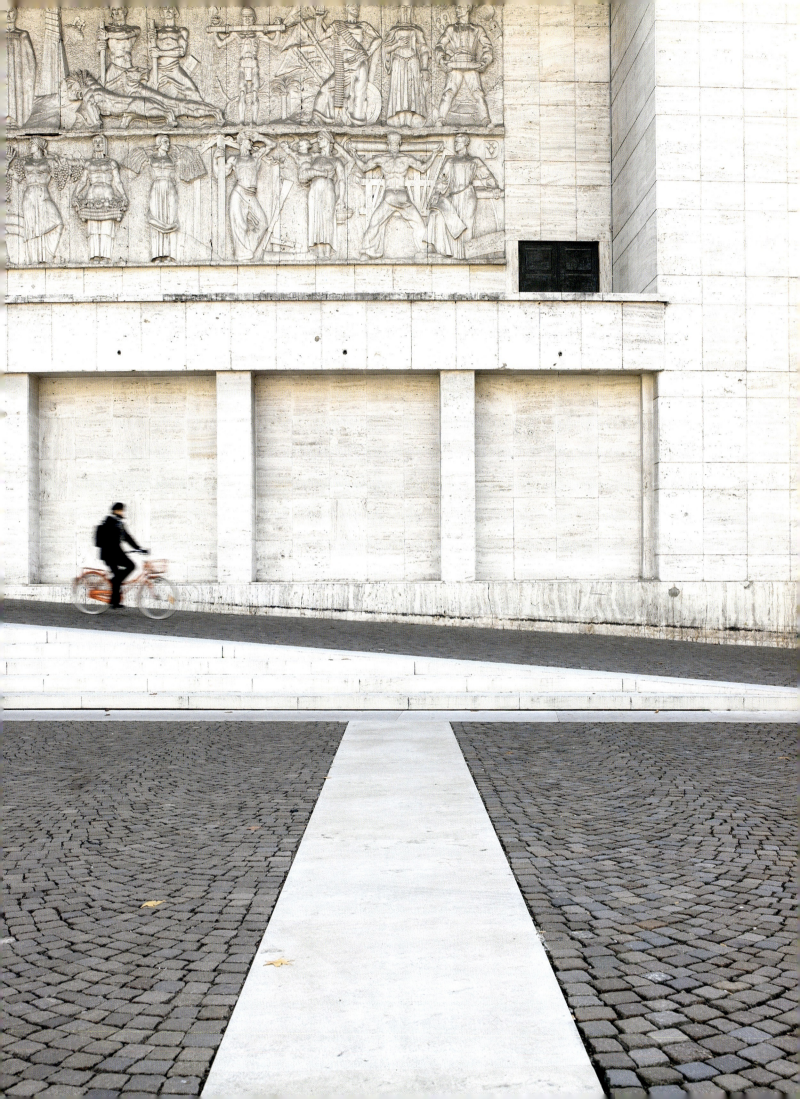

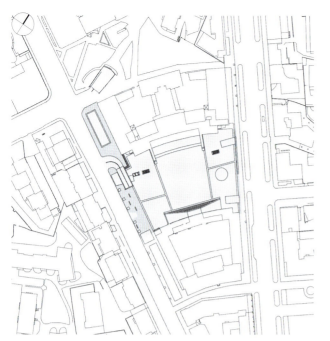

überhöht. Indem die Aufgangstreppe in das Finanzamt vorgerückt wurde, konnte das Gebäude behindertengerecht mit einer Rampe ausgestattet werden. Der Eleganz des auf Straßenniveau realisierten Teils des Projekts entspricht auch die Gestaltung der darunter liegenden Tiefgarage mit ihrem feinen Tageslicht-, Farb- und Grafikkonzept.

cautela la scenografia di un tempo, senza declamarla. Spostando in avanti la scalinata degli Uffici Finanziari, questo edificio è stato reso accessibile ai disabili da una rampa. L'eleganza del progetto si eguaglia sia in superficie che nell'interrato per la sua fine concezione della luce, del colore e della grafica.

exaggerating it. By moving the staircase exit into the tax office it was possible to make a disabled ramp for the building. The elegance of the part of the project at street level is matched by the design of the underground garage with its carefully considered use of daylight, colour and graphic design.

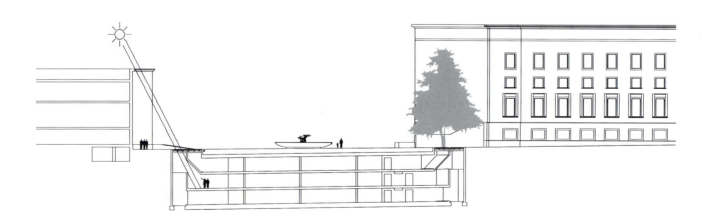

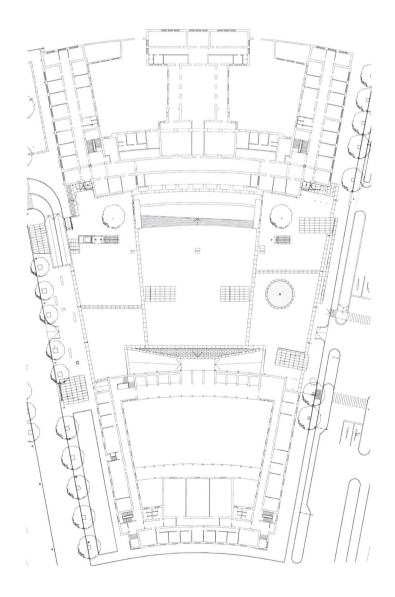

Klaus Kada
Europäische Akademie Bozen (EURAC), Bozen
2002
Kunst am Bau: Manfred Alois Mayr

Die „Casa della Giovane Italiana" (GIL) der Architekten Mansutti und Miozzo aus Padua wurde 1935 vollendet. Seither zählt der Bau zu den wichtigsten Beispielen rationaler Architektur in Südtirol. In der Nachfolge eines international besetzten Wettbewerbes ist Klaus Kada mit der Aufgabe betraut worden, dieses Gelände für die EURAC (Akademie für angewandte Forschung und Postgraduate-Studien) zu renovieren und zu erweitern. Auditorium, Bürogebäude und ehemalige Turnhalle (heute Bibliothek) wurden nach historischen Plänen in ihren Erstzustand zurückgeführt: Tragende Strukturen wurden saniert, Fenstergesimse und Pfeiler erhielten ihre ursprünglich helle Färbung und die Fassaden ihr spezifisches Rot zurück.

Auf der Seite des Talfer-Flusses wurde ein neuer Bauteil errichtet, der ein Foyer, ein weiteres Auditorium, Büros und ein Café enthält. Dieser Bauteil erstreckt sich von der Drususbrücke in Richtung des bestehenden, oval geformten Saales, also von einer Hauptverkehrsader Bozens zu einer Ruhezone am Flussufer. An seiner Rückseite, dem Park, wurden weitere Zubauten angefügt. An die Bibliothek schließt ein neuer Bauteil an, der in ein zweihüftiges Institutsgebäude übergeht. Die Architektur des alten GIL-Komplexes war wegen ihrer städtebaulichen Qualität und ihrer starken,

Klaus Kada
Accademia Europea Bolzano (EURAC), Bolzano
2002
Intervento artistico: Manfred Alois Mayr

La "Casa della Giovane Italiana" (GIL) degli architetti Mansutti e Miozzo di Padova fu terminata nel 1935. Da allora l'edificio è annoverato tra i più importanti esempi dell'architettura razionalista in Alto Adige. In seguito ad un concorso internazionale Klaus Kada è stato incaricato di ristrutturare ed ampliare questo complesso per la sede dell'EURAC (Accademia di ricerca applicata e studi Postgraduate). L'auditorium, la palazzina degli uffici e la palestra (oggi biblioteca) sono stati riportati allo stato originale rispettando i disegni storici. Le strutture portanti sono state restaurate, cornici e pilastri delle finestre sono stati riportati al colore chiaro originale e le facciate alla loro specifica tinta rosso pompeiano.

Sul lato del fiume Talvera è stato eretto un nuovo corpo di fabbrica contenente un atrio d'ingresso, un altro auditorium, degli uffici e una caffetteria. Questo edificio si estende dal Ponte Druso fino alla sala ovale preesistente, ovvero da un'arteria principale di traffico sino ad una zona riparata, affacciata sull'argine del fiume. Sul suo retro, il parco, sono stati aggiunti altri corpi di fabbrica. Alla biblioteca si allaccia un nuovo edificio che si prolunga nella sede dell'istituto a due fiancate. L'architettura del vecchio complesso GIL è da sempre famosa per l'efficacia del suo inserimento ur-

Klaus Kada
European Academy Bolzano (EURAC), Bolzano
2002
Site-specific artwork: Manfred Alois Mayr

The "Casa della Giovane Italiana" (GIL) by architects Mansutti und Miozzo from Padova was completed in 1935. The building has long been numbered among the most important examples of rationalist architecture in South Tyrol. Following an international competition Klaus Kada was entrusted with the task of renovating and extending this complex for the EURAC (academy for applied research and postgraduate studies). The auditorium, office building and former gymnasium (today the library) were restored to their original state according to the historic plans. Load-bearing structures were renovated; window cornices and piers were restored to their original light colouring and the facades to their specific red colour.

On the river side a new building was erected that contains a foyer, a further auditorium, offices and a café. This building extends from the bridge in the direction of the existing oval hall, that is to say from one of Bolzano's main traffic arteries to a quiet area on the bank of the river. At the rear, facing towards the park, further extensions were added. A new element that adjoins the library is continued into the institute building, which is based on a double-loaded corridor plan. The architecture of the old GIL complex has long been legendary on ac-

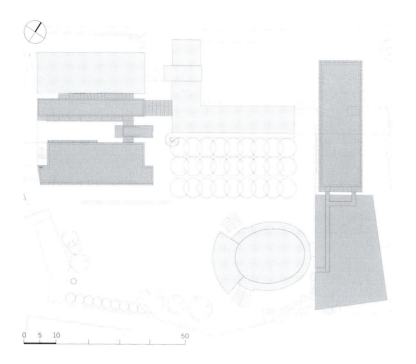

fast theatralischen Gestik immer schon legendär. Im Zuge der Revitalisierung ist es gelungen, dieses Potenzial zu erhalten und durch den effektvoll verglasten Zubau an der Drususstraße noch zu verstärken.

banistico e per la sua forte e quasi teatrale simbologia. La ristrutturazione è riuscita a conservare questo potenziale ed il corpo vetrato dell'ampliamento lo ha addirittura rafforzato con notevole effetto.

count of its urban qualities and its strong, almost theatrical gestures. In the course of the renovation work it proved possible to retain this potential and to strengthen it through the dramatically glazed building on Via Druso.

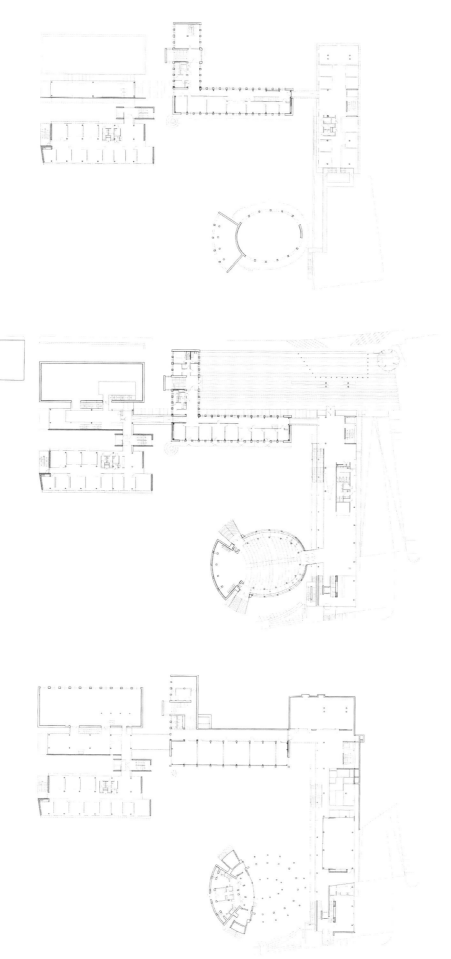

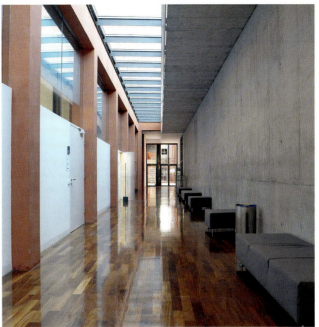
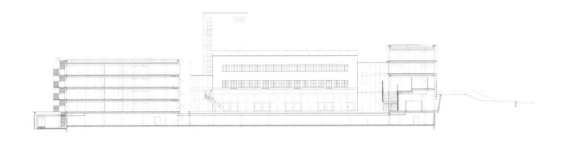
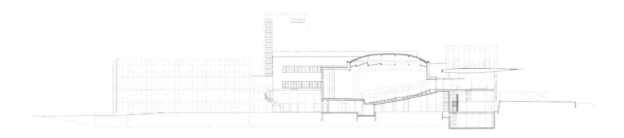

Höller & Klotzner
Abbruch und Neubau Landesberufsschule, Bozen
2005 (1. Baulos)
Kunst am Bau: Heimo Zobernig

Höller & Klotzner
Demolizione e nuova edificazione Scuola Professionale Provinciale, Bolzano.
2005 (1° lotto)
Intervento artistico: Heimo Zobernig

Höller & Klotzner
Demolition and new building, Regional Vocational School, Bolzano
2005 (1st construction phase)
Site-specific artwork: Heimo Zobernig

Das alte Messegelände Bozens sollte dem Neubau einer Berufsschule weichen. Die Umwidmung des Geländes nahm aber fast zehn Jahre in Anspruch, bevor der erste Bauabschnitt der Schule in Angriff genommen werden konnte.
Die Stirnseiten der lang gezogenen, aneinander gereihten und miteinander in Verbindung gesetzten Riegel befinden sich an der Romstraße, von wo die gewaltige Dimension der Baukörper bereits erahnt werden kann. Die Erschließungshalle im Erdgeschoss wurde auf die Decke des Turnsaales gesetzt. Deshalb kann durch am Boden verlegte Glasbausteine effektvoll Kunstlicht in das große, glasüberdachte Atrium dringen. Um diesen zentralen Lichthof wurden auf insgesamt fünf Ebenen Werkstätten und Klassenräume gruppiert. Sichtbeton, Glas (mit Lamellen zur Beschattung) und Gipsfaser sind die drei wesentlichen Werkstoffe, mit denen dieser Bau ausgeführt wurde. Dabei war die Verwendung von Gipsfaser für die Verkleidung von Böden, Wänden und Decken wohl europaweit einmalig, denn das neue Material zählt in puncto Schalldämmung und Brandsicherheit zu den besten Produkten, die der Baumarkt derzeit zu bieten hat. Auch die Möglichkeit, viele Baustoffe auf einen einzigen

Il vecchio areale della fiera doveva fare spazio al nuovo edificio di una scuola professionale. La trasformazione dell'area è durata quasi dieci anni, prima che si potesse avviare l'edificazione del primo lotto.
I fronti dei lunghi edifici, che corrono paralleli e sono reciprocamente collegati, si affacciano sulla via Roma, da dove si possono percepire le grandiose dimensioni dei corpi di fabbrica. L'atrio di distribuzione a piano terra sorge sul solaio della palestra. Il vetro-mattone inserito nel pavimento lascia filtrare la luce proveniente dal tetto vetrato dell'atrio. Intorno a questa corte centrale di cinque piani illuminata dall'alto sono distribuite le classi ed i laboratori. I tre materiali principali con cui è realizzata l'opera sono il cemento a vista, il vetro (con le lame vetrate per la protezione dal sole) e il cartongesso. L'impiego massiccio della fibra di gesso per il rivestimento sia dei pavimenti, che di pareti e soffitti, uno tra i migliori prodotti per l'isolamento acustico ed antincendio che il mercato può offrire al momento, è stato unico a livello europeo. Il vantaggio è stato anche quello di poter

It was planned to erect a new vocational school on the old trade fair grounds in Bolzano. The official rezoning of the site took almost ten years before the first construction phase of the school could begin.
The ends of the elongated blocks arranged in a row and linked to each other face onto Via Roma from where one has a first intimation of the impressive dimensions of this building. The circulation and access hall at ground floor level was placed on the roof of the gymnasium. This means that effective artificial light can enter the large glass-roofed atrium through glass blocks set in the floor. Workshops and classrooms were organised on a total of five levels around this central light well. Exposed concrete, glass (with louvers to provide shade) and plaster fibre panels are the three most important materials used in this building. The use of plaster fibre to clad walls, floors and ceilings was unique in Europe. In terms of acoustic insulation and resistance to fire this new material is one of the best products on the market. As it has many different applications it allows the number of

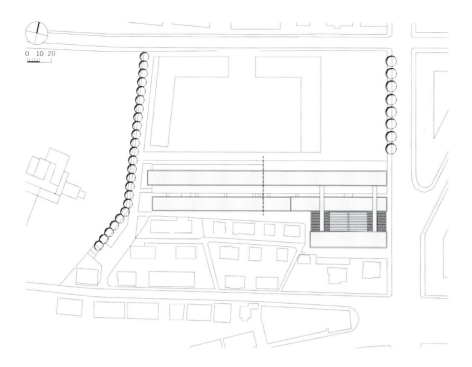

reduzieren zu können, ist einer seiner Vorteile.

Öffentliche Großbauten benötigen auch Wegleitsysteme. Hier wurde es nicht von einem Grafik-Büro gestaltet, sondern von einem Künstler entworfen. Das beste Grafik-Konzept wurde im Zuge eines Kunst-am-Bau-Wettbewerbs ermittelt.

concentrare in uno solo l'impiego di molti materiali.

Gli edifici pubblici di grandi dimensioni richiedono un sistema segnaletico di orientamento: qui non è stato progettato da uno studio grafico, bensì da un artista il cui concetto grafico è stato premiato nell'apposito concorso per gli interventi d'arte in architettura.

materials used in a building to be reduced considerably, which is a major advantage. Large public buildings need a directional system. In this case a graphic design office was not employed, instead the system was designed by an artist. The best graphic concept was selected by means of a competition for the site-specific artwork.

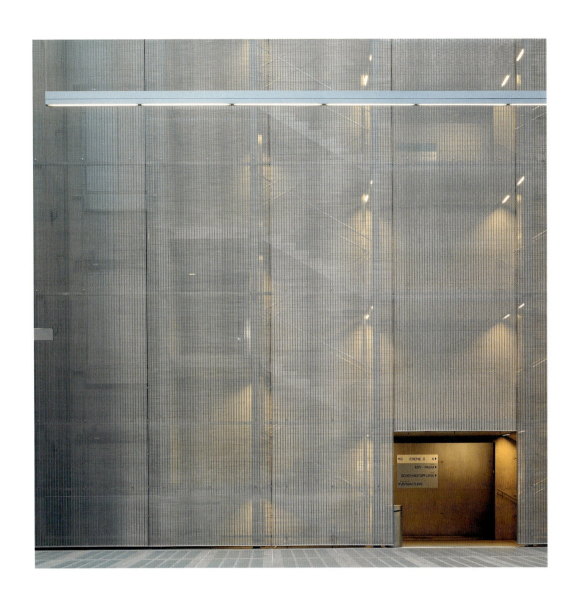

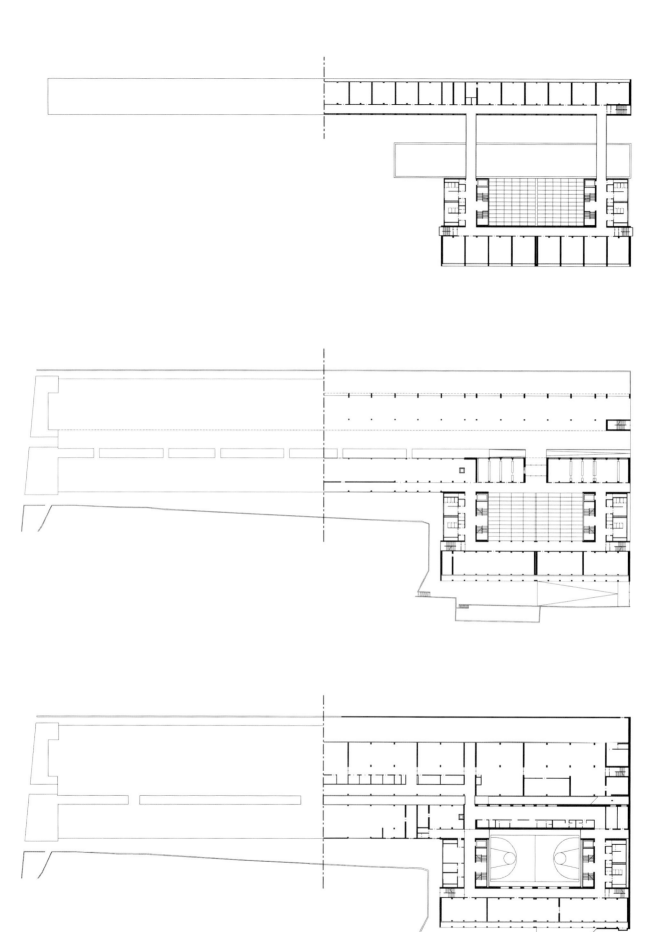

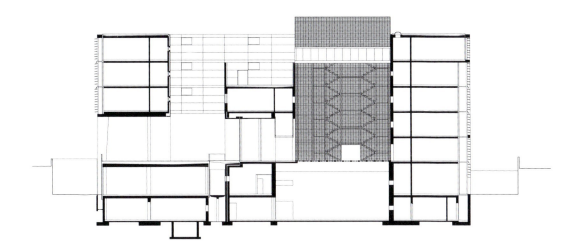

Bischoff Azzola Architekten
Freie Universität Bozen, Bozen
2002 (1. Baulos), 2005 (2. Baulos, nach den Ausführungsplänen der Architekten)
Kunst am Bau: Erik Steinbrecher (Konzept und Koordination)

Architetti Bischoff Azzola
Libera Università di Bolzano, Bolzano
2002 (1° lotto), 2005 (2° lotto come da progetto esecutivo degli architetti)
Intervento artistico: Erik Steinbecher (concezione e coordinamento)

Bischoff Azzola Architekten
Free University of Bolzano, Bolzano
2002 (1st development phase), 2005 (2nd development phase according to the architects' detail drawings)
Site-specific artwork: Erik Steinbrecher (concept and coordination)

1998 wurde für die Errichtung der Universität Bozen ein Wettbewerb mit anspruchsvollem Programm ausgeschrieben: Es sollten zwei Fakultäten (Wirtschafts- und Agrarwissenschaften) und zwei Fachhochschulen (Design und Sozialwesen) mit allen Nebeneinrichtungen (Bibliothek, Mensa u. a.) für 3.000 Studenten auf einem Areal nahe der Bozner Altstadt realisiert werden. Dabei reüssierte ein Projekt, das sich auf städtebauliche Aspekte konzentriert: Zwischen Sparkassenstraße, Spitalgasse und Sernesistraße sollten drei Plätze bzw. Höfe für Durchlässigkeit in dem – seit dem 19. Jahrhundert ständig erweiterten – Viertel sorgen. Durch die Umwidmung bestehender und die Errichtung neuer Bauten wollte man im Gegensatz dazu erreichen, dass sich alle Gebäude positiv auf den „Zusammenhalt" des Stadtteils auswirken und die Entstehung eines innerstädtischen Campus zulassen.

Zu den bisher realisierten neuen Baukörpern zählt ein Gebäude mit Bibliothek und Mensa an der Sernesistraße, dessen kühles äußere Erscheinungsbild (Kunststeinplatten) viele Südtiroler noch nicht überzeugen konnte. Im Erdgeschoss befindet

Nel 1998 fu indetto un concorso caratterizzato da un ambizioso programma per la costruzione dell'università di Bolzano. Si dovevano realizzare due facoltà (Economia ed Agronomia) e due scuole professionali (Design e Professioni sociali) per 3000 studenti, dotate di tutte le attrezzature accessorie (biblioteca, mensa, ecc.) su di un'area del centro storico di Bolzano. Vinse un progetto che si concentrò sugli aspetti urbanistici: tre piazze, o meglio tre corti, poste tra via Cassa di Risparmio, via Ospedale e via Sernesi, dovevano garantire l'apertura di un quartiere che a partire dal XIX secolo si è sempre ampliato.

Contrariamente a questa impostazione, con la conversione degli edifici esistenti e l'edificazione di nuove costruzioni, si é voluto fare in modo che questi interventi agissero in positivo sulla "coesione" del quartiere e realizzare un campus interno alla città stessa. Uno dei corpi di fabbrica sinora realizzati é l'edificio per la mensa e la biblioteca, disposto lungo via Sernesi, la cui fredda immagine esterna (lastre di pietra artificiale) non è ancora riuscita a convincere molti altoatesini. Gli spazi di lavoro sono raggruppati intorno ad una corte

In 1998 a competition with a challenging brief was set up for the design of the University of Bolzano. The intention was to create two faculties (Economics and Agricultural Science) and two specialist schools (Design and Social Studies), with all the required facilities (library, cafeteria, etc.) for 3000 students on a site near the centre of Bolzano. The successful project concentrated on urban aspects: three squares or courtyards between Via Cassa di Risparmio, Via Ospedale and Via Sernesi were intended to provide permeability in a district that has grown continuously since the 19th century. Through rezoning surrounding buildings and erecting new buildings the aim was to achieve a positive effect on the ‚cohesion' of this district and to encourage the development of an inner city campus.

The structures erected to date include the library and cafeteria building on Via Sernesi with a cool exterior (artificial stone slabs) that to date has not won the hearts of many South Tyrolese. The cafeteria is on

sich die Mensa, in den Ebenen darüber die Bibliothek. Die Arbeitsplätze sind um einen Lichthof gruppiert, was ein Lesen und Lernen bei Tageslicht ermöglicht. Ein breiter Gang verbindet diesen Bauteil mit dem Fakultätsgebäude an der Sparkassenstraße. Die hier abgebildeten Pläne zeigen den geplanten Zustand des zweiten Bauabschnitts.	illuminata dall'alto che consente di leggere e studiare con luce diurna. Un ampio corridoio collega questo corpo di fabbrica con l'edificio della facoltà, disposto su via Cassa di Risparmio. Le tavole di progetto qui riportate descrivono il secondo lotto.	ground floor level, the library is on the floor above the workstations are grouped around a light well thus allowing students to study and read by natural light. A broad corridor connects this building with the faculty building on Via Cassa di Risparmio. The plans reproduced here show the planned second development phase.

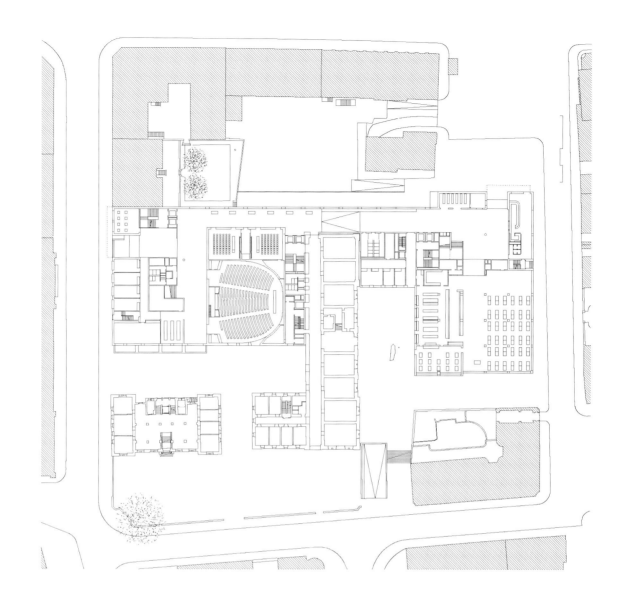

195

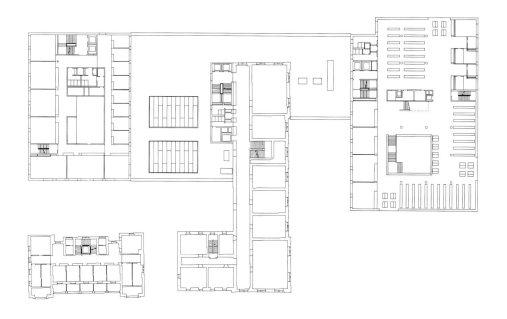

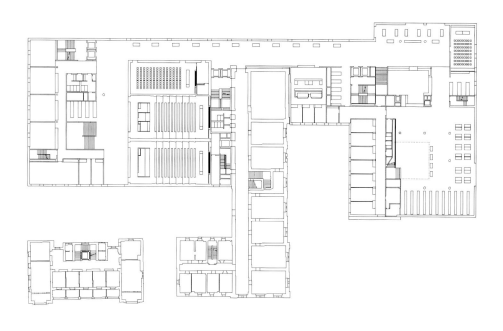

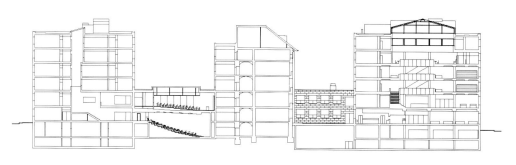

Elisa Seitt, Studentin

„Von Anfang an hat es mir gut gefallen, obwohl viele sagen, dass es so klotzig ist. Vor allem die Bibliothek ist sehr intim und trotzdem groß und hell."

Elisa Seitt, studentessa.

"Sin dall'inizio mi è piaciuta, nonostante molti dicano che abbia un effetto massiccio. Soprattutto la biblioteca è uno spazio intimo, eppure è grandiosa e luminosa."

Elisa Seitt, student

"I liked it from the very start, although lots of people do say that it's too block-like. But the library in particular is very intimate and yet large and bright."

Peter Plattner
Sanierung und Erweiterung Haus Amonn, Bozen
2001

Peter Plattner
Restauro e ampliamento di Casa Amonn, Bolzano
2001

Peter Plattner
Renovation and extension to the Amonn House, Bolzano
2001

Das in seinem Kern aus dem 13. Jahrhundert stammende Bozner Stadthaus verfügt über einen mehrgeschossigen Keller, von dem aus ein an der Hofseite liegender Anbau erreichbar ist. Die Stockwerke über dem Keller haben keine durchgehenden Geschossebenen, was auf die wechselvolle Bau- und Umbaugeschichte des Gebäudes zurückzuführen ist. Der Gebäudeteil an der Hofseite stammt aus einer anderen Bauperiode als der an der Straßenseite. In ihrer Mitte befindet sich der für die Bozner Stadthäuser typische Lichthof mit Laterne. Der Bau stand lange Zeit leer, ehe sich sein Besitzer gemeinsam mit dem Architekten und dem Denkmalamt zur Sanierung entschloss. Nach einer Bauanalyse wurden manche dem Charakter der Bausubstanz nicht zuträgliche Einbauten und Schichten von Wandoberflächen entfernt. Damit war die Basis für die Erhaltung der Substanz bzw. das Einbringen neuer Gestaltungselemente gelegt. Freigelegte Details wurden vielfach in ihrer („nackten") Form fixiert und nur lückenhaft Gebliebenes wurde durch Neues ergänzt. Das hatte zur Folge, dass überall dort, wo Fehlendes ersetzt werden musste, die Materialsprache des Neuen voll zur Geltung gebracht werden konnte. War es im Inneren des Amonnhauses bis vor kurzem nicht mehr nachvollziehbar,

L'edificio bolzanino il cui nucleo risale al XIII secolo si erge su una cantina a più livelli. Da qui si può raggiungere un corpo di fabbrica annesso sul lato del cortile. A causa delle alterne vicende legate alla storia della costruzione e ristrutturazione dell'edificio, i piani sopra la cantina non posseggono una superficie continua. La parte di edificio sul lato del cortile risale ad un periodo diverso da quello della parte prospiciente alla strada. Al centro si erge la corte interna con lucernario tipica delle residenze urbane di Bolzano. La costruzione rimase a lungo vuota fino a quando i proprietari, assieme all'architetto ed alla Soprintendenza ai Beni Culturali, si convinsero per il restauro.
In seguito ad un'analisi dell'edificio, alcuni interventi costruttivi ed alcuni strati delle pareti, ritenuti non pertinenti al carattere dell'architettura, sono stati rimossi. Con questo si sono poste le basi per la conservazione e per l'introduzione di nuovi elementi compositivi. I dettagli costruttivi liberati da questi interventi sono stati fissati nella loro "nuda" forma, e lì dove mancavano degli elementi, si è intervenuto con il nuovo. Così l'espressione materica del nuovo si manifesta al meglio, proprio lì dove le parti mancanti dovevano essere sostituite. Se la mancanza di chiarezza

The core of this town house in Bolzano dates from the 13th century and it has a basement consisting of several levels from which a building added on the courtyard side can be reached. The floors above the basement are not continuous levels, reflecting the long and complex history of construction and conversion that this building has undergone. The part of the building on the courtyard side dates from a different period to the street front. At the centre there is a typical light-well with a glazed roof lantern usually found in town houses in Bolzano.
This building stood empty for a long time before the owner together with the architect and the building conservation authorities decided to restore it. Following a building analysis several insertions and layers of wall that detracted from the character of the building fabric were removed. This created a basis for preserving the substance and for the introduction of new design elements. In a number of cases exposed details were left in their "naked" form, and where only remnants survived these were augmented by new additions. The result was that wherever missing elements had to be replaced the idiom of the new materials could develop fully. Whereas previously in the Amonn house it was no longer possible

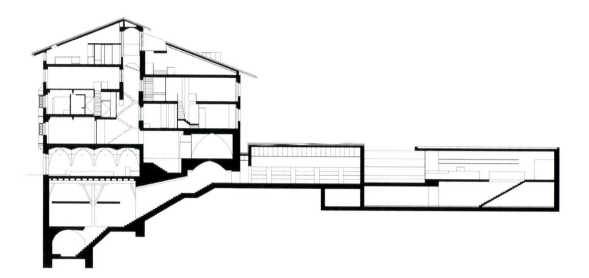

welche Bestandteile des Gebäudes aus der Gotik, der Renaissance, dem Barock oder einer späteren Epoche stammen, so ist heute gerade das detailreiche Herauszeichnen der einzelnen Bauperioden der Grund für die Stimmigkeit der Sanierung.

che precedentemente regnava all'interno di casa Ammon, non consentiva di riconoscere quali parti dell'esistente appartenessero al periodo gotico, rinascimentale, barocco o di epoche successive, oggi, proprio il manifestarsi della ricchezza di dettagli dei singoli periodi costruttivi, diventa il motivo di coerenza della ristrutturazione.

to identify which elements came from the Gothic, Renaissance, Baroque or later periods, today the richly detailed illustration of the individual building periods is the reason for the particularly harmonious quality of this renovation.

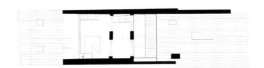

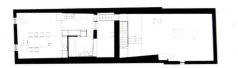

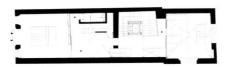

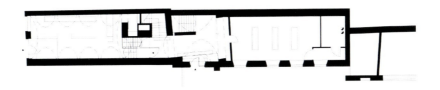

201

Luigi Scolari
Neubau einer Industriehalle mit Bürotrakt, Firma BEL Bozen
2004

Der Klebeetiketten-Erzeuger BEL vergab den Auftrag zum Bau einer massiven Industriehalle mit einem Dachgeschoss in Leichtbauweise. Das Gebäude entstand in Bozen-Süd, wo sich bereits eine ganze Reihe von Firmen niedergelassen hat, Architektur und Städtebau bisher jedoch noch kaum Fuß fassen konnten.

Auf der untersten Ebene des Bauwerks befinden sich eine Garage und ein Zusatzlager, in der Etage darüber das Hauptlager und im zweiten Stock die Produktion mit angeschlossenen Büroräumlichkeiten. Die zum Teil in Ortbeton ausgeführte Industriehalle soll schlicht und funktional wirken. In architektonischer Hinsicht wurde aber viel Wert darauf gelegt, ihr großes Volumen geometrisch aufzulösen und so zu strukturieren, dass der Kubus als Ensemble aus vor- und zurückspringenden Gebäudeteilen in Erscheinung tritt. Das bewirkt, dass selbst eine Industriehalle den Charakter einer – wenn auch künstlich geschaffenen – Landschaft annimmt. Auf die Decke der Halle wurde ein weiterer Bauteil gesetzt, der einem großen Penthouse gleicht. In diesem teilweise verglasten Stahlkörper befindet sich die Verwaltung des Unternehmens. Durch die Mitte dieses Dachgeschosses

Luigi Scolari
Nuova edificazione di un edificio industriale con uffici, ditta BEL, Bolzano
2004

Il produttore di etichette BEL ha affidato l'incarico per la realizzazione di un capannone a struttura massiccia con un piano di copertura a struttura leggera. L'edificio sorge nella zona di Bolzano-sud, dove si sono insediate molte aziende, ma dove, finora, architettura ed urbanistica non hanno potuto attecchire.

Nell'interrato si trovano l'autorimessa ed un deposito secondario, al piano superiore il magazzino principale e al secondo piano la produzione con i relativi uffici. L'edificio industriale realizzato in parte con calcestruzzo a vista, deve apparire sobrio e funzionale. Il progetto architettonico ha dato risalto alla dissoluzione geometrica del grande volume, ed ha strutturato il cubo in modo che risulti composto da un insieme di corpi di fabbrica che alternativamente aggettano o retrocedono. Ciò consente persino ad un capannone industriale di assumere il carattere, seppur artificiale, di un paesaggio.

Sul solaio del capannone è stato posto un ulteriore elemento costruttivo, che assomiglia ad un'enorme attico.

All'interno di questa struttura d'acciaio, parzialmente vetrata, è ospitata l'amministrazione dell'azienda. Un asse verde l'at-

Luigi Scolari
New industrial building with office wing, BEL Company, Bolzano
2004

The BEL Company, a manufacturer of adhesive labels, commissioned the construction of a large industrial shed with an attic level using a lightweight construction system. The building was erected in Bolzano-South, a district where there are already a considerable number of company buildings, but where an awareness of architecture and urban planning has managed to gain a foothold.

The lowest level of the building contains a garage and the extra storeroom, the floor directly above contains the main storeroom, while the manufacturing area with the adjoining office spaces are located on the floor above that. The shed is built of in-situ concrete and was intended to be plain and functional in appearance. But in architectural terms considerable effort was made to break up the large volume geometrically and to structure it in such a way that it seems to be made up of projecting and recessed parts. This has given the industrial building the character of a landscape, albeit an artificially created one. An element placed on the roof of the building resembles a large penthouse. The administrative offices of the company are housed in this partly glazed steel-built element. A

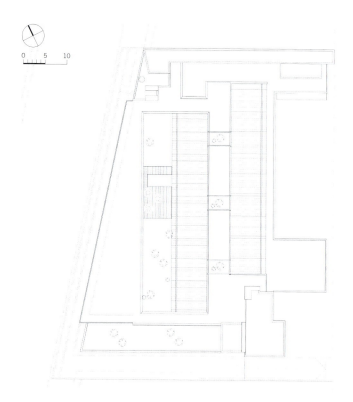

verläuft eine begrünte Achse, die eine Art Präsentationszone mit Cafeteria und die Büros voneinander trennt. Aufgrund der strategisch günstigen Lage des neuen Unternehmenssitzes an der Autobahnausfahrt Bozen-Süd fungiert die Architektur auch als Werbung.

traversa al centro e divide la zona destinata alle presentazioni, con caffetteria, dagli uffici. Grazie alla posizione strategica della nuova sede, all'uscita dell'autostrada di Bolzano-sud, l'architettura assume anche una valenza pubblicitaria.

"green" axis running through the middle of this roof top level separates a kind of presentation zone with cafeteria from the office spaces. Thanks to the new company building's strategically favourable location on the motorway exit Bolzano-South, the architecture also functions as a kind of advertising.

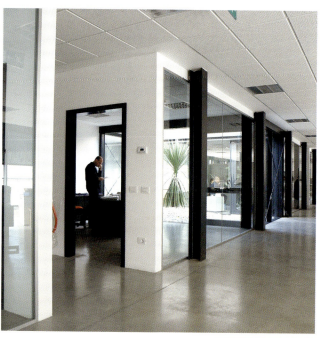

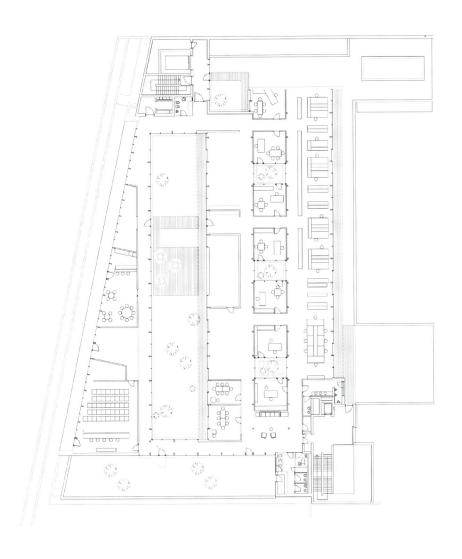

Lunz & Zöschg Architekten
Kindergarten Maria Rast, St. Michael, Eppan
2005

Das Projekt ging aus einem geladenen Wettbewerb als Sieger hervor. Die Preisrichter überzeugte die Ausgangsidee des Beitrags, wonach eine zeitgemäße Kindergarten-Architektur auch auf die in Südtirol gegebene Mehrsprachigkeit eingehen soll. Üblicherweise werden die Kinder je nach Muttersprache in italienische und deutsche Kindergarten-Gruppen eingeschrieben. In den Tagesbetreuungsstätten haben die italienischen Gruppen dann auch andere Programme als die deutschen. Das alte Bild von den gesondert zu behandelnden Bevölkerungsgruppen verschwimmt aber unter den jungen und jüngsten Südtirolern zunehmend, was die Architekten veranlasste, bei der Planung des Kindergartens in Eppan das Thema der Sprachintegration auch architektonisch umzusetzen. Dabei war die Schaffung von fließenden Übergängen besonders wichtig. Zwar sieht es von außen so aus, als bestünde der Kindergarten aus je einem „Reihenhäuschen" pro Kindergruppe – grundsätzlich stimmt das auch, denn die Gruppen- und Ruheräume sind in vier bunt eingefärbten Würfeln übereinander angeordnet. Die Gänge zwischen den Gruppenräumen wurden aber so großzügig gestaltet, dass sie die Kinder dazu einladen, sich auch in diesen Zwischenräumen

Lunz & Zöschg architetti
Scuola materna Maria Rast, S. Michele, Appiano
2005

Il progetto ha vinto un concorso ad invito. La sua impostazione ha convinto la giuria del contributo positivo che l'architettura contemporanea per gli asili può dare alla reale condizione di plurilinguismo di cui gode l'Alto Adige.
Di norma i bambini vengono iscritti nelle diverse sezioni secondo la loro madrelingua. I bambini italiani seguono programmi differenti da quelli tedeschi all'interno dei gruppi di affidamento. Il vecchio concetto pedagogico secondo il quale i gruppi linguistici devono essere trattati diversamente va sempre più scemando tra le giovani e giovanissime generazioni altoatesine, cosa che ha consentito agli architetti di interpretare con il progetto il tema dell'integrazione linguistica. La realizzazione di passaggi fluidi tra zone ne è stata un presupposto. In realtà dall'esterno sembra che la scuola materna si componga di singole "casette a schiera", una per ogni sezione, e questo corrisponde al vero, infatti, gli spazi per i gruppi e per il riposo sono allineati uno sull'altro in quattro "cubetti" vivacemente colorati. I corridoi tra i locali di gruppo, però,

Lunz & Zöschg Architekten
Maria Rast kindergarten, S. Michele, Appiano
2005

This project emerged as the winner from an invited entry competition. The jury was impressed by the starting point of this design, which reflected the belief that contemporary kindergarten architecture should also exert a positive influence on the existing multi-lingual situation in South Tyrol.
Usually children are registered according to their native language in either Italian or German language kindergarten groups. In the children's day care centres the Italian groups have a different programme to the German-language ones. The traditional idea that the different population groups should be treated differently is gradually fading among young and very young South Tyroleans, a fact that led these architects to apply the theme of linguistic integration to their design for the kindergarten in Appiano. To achieve their goal the creation of flowing transitions was most important. It looks from outside as if the kindergarten consists of a "little terraced house" for each group of children and, in fact, this is essentially the case, as the group and relaxation rooms are arranged above each other in four colourful cubes. But the corridors between the group rooms are so generously

Spielplätze zu schaffen. Darüber hinaus benützen alle Kinder denselben Eingang ins Gebäude und denselben Mehrzwecksaal, was für Südtiroler Kindergärten ebenfalls ein Novum ist.

sono stati realizzati con tale ampiezza, che i bambini sono portati a giocare anche in questi spazi interstiziali. Inoltre, i bambini utilizzano tutti lo stesso ingresso e la medesima sala polivalente: una novità per gli asili in Alto Adige.

dimensioned that they invite the children to create play areas in these intermediate zones. In addition all the children use the same entrance to the building and the same multi-purpose hall, something of a novelty for a kindergarten in South Tyrol.

Forer Unterpertinger Architekten
Sanierung und Erweiterung Lanserhaus, St. Michael, Eppan
2005

Ende der 90er Jahre kaufte die Gemeinde Eppan das bis dahin in Privatbesitz stehende Lanserhaus mit seiner Freifläche an und schrieb einen Ideenwettbewerb für seine Sanierung und Erweiterung aus. Die auf das 16. Jahrhundert zurückgehende Gebäudegruppe, bestehend aus Gutshaus an der Straßenseite, Ställen und anderen Wirtschaftsgebäuden im Innenhof, sollte in einen vielfältig nutzbaren Veranstaltungsort umgewandelt werden. Da es sich bei der Substanz um eine Reihe höchst unterschiedlicher Bauten bzw. Räume handelte, sollten nicht nur ihre Sanierung und Revitalisierung vorgenommen, sondern die verschiedenen Veranstaltungsorte innerhalb des Ensembles auch von einem zentralen Verteilergebäude aus (behindertengerecht) erschlossen werden. Aus diesem Grund wurde im Hof ein kleiner Neubau für den Empfangsbereich geschaffen. Von hier aus führt ein unterirdischer Gang in den gotischen Keller des Lanserhauses, wo u. a. Weinverkostungen stattfinden. In den Geschossen darüber wurden Ausstellungsräume und ein Atelier für Gastkünstler eingerichtet. An den Seiten des Verteilergebäudes befinden sich Konzertsäle, Seminarräume und Büros. Da an derartigen

Forer Unterpertinger Architekten
Restauro ed ampliamento Lanserhaus, S. Michele, Appiano
2005

Alla fine degli anni Novanta il comune di Appiano acquistò l'edificio Lanserhaus con annessi gli spazi esterni, che sino ad allora erano stati di proprietà privata, e bandì un concorso per la sua ristrutturazione. Il complesso di edifici che risale al sedicesimo secolo e si compone di una casa padronale sul lato strada, stalle ed altri annessi agricoli nella corte interna, doveva essere trasformato in un luogo per molteplici e differenti manifestazioni. Trattandosi di un gruppo di edifici e di spazi molto differenti, non bastava una ristrutturazione per portarli a nuova vita: i diversi luoghi per manifestazioni all'interno del complesso dovevano essere collegati da un corpo di fabbrica centrale destinato alla distribuzione e fruibile anche dai disabili. Nel cortile si è pertanto realizzato un piccolo edificio da destinare all'ingresso e ricezione, e dal quale lungo un corridoio sotterraneo si raggiunge la cantina gotica del Lanserhaus, dove tra l'altro si posso degustare vini. Ai piani superiori sono stati allestiti locali espositivi e un atelier per ospitare gli artisti. Sui lati dell'edificio di distribuzione si trovano sale da concerto, locali per seminari ed uffici. Poiché a questi tipi di case padronali si sono sempre aggiunte altre co-

Forer Unterpertinger Architekten
Renovation and extension of the Lanserhaus, S. Michele, Appiano
2005

At the end of the 1990s the local authority of Appiano acquired the Lanserhaus and surrounding land that had previously been in private ownership and set up an ideas competition for its renovation and extension. The group of buildings that dates back to the 16th century and consists of the farmhouse on the road, with the stables and other outhouses in an internal yard was to be transformed into a flexible location for events of different kinds. As the existing fabric consists of a series of diverse buildings and spaces the intention was not only to renovate and revitalise it, but to provide a central distributor building, easily used by the disabled, which offers access to the various locations within the ensemble. Consequently a small new building for the reception area was erected in the courtyard. From here an underground corridor leads to the Gothic cellar of the Lanserhaus where wine-tastings and other events are held. On the floors above there are concert rooms, seminar rooms and offices. As traditionally buildings were added from time to time to farms of this kind, the fact that the distributor building is fully glazed on the courtyard side and clad in copper at the rear is not disturbing; it is

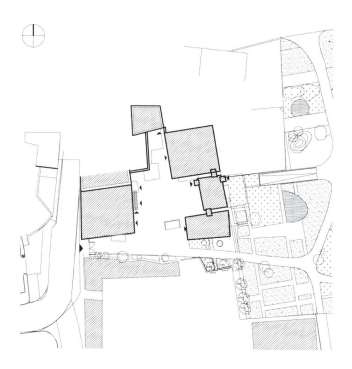

Gutshöfen schon immer von Zeit zu Zeit angebaut wurde, stört es nicht, dass das Verteilergebäude zum Hof hin vollständig verglast und an seiner Rückseite mit Kupfer beschichtet wurde. Man nimmt es nicht als Fremdkörper, sondern als eine aus dem Wandel der Bedürfnisse entstandene Einfügung in das Ensemble wahr.

struzioni, non disturba che l'edificio di distribuzione sia completamente vetrato verso il cortile e rivestito in rame sulla facciata posteriore, non lo si percepisce come un corpo estraneo, bensì come un intervento dovuto alle mutate esigenze dell'edificio.

not perceived as a foreign element but as something introduced into the ensemble to meet changing needs.

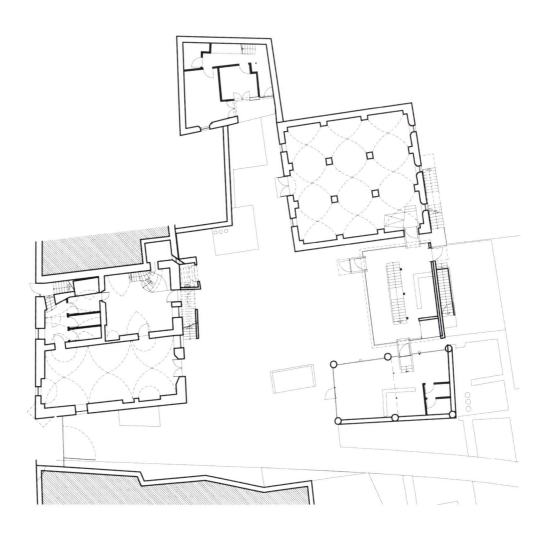

Walter Angonese, Silvia Boday, Rainer Köberl

Weingut Manincor, Kaltern

2004

Kunst am Bau: Manfred Alois Mayr, Erik Steinbrecher

Seit 1996 keltert die Familie Goëss-Enzenberg aus dem Ertrag der eigenen 45 ha Rebgärten edle Weine. In den vorhandenen Weinkellern reichte der Platz bald nicht mehr aus, was zum Entschluss führte, sie zu vergrößern. Das der Bauaufgabe zugrunde liegende architektonische Konzept ging vom Gedanken aus, dass der Charakter des Kulturlandes Südtirol von seinen Weinbergen geprägt wird. Da diese von Menschenhand gestaltet wurden und somit künstliche Bestandteile der Landschaft darstellen, sollte für die Kellerei Manincor ein Gebäude entworfen werden, das sich in diese historisch gewachsene Struktur der Weingüter am Kalterer See mimetisch einfügt. An das bestehende Renaissancegut wurden so genannte Funktionskeller angebaut. Ihr Bauprogramm umfasste u. a. Räume für Pressen und Tanks, Barrique- und Gärkeller, Lager, Garagen für Landwirtschaftsmaschinen, Abfüllanlagen, Verwaltung und Verkauf. Die Nutzflächen haben ein Gesamtausmaß von ca. 3.000 m^2 und wurden fast zur Gänze unterirdisch angelegt bzw. in einem mit Reben bepflanzten Hügel verborgen. Um dem großen mehrstöckigen Bauvolumen aber nicht die Wirkung zu verleihen, es wolle seine „natürliche" Umgebung nachahmen, wurde es derart konzipiert, dass es nur an wenigen Stellen seine Aufgabe verrät: Einschnitte für die Zufahrten und die Anhebung einer Deckenplatte zur Errichtung einer Aussichtsterrasse verleihen dem Weinberg einen denkwürdig funktionalen Charakter.

Walter Angonese, Silvia Boday, Rainer Köberl

Tenuta vinicola Manincor, Caldaro

2004

Intervento artistico: Manfred Alois Mayr, Erik Steinbrecher

Dal 1996 la famiglia Goëss-Enzenberg produce vini pregiati dalla vendemmia dei suoi quarantacinque ettari di vigneto. Poichè le dimensioni della cantina vinicola esistente non erano più sufficienti e si è deciso di ampliarla. Il progetto si basa sul presupposto che il paesaggio agricolo altoatesino è fortemente caratterizzato dal segno delle colline coltivate a vigneto e riconosce che, essendo un paesaggio tracciato dalla mano dell'uomo, esso è un elemento artificiale.

Il nuovo edificio della cantina Manincor è concepito per inserirsi mimeticamente nella struttura storicamente stratificata dei vigneti sul lago di Caldaro. Al complesso rinascimentale della tenuta sono state aggiunte delle cantine cosiddette "funzionali". Il programma previsto per la costruzione ha incluso, tra l'altro, spazi per le presse, per i serbatoi, le cantine per le barrique e la fermentazione, depositi, rimesse per macchine agricole, impianti d'imbottigliamento, l'amministrazione e la vendita. La superficie utile ammonta a circa 3.000 mq, quasi tutti disposti sotto terra o nascosti sotto la collina coltivata a vigneto. Per nascondere la dimensione del grande volume a più piani, volendo riprodurre un paesaggio "naturale", l'edificio è stato concepito in modo da emergere solo in pochi punti. I tagli per le rampe d'ingresso, l'inarcamento di un solaio per realizzare una terrazza panoramica, conferiscono al vigneto un carattere memorabile.

Walter Angonese, Silvia Boday, Rainer Köberl

Manincor vineyard, Caldaro

2004

Site-specific artwork: Manfred Alois Mayr, Erik Steinbrecher

Since 1996 the Goëss-Enzenberg family has produced fine wines from the grapes yielded by their 45 hectares of vineyards. The increasing shortage of space in their wine cellars led to a decision to expand. The architectural concept behind this project is derived from the idea that the character of the cultivated landscape of South Tyrol is shaped by its vineyards. As these were laid out by man and are therefore artificial elements of the landscape, it was planned to design a winery building for the Manicor vineyard that would integrate itself in the historically developed structure of the vineyards around Lago di Caldaro. So-called functional wine cellars were attached to the existing Renaissance building. The brief included spaces for the wine presses and tanks, barrique and fermentation cellar, storeroom, garages for agricultural machinery, filling plant, administration and sales. The floor area is about 3,000 m^2 and was laid out almost entirely below ground level or concealed in a hill planted with vines. To avoid any impression that this large building volume of several storeys attempts to mimic its "natural" environment it reveals its function at a few places: incisions made for the approach routes and the roof slab lifted to form a viewing terrace give the vineyard hill a memorably functional character.

Silvia Boday
Haus an der Weinstraße, Tramin
2005

Silvia Boday
Casa sulla Strada del Vino, Termeno
2005

Silvia Boday
House on the Weinstraße (wine road), Termeno
2005

Eine Scheune mit Hof und Querverbindung zum Nachbargebäude sollte abgerissen und durch ein kleines Haus ersetzt werden. In so einem Fall schreiben die Südtiroler Baugesetze vor, dass auf einem Baugrund in einer (quasi historisch) gewachsenen Ensemblestruktur bereits bestehende Höhen, Breiten und Abstände eines Altbaues auch bei einem Neubau erhalten bleiben müssen. Vor diesem Hintergrund schien wenig Freiraum für eine architektonische Gestaltung zu bestehen, dennoch ist es gelungen, das restriktive Reglement einzuhalten und dazu zu nützen, das Wohnhaus von Straßenlärm und Staub abzuschotten: Die Fassade wurde – ähnlich jener des Bestandes – bis auf ein kleines, rautenförmiges Fenster geschlossen. Mit seinen vorgegebenen Ankermustern am Sichtbeton und den abgeschnittenen Vordächern spielt das architektonische Konzept, so scheint es zumindest, auf das Vorbild des „Knusperhäuschens" im Märchen „Hänsel und Gretel" an.

Die massive Sichtbetonmauer wurde um die eine Hälfte des Hauses herumgezogen und im Unterschied dazu die Aussichtsseite völlig geöffnet. Im Erdgeschoss befinden sich die Schlafzimmer. Die Kinder gelangen von ihren Räumen in den geschützten Innenhof, der ihnen als Spielzimmer im Freien dient. Obergeschoss und Dachraum

Per fare spazio ad una piccola casa sono stati demoliti un fienile ed il corpo di collegamento all'edificio vicino. In questi casi la normativa edilizia altoatesina prescrive che sul lotto dove sorge l'insieme (storicamente) stratificato, le dimensioni e le distanze dell'edificio preesistente siano ripristinate nella nuova costruzione.

Le condizioni per un gesto architettonico, visti i presupposti, sembravano limitate, eppure l'intervento è riuscito nel rispetto del rigido regolamento che è stato utilizzato per proteggere la casa dalle polveri e dal rumore della strada: la facciata è stata chiusa come quella dell'edificio preesistente ad eccezione di una piccola finestra a losanga. Con il suo reticolo disegnato dai punti di ancoraggio dei casseri del cemento faccia a vista e il taglio degli spioventi del tetto, l'edificio sembra citare la casetta di pan pepato della fiaba di "Hansel e Gretel".

La muratura in cemento faccia a vista avvolge metà della casa; in antitesi, la parte panoramica con vista è completamente aperta. Le stanze da letto sono al piano terra e da lì i bambini possono raggiungere il cortile interno protetto, che è utilizzato come stanza da gioco all'aperto. Il piano superiore ed il sottotetto sono riuniti in un unico livello per recuperare l'altezza mancante. A questo piano si trovano una

A barn with a yard and a transverse connection to a neighbouring building was to be torn down and replaced by a small house. In such cases the building regulations in South Tyrol require that where an ensemble has developed historically on a site any new building erected must maintain the existing heights, widths and distances apart of the old buildings. While this situation may appear to restrict the scope for architectural design, in this particular case the restrictive regulation has been observed and indeed utilized to screen the dwelling house from the noise and dust of the road. The new façade, like that of the old building, is closed apart from a small diamond-shaped window. With the pattern of the anchor bolts for the shuttering used in making the exposed concrete walls and the abbreviated canopy roofs the architectural concept seems perhaps to refer to the model of a "gingerbread house" like in the fairy-tale "Hansel and Gretel".

A solid exposed concrete wall was extended around one half of the house, whereas the side of the building facing towards the view was opened up completely. The bedrooms are at ground floor level. The children can go directly from their rooms into a sheltered courtyard that they can use as a kind of outdoor playroom. The upper floor and the attic space were combined to compensate

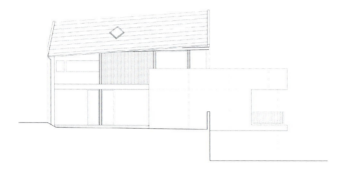

sind aufgrund fehlender Höhen zu einer Ebene zusammengezogen worden. Hier befinden sich eine Terrasse (am Dach des Elternschlafzimmers), der Wohnraum und die Küche. Auf einem eingebauten „Möbel" mit Nebenräumen konnte noch eine Bibliothek Platz finden.

terrazza (sul tetto della stanza da letto dei genitori), il soggiorno e la cucina. Un "mobile" ad incasso con spazi accessori ospita la biblioteca.

for the lack of height. There is a terrace at this level (on the roof of the parents' bedroom), as well as the living room and the kitchen. Space was found for a library on a piece of built-in "furniture" containing service rooms.

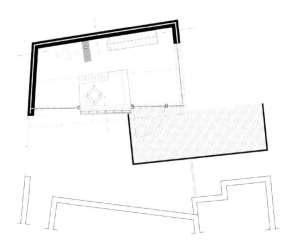

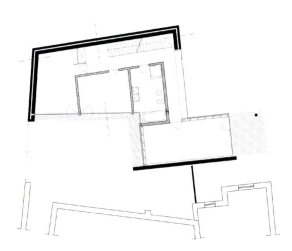

Wolfgang Piller
Oberschule für Landwirtschaft, Ansitz Baumgarten, Auer
2001
Kunst am Bau: Margit Klammer

Der in seinem Kern auf das 13. Jahrhundert zurückgehende Komplex durchlebte eine wechselvolle Geschichte und drohte zu verfallen, doch seine Umwidmung in eine Schule ging weit über eine Sanierung hinaus: Ursprünglich bestand das Ensemble aus vier Baukörpern, auf die völlig neue Nutzungsformen geschickt aufzuteilen und diese anschließend in eine funktionstüchtige Verbindung zueinander zu bringen waren. Für die Schaffung einer allen Bedürfnissen entsprechenden Organisation des Schulbetriebs wurden die notwendigen technischen und sanitären Einrichtungen in das Gebäude regelrecht implantiert. Wie im Verlauf einer Operation sind 25 km Stromkabel, 20 km Fußbodenheizung u. a. m. in die alten Mauern eingesetzt worden. Ein neuer Anbau verbindet das Schloss (Schulräume, Verwaltung) auf allen Ebenen mit einem vorgelagerten, ebenfalls zum Altbestand gehörenden Baukörper (Cafeteria) und einem früheren Wirtschaftsgebäude (Bibliothek). Heute bildet dieser aus vielen Tonnen Stahl und Beton bestehende Zubau das „Rückgrat" des Ansitzes. Seine architektonische Formensprache eines Riegels grenzt sich vom Altbestand optisch klar ab, ohne wie ein Fremdkörper zu wirken. Das milde Klima von Auer und der anziehende

Wolfgang Piller
Istituto Tecnico Agrario, Castel Baumgarten, Ora
2001
Intervento artistico: Margit Klammer

Il complesso, il cui nucleo risale al XIII secolo, ha sperimentato vicende alterne e minacciato di andare in rovina, ma la nuova destinazione d'uso ad edificio scolastico è andata ben oltre un intervento di restauro. Inizialmente l'insieme era composto da quattro edifici. Si è deciso di destinarli a nuovi usi e di collegarli in modo funzionale. Per realizzare un complesso scolastico la cui organizzazione soddisfacesse qualsiasi esigenza, sono stati installati secondo la normativa tutti gli impianti tecnico-sanitari necessari al funzionamento dell'edificio. Analogamente ad un'operazione chirurgica, sono stati inseriti nelle vecchie murature 25 km di cavi elettrici, 20 km di serpentine termiche ed altri impianti.
Un nuovo corpo di fabbrica per la distribuzione collega il castello (classi ed amministrazione) a tutti i livelli con l'edificio antistante (caffetteria), e con un deposito agricolo (biblioteca), entrambi già appartenenti al complesso.
Questo nuovo corpo di fabbrica, frapposto agli edifici, con le sue tonnellate d'acciaio e cemento, costituisce la "spina dorsale" della vecchia residenza. L'espressione formale della sua tipologia a stecca lo differenzia con chiarezza dalla preesistenza, senza farlo apparire un corpo estraneo.

Wolfgang Piller
Agricultural school, Baumgarten estate, Ora
2001
Site-specific artwork: Margit Klammer

This complex, with a core dating back to the 13th century experienced an eventful history and was even threatened by decay. However its conversion into a school went far further than a mere renovation. The original ensemble consisted of four buildings; the task was to distribute completely new uses among these buildings in an intelligent way and to combine these uses functionally. To organize the school in a way that would meet all requirements the necessary technical and sanitary facilities were truly "implanted" in the building. Like in a surgical operation 25 kilometres of electric cables, 20 kilometres of underfloor heating, and other services were inserted in the old walls. A new addition connects the Schloss (classrooms, administration) on all levels with an existing building in front of it (cafeteria) and a former outhouse (library). Today this addition consisting of many tons of steel and concrete forms the "spine" of the estate. Its particular architectural idiom clearly distinguishes it visually from the old buildings, yet it does not seem like an alien element. The mild climate in Ora and the

Charme des Ansitzes bestimmen die Topografie des Ortes. Die Modernisierung führte nun dazu, dass hier eine angenehme Campus-Atmosphäre eingezogen ist, die infolge einer künstlerischen Intervention auch eine poetische Note besitzt.

Il clima mite di Ora e lo charme attraente del castello caratterizzano la topografia del luogo. L'ammodernamento ha donato al complesso una piacevole atmosfera da campus scolastico e, grazie all'intervento artistico, anche una nota poetica.

attractive charms of the estate determine the topography of the place. The modernisation has led to development of a kind of campus atmosphere that is lent a poetic note by an artistic intervention.

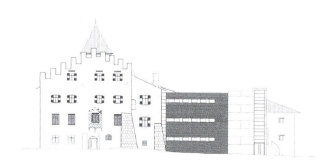 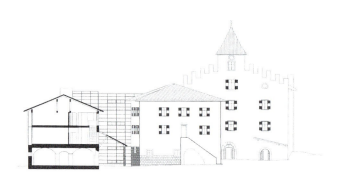

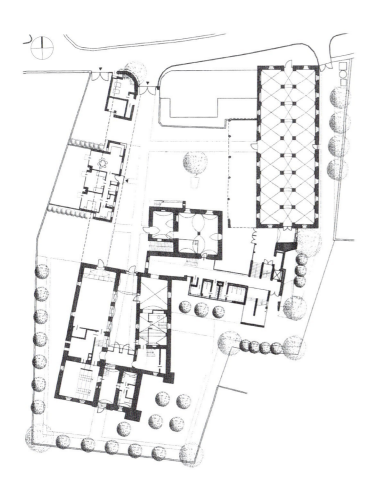
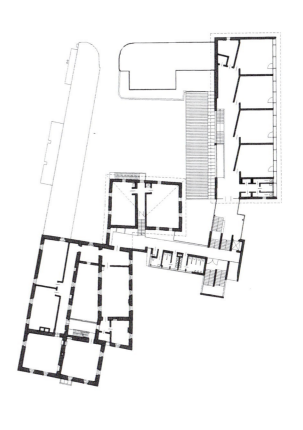

0 10 20

Höller & Klotzner Architekten
Erweiterung Pfarrkirche, Leifers
2003
Kunst am Bau: Carmen Müller und Manfred Alois Mayr

Bei der Kirchenerweiterung wurde ein minimiertes Material-Repertoire eingesetzt, um dem Ideal einer Kirche als Ort der inneren Einkehr gerecht zu werden: Die äußere Schale des Baues besteht aus Tombak-Platten (Kupfer-Zink-Legierung), die Innenraumgestaltung wird von Ahorn bestimmt und verschiedene Glasarten sorgen für gezielte Lichtinszenierungen. Der Bau wurde über einem unregelmäßigen Grundriss errichtet, der sich am Verlauf der nördlichen Grundstücksgrenze orientiert. Daher mündet der angebaute Körper auch formal in einen spitzen Winkel in Richtung der hinter ein Holzgerüst gesetzten Orgel und des Platzes für den Chor. Diese Zone ist die hellste im neuen Kirchenraum, so gehen vor dem matt leuchtenden Hintergrund alle hervorgebrachten Klänge bildlich sofort in höhere Sphären über.
An den Eingang zum Neubau wurde eine Lichtschleuse gesetzt. Von dort werden die Blicke der Besucher regelrecht zum Altar hingezogen – ein Wahrnehmungseffekt, der durch nach innen geneigte Wände, einen zum Altar leicht abfallenden Boden und die wie eine Zeltplane durchhängende Decke erzeugt wird. Mit dem über dem Altar abgehängten Kreuz erreicht das dramaturgische Konzept seinen Höhepunkt. Verstärkt

Höller & Klotzner architetti
Ampliamento della Chiesa Parrocchiale, Laives
2003
Intervento artistico: Carmen Müller e Manfred Alois Mayr

L'ampliamento della parrocchiale utilizza un repertorio ridotto di materiali per corrispondere all'idea della chiesa come luogo di raccoglimento interiore: la pelle esterna dell'edificio è realizzata in piastre di Tombak, una lega di rame ed alluminio, l'allestimento interno è caratterizzato dall'uso del legno d'acero, mentre l'uso di diversi tipi di vetro soddisfa una mirata messinscena della luce. La costruzione sorge su un lotto di forma irregolare che si orienta secondo l'andamento del confine settentrionale del lotto. Il corpo di fabbrica annesso sfocia pertanto anche formalmente in un angolo acuto, rivolto in direzione dello spazio destinato al coro e dell'impalcatura lignea, dietro alla quale è disposto l'organo. Questa zona è la più luminosa del nuovo spazio della chiesa, realizzata in modo tale che, davanti alla quinta da cui si diffonde una luce opaca, tutti i suoni risalgano figurativamente alle più alte sfere.
Sopra all'ingresso della nuova costruzione è posto un taglio di luce. Da qui lo sguardo dei visitatori è attirato all'altare – un effetto percettivo che si realizza grazie all'inclinazione verso l'interno delle pareti, ad un pavimento lievemente in discesa verso l'altare e alla copertura che come un tendone appeso scende verso il basso.

Höller & Klotzner Architekten
Extension to Laives Parish Church, Laives
2003
Site-specific artwork: Carmen Müller and Manfred Alois Mayr

To achieve the ideal of a church as a place of inner contemplation this substantial addition to an existing church employs a minimised repertoire of materials: the external envelope of the building consists of tombac panels (an alloy of copper and zinc), while the interior is dominated by maple wood and various kinds of glass that produce a focussed use of light. The building was erected on an irregular plan that follows the line of the northern site boundary. Therefore the new volume tapers in an acute angle towards the organ (behind a wooden frame) and the space for the choir. This zone is the brightest in the new church space; against the matt shining background all the tones produced immediately pass visually into a higher sphere.
From the "gateway of light" positioned at the entrance to the new building the visitors' gaze is drawn towards the altar, an effect that is created by the inward tilted walls, the floor that slopes slightly downwards to the altar and the ceiling that is suspended like a piece of tarpaulin. The cross hanging above the altar is the highpoint in this dramaturgical concept. According to the

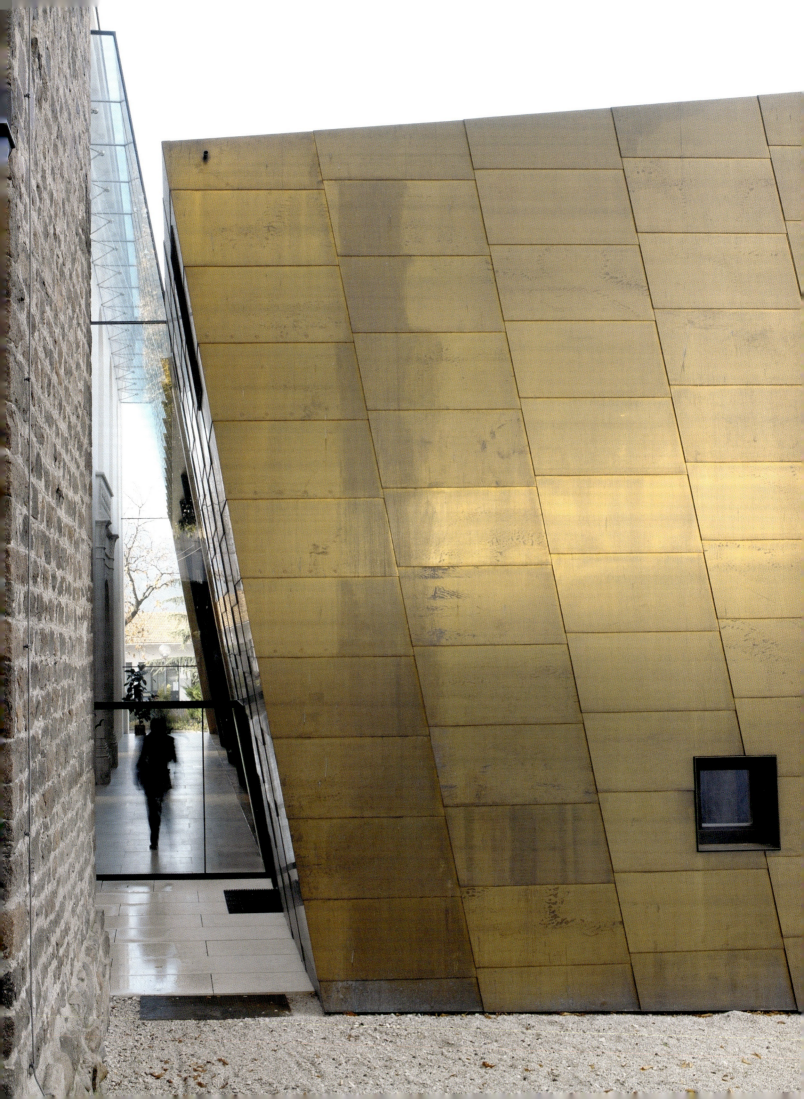

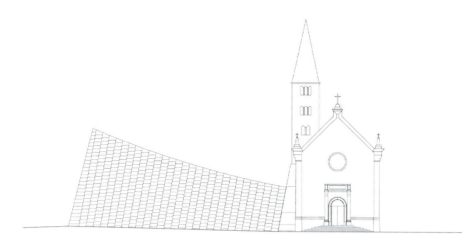

wird diese Wirkung noch durch ein – je nach Tageszeit – wechselndes Streiflicht im Hintergrund und eine optische Täuschung, die beim Betrachter den Eindruck erweckt, ihm sei das Kreuz wie ein „Fingerzeig Gottes" zugeneigt.

L'effetto scenografico raggiunge l'apice con la croce appesa sull'altare. Questa tensione è rafforzata dalla lama di luce retrostante che muta secondo le ore del giorno, e dall'illusione ottica che incute nell'osservatore l'impressione che la croce penda su di lui come un "cenno divino".

time of day the slanting light in the background further heightens the overall effect, as does the visual illusion that the cross is tilted towards visitors like the pointing finger of God.

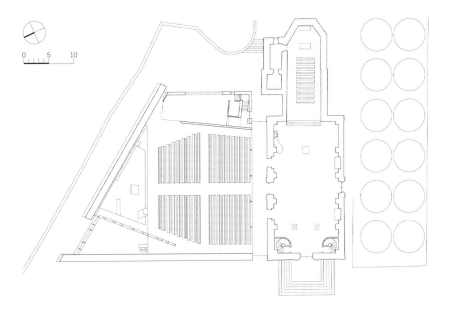

Bruno Endrizzi, Kirchgänger

„Wenn man sich einmal daran gewöhnt hat, ist die neue Kirche wunderbar."

Bruno Endrizzi, cattolico osservante

"Dopo che ci si è abituati, la chiesa è splendida!"

Bruno Endrizzi, church-goer

"Once you have grown used to it the new church is wonderful."

Eisacktal   **Valle d'Isarco**

Brennerautobahn im Wipptal
Autostrada del Brennero presso l'Alta Val d'Isarco
Brenner motorway in Alta Val d'Isarco

Benno Barth
Haus Kaser, Brixen
2004
Kunst am Bau: Designer Societät Stuttgart (Farb- und Materialkonzept)

Benno Barh
Casa Kaser, Bressanone
2004
Intervento artistico: Designer Societät Stuttgart (concetto per i materiali ed il colore)

Benno Barth
Kaser House, Bressanone
2004
Site-specific artwork: Designer Societät Stuttgart (colour and material concept)

Das Wohnhaus befindet sich auf leicht ansteigendem Terrain im ländlichen Ortsteil Milland bei Brixen. Auf der einen Seite der Parzelle verläuft ein Bach, auf der anderen erstrecken sich im Anschluss an die Zufahrtsstraße weitläufige Wiesen. Ober- und unterhalb des Bauplatzes wurden schon früher Wohnhäuser errichtet. Da auch noch entsprechende Abstände zu den Nachbargebäuden einzuhalten waren, führte diese Ausgangslage zum Entwurf eines lang gestreckten Baukörpers von ca. 4,20 x 20 m. Unter den relativ eingeschränkten Bedingungen – die vorgegebenen Maße des Einfamilienhauses betreffend – war es nur durch die Anwendung eines Kunstgriffs möglich, neben dem üblichen Raumprogramm auch noch einen Gästetrakt unterzubringen: Aufgrund der Neigung des Geländes konnte die Hälfte des Erdgeschosses unterirdisch angelegt werden. Von den hier liegenden Schlafzimmern der Familie gelangt man direkt in den Garten, wohingegen der hangseitig angelegte Gästetrakt sein Tageslicht über einen kleinen Lichthof bezieht. Da das Dach dieses Bereiches begrünt wurde und es somit zum Garten gehört, ist die Einhaltung seines Abstandes zum Nachbarhaus nicht mehr von Bedeutung.

L'edificio residenziale è collocato su un terreno in leggero pendio nella frazione più rurale di Milland a Bressanone. Su un lato del lotto scorre un torrente, sull'altro lato oltre la strada di accesso si estendono ampie distese di prati, mentre a monte e a valle esistevano già degli altri edifici residenziali. Dovendo rispettare anche le distanze dagli edifici limitrofi, questa condizione iniziale ha determinato il progetto di un corpo di fabbrica allungato delle dimensioni di ca. 4,20 x 20 metri. A causa delle limitate condizioni – quelle imposte dalle dimensioni prestabilite per una casa unifamiliare – è stato possibile realizzare solo con un artificio, oltre al solito programma funzionale, anche un'ala per gli ospiti. Grazie all'inclinazione del terreno, metà del piano terra è stato interrato. Qui, dalle stanze da letto della famiglia si può raggiungere direttamente il giardino. L' ala destinata agli ospiti è disposta sotto il pendio e prende luce da una corte.
Il rispetto delle distanze dalla casa vicina non ha più rilevanza, perché la copertura di questa zona trattata a verde appartiene al giardino.
Il piano superiore della casa confina su questo lato del giardino con la cucina, la zona pranzo ed il soggiorno. Sul tetto è sta-

This residence is situated on a slightly rising slope in the rural area of Milland, near Bressanone. A stream runs along one side of the site, on the other extensive meadows flank the approach road. Houses had been already erected above and below the site. The necessity of keeping the required distance to the neighbouring buildings led to the design of an elongated volume measuring approximately 4.20 x 20 metres.
Given these relatively restricted conditions – as far as the predetermined dimensions of the single-family house were concerned – only the use of considerable ingenuity made it possible to include a guest wing as well the normal spatial programme. Thanks to the slope of the site half of the ground floor could be embedded below ground level. The family bedrooms, which are on this level, have direct access to the garden, whereas the guest wing added up the slope gets daylight from a small light well. As the roof of this latter area was planted and therefore forms part of the garden, preserving the stipulated distance to the neighbouring house was no longer a concern.
The upper floor of the house that contains the kitchen, dining area and living room adjoins this part of the garden. A library made

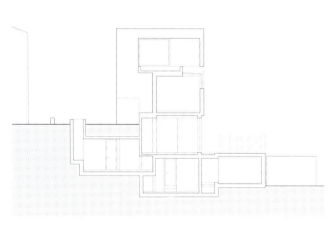

An diesen Teil des Gartens grenzt das Obergeschoss des Hauses mit Küche, Essplatz und Wohnzimmer. Im Dachgeschoss wurde eine Bibliothek eingerichtet, an die eine Dachterrasse anschließt. Diese Freifläche wird von einer lustvoll geschwungenen „Bambus-Reling" umfangen, die ihre Benutzer vor neugierigen Blicken von außen schützen soll.

ta allestita la biblioteca che si apre su un terrazzo. Un parapetto ondulato in canne di bambù delimita questo spazio all'aperto e protegge gli abitanti da sguardi indiscreti.

in the attic adjoins a roof terrace. This outdoor area is enclosed by a playfully curving bamboo railing intended to shield the residents from outsiders' prying glances.

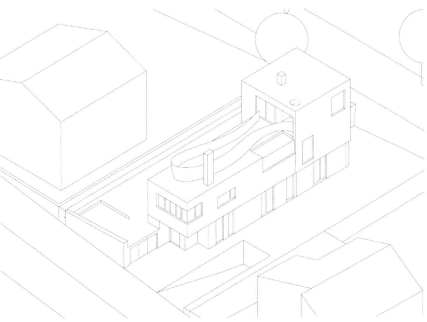

Sabine Kaser, Bauherrin (mit Tochter Greta)	**Sabine Kaser, committente (con la figlia Greta)**	**Sabine Kaser, client (with daughter Greta)**
„Ja, wunderbar! Wir genießen es sehr – diese Offenheit der Räume."	"E' magnifico! Siamo soddisfatti di questi spazi ariosi."	"Yes, wonderful! We really enjoy the openness of the spaces."

Siegfried Delueg
Landesberufsschule und Studentenhaus, Brixen
2002/2003
Kunst am Bau: Designer Societät Stuttgart mit Hans Knapp, Josef Rainer

Am südlichen Rand von Brixen entstand ein Stadtteil, der ganz von jungen Menschen bevölkert ist, die hier attraktive Lernangebote vorfinden. Unter anderem wurde zwischen der viel befahrenen Brennerstraße und dem ruhigen Fischzuchtweg eine Landesberufsschule realisiert, deren Baukörper so am Gelände verteilt wurden, dass die Lärm erzeugenden von den Ruhe benötigenden getrennt sind: Die Werkstätten liegen an der Durchzugsstraße, die Klassentrakte auf der anderen Seite. In der Mitte der beiden Riegel erstreckt sich eine Sporthalle, die auch von außen begehbar ist. Aus der Vogelperspektive betrachtet, ergibt das ganze Ensemble ein Quadrat – das allerdings durch die geschickte Aufteilung der Nutzungsformen auf verschiedene Volumen keinerlei Behäbigkeit aufweist. Am Campus befinden sich ferner ein Pausengarten und ein weitläufiger Vorplatz. Die Schüler nützen beide Zonen, z. B. zur Präsentation von temporären Installationen, die im Werkstatt-Unterricht entstanden sind.

In nächster Nähe befindet sich ein weiteres Gebäude mit quadratischem Grundriss. Es beherbergt eine Mensa und ein Wohnheim für Studenten, dessen Zimmer in U-Form um einen Erschließungskern und eine Gemeinschaftszone gruppiert wurden. Dieser

Sigfried Delueg
Scuola Professionale Provinciale e studentato, Bressanone
2002/2003
Intervento artistico: Designer Societät Stuttgart con Hans Knapp, Josef Rainer

Lungo il margine meridionale della cittadina di Bressanone è sorto un quartiere frequentato prevalentemente da giovani che vi trovano un'interessante offerta scolastica. Compresa tra la statale del Brennero, fortemente trafficata, e la più tranquilla via del laghetto, insieme agli altri edifici è stata realizzata una scuola professionale i cui corpi di fabbrica sono distribuiti sul lotto in modo da distinguere quelli che provocano rumore da quelli che necessitano di quiete. I laboratori si trovano lungo la strada di transito, le classi sull'altro lato. Al centro delle due stecche edilizie si estende la palestra accessibile anche dall'esterno. Osservato da una prospettiva a volo d'uccello, tutto l'insieme rimanda ad un quadrato che però, grazie alla sapiente distribuzione dei diversi volumi funzionali, non suscita alcun senso di pesantezza. Nel campus si trovano anche il giardino per la pausa ed un ampio piazzale d'ingresso. Gli studenti utilizzano entrambe le zone anche per la presentazione delle installazioni temporanee realizzate durante le lezioni di laboratorio.

Poco distante si trova un altro edificio a pianta quadrata. Esso ospita una mensa ed uno studentato le cui stanze si dispongono per gruppi a "U" intorno a un nucleo per la distribuzione e a uno spazio collettivo.

Siegfried Delueg
Regional vocational school and student residence, Bressanone
2002/2003
Site-specific artwork: Designer Societät Stuttgart with Hans Knapp, Josef Rainer

On the southern periphery of Bressanone an urban district has been created that is populated entirely by young people who can avail of attractive educational facilities here. These include a regional vocational school built between Via Brennero with its heavy traffic and Via Piscicoltura, a far quieter road. In distributing the volume of the building on the site the areas that create noise were separated from those that require quiet: the workshops are on the main road, the classrooms on the other side. The sports hall that stands between the two blocks can also be entered separately from outside. Seen from a birds-eye view the entire ensemble is a square – but due to the intelligent distribution of the functions in different volumes it avoids making a sedate impression. There is a garden on the campus that is used during breaks, as well as an extensive forecourt. The students use both zones, for instance to present temporary installations that have been made during classes in the workshops.

Nearby there is another building with a square floor plan containing the cafeteria and a student residence. The students' rooms are grouped around an internal circulation core and communal zone. This core, which is rounded in plan, contains a

Bereich, der an seinen Ecken abgerundet ist, enthält ein Fernsehzimmer bzw. einen Fitnessraum, an seiner Außenwand ist in jedem Stockwerk eine Gemeinschaftsküche eingerichtet worden.

Questo ambiente, arrotondato agli angoli, contiene una sala video o un locale per l'esercizio fisico, mentre sulla sua parete esterna è allestita ad ogni piano una cucina comunitaria.

television room, a fitness room and on each floor there is a communal kitchen running along the outside of the enclosing wall.

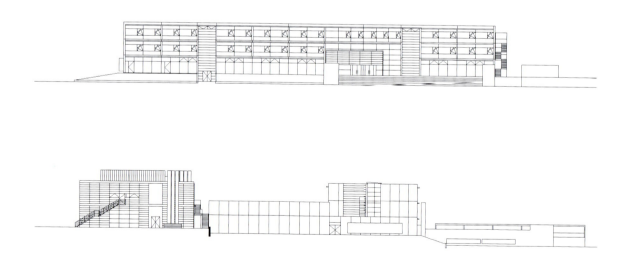

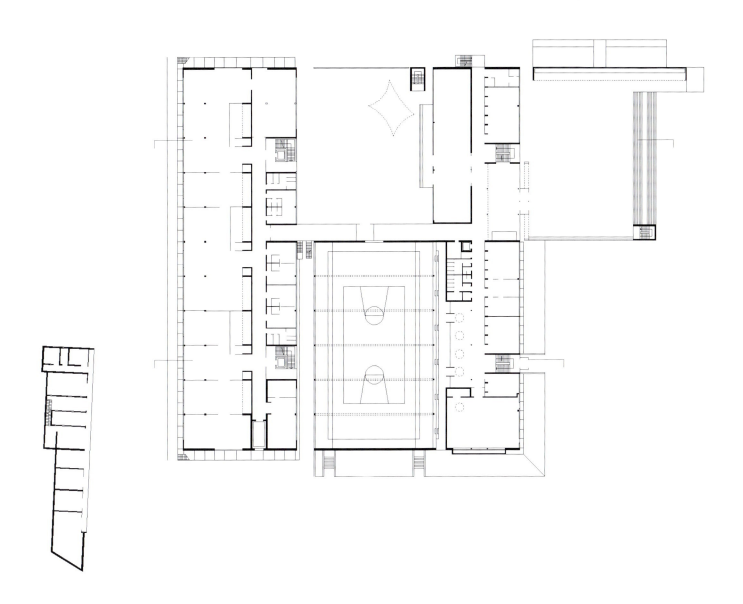
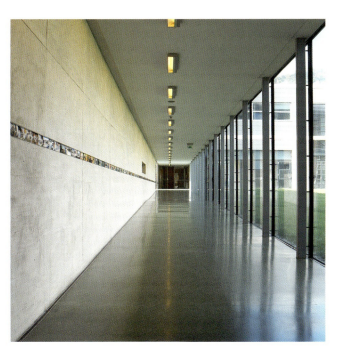

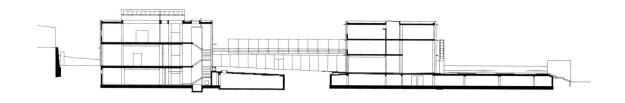
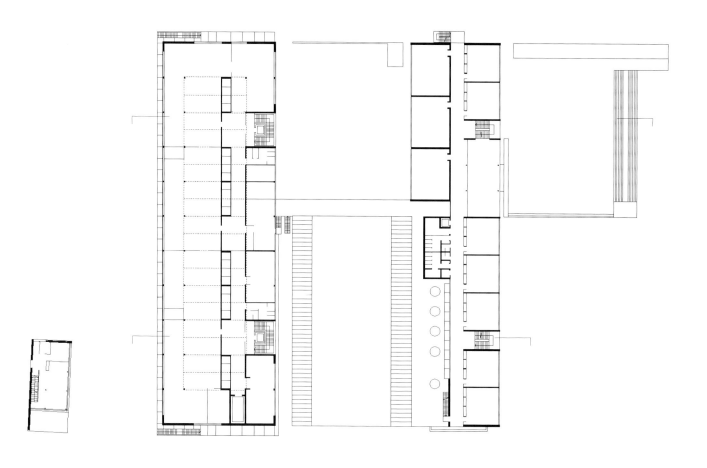
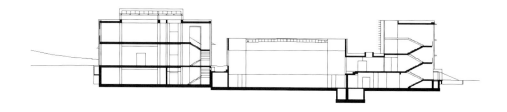

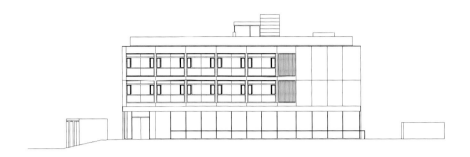

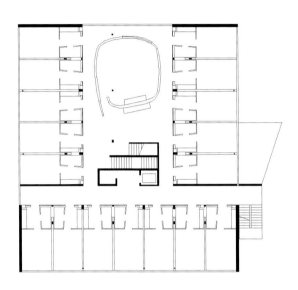

Studentenhaus
Studentato
Student residence

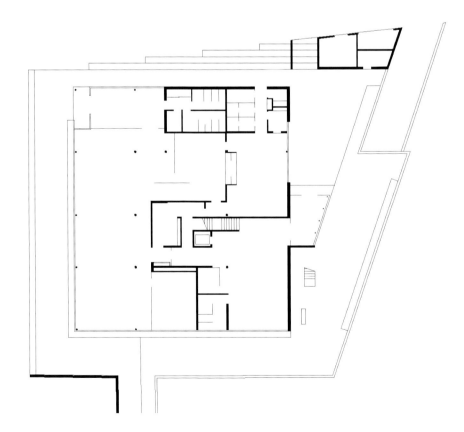

MODUS architects (Matteo Scagnol, Sandy Attia)
Kinder-Tagesbetreuungsstätte im Krankenhaus, Brixen
2005

Mit der Ausschreibung eines Unternehmer-Ideenwettbewerbs verfolgte der Sanitätsbetrieb Brixen das Ziel, einen Entwurf für eine Kinder-Tagesbetreuungsstätte zu erhalten und zugleich das kostengünstigste Projekt zu ermitteln. Es wurde der Vorschlag realisiert, der u. a. durch die Einsparung von Bautagen – der Kinderhort wurde in nur 90 Tagen schlüsselfertig realisiert – die Errichtungskosten besonders niedrig halten konnte.

Der Kindergarten entstand auf dem Areal des Krankenhauses, wo man ihn für die Kinder der Angestellten und die stundenweise Betreuung der Kinder von Patienten benötigt. Vorgefertigte Bauteile wurden in Trockenbauweise auf einer massiven Betonplatte montiert. Das Gebäude gleicht einem Gartenpavillon, dessen Raumprogramm in zwei Bereiche geteilt wurde, in eine Ruhezone mit Schlafräumen im rückwärtigen Teil und eine Aufenthalts- bzw. Spielzone im vorderen Teil des Baukörpers. Eine Glasfront grenzt die Innenräume zum Park hin ab. Die Innenraumgestaltung von Kindergärten ist ein problematisches Arbeitsgebiet, weil viele Designer und Hersteller keinen Bezug zur Ideenwelt von Kindern finden und ihnen mit ihren Entwürfen häufig das Kindsein wegnehmen. Bei der

MODUS architects (Matteo Scagnol, Sandy Attia)
Centro bambino dell'ospedale, Bressanone
2005

Con il bando di un appalto concorso l'unità sanitaria di Bressanone ha ottenuto due obbiettivi, il progetto preliminare per il centro assistenza diurna all'infanzia e allo stesso tempo l'offerta più economica per la sua realizzazione. E' stata realizzata la proposta che è riuscita in modo particolare a contenere i costi e tra l'altro i tempi d'esecuzione, l'asilo nido è stato realizzato in soli novanta giorni. L'asilo è stato edificato su un'area dell'ospedale e viene utilizzato per i figli dei dipendenti e per l'affidamento temporaneo dei bambini dei pazienti. Gli elementi prefabbricati a secco sono stati montati su di un basamento massiccio in calcestruzzo. La costruzione assomiglia ad un padiglione per giardini ed il suo programma funzionale è stato suddiviso in due: sul retro una zona riparata con gli spazi per il riposo, sul davanti una zona di intrattenimento e per il gioco. Un fronte vetrato delimita gli spazi interni verso il parco. L'arredo degli interni delle scuole per l'infanzia è un tema problematico, infatti molti designer e produttori non trovano riferimenti all'immaginario dei bambini e spesso li privano dell'espe-

MODUS architects (Matteo Scagnol, Sandy Attia)
Children's day-care centre in the hospital, Bressanone
2005

The health authorities in Bressanone set up an ideas competition to find the most economically viable design for a children's day-care centre. The proposal that was eventually carried out involved a construction period of only 90 days thus keeping building costs to an absolute minimum.

The kindergarten was erected on a site in the hospital and caters for the children of hospital staff as well as looking after patients' children on an hourly basis. Prefabricated building elements were mounted on a solid concrete slab using a dry construction system. The building resembles a garden pavilion, with a spatial programme split into two parts: a rest zone with sleeping areas at the rear and a play area at the front. A glass wall separates the interior spaces from the park. The design of a kindergarten interior is often problematic, as many designers and producers cannot relate to the children's world of ideas and hence their designs often deprive children of the experience of being a child. In the interior design of the Bressanone kindergarten, however, the children have been given exactly what they need for their intellectual

innenarchitektonischen Gestaltung des Brixner Kindergartens ist es jedoch gelungen, den Kindern genau das zu bieten, was sie für ihre geistige und emotionale Entfaltung benötigen: formal klar strukturierte Räume, Möbel mit eindeutig erkennbaren Funktionen und eine nicht mit Farben überfrachtete Umwelt.

rienza di essere bimbi. Nel progetto d'interni dell'asilo di Bressanone si è riusciti ad offrire ai bambini, proprio quanto loro necessario per un corretto sviluppo spirituale ed emozionale: spazi formali chiaramente strutturati, mobili dalla funzione inequivocabile ed un ambiente non sovracarico di colore.

and emotional development: spaces that are clearly structured in the formal sense, furniture with unambiguously defined functions rather than an environment characterised by the excessive use of different colours.

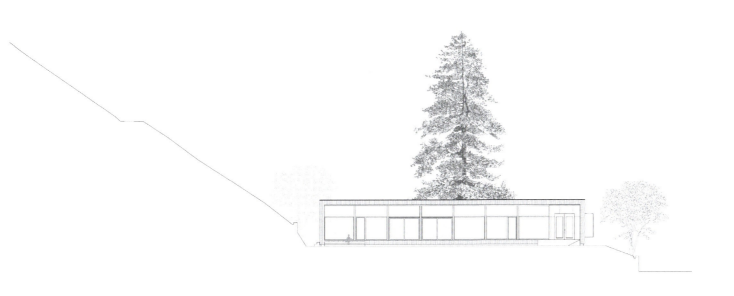

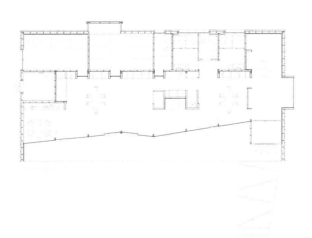

Gerd Bergmeister
Haus Sachsenklemme, Franzensfeste
2004

Im Transitland Südtirol gibt es heute viele Wohngegenden, die einer enormen Lärm-, Staub- und Giftbelastung ausgesetzt sind. Mit diesen negativen Auswirkungen des Verkehrs auf ihre Lebensräume muss die Bevölkerung zwangsläufig zurechtkommen. Ein regelrechtes Arrangement mit der Umwelt wollte der Besitzer des Hotels Sachsenklemme eingehen und gab den Auftrag zur Gestaltung eines Hauses neben seinem Gasthof, das allen Einflüssen von außen trotzt. Dem Bauplatz „Sachsenklemme" kommt dabei sogar symbolische Bedeutung zu, denn wie der Bauherr Staub und Lärm draußen halten möchte, trotzten an der selben Stelle schon 1809 die Tiroler Freiheitshelden den Verbündeten Napoleons.

Das Wohnhaus steht wie eine Festung zwischen Autobahn, Staatsstraße und Eisack-Fluss. Es ist in Sichtbeton ausgeführt und nur die obere Zone wurde mit rot emailliertem Glas beplankt, um das Gebäude an die rot-weißen Fensterläden des Hotels anzupassen. Das Erdgeschoss ist als offene Wohnebene mit Küche und Sitzplätzen gestaltet, im Obergeschoss befinden sich Schlaf- und Sanitärräume. In allen Bereichen des Hauses ist spürbar, dass der Architekt bisher als Innenraumgestalter tätig war. Doch nirgends – auch nicht auf der Terrasse – würde man annehmen, dass sich in nächster Nähe zu diesem gediegenen

Gerd Bergmeister
Casa Sachsenklemme, Fortezza
2004

L'Alto Adige è una provincia di transito e pertanto molte zone residenziali sono esposte ad un'elevata quantità di rumore, polveri ed inquinamento. La popolazione è costretta a confrontarsi con gli effetti negativi del traffico sul suo ambiente. Il proprietario dell'albergo Sachsenklemme ha cercato un confronto in piena regola ed ha affidato l'incarico per il progetto della sua casa affinché venisse costruita proprio a fianco del suo albergo, indifferente alle conseguenze del traffico.

L'area di edificazione "Sachsenklemme" assume così un significato simbolico: come il committente ha voluto tenere all'esterno polveri e rumori, così nel 1809 i combattenti per la libertà tirolese si opposero agli alleati di Napoleone. La casa d'abitazione si erge come una fortezza tra l'autostrada, la strada statale e il fiume Isarco. E' costruita in calcestruzzo a vista, e solo la parte superiore è rivestita in lastre di vetro smaltate di rosso in sintonia con le imposte rosse e bianche dell'albergo. Il piano terra è allestito come spazio aperto con cucina e zona pranzo, al piano superiore si trovano le stanze da letto ed i bagni. In tutti gli ambienti della casa risulta evidente la specializzazione per gli interni, che finora ha caratterizzato l'attività dell'architetto. Eppure in nessun luogo, neanche sulla terrazza, si percepisce che questa studia-

Gerd Bergmeister
Sachsenklemme House, Fortezza
2004

In South Tyrol, a region with an enormous volume of through traffic, many residential areas are exposed to extremely high levels of noise, dust and toxic pollution. The populace has been obliged to come to terms with the negative impact of traffic on the space in which they live. The owner of the Hotel Sachsenklemme wanted to enter into an arrangement with the environment and commissioned the design of a house beside his hotel that resists all external influences. As a consequence the site Sachsenklemme acquires a symbolic meaning, for in much the same way as the client attempts to resist the invasion of dust and noise, in 1809 on the same site heroic Tyrolean freedom fighters defied Napoleon's allies.

The house stands like a fortress between the highway, main road and the River Isarco. It is built in exposed concrete; only the upper zone was clad with red enamelled glass to harmonise with the red and white shutters of the hotel. The ground floor is designed as an open living area with kitchen and seating, the bedrooms and bathrooms are on the upper floor. Throughout the house one notices the fact that the architect previously worked as an interior designer. But nowhere, not even on the terrace, would one guess that a busy road runs close to this dignified residence. The massiveness of the concrete repels the noise of traffic,

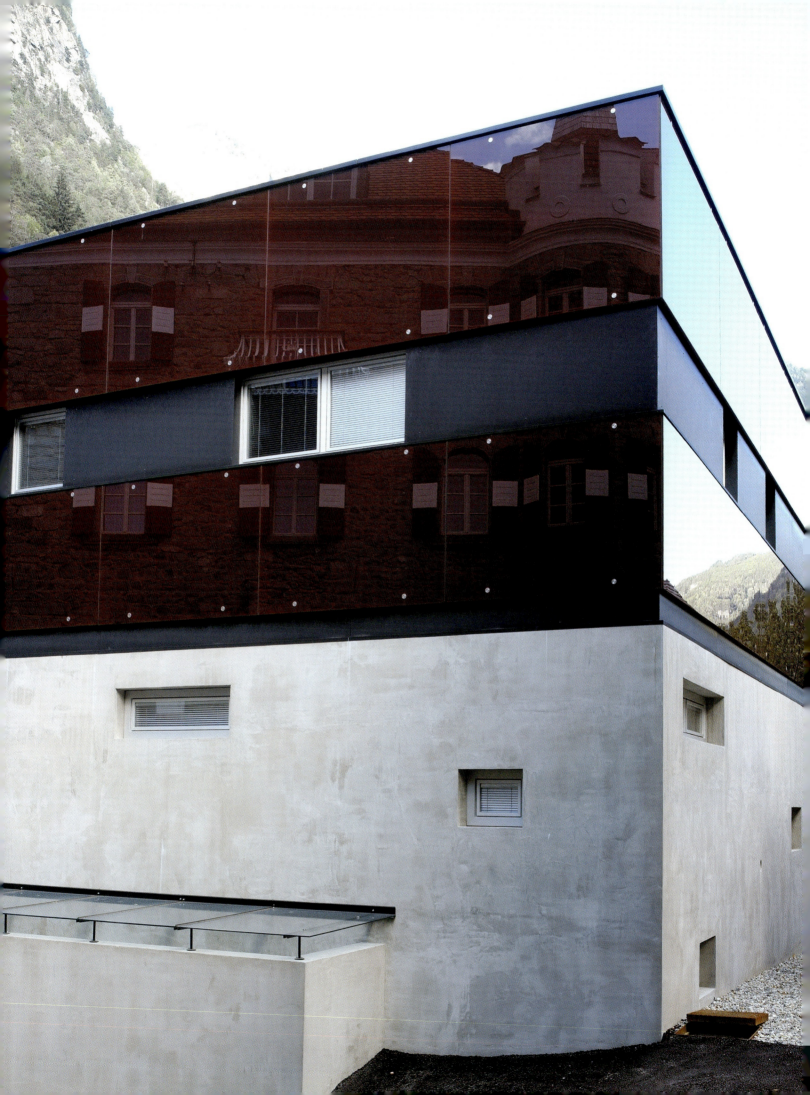

Wohnort viel befahrene Straßen befinden. Der massive Beton hält den Autolärm gut ab und die hier so extrem schlechte Luftqualität wird verbessert, indem ein Lüftungssystem Frischluft aus dem Wald ansaugt, filtert und in die Innenräume abgibt.

ta residenza si trova nelle vicinanze di vie fortemente trafficate. La massa del calcestruzzo trattiene efficacemente il rumore delle automobili, e la qualità dell'aria, qui molto scadente, è migliorata da un sistema di ventilazione che aspira l'aria dal bosco, la filtra e la reinserisce nei locali.

while the air quality, which is generally so poor here, is improved through a ventilation system that draws fresh air from the woods, filters it and introduces it into the interior.

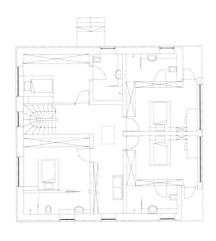

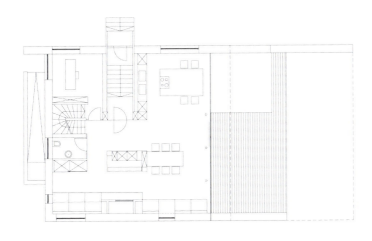

Christian Schwienbacher
Wohnhaus in Stilfes, Freienfeld
2004

Der kleine Wohnbau wurde auf einem Teil des elterlichen Grundstückes errichtet. Im Zuge der Planung kam ein vom Architekten ausgearbeiteter Fragebogen zum Einsatz, der zur Analyse der Bedürfnisse der zukünftigen Bewohner diente und sich den Themen Wohnen, Gäste, Baden u. a. m. widmete. Anhand der Fragen über Wünsche, Lebenspläne und Empfindungen setzten sich die Bauherren mit dem von ihnen geplanten Wohnraum in einer Weise auseinander, die nicht schon von visuellen Vor-Urteilen geprägt war, bevor der Architekt zum Zeichenstift greifen konnte. Auch gelang es mithilfe der Fragen, die Aufgabenstellung für den Architekten zu klären – hier mit dem Resultat, dass er dieser Familie ein Haus „kochen" sollte:
Im Erdgeschoss bilden Küche und Essplatz die zentralen Wohneinheiten des ganzen Hauses, wobei ein fließender Übergang zwischen dem Garten, der Terrasse und dem Innenraum hergestellt wurde. Im rückwärtigen Teil dieser Ebene befindet sich sonst nur noch ein abgeteilter Wohnbereich, während die Schlafzimmer im oberen Stockwerk untergebracht wurden. Von jedem dieser Schlafräume gelangt man auf den umlaufenden Balkon. Beton, Lärchenholz im Außenbereich und Eichenholz in den Innenräumen sind die wichtigsten Materialien, aus denen dieses Haus besteht.

Christian Schwienbacher
Casa d'abitazione a Stilves, Campo di Trens
2004

La piccola costruzione residenziale è stata costruita su una parte del terreno appartenente ai genitori. Il progetto è stato affiancato dall'elaborazione da parte dell'architetto di un questionario sulle esigenze dei futuri abitanti, dedicato tra gli altri, ai temi dell'abitare, dell'ospitalità e dell'igiene. Sulla scorta delle domande riguardo i propri desideri, percezioni e progetti di vita, i committenti si sono confrontati con lo spazio abitativo da loro pensato senza essere influenzati da pregiudizi visivi, ancor prima che l'architetto potesse toccare la matita. Il questionario è stato d'aiuto anche all'architetto per meglio definire il compito progettuale, con il risultato che egli ha dovuto "cucinare" una casa per questa famiglia: al piano terreno la cucina e la zona pranzo costituiscono l'unità abitativa centrale della casa, nonostante si sia realizzato un passaggio fluido tra il giardino, la terrazza e lo spazio interno. A questo piano sul retro c'è solo un altro ambito soggiorno separato. Le stanze da letto sono al piano superiore. Da ogni stanza si può raggiungere il balcone, che gira intorno all'edificio. Il calcestruzzo, il legno di larice per gli esterni e il rovere per gli interni, sono i materiali principali di questa costruzione. Sono pochi materiali da costruzione, ma vi si può riconoscere

Christian Schwienbacher
House in Stilves, Campo di Trens
2004

This small house was erected on part of a site belonging to the client's parents. In the course of planning the architects used a kind of questionnaire to analyse the needs of the future residents. It dealt with themes such as living, guests, the role of the bathroom etc. Before the architect even started to draw in answering these questions about their wishes, plans and sensibilities the clients examined their future living space in a way that was not influenced by visual preconceptions. This questionnaire also enabled the architect to clarify his task, with the outcome that his job here was to "cook" a house for the family.
On the ground floor the kitchen and dining room form the central living unit of the entire house, whereby a flowing transition was created between the garden, the terrace and the interior. At the rear of this level there is a separate living area, the bedrooms are located on the first floor. Each of these bedrooms has access to a continuous balcony. Concrete, larch wood used externally and oak indoors are the most important building materials employed in this house. One can discern a relationship between this restricted number of materials and the approach to life of the people who live here: the family wanted to build a solid, modern house, but everything was to revolve around the kitchen.

Das sind nur wenige Werkstoffe, doch man kann zwischen ihnen und dem Lebensgefühl der hier wohnenden Menschen auch eine übergeordnete Beziehung erkennen: Die Familie wollte ein solides und modernes Haus bauen, es sollte sich nur alles um die Küche drehen.

una relazione con lo spirito degli abitanti della casa: la famiglia desiderava costruire una casa solida e moderna e tutto doveva ruotare intorno alla cucina.

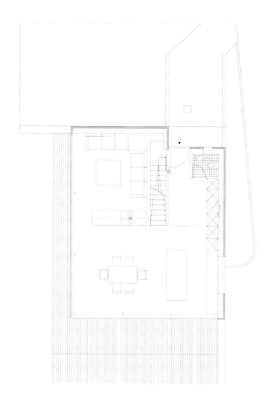
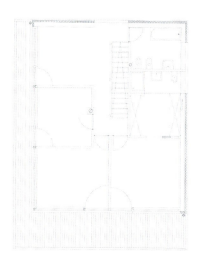

Richard und Beatrix Holzer, Eltern und Nachbarn

„Inzwischen haben wir uns an die neue Architektur gewöhnt. Wir haben es uns zuerst anders vorgestellt, aber es gefällt uns schon gut."

Richard e Beatrix Holzer, genitori confinanti.

"Nel frattempo ci siamo abituati alla nuova architettura. Ce l'eravamo immaginata diversa, ma ci piace comunque"

Richard and Beatrix Holzer, parents and neighbours

"By now we have become used to the new architecture. At first we expected something else but now we really like it."

Pustertal **Val Pusteria**

Begräbnis in Luttach
Funerale a Luttago
Funeral in Luttago

Mutschlechner & Mahlknecht
Neubau Mehrzweckgebäude am Bühel, St. Jakob im Ahrntal
2005

An der Stelle des heutigen Mehrzweckgebäudes befand sich eines aus der Zwischenkriegszeit, das schon immer ein Provisorium gewesen sein dürfte und einfach so lange als Pfarrsaal diente, bis es zu verfallen drohte. Vielen Dorfbewohnern ist wohl erst nach seinem Abriss aufgefallen, dass es die Sicht auf die Kirche verstellt hatte. Nun ist die Kirche ein weithin sichtbares Element der Landschaft, und beim ersten Anblick aus der Ferne scheint es, als ob der Friedhof, das Widum und das neue Gebäude neben ihr auf der Hügelkuppe gerade noch Platz hätten.

Der Neubau wurde schräg neben die Kirche gesetzt, wodurch sich nicht nur freie Sicht auf das Gotteshaus, sondern auch ein kleiner Versammlungsort vor dem Friedhof ergab. An die Rückseite des Gebäudes grenzt ebenfalls ein neuer Platz. Er liegt tiefer, daher wurde hier ein zweiter Eingang in das Mehrzweckgebäude geschaffen: der südseitige führt in den Pfarrsaal, der nordseitige in das Probelokal der Blasmusiker. Neben den beiden Sälen bietet das Gebäude Lagerräume, ein Zimmer für die mobile Krankenversorgung und WCs für die Kirchenbesucher. Das architektonische Konzept berücksichtigte die Fernwirkung

Mutschlechner & Mahlknecht
Nuovo edificio polifunzionale a Monte, S. Giacomo in Valle Aurina
2005

Nel posto dove oggi si erge l'edificio polifunzionale, si trovava una costruzione risalente al periodo tra le due guerre e che è stata a lungo utilizzata come sala parrocchiale provvisoria, fino a quando non mostrò evidenti segni di decadimento. Solo dopo la sua demolizione molti abitanti del paese si sono accorti che la vista sulla chiesa si era spostata. Oggi la chiesa è un elemento chiaramente distinguibile nel paesaggio, e da lontano di primo acchito sembra che lì accanto, il cimitero, la canonica ed il nuovo edificio trovino appena posto sul crinale della collina.

Il nuovo edificio è posizionato obliquamente accanto alla chiesa, offrendone una veduta aperta e realizzando al contempo un piccolo spazio di raccoglimento davanti al cimitero. Anche il retro dell'edificio è delimitato da una nuova piazza. Poiché essa si trova ad un livello inferiore, si è provvisto l'edificio di un secondo ingresso: l'ingresso sul lato meridionale conduce alla sala parrocchiale, quello sul lato settentrionale alla sala prova degli strumenti da fiato. Oltre alle due sale, l'edificio dispone di locali per deposito, una stanza per l'infermeria ed i bagni per i credenti. Il progetto architettonico ha tenuto conto dell'effetto prospetti-

Mutschlechner & Mahlknecht
New multi-purpose building at Bühel, S. Giacomo in Valle Aurina
2005

The site of the present multi-purpose building was previously occupied by a structure from the interwar period that had always been intended as provisional but which served as a parish hall until it threatened to collapse. Only after it had been demolished did many people in the village notice that it had blocked the view of the church. Now the church forms an element in the landscape that is visible from afar and, when first seen from a distance, it looks as if the cemetery, the presbytery and the new building beside it have just enough space on the hill.

The new building was placed at an angle to the church, which not only allows an unobstructed view of the house of prayer but also creates a small gathering place in front of the cemetery. The rear of the building is also adjoined by new square. It lies somewhat lower, and therefore a second entrance to the multi-purpose building was made there: the entrance on the south side leads into the parish hall, while the northern entrance provides access to a rehearsal room for the brass band. In addition to these two halls the building accommodates storerooms, a room for facilities for the mobile care of the sick and WCs for

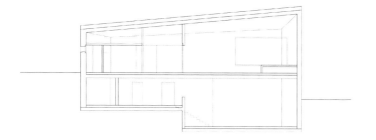

des Mehrzweckgebäudes und nützte dabei die Möglichkeit einer optischen Verkürzung. Sie verhindert, dass sich der Bau in den Vordergrund des Ensembles am Hügel drängt. Geschickt richteten die Architekten auch ein Eckfenster talauswärts: Von innen kann man das Panorama genießen, von außen die Durchsicht auf die Kirche.

co dell'edificio polifunzionale ed ha sfruttato la possibilità di una compressione ottica del volume. In questo modo la costruzione non incombe sull'insieme della collina. Gli architetti hanno posizionato abilmente anche una finestra d'angolo direzionata verso valle, da cui si può godere il panorama e scorgere la chiesa.

church-goers. The architectural concept took into account the impression made by the multi-purpose building when seen from a distance and utilized visual foreshortening. This prevents the building from projecting visually too far into the foreground of the ensemble on the hill. The architects cleverly placed a corner window facing down the valley, so that from inside one can enjoy the panorama, while from outside there is a view of the church through the building.

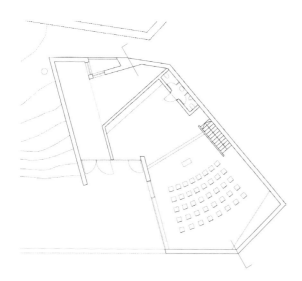
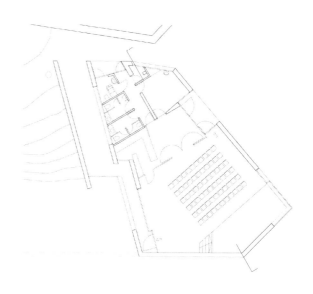

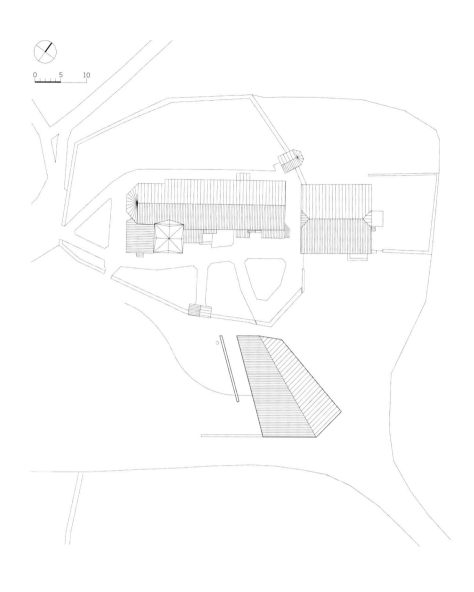

Mutschlechner & Mahlknecht
Sanierung Stein- und Holzhaus Dr. Tasser, Steinhaus im Ahrntal
2004

Ein um 1719 errichteter Stall aus Holz und Stein an der Durchzugsstraße durch das Ahrntal war Teil des Erbes der Bauherrin. Da sie und ihr Ehemann – er ist Historiker – dem Thema Geschichte sehr zugetan sind, sollte das Vermächtnis nicht verfallen. Viele Vorschläge für die Sanierung und den Umbau des Stalles zu einem Zweitwohnsitz wurden vor Ort und gemäß dem Zustand der denkmalgeschützten Bausubstanz erarbeitet. Dabei mussten ihr Erscheinungsbild und ihre Ausmaße erhalten bleiben, weshalb z. B. die Wärmedämmung innen verlegt wurde.

Im aus Bruchsteinen gemauerten Sockel des Gebäudes befinden sich heute Küche, Bad und Abstellraum, im aus Holz mit steinernen Eckpfeilern bestehenden Obergeschoss der Wohnraum mit Essplatz und Schlafnische. Das Kopfende dieser Nische ragt über die Seitenwand des Gebäudes hinaus. Die Auskragung rührt von der ursprünglichen Nutzung der Stelle als Getreidesöller her. Auf der gegenüberliegenden Seite dieser Ebene lässt sich eine Lamellenkonstruktion aus Holz so nach außen drehen, dass sie bei Bedarf als Sichtschutz für die Terrasse dient. Für den Umbau des Liebhaberobjekts wurden möglichst naturbelassene, einheimische Materialien verwendet: Fichtenholz für

Mutschlechner & Mahlknecht
Restauro della casa in pietra e legno del Dr. Tasser, Cadipietra in Valle Aurina
2004

La stalla in legno e pietra, eretta intorno al 1719 lungo la via di attraversamento della Valle Aurina, faceva parte di un'eredità della committente. Poiché la signora ed il marito, storico di professione, sono molto sensibili all'argomento storico, il lascito testamentario non doveva assolutamente andare in rovina. Molte proposte di restauro e ristrutturazione per trasformare la stalla in seconda casa sono state realizzate direttamente sul posto e nel rispetto del manufatto vincolato dalla Soprintendenza. Dimensioni e fattura dell'edificio dovevano essere conservate e per raggiungere questo obbiettivo si è dovuto, ad esempio, porre la coibentazione all'interno. Nel basamento eseguito con pietra a spacco si trovano oggi la cucina, il bagno ed il ripostiglio, nella soprastante parte in legno sorretta da pilastri d'angolo in pietra, si trovano il soggiorno con uno spazio per il pranzo e la nicchia per la stanza da letto. La testata della nicchia aggetta sulla facciata laterale. L'aggetto muove dall'originaria posizione del solaio per le granaglie. Sul fronte opposto, uno schermo a lamelle in legno può essere ruotato verso l'esterno e servire come protezione visiva della terrazza dalla strada. Nella ristrutturazione di quest'opera per appassionati sono stati utilizzati materiali locali non trattati: legno di pino per

Mutschlechner & Mahlknecht
Renovation of the stone and timber built Dr. Tasser house, Cadipietra in Valle Aurina
2004

A stables building made of timber and stone and erected in 1719, lying on the main road leading through the Valle Aurina, formed a part of the client's inheritance. As she and her husband, who is a historian, are greatly interested in the theme of history they wanted to preserve this legacy. Many of the suggestions for the renovation and conversion of the stables into a second home were worked out on site, taking into account the condition of this building, which is under a preservation order. The appearance and dimensions had to be preserved, which explains, for example, why the thermal insulation was fitted internally.

The plinth of the building made of quarry stone now contains the kitchen, bathroom and storage space. The upper floor, which is built of timber with stone corner piers, contains the living room with dining area and niche for sleeping. The end of this niche extends beyond the end wall of the building. This projection is an indication of the building's original use as a grain loft. On the other side of this level a construction of timber louvers can be swivelled outwards to screen the terrace. As far as possible natural local materials were used for the conversion of this treasured building: spruce for the panelling, larch for the furniture, black slate for the floor of the lower

die Täfelung, Lärchenholz für die Möbel, schwarzer Schiefer für den Bodenbelag des Tiefgeschosses und schwarzes, unbehandeltes Stahlblech, das schon ausreichend Rost angesetzt hat, um sich farblich nicht mehr allzu stark vom Altbestand abzuheben.

i tavolati, di larice per i mobili, scisto nero per la pavimentazione del piano inferiore e lamiera al naturale, che con il passare del tempo ha già assunto la sua patina rugginosa, non molto diversa da quella dell'edificio preesistente.

level and black untreated steel sheeting that has already rusted to such a degree that, in terms of colour, it does not differ excessively from the old building.

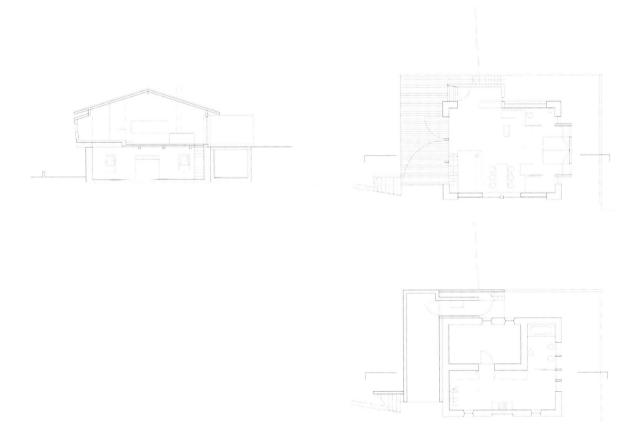

Mutschlechner & Mahlknecht
Friedhofserweiterung, Luttach im Ahrntal
2004
Kunst am Bau: Alois Steger

Im Ortsbild ist der im Zuge der Friedhofserweiterung gerodete Kirchhügel heute präsenter als früher. Eine Erschließungstreppe führt direkt zur Kirche, wo der alte Gottesacker unmittelbar in den – einen Niveausprung tiefer liegenden – neuen übergeht. Dort befinden sich nun auch Urnengräber, ein Brunnen und WCs. An der Nordseite des Kirchhügels verläuft eine behindertengerecht angelegte Rampe, die auf der Höhe der ebenfalls neuen Einsegnungskapelle auch als Versammlungsplatz dient. Die Kapelle wurde mit einer mobilen Glasfront ausgestattet, die bei Bedarf fast vollständig geöffnet werden kann, während die übrigen Bauteile in (zum Teil eingefärbtem) Sichtbeton ausgeführt wurden. So bilden die alten und neuen Mauern eine harmonische Einheit.

Im Inneren der Kapelle sorgt ein dunkles Braunschwarz für Tiefenwirkung und erzeugt einen Kontrast zu den farbigen Grabkränzen. Die Verwendung des Sichtbetons für eine religiöse Einrichtung und die Farbe des Innenanstrichs der Einsegnungskapelle stießen aber auf heftige Gegenwehr in der Bevölkerung. Das ist unerklärlich, da Beton heute zu den wichtigsten Baustoffen gehört und bildhaft gesprochen auch als „zeitgenössischer Stein" betrachtet werden kann. Ähnliches gilt in Bezug auf die

Mutschlechner & Mahlknecht
Ampliamento del cimitero, Luttago in Valle Aurina
2004
Intervento artistico: Alois Steger

La collina della chiesa, scavata dall'ampliamento del cimitero, risulta oggi più presente nell'immagine del paese. Una scalinata collega direttamente alla chiesa, dove il vecchio cimitero, posto appena un livello più in basso, si congiunge a quello nuovo senza soluzione di continuità. Qui si trovano anche i loculi per le urne, una fontana ed i locali igienici. Sul lato nord della collina della chiesa corre una rampa per i disabili, che all'altezza della nuova cappella funeraria è utilizzata anche come luogo di riunione. La cappella è stata dotata di una vetrata scorrevole che, secondo necessità, può essere aperta del tutto, mentre la rimanente struttura è realizzata in cemento a vista in parte colorato. In questo modo, vecchie e nuove murature compongono un insieme armonioso.

All'interno della cappella la scura tinta nero/marrone crea un senso di profondità e contrasta con i colori delle corone funebri. L'uso del cemento a vista per una costruzione religiosa e della pittura nera alle pareti interne alla cappella funebre ha però incontrato le forti proteste della popolazione. Sembra incomprensibile, poiché il cemento si presenta oggi come uno dei materiali da costruzione più importanti e può essere considerato, metaforicamente parlando, come la "pietra contemporanea".

Mutschlechner & Mahlknecht
Cemetery extension, Luttago in Valle Aurina
2004
Site-specific art work: Alois Steger

In the overall appearance of the village the church hill, which was cleared of trees for the extension to the cemetery, is now more clearly present than previously. A flight of steps leads directly to the church, where the old cemetery flows directly into the new one that lies somewhat lower. The new cemetery also contains urn graves, a fountain and WCs. A ramp for the disabled runs up the north side of the church hill and also serves as a gathering place at the level of the new chapel of rest. This chapel has a glass front that, when required, can be opened almost completely, whereas the other parts of the building are made of exposed concrete (coloured in part). The old and new walls thus form a harmonious unity.

Inside the chapel a dark black-brown colour provides a feeling of depth and contrasts with the colours of the funeral wreaths. The use of exposed concrete for a religious building and the colour employed for the interior met with stern resistance from the local population. This is difficult to understand, as concrete is one of the most important modern building materials and in symbolic terms could be seen as a kind of "contemporary stone". The same applies to dark colour used for the interior of the chapel, as in religion and society black is

dunkle Farbe im Inneren der Kapelle, denn in Religion und Gesellschaft ist Schwarz traditionell die Farbe der Trauer. Hier wurde sie übrigens auch dazu verwendet, den kleinen Innenraum optisch größer erscheinen zu lassen.

Altrettanto vale per l'uso del colore scuro all'interno della cappella, infatti, sia nella tradizione religiosa che nella società, il nero è il colore del lutto. Qui è stato inoltre adottato per ampliare le dimensioni percettive del piccolo spazio interno.

traditionally the colour of mourning. Here, incidentally, it was also used to make the small interior seem larger.

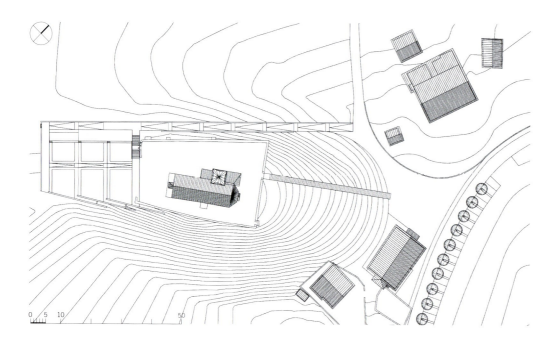

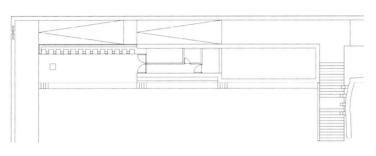

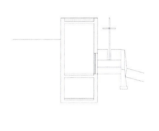

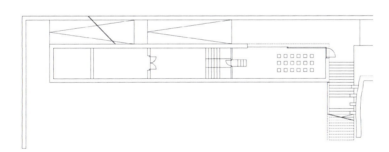

Mag. Franz-Josef Campidell, Pfarrer von Luttach und Weißenbach

„Wir haben fünf Bürgerversammlungen im Vorfeld gehabt. Da hat es in der Bevölkerung große Meinungsverschiedenheiten gegeben, sehr emotionsreich, einige haben sich in Leserbriefen geäußert, es gab eine Unterschriftenaktion, es kam zu Nacht- und Nebelaktionen und Vandalenakten. Die Kunst ist umgeworfen worden, es kam zu Anzeigen und alles hat ein großes mediales Echo hervorgerufen."

Mag. Franz-Josef Campidell, parroco di Luttago e Weißenbach

"Prima abbiamo fatto cinque assemblee con la popolazione del paese. C'erano opinioni diversissime tra la popolazione, molto appassionate, alcuni hanno inviato lettere ai giornali, c'è stata una sottoscrizione, ci sono state azioni di disturbo e atti vandalici. L'intervento artistico è stato danneggiato, ci sono state denunce, e tutto è stato accompagnato da una grande eco mediatico."

Mag. Franz-Josef Campidell, parish priest of Luttago and Weissenbach

"We held five local community meetings beforehand. There were highly divergent opinions among the local people and a great deal of emotion, some sent readers letters to the newspaper, there was a campaign to collect signatures, a cloak-and-dagger operation and some vandalism. The art was knocked over, there were complaints to the police and the whole thing received considerable publicity in the media."

Bruno Rubner, dkp-architektur, dreiplus-architektur
Wohnanlage G3D, Bruneck-Stegen
2003

Auf dem Grund der Wohnanlage befand sich früher ein Recyclinghof. Nachdem dieser verlegt und das Areal zur Bauzone erklärt worden war, entwickelte die Gemeinde einen Durchführungsplan für einen geförderten Wohnbau. In Italien teilen die Wohnbauförderungs-Stellen Wohnungssuchenden Bauplätze zu. Das hat zur Folge, dass unter Berücksichtigung der behördlichen Bebauungspläne wenig Freiraum für gute Architektur besteht, zumal jedem Mitglied einer neu gebildeten Wohngemeinschaft auch Mitsprache bei der Gestaltung des Wohnhauses eingeräumt werden muss.

Die für den Wohnbau in Stegen gebildete Gemeinschaft von 16 Bauherren betrieb ihr Bauprojekt sehr engagiert und schrieb unter zehn Büros einen privaten Wettbewerb aus. Nach der Ermittlung des besten Projekts hatten auch die Architekten viel Glück, denn ihre Bauherren hatten zwar fixe Budgetvorstellungen (Baukosten 2.000,– € pro m²), sonst aber kaum Änderungswünsche am vorgeschlagenen Projekt. Es entstand ein Baukörper in Ost-West-Ausrichtung, der sechs Maisonetten mit Dachterrassen, acht Geschosswohnungen und zwei Duplex-Wohnungen zwischen Erdgeschoss und erstem Stock enthält. Den Wünschen der Bauherren entsprechend,

Bruno Rubner, dkp-architektur, dreiplus-architektur
Complesso residenziale G3D, Brunico-Stegona
2003

Sul lotto del complesso residenziale esisteva un deposito di riciclaggio. Dopo che il deposito è stato trasferito e la zona dichiarata edificabile, il comune ha redatto un piano di attuazione per l'edilizia residenziale sovvenzionata. In Italia gli istituti per l'edilizia sovvenzionata distribuiscono i terreni edificabili tra coloro che fanno richiesta di un alloggio. Pertanto, tenendo conto dei piani di edificazione pubblici, non rimane molto spazio per una buona architettura e inoltre si deve concedere al singolo socio di ogni cooperativa edilizia appena formata, il diritto di partecipare alla definizione formale dell'edificio.

Il gruppo di sedici committenti formatosi per la costruzione dell'edificio residenziale di Stegona, ha seguito il progetto con molto impegno ed ha bandito un concorso ad invito per dieci studi di progettazione. Definito il progetto migliore, gli architetti incaricati hanno avuto molta fortuna: infatti, al di là di un budget fisso di spesa (costo di costruzione di 2.000,00/m²) non sono state avanzate richieste di variazioni al progetto proposto.

Si è realizzato un corpo di fabbrica con orientamento est-ovest, sei "maisonettes" con terrazza pensile, otto appartamenti ad un piano, e due appartamenti "duplex" tra piano terreno e primo piano. Su desiderio

Bruno Rubner, dkp-architektur, dreiplus-architektur
G3D housing development, Brunico-Stegona
2003

The site of this housing development was previously occupied by a recycling yard. After this yard had been relocated and the site rezoned as building land, the local authorities developed a plan for building subsidised housing here. In Italy it is the housing subsidy offices that allot building sites to those looking for a home. This leads to the situation that, once the requirements of local development plans have been observed, there is little scope left for good architecture, especially because every member of a newly founded housing association also has the right to have a say in the design of the residential building.

The association of 16 clients that was formed for the construction of the housing project in Stegona carried out the project in a highly committed way, setting up a private competition among ten architects offices. After the best project had been selected the architects were fortunate in that, although their clients had fixed ideas about budget (building costs of 2,000 per m²), they required changes to the proposed project. A two-storey east/west oriented building was erected that contains six maisonettes with roof terraces, eight single-storey apartments and two duplex flats. In response to the clients' wishes the project is based on ecological considerations.

wurde das Bauvorhaben nach ökologischen Gesichtspunkten ausgerichtet. Für die Ausführung wurden viele natürliche Baustoffe verwendet und das Gebäude an das lokale Fernwärme-Netz angeschlossen. Das Niedrig-Energiehaus ist sowohl mit Fußbodenheizungen als auch mit einem Wandheizungssystem ausgestattet.

dei committenti la costruzione persegue principi ecologici: è stata costruita con materiali naturali e allacciata alla locale rete di teleriscaldamento. L'edificio a risparmio energetico è dotato di riscaldamento a pavimento e a parete.

Many natural building materials were used and the building was connected to the local district heating system. This low energy building has underfloor heating as well as a wall-enclosed heating system.

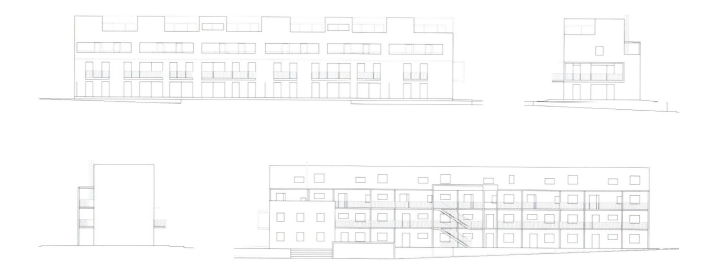

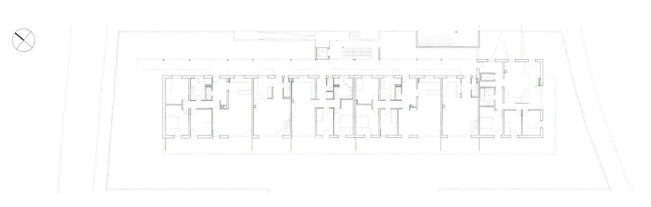

Comfort_Architecten
Haus Sonne, St. Lorenzen
2003

Das Wohnhaus schließt eine Baulücke an der Rückseite eines Hotels und dient dem Hotelier als „Betriebswohnung für einen Gewerbebetrieb". Dieser in Südtirol relativ häufige Bautyp darf die Größe von 110 m² nicht überschreiten. Dazu kam im Fall des Hauses Sonne, dass glatte Fronten ohne Balkone gefordert und die unterschiedlichen Firsthöhen der seitlich angrenzenden Häuser auszugleichen waren. Außerdem mussten drei Parkplätze nachgewiesen werden.
Die Bauaufgabe wurde auf einem Mini-Grundstück von 7 x 7 m wie folgt gelöst: Zwei der drei erforderlichen Parkplätze wurden im Keller untergebracht, wobei die Tiefgarage des Nachbarhauses als Zufahrt genützt wird. Der dritte Parkplatz wurde seitlich vom Eingang im Freien angelegt. Die Einfügung einer Dachterrasse im Ausmaß einer halben Geschossebene führte zum Ausgleich zwischen den Niveaus der Firsthöhen. Für die weitere Planung hatte das zur Folge, dass das Haus über zueinander versetzte Stockwerke verfügt. Solche „Split Levels" sind ein Import aus den USA, wo sie in den 50er Jahren modern wurden. Sie haben den Vorteil, dass sie eine kompakte Verbindung verschiedener Ebenen in einem Haus ermöglichen. Den Architekten war es ein Anliegen, diese Abwicklung der Innenräume äußerlich sichtbar zu machen. Sie schrägten die Ecken

Comfort_Architecten
Casa Sonne, S. Lorenzo di Sebato
2003

La casa d'abitazione chiude un vuoto edilizio sul retro di un albergo e serve all'albergatore come "appartamento di servizio per l'azienda". Questa tipologia residenziale, abbastanza diffusa in Alto Adige, non può superare la superficie di 110 mq. Per casa Sonne era richiesto specificatamente di realizzare facciate lineari prive di balconi, e di compensare le diverse quote di colmo degli edifici adiacenti. In aggiunta dovevano essere dichiarati tre posti auto.
Il tema progettuale è stato risolto su un mini-lotto di 7x7 metri com'è descritto qui di seguito: due dei parcheggi richiesti sono stati realizzati in cantina utilizzando l'ingresso del garage interrato del vicino.
Il terzo posto auto è collocato all'aperto, a fianco dell'entrata.
Inserendo sul tetto una terrazza con superficie pari a metà di un piano, si sono compensate le quote tra i colmi.
La parte restante dell'edificio è stata pertanto impostata su piani reciprocamente sfalsati. Questa tipologia importata dagli Stati Uniti è un retaggio moderno degli anni Cinquanta; gli "split levels" hanno il vantaggio di rendere possibile un collegamento compatto tra diversi livelli all'interno dell'abitazione. Gli architetti hanno voluto rendere visibile anche dall'esterno il fluire degli spazi interni. Tagliando in diagonale gli angoli delle finestre, hanno disegnato

Comfort_Architecten
Sonne House, S. Lorenzo di Sebato
2003

The house fills a vacant site at the rear of a hotel and serves the proprietor as a "company apartment for a commercial business". This kind of building, found relatively often in South Tyrol, is not permitted to exceed 110 square metres in size. In the case of the Sonne House the authorities also required that the façade should be flat, without balconies, and that the new building should reconcile the different ridge heights of the buildings on either side of it. Furthermore, three car parking spaces had to be specified.
On a minimal site measuring only 7 x 7 metres the problem was solved as follows: two of the three required car parking spaces were located in the basement, whereby the underground car park of the neighbouring building was used as the approach. The third parking space was placed outdoors, beside the entrance. The introduction of a roof terrace, half a standard storey in area, created the required balance between the different ridge heights. In planning terms the consequence of this move was that the floor levels in the house are staggered. Split-levels, as this kind of planning is known, were imported from the USA where they became popular in the 1950s. Their principal advantage is that they allow the compact connection of the different floor levels in a building. A major concern of

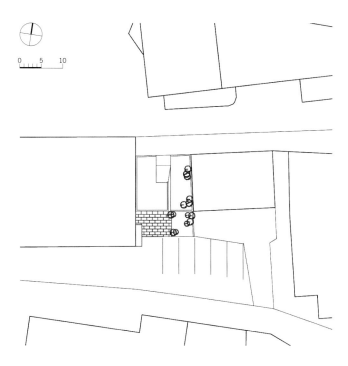

der Fensteröffnungen ab und zeichneten auf diese Weise ein Fassadenbild, das den quasi nahtlosen Übergang der Etagen im Inneren wiedergibt.

un'immagine della facciata che riproduce la transizione continua da un piano all'altro dell'interno dell'edificio.

the architects was that this internal layout should be visible from the outside. They chamfered the corners of the window openings and in this way created a façade that reflects the almost seamless transition between the floor levels inside the building.

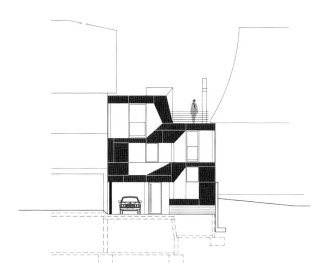
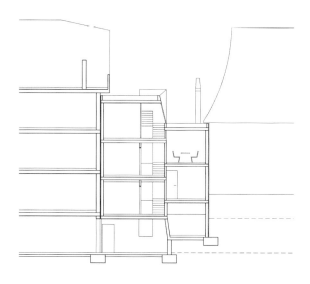

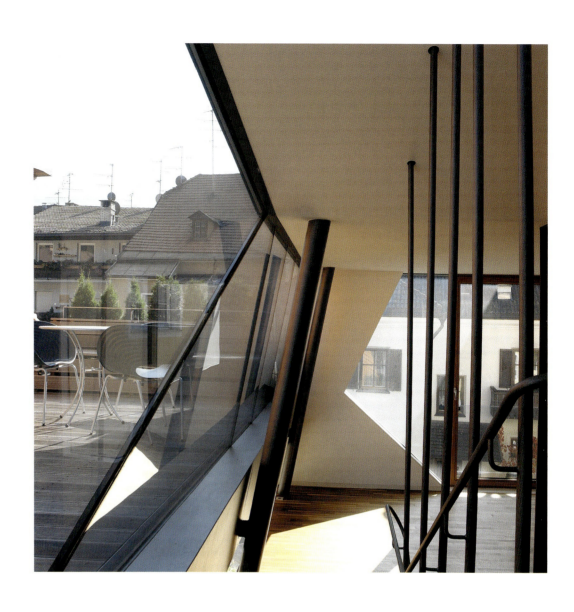

Architekturbüro D3
(Robert Veneri, Richard Veneri, Armin Kienzl, Kathrin Gruber)
Gesundheits- und Sozialsprengel Gadertal, Pikolein, St. Martin in Thurn
2001

Studio di architettura D3
(Robert Veneri, Richard Veneri, Armin Kienzl, Kathrin Gruber)
Unità socio-sanitaria locale Val Badia, Piccolino, S. Martino in Badia
2001

Architekturbüro D3
(Robert Veneri, Richard Veneri, Armin Kienzl, Kathrin Gruber)
Gadertal health and social services centre, Piccolino, S. Martino in Badia
2001

Als Sprengel bezeichnet man in Südtirol die Verwaltungsbezirke im Gesundheits- und Sozialbereich. In so genannten Sprengelsitzen wird die gesamte Nahversorgung im Gesundheits- und Sozialwesen entlegener Regionen organisiert und abgewickelt, z. B. die Mutter-Kind-Beratung, die Betreuung älterer Menschen und die medizinische Grundversorgung.

Das Architekturbüro D3 gewann den Wettbewerb für den Neubau des Sprengelsitzes in Pikolein, einem Weiler von St. Martin in Thurn, und realisierte im Anschluss einen V-förmigen Bau an der Hauptstraße durch das Gadertal. Das Grundstück befindet sich unterhalb von historischen Bergbauernhöfen mit sonnenverbrannten Holzfassaden, was Auswirkungen auf die Gestaltung der Außenflächen hatte.

Im dreigeschossigen Schenkel des Gebäudes sind die sozialen Dienste untergebracht, im zweigeschossigen die Arztpraxen mit ihren Nebenräumen. Zwischen den zwei im spitzen Winkel zueinander stehenden Riegeln befindet sich ein glasüberdachtes Atrium. Aufgrund der Hanglage des Baukörpers steigt der Lichthof an. Die hier verlaufende Treppenstraße ist so angelegt worden, dass sie wie ein Gebirgs-

In Alto Adige l'amministrazione circondariale per i servizi sociali e sanitari viene denominata Sprengel, distretto. Nei centri distrettuali si organizza e svolge tutta l'assistenza sociale e sanitaria delle zone decentrate: per esempio la consulenza alle mamme e all'infanzia, l'assistenza agli anziani e quella farmaceutica di base. Lo studio di architettura D3 ha vinto il concorso per la nuova edificazione della sede del distretto di Piccolino poco distante da S. Martino in Badia, e ha poi realizzato un edificio dalla pianta a "V" collocato sulla strada principale della Val Badia. Il lotto di edificazione si trova sotto a dei masi storici con le loro facciate in legno bruciate dal sole, fatto che ha avuto una sua influenza sulla definizione estetica delle superfici esterne dell'edificio. Il "braccio" a tre piani dell'edificio ospita i servizi sociali, il "braccio" a due piani gli ambulatori medici e gli spazi di servizio. Dove i due corpi di fabbrica si incontrano ad angolo retto, si colloca un atrio con copertura vetrata. La corte con lucernario sale rispettando la pendenza dei corpi di fabbrica lungo il pendio. La scala di distribuzione si inoltra nell'edificio come lo scorrere di un torrente montano.

Per instaurare altri rimandi tra i corpi di

In South Tyrol administrative districts in the field of health and social services are known as "Sprengel". In so-called "Sprengelsitzen" the entire range of local health and other social services for remote regions are organized and administered, for example mother and child care, care of the elderly and basic medical services.

The architects practice D3 won the competition for the new "Sprengel" building in Piccolino, a hamlet outside S. Martino in Badia. They planned a V-shaped building located on the main road through the Val Badia. The site lies below a number of historic mountain farmhouses with timber facades singed by the sun, which had an influence on the design of the exterior of the new building.

The social services are accommodated in a three-storey wing, while the doctors' surgeries and the service rooms are housed in a two-storey block. A glass-roofed atrium was placed in the acute angle formed by the two blocks. As the site slopes this courtyard has a change in level. The stepped path laid out seems to flow through the interior of the building like a mountain stream. To establish a further reference to the building's surroundings the side facades of the

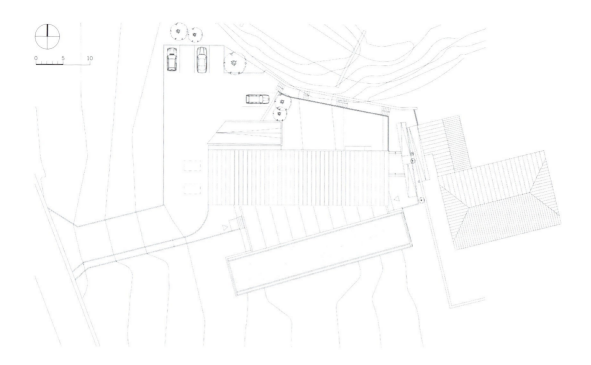

bach durch das Innere des Gebäudes zu fließen scheint. Um einen weiteren Bezug zwischen dem Baukörper und dem Standort des Gebäudes herzustellen, wurden die Seitenfassaden der Riegel senkrecht mit Holz beplankt bzw. waagrecht verlaufende, hölzerne Lamellen vor ihre Fenster gesetzt.

fabbrica ed il luogo di costruzione dell'edificio, le facciate laterali possiedono un rivestimento verticale in legno, mentre davanti alle finestre sono state fissate lamelle orizzontali dello stesso materiale.

blocks are clad vertically with timber and have horizontal wooden louvers in front of the windows.

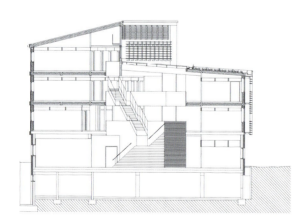

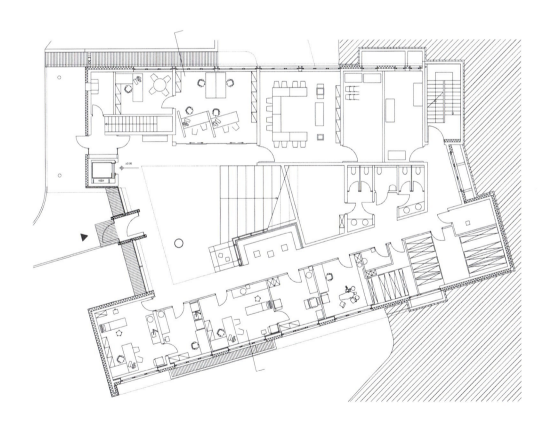

aichner-seidl ARCHITEKTEN
Haus Huber Schnarf, Olang
2004

Für eine kinderreiche Familie entstand im Dorfzentrum von Olang ein Niedrigenergie-Haus der Klasse A+. Das entspricht dem Standard eines so genannten „3-Liter-Hauses" (Öl- bzw. Stromverbrauch pro m^2 und Jahr weniger als 3 l bzw. 30 kWh). Vereinfacht ausgedrückt, ist es in diesem Niedrigenergie-Haus möglich, bereits im Januar die Heizung auszuschalten. Am Beispiel dieses Baues lässt sich aber auch demonstrieren, dass ein niedriger Energieverbrauch direkte Auswirkungen auf die Architektur eines Hauses hat, da z. B. die Durchmesser der Außenwände viel stärker sein müssen als bei Bauten, bei denen der Umweltschutzgedanke eine geringere Rolle spielt. Dennoch gelang es den Architekten, eine Ruhe ausstrahlende Struktur zu entwickeln, die sich sowohl auf das innere als auch auf das äußere Erscheinungsbild des Hauses auswirkt. Man könnte fast von einem „Hausboot" sprechen, das die Architekten hier am Rand einer Wiese verankerten. Das Bild vom schwimmenden Haus wird von einer Betonplatte erzeugt, auf die eine zweigeschossige Holzkonstruktion gesetzt wurde. Ein leichter Niveauunterschied des Bauplatzes, über den die waagrechte Platte hinausragt, verstärkt diesen Eindruck.

aichner-seidl ARCHITETTI
Casa Huber Schnarf, Valdaora
2004

Nel centro del paese di Valdaora è stata realizzata una casa a basso consumo energetico, di classe A+, per una famiglia con bambini. La classificazione corrisponde allo standard di una cosiddetta "casa da 3 litri", con un fabbisogno energetico annuo inferiore a 3 l se a combustibile ad olio, o 30 kWh se elettrico. In pratica, in questa casa a basso consumo energetico si può spegnere il riscaldamento già a gennaio. Questa costruzione esemplifica come i requisiti previsti per un basso consumo energetico siano determinanti per la composizione architettonica dell'edificio: ad esempio lo spessore delle pareti esterne deve essere molto maggiore di quello di edifici in cui la componente ecologica giochi un ruolo ininfluente.
Ciononostante gli architetti sono riusciti a proporre una costruzione che comunica un'immagine armoniosa sia all'esterno che all'interno della casa. Viene da pensare ad una "houseboat" ancorata al limitare di un prato. L'immagine di una casa galleggiante è suggerita dallo zoccolo in calcestruzzo su cui è posto l'edificio a due piani ed il leggero dislivello del terreno, sul quale aggetta la piattaforma, ne rafforza il riferimento. Dal basamento ricevono luce alcuni locali dello scantinato, per la gioia dei bambini

aichner-seidl ARCHITEKTEN
Huber Schnarf House, Valdaora
2004

A low-energy house (category A+) for a large family was built in the village centre of Valdaora. This is the standard for a so-called "3 litre house" (oil or electricity consumption per m^2 per year less than 3 l or 30 kWh). To put it more simply: in this low energy house you can turn off the heating as early as January. This building demonstrates that low energy use has a direct effect on the architecture of a house as, for example, the external walls must be far thicker than in buildings where environmental considerations play a less important role. Nevertheless, the architects have succeeded in creating a building that emanates a calm that is evident both externally and internally. One could almost speak of a "houseboat", which the architects have anchored here at the edge of a meadow. A concrete slab on which the two-storey timber structure was placed creates the image of a floating house. The fact that the horizontal slab continues uninterrupted across a slight change of level in the site strengthens this impression. Several spaces in the cellar below receive direct daylight – much to the delight of the children who have a large play space there. The concrete slab also serves as a terrace and has a railing on all sides – as befits a houseboat.

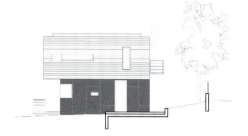

Manche Räume im darunter liegenden Keller können Tageslicht beziehen – sehr zur Freude der Kinder, denn sie haben hier ein großes Spielzimmer erhalten. Die Betonplatte dient auch als Terrasse und wurde – weil das eben zu einem Hausboot so gehört – mit einer umlaufenden Reling ausgestattet.

che lì hanno la loro sala giochi. La piattaforma è utilizzata anche come terrazza ed è stata dotata di un parapetto, come è usanza sulle "houseboat".

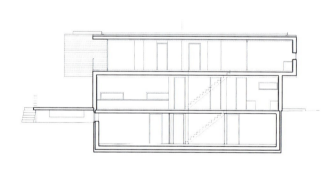

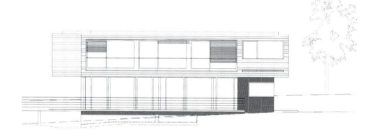

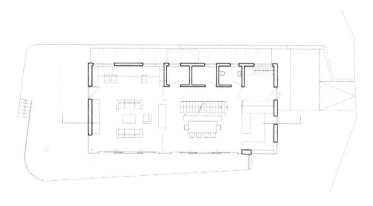

Lea, Hannah und Sarah Huber Schnarf (v. l. n. r.), Kinder der Familie

„Mein eigenes Zimmer – und die große Bank!"

Lea, Hannah e Sarah Huber Schnarf (da destra a sin.), i figli della famiglia

"La mia stanza privata – e la grande panca!"

Lea, Hannah and Sarah Huber Schnarf (from left to right), the children of the family

"My own room – and the big bench!"

Siegfried Delueg
Fernheizwerk, Sexten
2005

Das Projekt ging als Sieger aus einem geladenen Wettbewerb zu einem kommunalen Gewerbebau in Südtirol hervor. Die Ausschreibung dieser Konkurrenz ist deshalb bemerkenswert, weil kleine Orte gemeindeeigene Bauvorhaben leider noch immer viel zu häufig direkt und dann nicht immer an Architekturbüros vergeben. Eine der Folgen davon ist, dass gerade das unkontrollierte Wachstum der überall aus dem Boden schießenden Gewerbezonen viele schöne ländliche Regionen und Orte zerstört. Das Beispiel des Architekturwettbewerbs in der Gemeinde Sexten muss daher zur Nachahmung weiterempfohlen werden.

Dem Fernheizwerk in der Gewerbezone von Sexten liegt die Idee zugrunde, dass der Übergang zwischen dem Industriebau und der ihn umgebenden Natur möglichst sanft sein sollte. Es wurde eine Aufteilung in zwei Baukörper gewählt, die im spitzen Winkel zueinander stehen. Da es der Architekt als optisches Problem ansah, wenn sich zwei gleich große Bauvolumen gegenüberstehen, wurde ein Teil der notwendigen Lagerflächen für die Hackschnitzel im Heizhaus untergebracht. Die ungleichmäßige Aufteilung der Kubaturen hat den Vorteil, dass sie das landschaftsbezogene Bauen unterstützt. Um dem Umweltschutz-Gedanken eines Fernheizwerks auch in architektonischer Hinsicht Ausdruck zu

Sigfried Delueg
Centrale di teleriscaldamento, Sesto
2005

Il progetto ha vinto il concorso ad invito altoatesino per un edificio destinato ad infrastruttura comunale. Il bando di questo concorso è degno di nota perché i piccoli paesi affidano, purtroppo ancora troppo spesso, gli incarichi edilizi comunali in modo diretto e non sempre a studi di architettura. Una conseguenza diretta di questa pratica è che le zone produttive, sottoposte ad una crescita incontrollata e diffuse su tutto il territorio, deturpano il paesaggio rurale di molti paesi e regioni. L'esempio del concorso di progettazione del Comune di Sesto merita di essere promosso perché possa essere imitato.

Alla base del progetto della centrale di teleriscaldamento di Sesto c'è l'idea che la transizione compositiva tra l'edificio industriale e il paesaggio naturale debba avvenire con la maggior gradualità possibile. Si é scelta la suddivisione della costruzione in due corpi edilizi disposti reciprocamente ad angolo acuto. L'architetto non era propenso a giustapporre due grandi volumi della stessa dimensione, e quindi una parte della superficie necessaria al deposito per i trucioli è stata trasferita all'edificio della centrale termica. La ripartizione differente della cubatura presenta il vantaggio di favorire un'edificazione attenta al paesaggio. L'immagine architettonica, corrispondente ad un approccio ecologico

Siegfried Delueg
District heating plant, Sesto
2005

This building was the winner of one of the entry competition to be held for a communal industrial building in South Tyrol. The fact that a competition was set up is worth remarking on here, as small towns still far too often commission building projects directly, on many occasions not even from architects. One of the consequences of this policy is the uncontrolled growth of commercial and industrial zones that seem to sprout out of the ground destroying many very beautiful rural regions and towns. Therefore the example set by this architecture competition organised by the local authorities in Sesto is worth following.

The basic concept behind the district heating plant in the industrial zone in Sesto is that the transition between the building and its natural surroundings should be as gentle as possible. It was decided to split the building into two parts standing at an acute angle to each other. As the architect regarded a situation where two volumes of equal size confront opposite each other as problematic, part of the storage area for wood chips (used as fuel) was incorporated in the boiler house. The advantage of this unequal division of the total volume is that it helps the building relate better to the landscape. To express in architectural terms the environmental aspects of a district heating plant the side walls and

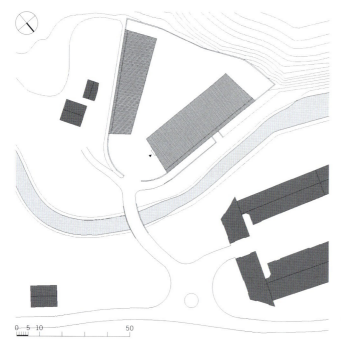

verleihen, wurden die Seitenwände und Dachflächen der Baukörper abgeschrägt und ihre Außenseiten mit rauen Lärchenbrettern verkleidet. Auch das erzeugt eine perfekte Anpassung des Industriebaues an das alpine Landschaftsbild.

alla progettazione di una centrale di teleriscaldamento, si è configurata in volumi obliqui le cui facciate sono rivestite con assi grezze di larice.
Anche queste soluzioni progettuali realizzano un inserimento perfetto dell'edificio destinato ad un'infrastruttura nel contesto paesaggistico.

roof of the building were angled and clad externally with rough larch boarding. This helps this industrial building to harmonise perfectly with the surrounding alpine landscape.

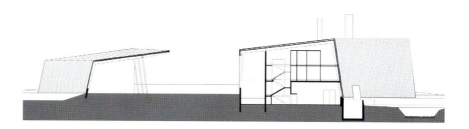

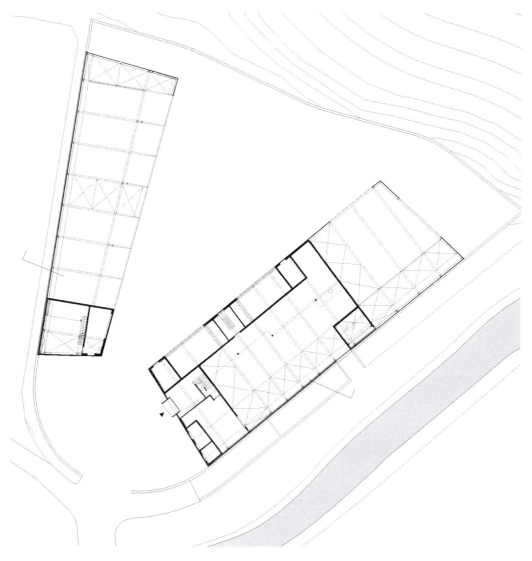

Baudaten **Dati dei progetti** **Construction data**

Projekt/progetto/project:
Messner Mountain Museum „Ortles"
Adresse/indirizzo/address:
Sulden Nr. 158A, I-39020 Stilfs
Architektur/architettura/architecture:
Arnold Gapp
Bauherr/committente/client:
Reinhold Messner
Planungszeit/tempi di progettazione/start of planning: 2003
Errichtungszeit/tempi di esecuzione/construction: 10/2003–11/2004
Statik/statica/structural consultant:
Siegfried Pohl
Lichtplanung/progetto illuminotecnico/lightning concept: Bartenbach Licht Labor GmbH, A-Innsbruck
Elektroplanung/ progettista impianto elettrico/electrical services: Bartenbach Licht Labor GmbH, A-Innsbruck
Heizungs-, Klima- und Sanitärplanung/progetto termo-sanitario/heating, air conditioning, plumbing:
Nischler – Planconsulting, Burgstall
Einrichtung, Möbel/arredo, mobili/facilities, furnishing: Zischg Christian Möbeldesign, Prad am Stilfser Joch
Nutzfläche/superficie netta/floor area: 510 m^2
Umbauter Raum/cubatura/cubage: 2.515 m^3
Baukosten/costi di costruzione/construction costs: 653.000 €

Projekt/progetto/project:
Kleinsportanlagen und Mehrzweckgebäude
Adresse/indirizzo/address: Tschengls, I-39023 Laas
Architektur/architettura/architecture:
Arnold Gapp
MitarbeiterInnen/collaboratori/assistance:
Christian Kapeller
Bauherr/committente/client:
Gemeinde Laas
Planungszeit/tempi di progettazione/start of planning: 01/2002–09/2002
Errichtungszeit/tempi di esecuzione/construction: 09/2002–08/2005
Statik/statica/structural consultant:
Siegfried Pohl
Elektroplanung/ progettista impianto elettrico/electrical services: M & N – Plan Consulting, Burgstall
Heizungs-, Klima- und Sanitärplanung/progetto termo-sanitario/heating, air conditioning, plumbing:
Nischler – Planconsulting, Burgstall
Einrichtung, Möbel/arredo, mobili/facilities, furnishing: Holzstudio Bachmann, Schlanders
Nutzfläche/superficie netta/floor area: 606 m^2 (Gebäude), 2.400 m^2 (Spielfeld)
Umbauter Raum/cubatura/cubage: 3.759 m^3
Baukosten/costi di costruzione/construction costs: 1.120.000 €

Projekt/progetto/project:
Aufstockungen von Betriebsgebäuden und Errichtung von zwei Betriebswohnungen
Adresse/indirizzo/address:
Stachelburgstr. 19, I-39028 Schlanders
Architektur/architettura/architecture:
ARCHITEKTEN Marx - Ladurner
Bauherr/committente/client:
Martin Fleischmann; Hannes Fleischmann
Planungszeit/tempi di progettazione/start of planning: 2003–2004
Errichtungszeit/tempi di esecuzione/construction: 09/2002–12/2002; 09/2004–12/2004
Statik/statica/structural consultant:
Bauteam, Latsch
Lichtplanung/progetto illuminotecnico/lightning concept: Lichtstudio, Marling
Heizungs-, Klima- und Sanitärplanung/progetto termo-sanitario/heating, air conditioning, plumbing:
Josef Mairösl, Schlanders
Nutzfläche/superficie netta/floor area: 150 m^2; 110 m^2
Umbauter Raum/cubatura/cubage: 975 m^3
Baukosten/costi di costruzione/construction costs: 250.000 €; 285.000 €

Projekt/progetto/project:
Haus Schöpf
Adresse/indirizzo/address:
I-39020 Vezzan 23
Architektur/architettura/architecture:
Werner Tscholl
MitarbeiterInnen/collaboratori/assistance:
Michaela Wunderer
Bauherr/committente/client:
Benedikta und Hanspeter Schöpf
Planungszeit/tempi di progettazione/start of planning: 2003
Errichtungszeit/tempi di esecuzione/construction: 2004
Statik/statica/structural consultant:
Thomas Schrentewein, Bozen
Einrichtung, Möbel/arredo, mobili/facilities, furnishing: Werner Tscholl
Nutzfläche/superficie netta/floor area: 320 m^2
Umbauter Raum/cubatura/cubage: 1.350 m^3 (über der Erde)
Baukosten/costi di costruzione/construction costs: –

Projekt/progetto/project:
Bergstation Seilbahn St. Martin
Adresse/indirizzo/address:
St. Martin am Kofel, I-39021 Latsch
Architektur/architettura/architecture:
Arnold Gapp
Bauherr/committente/client:
Gemeinde Latsch
Planungszeit/tempi di progettazione/start of planning: 2001
Errichtungszeit/tempi di esecuzione/construction: 01/2002–10/2002
Generalunternehmer/impresa di costruzioni/building contractor:
Hölzl – Seilbahnbau GmbH
Elektroplanung/ progettista impianto elettrico/electrical services: Arnold Gapp
Nutzfläche/superficie netta/floor area: 155 m^2
Umbauter Raum/cubatura/cubage: 980 m^3
Baukosten/costi di costruzione/construction costs: 439.200 €

Projekt/progetto/project:
Vinschgerbahn, Wiederinbetriebnahme Eisenbahnlinie Meran-Mals, Haltestellen, Erweiterung Remise Mals
Haltestellen:
Adresse/indirizzo/address: Haltestellen der Eisenbahnlinie Meran-Mals, Vinschgau

Architektur/architettura/architecture:
Walter Dietl
MitarbeiterInnen/collaboratori/assistance:
Thomas Hickmann, Patrik Fössinger, Martin Thoma, Heiko Mehlmann, Monika Siller
Bauherr/committente/client:
STA – Südtiroler Transportstrukturen AG, Bozen (Helmuth Moroder)
Planungszeit/tempi di progettazione/start of planning: 08/2004–10/2004
Errichtungszeit/tempi di esecuzione/construction: 11/2004–08/2005
Statik/statica/structural consultant:
Siegfried Pohl, Latsch
Lichtplanung/progetto illuminotecnico/lightning concept: Walter Dietl
Elektroplanung/ progettista impianto elettrico/electrical services: Ingenieurbüro Dr. Fleischmann & Dr. Janser, Latsch
Einrichtung, Möbel/arredo, mobili/facilities, furnishing: Walter Dietl
Baukosten/costi di costruzione/construction costs: ca. 2.600.000 € (o. Mwst.)
Remise Mals:
Adresse/indirizzo/adress:
Bahnhofsgelände Mals
Architektur/architettura/architecture:
Walter Dietl
MitarbeiterInnen/collaboratori/assistance:
Thomas Hickmann,
Geom. Andreas Kaserer
Bauherr/committente/client:
STA – Südtiroler Transportstrukturen AG, Bozen (Helmuth Moroder)
Planungszeit/tempi di progettazione/start of planning: 09/2003–10/2003
Errichtungszeit/tempi di esecuzione/construction: 02/2004–11/2004
Statik/statica/structural consultant:
Wolfgang Oberdörfer, Latsch
Lichtplanung/progetto illuminotecnico/lightning concept: Walter Dietl
Elektroplanung/ progettista impianto elettrico/electrical services: Ingenieurbüro Dr. Fleischmann & Dr. Janser, Latsch
Heizungs-, Klima- und Sanitärplanung/progetto termo-sanitario/heating, air conditioning, plumbing: Ingenieurbüro Dr. Fleischmann & Dr. Janser, Latsch
Nutzfl./sup. netta/floor area: 588,24 m^2
Umbauter Raum/cubatura/cubage: 5.301,91 m^3
Baukosten/costi di costruzione/construction costs: 1.065.000 € (o. MwSt.)

Projekt/progetto/project:
Fahrradverleih Vinschgerbahn, Schlanders
Adresse/indirizzo/address:
Bahnhofstraße, I-39028 Schlanders
Architektur/architettura/architecture:
Karl Spitaler
Bauherr/committente/client:
Gemeinde Schlanders
Planungszeit/tempi di progettazione/start of planning: 2003–2004
Errichtungszeit/tempi di esecuzione/construction: 03/2005–05/2005
Generalunternehmer/impresa di costruzioni/building contractor:
Richard Gamper OHG
Statik/statica/structural consultant:
Karl Spitaler
Elektroplanung/ progettista impianto elettrico/electrical services: Karl Spitaler
Heizungs-, Klima- und Sanitärplanung/progetto termo-sanitario/heating, air conditioning, plumbing: Ingenieurbüro Dr. Fleischmann & Dr. Janser, Latsch
Einrichtung, Möbel/arredo, mobili/facilities, furnishing: Karl Spitaler
Nutzfläche/superficie netta/floor area: 82,50 m^2
Umbauter Raum/cubatura/cubage: 127,50 m^3
Baukosten/costi di costruzione/construction costs: ca. 180.000 €

Projekt/progetto/project:
Bahnhof mit Jugendraum
Adresse/indirizzo/address:
Bahnhofstrasse, I-39025 Plaus
Architektur/architettura/architecture:
Architketurbüro D3 (Kathrin Gruber, Richard Veneri)
Bauherr/committente/client:
Gemeinde Plaus
Planungszeit/tempi di progettazione/start of planning: 01/2004–01/2005
Errichtungszeit/tempi di esecuzione/construction: 03/2005–12/2005
Generalunternehmer/impresa di costruzioni/building contractor:
Baumeister Baumänner, Kastelbell; Schlosser Fischnaller, Teis, Vilnöss; u. a.
Statik/statica/structural consultant:
Ingenieurbüro "Bauteam", Latsch
Lichtplanung/progetto illuminotecnico/lightning concept: Architketurbüro D3
Elektroplanung/ progettista impianto elettrico/electrical services:
Architekturbüro D3; Jürgen Klotz, Plaus
Heizungs-, Klima- und Sanitärplanung/progetto termo-sanitario/heating, air conditioning, plumbing:
Franz Blaas GmbH, Naturns
Nutzfläche/superficie netta/floor area: 227 m^2
Umbauter Raum/cubatura/cubage: ca. 650 m^3
Baukosten/costi di costruzione/construction costs: 360.000 €

Projekt/progetto/project:
Pergola Residence
Adresse/indirizzo/address:
St. Kassianweg 40, I-39022 Algund
Architektur/architettura/architecture:
Studio Thun (Matteo Thun)
MitarbeiterInnen/collaboratori/assistance:
Bruno Franchi, Christina Biasi-von Berg, Elisa Catoir
Bauherr/committente/client:
Ruth und Josef Innerhofer
Planungszeit/tempi di progettazione/start of planning: 09/2001–12/2002
Errichtungszeit/tempi di esecuzione/construction: 09/2002–09/2004
Statik/statica/structural consultant:
Holzbau Schrentewein;
Statik Massivbau: Holzner, St. Pankraz
Lichtplanung/progetto illuminotecnico/lightning concept: Studio Thun
Elektroplanung/ progettista impianto elettrico/electrical services:
Helmut Stuppner, Bozen
Heizungs-, Klima- und Sanitärplanung/progetto termo-sanitario/heating, air conditioning, plumbing: Klammsteiner, Bozen
Einrichtung, Möbel/arredo, mobili/facilities, furnishing: Studio Thun
Nutzfläche/superficie netta/floor area: 2.400 m^2
Umbauter Raum/cubatura/cubage: 8.000 m^3
Baukosten/costi di costruzione/construction costs: ca. 5,2 Mio. €

Projekt/progetto/project:
Südtiroler Landesmuseum für Kultur- und Landesgeschichte Schloss Tirol
Adresse/indirizzo/address:
Schlossweg 1, I-39019 Tirol
Architektur/architettura/architecture:
Markus Scherer, Walter Angonese,
Klaus Hellweger
MitarbeiterInnen/collaboratori/assistance:
Alessia Carlotto, Sanja Balta,
Yvonne Garbukas
Bauherr/committente/client:
Autonome Provinz Bozen-Südtirol,
Abteilung Hochbau
Planungszeit/tempi di progettazione/start of planning: 1998–03/2003
Errichtungszeit/tempi di esecuzione/construction: 09/2000–06/2003
Generalunternehmer/impresa di costruzioni/building contractor: Bauarbeiten: Unionbau, Sand in Taufers, in Bietergemeinschaft mit Normbau, Meran; Einrichtung: Innenausbau Barth, Brixen, in Bietergemeinschaft mit Glasbau Hahn, D-Frankfurt/Main
Statik/statica/structural consultant:
Ingenieurteam Maia, Meran
(Hartmuth Theiner)
Lichtplanung/progetto illuminotecnico/lightning concept: Conceptlicht GmbH, A-Mils (Manfred Draxl);
Tecnology Innovation, Bruneck
Elektroplanung/ progettista impianto elettrico/electrical services:
Studio H., Bozen (P. I. Helmut Stuppner)
Heizungs-, Klima- und Sanitärplanung/progetto termo-sanitario/heating, air conditioning, plumbing:
Thermoplan, Bozen (Hubert Vilotti)
Medienplaung/tecnica audio e video/audio-visual technology:
Ton & Bild, Bregenz (Martin Beck)
Grafische Gestaltung/grafica/graphic design: Gruppe Circus, A-Innsbruck (Kurt Hoeretzeder)
Museumspädagogik/didattica museale/museum didactics:
Petra Paolazzi, A-Innsbruck
Einrichtung, Möbel/arredo, mobili/facilities, furnishing: Möbel: Barth Innenausbau, Brixen; Vitrinen: Glasbau Hahn, D-Frankfurt/Main; Siebdruckarbeiten: Serima, Brixen; Schlosserarbeiten Einrichtung: Metallbau Ritten, Ritten; Tapezierarbeiten: Raumausstatter Wolf, Brixen; Beleuchtung Vitrinen: Klaus Faller, Brixen
Nutzfläche/superficie netta/floor area:
3.300 m² (Museum 2.000 m²)
Umbauter Raum/cubatura/cubage:
24.000 m³
Baukosten/costi di costruzione/construction costs: 4.970.000 € (Einrichtung inkl. Beleuchtung und Medientechnik: 5.780.000 €)

Projekt/progetto/project:
„kunst Meran im Haus der Sparkasse"
Adresse/indirizzo/address:
Laubengasse 163, I-39012 Meran
Architektur/architettura/architecture:
Höller & Klotzner – Architekten
Bauherr/committente/client: Sparim AG
Planungszeit/tempi di progettazione/start of planning: 1999
Errichtungszeit/tempi di esecuzione/construction: 2000–2001
Generalunternehmer/impresa di costruzioni/building contractor: Serra, Meran
Statik/statica/structural consultant:
Mario Volante, Meran
Lichtplanung/progetto illuminotecnico/lightning concept: Conceptlicht GmbH, A-Mils (Manfred Draxl)
Elektroplanung/ progettista impianto elettrico/electrical services:
Roland Zuegg, Lana
Heizungs-, Klima- und Sanitärplanung/progetto termo-sanitario/heating, air conditioning, plumbing: Roland Zuegg, Lana
Einrichtung, Möbel/arredo, mobili/facilities, furnishing:
Gufler Holzwerkstatt, Meran (Maßmöbel), Trias, Meran (Serienmöbel)
Nutzfläche/superficie netta/floor area:
1.100 m²
Umbauter Raum/cubatura/cubage:
4.800 m³
Baukosten/costi di costruzione/construction costs: 2,4 Mio. € (inkl. Einrichtung)

Projekt/progetto/project:
Kurhauspassage
Adresse/indirizzo/address: Freiheitsstrasse 20 – Lauben 24, I-39012 Meran
Architektur/architettura/architecture:
Abram & Schnabl
MitarbeiterInnen/collaboratori/assistance:
Elmar Unterhauser, Partner, Ulrike Mühlberger, Thilo Doldi, Mario Festa, Petra Breddermann
Bauherr/committente/client: Karl und Erika Weithaler, Caser & Corona S.r.l.
Planungszeit/tempi di progettazione/start of planning: 09/1998
Errichtungszeit/tempi di esecuzione/construction: 12/2003
Generalunternehmer/impresa di costruzioni/building contractor: C.L.E. Gen.m.b.H
Statik/statica/structural consultant:
Bruno Marth
Elektroplanung/ progettista impianto elettrico/electrical services:
Georg Mutschlechner, St. Vigil/Enneberg
Heizungs-, Klima- und Sanitärplanung/progetto termo-sanitario/heating, air conditioning, plumbing:
Thermostudio P.I. Miori
Nutzfläche/superficie netta/floor area:
3860 m²
Umbauter Raum/cubatura/cubage:
22.960 m³
Baukosten/costi di costruzione/construction costs: 6,87 Mio. €

Projekt/progetto/project:
Wohnanlage Wolkenstein
Adresse/indirizzo/address: Oswald von Wolkensteinstrasse 8, I-39012 Meran
Architektur/architettura/architecture:
HolzBox, A-Innsbruck; Vorarlberger Ökohaus GmbH, A-Ludesch
Bauherr/committente/client:
Baugesellschaft Wolkenstein & Co. KG, Ellemunter Helmut, Meran
Planungszeit/tempi di progettazione/start of planning: 16 Monate
Errichtungszeit/tempi di esecuzione/construction: 04/2002–08/2003
Generalunternehmer/impresa di costruzioni/building contractor:
Vorarlberger Ökohaus GmbH, A-Ludesch; Baugesellschaft Wolkenstein & Co. KG, Meran
Statik/statica/structural consultant:
Robert Baldini, Marling
Bauleitung/direttore di lavoro/ construction management: Baldini Stefan, Marling

Lichtplanung/progetto illuminotecnico/
lightning concept:
Elektro Lochmann, Lana
Elektroplanung/ progettista impianto elettrico/electrical services:
HolzBox, A-Innsbruck; Vorarlberger
Ökohaus GmbH, A-Ludesch
Heizungs-, Klima- und Sanitärplanung/
progetto termo-sanitario/heating, air conditioning, plumbing: Konrad Hafner, Algund; Walter Malleier, Lana
Nutzfläche/superficie netta/floor area:
899 m^2
Umbauter Raum/cubatura/cubage:
1.899 m^3
Baukosten/costi di costruzione/construction costs: –

Projekt/progetto/project:
Villa Mozart
Adresse/indirizzo/address:
Markusstraße 26, I-39012 Meran
Architektur/architettura/architecture:
Oswald Zoeggeler
MitarbeiterInnen/collaboratori/assistance:
Umberto Bonagrua, Domenico Mariani,
Alessandro Scavazza, Alessandra Turri,
Alexander Zoeggeler
Bauherr/committente/client:
Christine Chizzali und Rinaldo Ghedina
Planungszeit/tempi di progettazione/start of planning: 09/1999
Errichtungszeit/tempi di esecuzione/construction: 2003–2005
Generalunternehmer/impresa di costruzioni/building contractor: Oswald Hafner
Statik/statica/structural consultant:
Planteam
Elektroplanung/progettista impianto elettrico/electrical services:
Manfred Tribus, Meran
Heizungs-, Klima- und Sanitärplanung/
progetto termo-sanitario/heating, air conditioning, plumbing:
Luis Egger GmBH, Schenna
Einrichtung, Möbel/arredo, mobili/facilities, furnishing: Dreika srl, Bozen
Wellness/spa:
Paul Hofer & C., St. Christina in Gröden
Nutzfläche/superficie netta/floor area:
2.050 m^2
Umbauter Raum/cubatura/cubage:
6.857 m^3

Baukosten/costi di costruzione/construction costs: 3.000.000,00 €

Projekt/progetto/project:
Die Gärten von Schloss Trauttmansdorff (Attraktionen, Pavillons, Einfriedung, Voliere)
Adresse/indirizzo/address:
St. Valentin Straße, I-39012 Meran
Architektur/architettura/architecture:
PVC – architects (Wolfram H. Pardatscher, Joachim M. Clemens, Alessandro Teti)
MitarbeiterInnen/collaboratori/assistance:
Margit Klammer (Konzept 5 Pavillons u. Voliere), SSS – Steiner Sarnen Schweiz (Konzept 6 Pavillons), B + B, Amsterdam (Konzept Einfriedung), Fiedrich Danglmaier, Salvo Di Silvestro, Marco De Fonzo
Bauherr/committente/client:
Autonome Provinz Bozen - Südtirol
Planungszeit/tempi di progettazione/start of planning: 1998–2000
Errichtungszeit/tempi di esecuzione/construction: 1999–2001
Generalunternehmer/impresa di costruzioni/building contractor: Amt für Wildbach- und Lawinenverbauung (Baumeister); Metallbau – Ritten (Schlosser); Paul Frener, Brixen (Schlosser); CMB, Bozen (Schlosser); Waldner – Bau, Meran (Baumeister); Paul Plunger, Eppan (Schlosser)
Statik/statica/structural consultant:
Alois Neulichedl, Meran
Lichtplanung/progetto illuminotecnico/
lightning concept:
ELE – Plan, Girlan (Thomas Meraner)
Heizungs-, Klima- und Sanitärplanung/
progetto termo-sanitario/heating, air conditioning, plumbing: M & N – Planconsulting, Burgstall (Mittelberger, Nischler)
Baukosten/costi di costruzione/construction costs: ca. 2.600.000 €

Projekt/progetto/project:
Besucherzentrum „Die Gärten von Schloss Trauttmansdorff"
Adresse/indirizzo/address:
St. Valentinstraße 51 a, I-39012 Meran
Architektur/architettura/architecture:
S.O.F.A. architekten mit Georg Mitterhofer
Bauherr/committente/client:

Autonome Provinz Bozen-Südtirol,
Land- und Forstwirtschaftliches Versuchszentrum Laimburg
Wettbewerb/concorso/competition:
1. Rang
Planungszeit/tempi di progettazione/start of planning: 01/2002–09/2002
Errichtungszeit/tempi di esecuzione/construction:01/2003–02/2004
Statik/statica/structural consultant:
Oswald Holzner
Lichtplanung/progetto illuminotecnico/
lightning concept:
Eleplan-Per. Ind. Thomas Meraner
Elektroplanung/ progettista impianto elettrico/electrical services:
Eleplan - Per. Ind. Thomas Meraner
Heizungs-, Klima- und Sanitärplanung/
progetto termo-sanitario/heating, air conditioning, plumbing: Energytech (Georg Felderer, Norbert Klammsteiner)
Einrichtung, Möbel/arredo, mobili/facilities, furnishing: Barth Innenausbau AG; Gogl GmbH
Nutzfläche/superficie netta/floor area:
658 m^2
Umbauter Raum/cubatura/cubage:
2.960 m^3
Baukosten/costi di costruzione/construction costs: 2,1 Mio. €

Projekt/progetto/project:
Landwirschaftliches Betriebsgebäude, Ladstätterhof
Adresse/indirizzo/address:
Sinich bei Meran
Architektur/architettura/architecture:
Peter Plattner
Bauherr/committente/client:
Autonome Provinz Bozen-Südtirol
Planungszeit/tempi di progettazione/start of planning: 2001
Errichtungszeit/tempi di esecuzione/construction: 2002–2003
Generalunternehmer/impresa di costruzioni/building contractor: Lancini costruzioni
Statik/statica/structural consultant:
Alois Neulichedl
Elektroplanung/ progettista impianto elettrico/electrical services:
per. Ind. Manfred Brugger
Heizungs-, Klima- und Sanitärplanung/
progetto termo-sanitario/heating, air con-

ditioning, plumbing: Gunther Langer
Nutzfläche/superficie netta/floor area:
ca. 1.320 m²
Umbauter Raum/cubatura/cubage:
4.800 m³
Baukosten/costi di costruzione/construction costs: 2.660.500,00 €

Projekt/progetto/project:
Mühlbauerhof
Adresse/indirizzo/address:
Mühlgraben 20, I-39010 Gargazon
Architektur/architettura/architecture:
Stefan Hitthaler
MitarbeiterInnen/collaboratori/assistance:
Thomas Niederwolfsgruber
Bauherr/committente/client:
Justine Gruber Kiem und Othmar Kiem
Planungszeit/tempi di progettazione/start of planning: 10/2002–10/2003
Errichtungszeit/tempi di esecuzione/construction: 10/2003–12/2004
Statik/statica/structural consultant:
Stefano Brunetti
Elektroplanung/ progettista impianto elettrico/electrical services: EKON, Bruneck
Heizungs-, Klima- und Sanitärplanung/progetto termo-sanitario/heating, air conditioning, plumbing: EKON, Bruneck
Nutzfläche/superficie netta/floor area:
301 m²
Umbauter Raum/cubatura/cubage:
3.323 m³
Baukosten/costi di costruzione/construction costs: 830.000 €

Projekt/progetto/project:
Haus Mumelter
Adresse/indirizzo/address:
Eisenkellerweg 8, I-39100 Bozen
Architektur/architettura/architecture:
Werner Tscholl
MitarbeiterInnen/collaboratori/assistance:
Albert Mascotti (Bauleitung)
Bauherr/committente/client:
Christa und Klaus Mumelter
Planungszeit/tempi di progettazione/start of planning: 1999
Errichtungszeit/tempi di esecuzione/construction: 2000
Statik/statica/structural consultant:
Holz & ko, Völs am Schlern
Einrichtung, Möbel/arredo, mobili/facilities, furnishing: Werner Tscholl
Nutzfläche/superficie netta/floor area:
180 m²
Umbauter Raum/cubatura/cubage:
865 m³
Baukosten/costi di costruzione/construction costs: –

Projekt/progetto/project:
Turnhalle der deutschsprachigen Grundschule „A. Rosmini", Bozen-Gries
Adresse/indirizzo/address: Martin Knoller Straße 9, I-39100 Bozen-Gries
Architektur/architettura/architecture:
Architekten Pardeller+Putzer+Scherer (Walter Pardeller, Josef Putzer, Michael Scherer)
MitarbeiterInnen/collaboratori/assistance:
Elisabeth Schatzer
Bauherr/committente/client: Gemeinde Bozen, Amt für öffentliche Arbeiten
Planungszeit/tempi di progettazione/start of planning: 01/2000–12/2000
Errichtungszeit/tempi di esecuzione/construction: 02/2001–01/2003
Generalunternehmer/impresa di costruzioni/building contractor:
Adanti S.p.A, Bologna
Statik/statica/structural consultant:
Helmuth Niedermair, Bozen
Lichtplanung/progetto illuminotecnico/lightning concept: Studio Masiero, Bozen
Elektroplanung/ progettista impianto elettrico/electrical services:
Architekten Pardeller+Putzer+Scherer; Studio Masiero, Bozen
Heizungs-, Klima- und Sanitärplanung/progetto termo-sanitario/heating, air conditioning, plumbing: Industrieteam, Terlan
Einrichtung, Möbel/arredo, mobili/facilities, furnishing:
Architekten Pardeller+Putzer+Scherer
Nutzfläche/superficie netta/floor area:
1.409 m²
Umbauter Raum/cubatura/cubage:
6.855 m³
Baukosten/costi di costruzione/construction costs: 3.115.976,00 €

Projekt/progetto/project:
Realgymnasium, Bozen
Adresse/indirizzo/address:
Fagenstraße 10, I-39100 Bozen
Architektur/architettura/architecture:
Christoph Mayr Fingerle (S. Leonardi und Geom. Nori Gruber, Mitarbeit bei der Bauleitung)
MitarbeiterInnen/collaboratori/assistance:
Sergio Leonardi, Renate Marchetti, Curdin Michael, Thomas Raschke, Susanne Waiz, Rolf Zimmermann
Bauherr/committente/client:
Autonome Provinz Bozen-Südtirol
Planungszeit/tempi di progettazione/start of planning: 1991–1993
Errichtungszeit/tempi di esecuzione/construction: 1994–2001
Generalunternehmer/impresa di costruzioni/building contractor: Leis S.P.A. (1994–1995); Longhin (1995); Betonbau (1996–1999); Zimmerhofer (1999–2000); Stampfer OHG (2000); Dana Costruzioni (2001) (Baufirmen)
Statik/statica/structural consultant:
Franco Letrari
Lichtkonzept/progetto illuminotecnico/lightning concept: Christoph Mayr Fingerle
Elektroplanung/ progettista impianto elettrico/electrical services:
Helmuth Stuppner, Bozen
Heizungs-, Klima- und Sanitärplanung/progetto termo-sanitario/heating, air conditioning, plumbing: Josef Reichhalter
Einrichtung, Möbel/arredo, mobili/facilities, furnishing: Christoph Mayr Fingerle
Umbauter Raum/cubatura/cubage:
40.000 m³
Baukosten/costi di costruzione/construction costs: 7,13 Mio. €

Projekt/progetto/project:
Tiefgarage und Neugestaltung Gerichtsplatz, Bozen
Adresse/indirizzo/address:
Piazza Tribunale, I-39100 Bozen
Architektur/architettura/architecture:
Studio Fierro (Stanislao Fierro)
MitarbeiterInnen/collaboratori/assistance:
Orazio Basso
Bauherr/committente/client:
Gemeinde Bozen

Wettbewerb/concorso/competition:
1. Rang
Planungszeit/tempi di progettazione/start of planning: 01/2000-06/2000
Errichtungszeit/tempi di esecuzione/construction: 07/2000–10/2004
Generalunternehmer/impresa di costruzioni/building contractor: PANA S.p.a
Statik/statica/structural consultant:
Klaus Plattner
Lichtplanung/progetto illuminotecnico/lightning concept: Stanislao Fierro
Elektroplanung/ progettista impianto elettrico/electrical services:
Heizungs-, Klima- und Sanitärplanung/ progetto termo-sanitario/heating, air conditioning, plumbing: Alfredo De Rivo
Einrichtung, Möbel/arredo, mobili/facilities, furnishing: Stanislao Fierro
Nutzfläche/superficie netta/floor area: 10.500 m^2
Umbauter Raum/cubatura/cubage: 29600 m^3
Baukosten/costi di costruzione/construction costs: 3.464.609,27 € (Tiefgarage), 1.500.000,00 € (Platz)

Projekt/progetto/project:
Europäische Akademie Bozen (EURAC)
Adresse/indirizzo/address:
I-39100 Bozen, Drususallee 1
Architektur/architettura/architecture:
Klaus Kada
MitarbeiterInnen/collaboratori/assistance:
Erwin Matzer – (Projektleitung), Heribert Altenbacher (Projektleitung), Helena Weber-Albrecher (Projektleitung), Ronald Schatz (IGO), Michael Dejori, Josef Ebner, Peter Eppich, Alexander Forsthofer, Irmgard Kolle, Rosi Kueng-Freiberger, Elia Nedkov, Martin Pallier-Rosenberger, Peter Rous, Claudia Schmidt, Herbert Schwarzmann, Peter Szammer, Angela Uhl, Gerhard Zehner, Hubert Schuller (Modell)
Bauherr/committente/client: Europäische Akademie Bozen (Werner Stuflesser)
Wettbewerb/concorso/competition:
1. Rang
Planungszeit/tempi di progettazione/start of planning: 1995–2002
Errichtungszeit/tempi di esecuzione/construction: 11/1998–09/2002

Statik/statica/structural consultant:
Konrad Bergmeister & Partner, Brixen-Wien
Lichtplanung/progetto illuminotecnico/lightning concept: Klaus Kada
Elektroplanung/ progettista impianto elettrico/electrical services: Roman Obexer und Reinhard Thaler, Bozen
Heizungs-, Klima- und Sanitärplanung/ progetto termo-sanitario/heating, airconditioning, plumbing: Erwin Mumelter und Michele Carlini, Bozen
Einrichtung, Möbel/arredo, mobili/facilities, furnishing: Klaus Kada
Bauphysik/fisica delle costruzioni/ construction physics:
Peter Kautsch, A-Graz
AV-Technik/tecnica audio e video/audio-visual technology:
Audio-Plan, CH-Müllheim-Wigoltingen
Nutzfläche/superficie netta/floor area: ca. 10.333,73 m^2
Baukosten/costi di costruzione/construction costs: ca. 42 Mio. € (inkl. Einrichtung, EDV, Multimedia)

Projekt/progetto/project:
Abbruch und Neubau der Landesberufsschule, Bozen, Abt. Handwerk und Industrie
Adresse/indirizzo/address:
Romstrasse 20, I-39100 Bozen
Architektur/architettura/architecture:
Höller & Klotzner – Architekten
Bauherr/committente/client:
Autonome Provinz Bozen-Südtirol
Wettbewerb/concorso/competition:
1. Rang
Planungszeit/tempi di progettazione/start of planning: 1997–1999
Errichtungszeit/tempi di esecuzione/construction: 2000–2005 (1. Bauphase)
Generalunternehmer/impresa di costruzioni/building contractor:
Rizzani de Eccher, Udine
Statik/statica/structural consultant:
Konrad Bergmeister & Partner, Brixen-Wien (Josef Taferner)
Lichtplanung/progetto illuminotecnico/lightning concept: Conceptlicht GmbH, A-Mils (Manfred Draxl)
Elektroplanung/ progettista impianto elettrico/electrical services: Elektrostudio p.i.

Gerhard Strobl, Bruneck
Heizungs-, Klima- und Sanitärplanung/ progetto termo-sanitario/heating, air conditioning, plumbing:
Erwin Mumelter, Bozen
Einrichtung, Möbel/arredo, mobili/facilities, furnishing: Höller, Leifers (Maßmöbel); Pedacta, Lana (Serienmöbel)
Nutzfläche/superficie netta/floor area: 20.600 m^2
Umbauter Raum/cubatura/cubage: 82.600 m^3
Baukosten/costi di costruzione/construction costs: 38 Mio. € (inkl. Einrichtung)

Projekt/progetto/project:
Freie Universität Bozen
Adresse/indirizzo/address:
Sernesistrasse 1, I-39100 Bozen
Architektur/architettura/architecture:
Bischoff Azzola Architekten
(Matthias Bischoff, Roberto Azzola)
MitarbeiterInnen/collaboratori/assistance:
Martin Litscher, Christoph Felder, Bernd Habersang, Roger Trottmann, Silvia Kopp
Bauherr/committente/client:
Autonome Provinz Bozen-Südtirol
Wettbewerb/concorso/competition:
1. Rang
Planungszeit/tempi di progettazione/start of planning: 1998 Vorprojekt; 1999–2003 Ausführungsplanung Baulose 1 und 2
Errichtungszeit/tempi di esecuzione/construction: 1. Baulos 2000–2002; 2. Baulos 2004–2005 (ohne Beteiligung Bischoff Azzola Architekten)
Generalunternehmer/impresa di costruzioni/building contractor:
Fietz AG Bauingenieure, CH-Zürich
Statik/statica/structural consultant:
Lichtplanung/progetto illuminotecnico/ lightning concept:
ARGE Kunstlicht, CH-Zürich
Elektroplanung/ progettista impianto elettrico/electrical services:
Ernst Basler + Partner, CH-Zürich
Heizungs-, Klima- und Sanitärplanung/ progetto termo-sanitario/heating, air conditioning, plumbing:
Ernst Basler + Partner, CH-Zürich
Einrichtung, Möbel/arredo, mobili/facilities, furnishing:
Bischoff Azzola Architekten

Nutzfläche/superficie netta/floor area:
ca. 12.500 m²
Umbauter Raum/cubatura/cubage:
123.000 m³
Baukosten/costi di costruzione/construction costs: 56 Mio. €

Projekt/progetto/project:
Sanierung und Erweiterung Haus Amonn
Adresse/indirizzo/address:
Bindergasse 37, I-39100 Bozen
Architektur/architettura/architecture:
Peter Plattner
MitarbeiterInnen/collaboratori/assistance:
Michaela Mair, Karin Triendl, Wolfgang Pröbstle
Bauherr/committente/client: Ander Amonn
Planungszeit/tempi di progettazione/start of planning: 1998
Errichtungszeit/tempi di esecuzione/construction: 2000–2001
Generalunternehmer/impresa di costruzioni/building contractor: Domus Residenz
Statik/statica/structural consultant:
Georg Kauer
Lichtplanung/progetto illuminotecnico/lightning concept: Halotech, A-Innsbruck
Elektroplanung/ progettista impianto elettrico/electrical services:
per. Ind. Manfred Brugger
Heizungs-, Klima- und Sanitärplanung/progetto termo-sanitario/heating, air conditioning, plumbing: per. Ind. Presutti
Einrichtung, Möbel/arredo, mobili/facilities, furnishing: Barth Innenausbau; Metallconcept
Nutzfläche/superficie netta/floor area:
867 m²
Umbauter Raum/cubatura/cubage:
3.410 m³
Baukosten/costi di costruzione/construction costs: 1.280.000,00 €

Projekt/progetto/project:
Neubau einer Industriehalle mit Bürotrakt, Firma Bel
Adresse/indirizzo/address:
Luis-Zuegg Straße 23, I-39100 Bozen
Architektur/architettura/architecture: Studio architetto Luigi Scolari (Luigi Scolari)
MitarbeiterInnen/collaboratori/assistance:
Guido Gentilli
Bauherr/committente/client: BEL s.r.l.
Planungszeit/tempi di progettazione/start of planning: 06/2001
Errichtungszeit/tempi di esecuzione/construction: 2006
Generalunternehmer/impresa di costruzioni/building contractor: Volcan s.r.l.
Statik/statica/structural consultant:
Giorgio Rizzo
Heizungs-, Klima- und Sanitärplanung/progetto termo-sanitario/heating, air conditioning, plumbing: Marina Bolzan
Nutzfläche/superficie netta/floor area:
9.850 m²
Umbauter Raum/cubatura/cubage:
49.000 m³
Baukosten/costi di costruzione/construction costs: 2.560.177 €

Projekt/progetto/project:
Kindergarten „Maria-Rast", St. Michael, Eppan
Adresse/indirizzo/address: Maria-Rast Weg, St. Michael, I-39057 Eppan
Architektur/architettura/architecture:
Lunz&Zöschg Architekten
(Markus Lunz und Hubert Zöschg)
MitarbeiterInnen/collaboratori/assistance:
Ilka Hesse, Manja Baudis, Sylvia Lehnig, Ulrike Mühlberger
Bauherr/committente/client:
Gemeinde Eppan
Wettbewerb/concorso/competition:
1. Rang
Planungszeit/tempi di progettazione/start of planning: 07/2003–05/2004
Errichtungszeit/tempi di esecuzione/construction: ca. 05/2004–08/2005
Statik/statica/structural consultant:
Oberrauch & Haller, Hoch- und Tiefbau, Bozen
Lichtplanung/progetto illuminotecnico/lightning concept: Techn. Büro
Per. Ind. Cristofoletti Jochen, Bozen
Elektroplanung/ progettista impianto elettrico/electrical services:
Jochen Cristofoletti, Bozen
Heizungs-, Klima- und Sanitärplanung/progetto termo-sanitario/heating, air conditioning, plumbing:
Einrichtung, Möbel/arredo, mobili/facilities, furnishing: Lunz&Zöschg Architekten
Nutzfläche/superficie netta/floor area:
ca. 1.850 m²
Umbauter Raum/cubatura/cubage:
ca. 9.200 m³
Baukosten/costi di costruzione/construction costs: 4.500.000 €

Projekt/progetto/project:
Haus an der Weinstraße, Tramin
Adresse/indirizzo/address:
Weinstrasse 100, I-39040 Tramin
Architektur/architettura/architecture:
Silvia Boday
MitarbeiterInnen/collaboratori/assistance:
M. Sc. Jurgen Groener
Bauherr/committente/client:
Inge Kerschbaumer
Planungszeit/tempi di progettazione/start of planning: 2003–2005
Errichtungszeit/tempi di esecuzione/construction: 01/2005–12/2005
Statik/statica/structural consultant:
Konrad Bergmeister & Partner, Brixen-Wien (Hermann Leitner)
Elektroplanung/ progettista impianto elettrico/electrical services: Manfred Prugger
Heizungs-, Klima- und Sanitärplanung/progetto termo-sanitario/heating, air conditioning, plumbing: Pfraumer Roland & Co.
Einrichtung, Möbel/arredo, mobili/facilities, furnishing:
Tischlerei Kofler des Oswald Kröss
Nutzfläche/superficie netta/floor area:
117 m²
Umbauter Raum/cubatura/cubage:
605,91 m³
Baukosten/costi di costruzione/construction costs: 380.000 €

Projekt/progetto/project:
Oberschule für Landwirtschaft, Ansitz Baugarten, Auer
Adresse/indirizzo/address:
Schlossweg 1, I-39040 Auer
Architektur/architettura/architecture:
Wolfgang Piller
MitarbeiterInnen/collaboratori/assistance:
Andreas Adelkirchner, Ilija Balta, Karoline Blaas, Joachim Clemens, Mauro Corradini, Wolfram Pardatscher, Luigi Scolari, Oliver Stadtmüller, Christoph Störck, Mathias

Trebo, Emil Wörndle
Bauherr/committente/client:
Autonome Provinz Bozen-Südtirol
Planungszeit/tempi di progettazione/start
of planning: 1996–1998
Errichtungszeit/tempi di esecuzione/
construction: 1999–2001
Generalunternehmer/impresa di costruzioni/building contractor:
Rizzani de Eccher S.p.a., Udine
Statik/statica/structural consultant:
Gerhard Rohrer, Bozen
Lichtplanung/progetto illuminotecnico/
lightning concept: Klaus Faller, Brixen
Elektroplanung/ progettista impianto elettrico/electrical services:
M & N Planconsulting, Burgstall
Heizungs-, Klima- und Sanitärplanung/
progetto termo-sanitario/heating, air conditioning, plumbing: Michele Carlini, Bozen
Einrichtung, Möbel/arredo, mobili/facilities, furnishing: Wolfgang Piller
Nutzfläche/superficie netta/floor area:
5.000 m²
Umbauter Raum/cubatura/cubage:
20.000 m³
Baukosten/costi di costruzione/construction costs: 8.800.000,00 € (inkl. Einrichtung)

Projekt/progetto/project:
Erweiterung Pfarrkirche Leifers
Adresse/indirizzo/address:
Weissensteinerstrasse, I-39055 Leifers
Architektur/architettura/architecture:
Höller & Klotzner – Architekten
Bauherr/committente/client: Pfarrei „Heiliger Antonius Abt und heiliger Nikolaus"
Wettbewerb/concorso/competition:
Preisträger
Planungszeit/tempi di progettazione/start
of planning: 1999
Errichtungszeit/tempi di esecuzione/
construction: 2000–2003
Generalunternehmer/impresa di costruzioni/building contractor: Zanella, Leifers
Statik/statica/structural consultant:
Konrad Bergmeister & Partner,
Brixen-Wien (Josef Taferner)
Lichtplanung/progetto illuminotecnico/
lightning concept: Conceptlicht GmbH,
A-Mils (Manfred Draxl)
Elektropl./progettista impianto elettrico/
electrical services: Roland Zuegg, Lana
Heizungs-, Klima- und Sanitärplanung/
progetto termo-sanitario/heating, air conditioning, plumbing: Thermoplan, Bozen
Einrichtung, Möbel/arredo, mobili/facilities, furnishing: Höller, Leifers
(lit. Elem/Innenausbau)
Nutzfläche/superficie netta/floor area:
960 m²
Umbauter Raum/cubatura/cubage:
9.200 m³
Baukosten/costi di costruzione/construction costs: 4,1 Mio. € (inkl. Einrichtung)

Projekt/progetto/project:
Haus Kaser
Adresse/indirizzo/address:
Platschweg 40 a, I-39042 Brixen-Milland
Architektur/architettura/architecture:
studio benno barth (Benno Barth)
Bauherr/committente/client:
Sabine und Rupert Kaser
Planungszeit/tempi di progettazione/start
of planning: 01/2002–06/2004
Errichtungszeit/tempi di esecuzione/
construction: 09/2003–11/2004
Statik/statica/structural consultant:
Benno Barth
Elektroplanung/ progettista impianto elettrico/electrical services:
Norbert Verginer, Brixen
Heizungs-, Klima- und Sanitärplanung/
progetto termo-sanitario/heating, air conditioning, plumbing:
Norbert Verginer, Brixen
Einrichtung, Möbel/arredo, mobili/facilities, furnishing: Benno Barth
Nutzfläche/superficie netta/floor area:
272 m²
Umbauter Raum/cubatura/cubage:
1.547 m³
Baukosten/costi di costruzione/construction costs: –

Projekt/progetto/project:
Landesberufsschule „Ch. J. Tschuggmall" und Studentenhaus „St. Michael", Brixen
Landesberufsschule „Ch. J. Tschuggmall":
Adresse/indirizzo/address:
Fischzuchtweg 18, I-39042 Brixen
Architektur/architettura/architecture:
Siegfried Delueg
MitarbeiterInnen/collaboratori/assistance:
Thomas Mahlknecht, Igor Comploi, Robert Margreiter (Wettbewerb), Manfred König, Raimund Wulz
Bauherr/committente/client:
Autonome Provinz Bozen-Südtirol
Wettbewerb/concorso/competition:
1. Rang
Planungszeit/tempi di progettazione/start
of planning: 01/1997–08/1998
Errichtungszeit/tempi di esecuzione/
construction: 03/1999–09/2002
Statik/statica/structural consultant:
Benno Barth, Brixen
Lichtplanung/progetto illuminotecnico/
lightning concept: Conceptlicht GmbH,
A-6068 Mils (Manfred Draxl)
Elektroplanung/ progettista impianto elettrico/electrical services:
Elektrostudio, Bruneck
Heizungs-, Klima- und Sanitärplanung/
progetto termo-sanitario/heating, air conditioning, plumbing:
Michele Carlini, Bozen
Einrichtung, Möbel/arredo, mobili/facilities, furnishing:
Barth/ Erlacher/ Schraffl (Maßmöbel)
Nutzfläche/superficie netta/floor area:
17.437 m²
Umbauter Raum/cubatura/cubage:
78.000 m³
Baukosten/costi di costruzione/construction costs: 37.050.000,00 € (Gesamtbaukosten)

Studentenhaus „St. Michael":
Adresse/indirizzo/address:
Fischzuchtweg 16, I-39042 Brixen
Architektur/architettura/architecture:
Siegfried Delueg
MitarbeiterInnen/collaboratori/assistance:
Thomas Mahlknecht, Igor Comploi,
Manfred König, Raimund Wulz
Bauherr/committente/client:
Autonome Provinz Bozen-Südtirol
Planungszeit/tempi di progettazione/start
of planning: 03/1998–12/1999
Errichtungszeit/tempi di esecuzione/
construction: 03/2001–10/2003
Generalunternehmer/impresa di costruzioni/building contractor: Guerrino Pivato

spa, Onè di Fonte (TV)
Statik/statica/structural consultant:
Benno Barth, Brixen
Lichtplanung/progetto illuminotecnico/
lightning concept: Conceptlicht GmbH,
A-Mils (Manfred Draxl)
Elektroplanung/ progettista impianto elettrico/electrical services:
Elektrostudio, Bruneck
Heizungs-, Klima- und Sanitärplanung/
progetto termo-sanitario/heating, air conditioning, plumbing:
Michele Carlini, Bozen
Einrichtung, Möbel/arredo, mobili/facilities, furnishing:
Berger Innenausbau (Maßmöbel)
Nutzfläche/superficie netta/floor area:
3.439 m^2
Umbauter Raum/cubatura/cubage:
13.293 m^3
Baukosten/costi di costruzione/construction costs: 8.200.000 € (Gesamtbaukosten)

Projekt/progetto/project:
Kinder-Tagesbetreuungsstätte im Krankenhaus, Brixen
Adresse/indirizzo/address:
Dantestraße 51, I-39042 Brixen
Architektur/architettura/architecture:
MODUS architects
Bauherr/committente/client:
Sanitätsbetrieb Brixen
Wettbewerb/concorso/competition:
1. Rang im Unternehmens-Ideenwettbewerb für die Projektierung (definitive und Ausführungsplanung) und Ausführung der Arbeiten schlüsselfertig, einschließlich Einrichtung
Planungszeit/tempi di progettazione/start of planning: 06/2004–09/2004
Errichtungszeit/tempi di esecuzione/
construction: 02/2005–05/2005
Generalunternehmer/impresa di costruzioni/building contractor: Zimmerhofer GmbH
Statik/statica/structural consultant:
Alois Dorfmann, Josef Taferner
Lichtplanung/progetto illuminotecnico/
lightning concept: Scagnol-Attia,
Gernot Hackhofer (Elpo srl)
Elektroplanung/ progettista impianto elettrico/electrical services: Elpo srl
Heizungs-, Klima- und Sanitärplanung/
progetto termo-sanitario/heating,
air conditioning, plumbing: Dieter Jung
(J. Schmidhammer srl)
Einrichtung, Möbel/arredo, mobili/facilities, furnishing: Tischlerei Krapf
Nutzfläche/superficie netta/floor area:
240 m^2
Umbauter Raum/cubatura/cubage: 320 m^3
Baukosten/costi di costruzione/construction costs: 375.000,00 €

Projekt/progetto/project:
„Haus Sachsenklemme"/ Haus Ganterer
Adresse/indirizzo/address:
Brennerstrasse 1, I-39045 Franzenfeste
Architektur/architettura/architecture:
Gerd Bergmeister
MitarbeiterInnen/collaboratori/assistance:
Markus Hofer; Stefan Griesser
Bauherr/committente/client:
Roland Ganterer
Planungszeit/tempi di progettazione/start of planning: Sommer 2003
Errichtungszeit/tempi di esecuzione/
construction: 01/2004–12/2004
Generalunternehmer/impresa di costruzioni/building contractor: Konrad Bergmeister & Partner, Brixen-Wien
Statik/statica/structural consultant: Konrad Bergmeister & Partner, Brixen-Wien
Lichtplanung/progetto illuminotecnico/
lightning concept: Light System,
Reischach; Gerd Bergmeister
Elektroplanung/ progettista impianto elettrico/electrical services:
Faller Alfred & Co. OHG, Brixen
Heizungs-, Klima- und Sanitärplanung/
progetto termo-sanitario/heating, air conditioning, plumbing: Mader, Sterzing
Einrichtung, Möbel/arredo, mobili/facilities, furnishing:
Barth Innenausbau, Brixen
Nutzfl./superficie netta/floor area: 180 m^2
Umbauter Raum/cubatura/cubage:
1.230 m^3
Baukosten/costi di costruzione/construction costs: –

Projekt/progetto/project:
Haus in Stilfes
Adresse/indirizzo/address:
Stilfes 83, I-39040 Freienfeld
Architektur/architettura/architecture:
Christian Schwienbacher
Bauherr/committente/client:
Nikolaus Holzer
Statik/statica/structural consultant:
Planteam, Bozen
Elektroplanung/ progettista impianto elettrico/electrical services:
Rudolf Bacher, Stilfes, Freienfeld
Heizungs-, Klima- und Sanitärplanung/
progetto termo-sanitario/heating, air conditioning, plumbing: Mader, Sterzing
Einrichtung, Möbel/arredo, mobili/facilities, furnishing: Tischlerei Brunner, Freienfeld
Baukosten/costi di costruzione/construction costs: –

Projekt/progetto/project:
Mehrzweckgebäude am Bühel
Adresse/indirizzo/address:
St. Jakob am Bühel, I-39030 Ahrntal
Architektur/architettura/architecture:
Mutschlechner & Mahlknecht architekten
Bauherr/committente/client:
Gemeinde Ahrntal
Planungszeit/tempi di progettazione/start of planning: 10/2003–05/2004
Errichtungszeit/tempi di esecuzione/
construction: 10/2004–08/2005
Generalunternehmer/impresa di costruzioni/building contractor:
Statik/statica/structural consultant:
Johann Mittermair, Bruneck
Lichtplanung/progetto illuminotecnico/
lightning concept:
Arno de Monte, Sand in Taufers
Elektroplanung/ progettista impianto elettrico/electrical services:
Arno de Monte, Sand in Taufers
Heizungs-, Klima- und Sanitärplanung/
progetto termo-sanitario/heating, air conditioning, plumbing:
Arno de Monte, Sand in Taufers
Einrichtung, Möbel/arredo, mobili/facilities, furnishing: Heinrich Mutschlechner
Nutzfläche/superficie netta/floor area:
375 m^2
Umbauter Raum/cubatura/cubage:
1.756 m^3

Baukosten/costi di costruzione/construction costs: 680.000,00 €

Projekt/progetto/project:
Sanierung Stein- und Holzhaus, Dr. Tasser
Adresse/indirizzo/address:
Steinhaus 57 A, I-39030 Ahrntal
Architektur/architettura/architecture:
Mutschlechner & Mahlknecht architekten
(Heinrich Mutschlechner und
Gerhard Mahlknecht)
Bauherr/committente/client: Josefine
Reichegger-Tasser und Dr. Rudolf Tasser
Planungszeit/tempi di progettazione/start of planning: 1996–2002
Errichtungszeit/tempi di esecuzione/construction: 1998–2004
Statik/statica/structural consultant:
Günther Schönegger, Bruneck
Lichtplanung/progetto illuminotecnico/lightning concept: Heinrich Mutschlechner
Elektroplanung/ progettista impianto elettrico/electrical services:
Heinrich Mutschlechner
Heizungs-, Klima- und Sanitärplanung/progetto termo-sanitario/heating, air conditioning, plumbing:
Heinrich Mutschlechner
Einrichtung, Möbel/arredo, mobili/facilities, furnishing: Heinrich Mutschlechner
Nutzfläche/superficie netta/floor area:
98 m^2
Umbauter Raum/cubatura/cubage:
360 m^3
Baukosten/costi di costruzione/construction costs: –

Projekt/progetto/project:
Friedhofserweiterung Luttach
Adresse/indirizzo/address:
Luttach, I-39030 Ahrntal
Architektur/architettura/architecture:
Mutschlechner & Mahlknecht architekten
(Heinrich Mutschlechner und Gerhard Mahlknecht)
Bauherr/committente/client:
Gemeinde Ahrntal, Pfarrei Hl. Sebastian
Wettbewerb/concorso/competition: 1997,
1. Rang
Planungszeit/tempi di progettazione/start of planning: 1998–2002
Errichtungszeit/tempi di esecuzione/construction: 2002–2004
Statik/statica/structural consultant:
Günther Schönegger, Bruneck
Lichtplanung/progetto illuminotecnico/lightning concept: Heinrich Mutschlechner
Elektroplanung/ progettista impianto elettrico/electrical services:
Arno de Monte, Sand in Taufers
Heizungs-, Klima- und Sanitärplanung/progetto termo-sanitario/heating, air conditioning, plumbing:
Arno de Monte, Sand in Taufers
Einrichtung, Möbel/arredo, mobili/facilities, furnishing: Heinrich Mutschlechner
Nutzfläche/superficie netta/floor area:
1.990 m^2
Umbauter Raum/cubatura/cubage:
775 m^3
Baukosten/costi di costruzione/construction costs: 1.080.000,00 €

Projekt/progetto/project:
Wohnanlage G3D
Adresse/indirizzo/address:
Althingstraße 32, I-39031Stegen-Bruneck
Architektur/architettura/architecture:
Projektgemeinschaft: Bruno Rubner,
dkp-architektur, dreiplus-architektur
Bauherr/committente/client:
Wohngemeinschaft, 16 private Bauherren
Wettbewerb/concorso/competition:
1. Rang
Planungszeit/tempi di progettazione/start of planning: 01/02-2002
Errichtungszeit/tempi di esecuzione/construction: 07/2002–09/2003
Statik/statica/structural consultant:
Günther Schönegger, Bruneck
Lichtplanung/progetto illuminotecnico/lightning concept: Ekon, Bruneck
Elektroplanung/ progettista impianto elettrico/electrical services: Ekon, Bruneck
Heizungs-, Klima- und Sanitärplanung/progetto termo-sanitario/heating, air conditioning, plumbing: Ekon, Bruneck
Nutzfläche/superficie netta/floor area:
2.800 m^2
Umbauter Raum/cubatura/cubage:
ca. 9.700 m^3
Baukosten/costi di costruzione/construction costs: 200.000,00 €–220.000,00 €
pro Einheit

Projekt/progetto/project:
Wohnhaus Sonne
Adresse/indirizzo/address: Josef-Renzler-Straße Nr. 24, I- 39030 St. Lorenzen
Architektur/architettura/architecture:
COMFORT_ARCHITECTEN
(Marco Micheli, Michael Mumelter)
Bauherr/committente/client:
Veronika Pichler-Oberhollenzer
Planungszeit/tempi di progettazione/start of planning: 01/2002–07/2002
Errichtungszeit/tempi di esecuzione/construction: 07/2002–07/2003
Statik/statica/structural consultant:
Stefan Brunetti, Bruneck
Lichtplanung/progetto illuminotecnico/lightning concept:
COMFORT_ARCHITECTEN
Elektroplanung/ progettista impianto elettrico/electrical services:
COMFORT_ARCHITECTEN
Einrichtung, Möbel/arredo, mobili/facilities, furnishing:
COMFORT_ARCHITECTEN
Nutzfläche/superficie netta/floor area:
110 m^2
Umbauter Raum/cubatura/cubage:
ca. 640 m^3
Baukosten/costi di costruzione/construction costs: 380.000,00 €

Projekt/progetto/project:
Gesundheits- und Sozialsprengel Gadertal
Adresse/indirizzo/address:
Picolin 71, I-39030 St. Martin in Thurn
Architektur/architettura/architecture:
Architekturbüro D3 (Kathrin Gruber, Armin Kienzl, Richard Veneri, Robert Veneri)
Bauherr/committente/client:
Gemeinde St. Martin in Thurn
Wettbewerb/concorso/competition:
1. Rang
Planungszeit/tempi di progettazione/start of planning: 06/1997–12/1998
Errichtungszeit/tempi di esecuzione/construction: 04/1999–07/2001
Generalunternehmer/impresa di costruzioni/building contractor: Clara Costruzioni,
La Villa (Baumeister); Holz & Haus,
St. Martin in Thurn(Holzbau); ARTE
GmbH, Bozen (Innenausbau)
Statik/statica/structural consultant:

Benno Barth, Brixen
Lichtplanung/progetto illuminotecnico/lightning concept: Franco Zanotto, Brixen
Elektroplanung/ progettista impianto elettrico/electrical services:
Franco Zanotto, Brixen
Heizungs-, Klima- und Sanitärplanung/progetto termo-sanitario/heating, air conditioning, plumbing: Luigi
Presutti, Bozen (in Zusammenarbeit mit Fraunhofer-Institut, D-Freiburg)
Einrichtung, Möbel/arredo, mobili/facilities, furnishing: Architekturbüro D3
Umbauter Raum/cubatura/cubage:
10.820 m^3
Baukosten/costi di costruzione/construction costs: 3.364.000,00 €

Projekt/progetto/project:
Haus Huber Schnarf
Adresse/indirizzo/address:
Pfarrstraße 18 D, I-39030 Olang
Architektur/architettura/architecture:
aichner_seidl ARCHITEKTEN
MitarbeiterInnen/collaboratori/assistance:
Robert Fischnaller, Christian Jurczyk, Sylvia Schwingshackl, Anton Treyer
Bauherr/committente/client:
Ursula Schnarf und Werner Huber
Planungszeit/tempi di progettazione/start of planning: 01/2003–06/2004
Errichtungszeit/tempi di esecuzione/construction: 06/2003–06/2004
Statik/statica/structural consultant:
Stefano Brunetti, Bruneck
Elektroplanung/ progettista impianto elettrico/electrical services:
Elektro Winkler, Olang
Heizungs-, Klima- und Sanitärplanung/progetto termo-sanitario/heating, air conditioning, plumbing:
Planungsteam E-Plus, A-Egg/Vorarlberg
Einrichtung, Möbel/arredo, mobili/facilities, furnishing:
aichner_seidl ARCHITEKTEN
Nutzfläche/superficie netta/floor area:
218 m^2
Umbauter Raum/cubatura/cubage:
ca. 1.100 m^3
Baukosten/costi di costruzione/construction costs: 450.000,00 € (ohne Einrichtung)

Projekt/progetto/project:
Fernheizwerk Sexten
Adresse/indirizzo/address:
Sextnerstraße, I-39030 Sexten
Architektur/architettura/architecture:
Siegfried Delueg
MitarbeiterInnen/collaboratori/assistance:
Thomas Mahlknecht, Igor Comploi
Bauherr/committente/client:
Fernheizwerk Sexten GmbH
Wettbewerb/concorso/competition:
11/2003, 1. Rang
Planungszeit/tempi di progettazione/start of planning: 01/2004–04/2004
Errichtungszeit/tempi di esecuzione/construction: 05/2004–09/2004
Generalunternehmer/impresa di costruzioni/building contractor:
Tschurtschentaler, Innichen
Statik/statica/structural consultant:
Team 4, Bruneck
Elektroplanung/ progettista impianto elettrico/electrical services:
VAS, Anlagensysteme, A-Großgmain
Heizungs-, Klima- und Sanitärplanung/progetto termo-sanitario/heating, air conditioning, plumbing: Seegen MBH
Nutzfläche/superficie netta/floor area:
2.229 m^2
Umbauter Raum/cubatura/cubage:
23.083 m^3
Baukosten/costi di costruzione/construction costs: 2.500.000,00 € (ohne Anlagen)

Architekten   **Architetti**   **Architects**

Name/nome/name:
Hanspeter Abler Trojer
Geboren/nato/born: 1956 Meran († 1998)
Studium/studi/education: TU Graz (A), Diplom 1988
Büro/studio professionale/office: seit 1991 in Algund
Lehrtätigkeit/attività didattica/teaching: –
Hauptwerke/progetti scelti/main projects: Bürogebäude Martin Geier

Name/nome/name:
abram&schnabl
Zeno Abram
Geboren/nato/born: 1941 Wien (A)
Studium/studi/education: TU München, Hochschule für Bildende Kunst, Berlin, Diplom München 1966, Promotion 1967, Postgraduate study urban design (Stadtplanung), Virginia State University, Blacksburg, USA 1969/70
Lehrtätigkeit/attività didattica/teaching: Universität Innsbruck, Gastprofessur 1990, 1993
Heiner Schnabl
Geboren/nato/born: 1941 Bozen (I)
Studium/studi/education: TU Wien, Universitätsinstitut für Architektur Venedig, Promotion Venedig 1967
Büro/studio professionale/office: Bürogemeinschaft abram & schnabl seit 1970
Hauptwerke/progetti scelti/main projects: Kurhauspassage, Meran; Behindertenzentrum „Pastor Angelicus", Meran/Obermais; Volksbank am Domplatz in Bozen; Kirche „Maria in der Au", Bozen Don Bosco; Weinkellerei Alois Lageder, Margreid; Landesberufschule „Luis Zuegg", Meran/Untermais; Grundschule und Musikschule, Tramin; Neues Rathaus und Parkgarage, Bruneck

Name/nome/name:
aichner_seidl ARCHITEKTEN
Werner Seidl
Geboren/nato/born: 1959 Lavamünd (A)
Studium/studi/education: TU Graz, Diplom 1989
Dora Aichner
Geboren/nato/born: 1957 Bruneck
Studium/studi/education: TU Graz, Diplom 1984
Büro/studio professionale/office: Bürogemeinschaft Kurt Egger & Dora Aichner 1989–2000 (nur Aichner); Bürogemeinschaft egger > aichner > seidl 2000–2002; Bürogemeinschaft aichner_seidl ARCHITEKTEN seit 2003
Lehrtätigkeit/attività didattica/teaching: –
Hauptwerke/progetti scelti/main projects: Haus Huber-Schnarf, Olang; Clubhaus TC Bruneck, Reischach; Grundschulerweiterung, St.Lorenzen; Grundschule, Bibliothek und Feuerwehr, Antholz Niedertal, 1. Preis; UFO Jugend- und Kulturzentrum, Bruneck, 1. Preis; Betriebsgebäude Elektro W&G, Bruneck; Betriebsgebäude BAUEXPERT, Bruneck; Betriebsgebäude SODECO, St.Vigil; Neubau des Athesia Buch- und Medienhauses in der Altstadt, Bruneck; Umbau und Umnutzung des Athesia Stammhauses, Bruneck; Altenwohnungen Söllstiftung, Bruneck; Hotelerweiterung Hotel PETRUS, Reischach; Betriebsgebäude Glasbau SEYR, Bruneck; Sportzentrum Aldein, 1. Preis

Name/nome/name:
Walter Angonese
Geboren/nato/born: 1961 Kaltern
Studium/studi/education: IUAV Venedig
Büro/studio professionale/office: 1987–2001 Bürogemeinschaft A5 Architekten in Bozen mit Markus Scherer und Elena Galvagnini; seit 2001 Büro Angonese2 in Kaltern
Lehrtätigkeit/attività didattica/teaching: Lehrbeauftragter für Entwerfen an der Universität Innsbruck; Gastkritiken und verschiedene Konferenzen an den Universitäten in Mailand, Venedig, Wien, Ferrara, Palermo, Reggio Calabria, Rom, München, Mendriso etc.
Hauptwerke/progetti scelti/main projects: Adaptierung Festung Kufstein „Josefsburg", A-Kufstein (mit Andreas Egger und Markus Scherer); Weingut Hofstätter, Tramin (mit Markus Scherer und Zeno Bampi); Südtiroler Landesmuseum für Kultur- und Landesgeschichte, Schloss Tirol bei Meran (mit Markus Scherer und Klaus Hellweger); Weingut Manincor, Kaltern (mit Rainer Köberl und Silvia Boday); Personalwohnhaus Goëss-Enzenberg, Siebeneich (mit Silvia Boday)

Name/nome/name:
ARCHITEKTEN Marx-Ladurner
Elke Ladurner
Geboren/nato/born: 1968 Meran
Studium/studi/education: Universität Innsbruck, IAUV Venedig, Diplom 1996
Stephan Marx
Geboren/nato/born: 1969 Schlanders
Studium/studi/education: Akademie der bildenden Künste Wien, Diplom 1999
Büro/studio professionale/office: Bürogemeinschaft ARCHITEKTEN Marx-Ladurner seit 2000
Lehrtätigkeit/attività didattica/teaching: –
Hauptwerke/progetti scelti/main projects: Aufstockungen von Betriebsgebäuden und Errichtung von zwei Betriebswohnungen, Schlanders; Wohnhaus Telser, Burgeis; Doppelwohnhaus Klotz, Algund; Wohnanlage Frischmann, Schlanders; Kindergarten, Bruneck, 2. Preis; Rathaus, Prad, 2. Preis; Grundschule Schlanders (in Zusammenarbeit mit Arnold Gapp), 1. Preis

Name/nome/name:
Architekturbüro D3, Veneri – Kienzl – Gruber
Kathrin Gruber
Geboren/nato/born: 1970 Meran
Studium/studi/education: Universität Innsbruck, Diplom 1995
Armin Kienzl
Geboren/nato/born: 1968 Bozen
Studium/studi/education: Universität Innsbruck, Diplom 1995
Richard Veneri
Geboren/nato/born: 1968 Bozen
Studium/studi/education: Universitäten Innsbruck und Delft, Diplom 1995
Robert Veneri
Geboren/nato/born: 1962 Bozen
Studium/studi/education: Universität Innsbruck und IUAV Venedig, Diplom 1988
Büro/studio professionale/office: Bürogemeinschaft Architekturbüro D3 seit 1997; Austritt Robert M. Veneri 2000; Austritt und eigenes Büro Armin Kienzl 2004
Lehrtätigkeit/attività didattica/teaching: Robert M. Veneri: IAUV, Assistenz 1991/92; Universität Innsbruck, Assistenz seit 1993; Fakultät für Design der Freien Universität Bozen, Professur 2002–2004; Institut für Architektur und Raumplanung,

Hochschule Liechtenstein, Dozentur seit 2004
Hauptwerke/progetti scelti/main projects: Gesundheits- und Sozialsprengel Gadertal, Picolin, St. Martin in Thurn; Friedhofserweiterung und Kapelle, St.Gertraud/Ulten; Altenwohn- und Pflegeheim, Villanders; Sanierung Widum, Plaus; Bahnhof mit Jugendraum, Plaus

Name/nome/name:
Benno Barth
Geboren/nato/born: 1962 Brixen
Studium/studi/education: Bauingenieur, Universität Innsbruck und Wien
Büro/studio professionale/office: seit 1992
Lehrtätigkeit/attività didattica/teaching: ADB Akademie für Design Bozen, Dozentur 1998–2002, Fakultät für Design und Künste (Freie Universität Bozen), Vertragsprofessur seit 2002
Hauptwerke/progetti scelti/main projects: Haus Kaser, Brixen-Milland

Name/nome/name:
Gerd Bergmeister
Geboren/nato/born: 1969 Brixen (I)
Studium/studi/education: IUAV Venedig und Universität Innsbruck, Diplom 1998
Büro/studio professionale/office: seit 2002
Lehrtätigkeit/attività didattica/teaching: –
Hauptwerke/ progetti scelti/main projects: Haus Sachsenklemme (Haus Ganterer), Franzensfeste; Das Nöckler, Bruneck; Pillhof, Frangart; Haus M., Girlan; Pitzock, Villnöss

Name/nome/name:
Bischoff Azzola Architekten
Matthias Bischoff
Geboren/nato/born: 1952 Thun (CH)
Studium/studi/education: ETH Zürich, Diplom 1976
Roberto Azzola
Geboren/nato/born: 1963 Zürich (CH)
Studium/studi/education: ETH Zürich, Diplom 1990
Büro/studio professionale/office: Bürogemeinschaft Bischoff Azzola Architekten 1998–2003, seither selbständige Tätigkeit
Lehrtätigkeit/attività didattica/teaching: –
Hauptwerke/progetti scelti/main projects: Freie Universität Bozen, Bozen

Name/nome/name:
Silvia Boday
Geboren/nato/born: 1975 Meran
Studium/studi/education: Universität Innsbruck, Diplom 2001
Büro/studio professionale/office: seit 2002
Lehrtätigkeit/attività didattica/teaching: –
Hauptwerke/progetti scelti/main projects: Haus an der Weinstraße, Tramin; Personalwohnhaus Goëss-Enzenberg, Siebeneich (mit Walter Angonese), Weingut Manincor (mit Walter Angonese und Rainer Köberl)

Name/nome/name:
COMFORT_ARCHITECTEN
Marco Micheli
Geboren/nato/born: 1969 Bruneck
Studium/studi/education: Universität Innsbruck, Staatsprüfung 1998
Michael Mumelter
Geboren/nato/born: 1972 Bozen
Studium/studi/education: Universität Innsbruck, Staatsprüfung 2000
Büro/studio professionale/office: Bürogemeinschaft COMFORT_ARCHITECTEN seit 2002
Lehrtätigkeit/attività didattica/teaching: –
Hauptwerke/progetti scelti/main projects: Aufstockung Tischlerei Baumgartner, Bruneck; Wohnhaus Sonne, St. Lorenzen/Bruneck; Gestaltung der Ausstellungsräume inkl. Innendesign, Burger GmbH, Welsberg; Mehrfamilienhaus, Olang; Dachaufbau Wohnhaus Röhrens, A-Volders; Wohnhaus Tasser, Percha; Wohnhaus Fender/Strobl, A-Innsbruck; Wohnhaus Röll, Bozen; Restaurant „Acquarium" im Hallenbad, Reischach; Betriebsgebäude Fa. Leimegger, St. Lorenzen (in Bau)

Name/nome/name:
Siegfried Delueg
Geboren/nato/born: 1958, Sterzing
Studium/studi/education: Universität Innsbruck, Diplom 1989
Büro/studio professionale/office: in Sterzing seit 1991, in Brixen seit 2004
Lehrtätigkeit/attività didattica/teaching: –
Hauptwerke/progetti scelti/main projects: Einfamilienhaus, Sterzing; Landesberufsschule „Ch. J. Tschuggmall", Brixen; Studentenhaus St. Michael, Brixen; Fernheizwerk, Sexten

Name/nome/name:
Walter Dietl
Geboren/nato/born: 1945 in Göflan, Schlanders
Studium/studi/education: TU Wien (Maschinenbau) und Universität Innsbruck
Büro/studio professionale/office: in Schlanders seit 1979
Lehrtätigkeit/attività didattica/teaching: –
Hauptwerke/progetti scelti/main projects: Rathaus, Mals; Berufsfachschule für Steinbearbeitung, Laas; Obstgenossenschaft, Schlanders; Wiederinbetriebnahme der Eisenbahnlinie von Meran nach Mals, Erweiterung Remise Mals und Haltestellen der Vinschgerbahn

Name/nome/name:
dkp_architektur pedevilla
Armin Pedevilla
Geboren/nato/born: 1973 Sterzing
Studium/studi/education: TU Graz, Diplom 2001
Büro/studio professionale/office: Bürogemeinschaft mit dreiplus Graz 2001–2003, dkp_architektur pedevilla seit 2003
Lehrtätigkeit/attività didattica/teaching: –
Hauptwerke/progetti scelti/main projects: Wohnanlage G3D, Stegen, Bruneck (mit Bruno Rubner und dreiplus Architektur); Wohnhaus Grunser, Neustift; Gemeindehaus, St. Lorenzen (mit Kurt Egger); Pflegeheim, Bruneck

Name/nome/name:
dreiplus Architektur
Thomas Heil
Geboren/nato/born: 1973 Hartberg (A)
Studium/studi/education: TU Graz, Diplom 2000

Stephan Hoinkes
Geboren/nato/born: 1974 Innsbruck (A)
Studium/studi/education: Universität Innsbruck, Diplom 2000
Büro/studio professionale/office: Bürogemeinschaft dreiplus Architektur seit 2000, dreiplus federspiel ZT KEG seit 2003 (Graz und Innsbruck)
Lehrtätigkeit/attività didattica/teaching: –
Hauptwerke/progetti scelti/main projects: Wohnanlage G3D, Stegen, Bruneck (mit Bruno Rubner und dkp_architektur pedevilla)

Name/nome/name:
Studio Fierro
Geboren/nato/born: 1961
Studium/studi/education: IUAV Venedig, Diplom 1988
Büro/studio professionale/office: seit 1989
Lehrtätigkeit/attività didattica/teaching: IUAV Venedig
Hauptwerke/progetti scelti/main projects: Tiefgarage und Neugestaltung Gerichtsplatz, Bozen; Mazziniplatz, Bozen; Expo 1992, Ausstellung in der Cartuja; Neue Adlerstraße, Brixen

Name/nome/name:
Forer Unterpertinger Architekten – komp(L)ott
Gert Forer
Geboren/nato/born: 1972 Bruneck
Studium/studi/education: Universität Innsbruck, Diplom 1998
Ursula Unterpertinger
Geboren/nato/born: 1974 Bruneck
Studium/studi/education: Universität Innsbruck, Diplom 2001
Büro/studio professionale/office: Bürogemeinschaft Forer Unterpertinger Architekten – komp(L)ott seit 2001
Lehrtätigkeit/attività didattica/teaching: –
Hauptwerke/progetti scelti/main projects: Umbau und Sanierung Lanserhaus, St. Michael, Eppan

Name/nome/name:
Arnold Gapp
Geboren/nato/born: 1951 Mals
Studium/studi/education: TU Wien 1975
Büro/studio professionale/office: seit 1976
Lehrtätigkeit/attività didattica/teaching: –
Hauptwerke/progetti scelti/main projects: Bergstation Seilbahn St. Martin, Latsch; Kleinsportanlage und Mehrzweckgebäude, Tschengls, Laas; Messner Mountain Museum „Ortles", Sulden

Name/nome/name:
Klaus Hellweger
Geboren/nato/born: 1961 Bruneck
Studium/studi/education: Universität Innsbruck und Wien
Büro/studio professionale/office: seit 1997
Lehrtätigkeit/attività didattica/teaching: Akademie für Design Bozen, 2000
Hauptwerke/progetti scelti/main projects: Südtiroler Landesmuseum für Kultur- und Landesgeschichte, Schloss Tirol bei Meran (mit Markus Scherer und Walter Angonese); Landesausstellung, Brixen (mit A5 Architekten); Diözesanmuseum Hofburg, Brixen; Messestand Damiani Holzindustrie, Architekturbiennale, Venedig 1996, Preise bei Wettbewerben: CD für Straßendienst Südtirol (mit Büro54, Innsbruck); Wege zum Museum, Bruneck (mit A. Laner); Sonderausstellungen Schloss Bruneck, Schneiderhof, Sexten

Name/nome/name:
Stefan Hitthaler
Geboren/nato/born: 1966 Bruneck
Studium/studi/education: Universität Innsbuck, Diplom 1991
Büro/studio professionale/office: seit 1992
Lehrtätigkeit/attività didattica/teaching: Referent: 4. Passivhaustagung in Kassel; Amt für Energieeinsparung; Amt für Luft und Lärm; Arbeitsgruppe „Zukunftsfähiges Bauen"; Klimahaus Kurse
Hauptwerke/progetti scelti/main projects: Mühlbauerhof, Gargazon; Wettbewerb „Intelligent Building" für Niedrigenergiehäuser, Kloster Neustift, 3. Preis (mit Haus Pescoller); Klimahauswettbewerb, Bruneck, 1. Preis (ex aequo); Südtiroler Architekturpreis, 1. Preis (ex aequo); Wohnbaugenossenschaft (Klimahaus B), Bruneck, 1. Preis; Stadtmuseum, Bozen (mit Arch. Schwienbacher), 1. Preis; Wohnbaugenossenschaft (Klimahaus A), Bruneck, 1. Preis

Name/nome/name:
HÖLLER & KLOTZNER – ARCHITEKTEN
Thomas Höller
Geboren/nato/born: 1959 Bozen
Studium/studi/education: Universität Innsbruck, Diplom 1985
Georg Klotzner
Geboren/nato/born: 1957 Meran
Studium/studi/education: Universität Innsbruck, Diplom 1982
Büro/studio professionale/office: Bürogemeinschaft HÖLLER & KLOTZNER – ARCHITEKTEN seit 1988
Lehrtätigkeit/attività didattica/teaching: –
Hauptwerke/progetti scelti/main projects: Neubau Realgymnasium, Sterzing; Erweiterung Pfarrkirche, Leifers; Abbruch und Neubau der Landesberufsschule, Bozen; „kunst Meran im Haus der Sparkasse", Meran

Name/nome/name:
Holzbox ZT GmbH & DI Anton Höss
Erich Strolz
Geboren/nato/born: 1959 Warth-Hochkrumbach (A)
Studium/studi/education: TU Graz, Universität Innsbruck
Armin Kathan
Geboren/nato/born: 1961 Lech (A)
Studium/studi/education: Universität Innsbruck, Universität für angewandte Kunst, Wien
Büro/studio professionale/office: Bürogemeinschaft Holzbox ZT GmbH & DI Anton Höss seit 1993
Lehrtätigkeit/attività didattica/teaching: –
Hauptwerke/progetti scelti/main projects: Wohnanlage Wolkenstein, Meran (mit Baugesellschaft Wolkenstein GmbH, Vorarlberger Ökohaus GmbH)

Name/nome/name:
Klaus Kada
Geboren/nato/born: 1940 Leibnitz (A)
Studium/studi/education: TU Graz, Diplom 1971
Büro/studio professionale/office: Bürogemeinschaft mit Gernot Laufer 1971–1976, Büro in Leibnitz 1976–2002, Büro in Graz seit 1988, Büro in Aachen seit 1996
Lehrtätigkeit/attività didattica/teaching: Fakultät für Architektur (Entwerfen von Hochbauten und Gebäudelehre) an der RWTH-Aachen, Professor seit 1995; Hochschule für Künste Bremen, Gastprofessur; Technische Universität München (Gastprofessur); Gastkritiken in Zürich, Wien und Graz; Workshop HDA „Die Stadt am Fluß" (1990); Workshop „Paesaggio alpino" Meran (1996); Workshop „Nuovi spazi del dialogo" Görz (1997)
Hauptwerke/progetti scelti/main projects: Europäische Akademie Bozen (EURAC); Sparkasse, Bad Radkersburg; Vermessungsamt, Leibnitz; Wohnanlage, Peggau; F + E Leykam, Gratkorn; Haus Tögl, Graz; Pflegeheim, Leibnitz; LKH, Hartberg; Stadthalle, Graz; Sparkasse, Bad Radkersburg; Vermessungsamt, Leibnitz; Glasmuseum, Bärnbach; Altenwohnheim, Neumarkt am Wallersee; WIST-Studentenheim; GERAMB-Medaille des Landes Steiermark; Preis des Landes Steiermark für Architektur; Architekturpreis Land Salzburg; Preis der Zentralvereinigung der Architekten; Piranesi-Preis; Architekturpreis der Zementindustrie; Staatspreis für Industriebau in Gold

Name/nome/name:
Margit Klammer
Geboren/nato/born: 1958 Innichen
Studium/studi/education: Universität für angewandte Kunst, Wien
Büro/studio professionale/office: Atelier seit 1994
Lehrtätigkeit/attività didattica/teaching: –
Hauptwerke/progetti scelti/main projects: Die Gärten von Schloss Trauttmansdorff (mit PVC – architects, Steiner Sarnen Schweiz)

Name/nome/name:
Rainer Köberl
Geboren/nato/born: 1956 Innsbruck (A)
Studium/studi/education: Universität Innsbruck und Haifa, Diplom 1984
Lehrtätigkeit/attività didattica/teaching: Institut für Raumgestaltung und Entwerfen an der Universität Innsbruck, Assistent 1986–1992; Institute für Städtebau, Gebäudelehre und Entwerfen an der Universität Innsbruck, Lehraufträge 1993–1999; Akademie für Design in Bozen, Dozentur 1998–2002
Hauptwerke/progetti scelti/main projects: Gastspieltheater „Treibhaus" (mit Gerhard Manzl und Raimund Rainer), A-Innsbruck; DOWAS Durchgangsort für Wohnungs- und Arbeitssuchende, A-Innsbruck; Büro der Lichtfabrik Halotech, A-Innsbruck; Haus Nofels – Alten- und Pflegeheim, A-Feldkirch; Haus Bramböck, A-Voldöp; Chillout – Übergangsheim für wohnungslose Jugendliche, A-Innsbruck; Forum der Lichtfabrik Halotech, Bozen; Buchhandlung Wiederin, A-Innsbruck; M_preis Supermarkt, A-Wenns, Pitztal; Ausstellungsraum/Werkstatt Halotech, A-Innsbruck; Stube Gasthof Lamm, A-St. Jodok; M_preis Supermarkt „Warentheater" Hauptbahnhof, A-Innsbruck; Kieferchirurgenordination im neuen „Rathaustor", A-Innsbruck; Weingut Manincor, Kaltern (mit Walter Angonese und Silvia Boday); Haus H., CH-Rorschach (mit Paul Pointecker); Sanierung und Umbau „Adambräu" zum „aut"-„Architektur und Tirol" und Architekturarchiv der Universität Innsbruck (mit Giner & Wucherer); „MANNA" Delikatessencafé, A-Innsbruck

Name/nome/name:
Lunz & Zöschg Architekten
Markus Lunz
Geboren/nato/born: 1968 Sterzing
Studium/studi/education: Universität Innsbruck, Diplom 1993
Hubert Zöschg
Geboren/nato/born: 1967 Bozen
Studium/studi/education: Universität Innsbruck, Diplom 1993
Büro/studio professionale/office: Bürogemeinschaft Lunz & Zöschg Architekten seit 1996
Lehrtätigkeit/attività didattica/teaching: –
Hauptwerke/progetti scelti/main projects: Kindergarten „Maria-Rast", St. Michael/Eppan; Gasserhof, Bozen/Gries; Hundegger Italia KG, Neumarkt; Widum St. Nikolaus; Dorfplatz, Andrian; Schulzentrum Stange, Ratschings; Karosserie, Andrian; Paulserhof

Name/nome/name:
Christoph Mayr Fingerle
Geboren/nato/born: 1951 Bozen
Studium/studi/education: Universität Innsbruck, Diplom 1978
Büro/studio professionale/office: seit 1981
Lehrtätigkeit/attività didattica/teaching: Vorträge in Wien, München, Ljubljana, Bergamo, Zürich, London
Hauptwerke/progetti scelti/main projects: Realgymnasium, Bozen

Name/nome/name:
Georg Mitterhofer
Geboren/nato/born: 1961 Meran
Studium/studi/education: TU Wien, Diplom 1988
Lehrtätigkeit/attività didattica/teaching: –
Hauptwerke/progetti scelti/main projects: Besucherzentrum „Die Gärten von Schloss Trauttmansdorff", Meran, 1. Preis (mit S.O.F.A. architekten); Schreibmaschinen-Museum Partschins (mit Luciano Delugan); Wohnhaus, Marling; Wohnanlage in Meran (mit Ruth Pinzger – in Planung)

Name/nome/name:
MODUS architects
Matteo Scagnol
Geboren/nato/born: 1968 Triest
Studium/studi/education: IUAV Venedig, Diplom 1995; Harvard University, Master of Architecture 1999
Sandy Attia
Geboren/nato/born: 1974 Kairo (ET)
Studium/studi/education: University of Virginia, Bachelor of Science in Architecture 1995, Harvard University, Master of Architecture 2000
Büro/studio professionale/office: Bürogemeinschaft MODUS architects seit 2000
Lehrtätigkeit/attività didattica/teaching: –

Hauptwerke/progetti scelti/main projects: Heizkraftwerk Brixen Süd, Brixen; Haus Jungmann in St. Andrä, Brixen; Kinderhort, Kindergarten, Elternkindzentrum, Grundschule, Stadtviertel Bibliothek und Platz Reschen 1, Bozen; Kinder-Tagesbetreuungsstätte im Krankenhaus, Brixen; Ursulinengebäude Bruneck, 3. Preis; Kindergarten „Bruder Willram", Bruneck, 4. Platz; Wiedergewinnung des ehemaligen Weißen-Kreuz-Areals in der Fagenstraße, Bozen, 1. Preis; Internationaler Planungswettbewerb Reschen 1, Bozen – Kinderhort, Kindergarten, Grundschule und Platz, 1. Preis; Städtebaulicher Wettbewerb Priel, Brixen, 3. Preis; Erweiterung der Landesberufsschule und Unterbringung der Schule für Sozialberufe, Meran, 2. Preis

Name/nome/name:
MUTSCHLECHNER & MAHLKNECHT architekten
Heinrich Mutschlechner
Geboren/nato/born: 1957 Bruneck
Studium/studi/education: Universität Innsbruck, IUAV Venedig, Diplom 1987
Gerhard Mahlknecht
Geboren/nato/born: 1956 Bruneck
Studium/studi/education: Universität Innsbruck, IUAV Venedig, Diplom 2001
Büro/studio professionale/office: Bürogemeinschaft MUTSCHLECHNER & MAHLKNECHT architekten seit 1988
Lehrtätigkeit/attività didattica/teaching: –
Hauptwerke/progetti scelti/main projects: Neubau Mehrzweckgebäude am Bühel, St. Jakob im Ahrntal; Sanierung Stein- und Holzhaus Dr. Tasser, Steinhaus im Ahrntal; Friedhofserweiterung, Luttach im Ahrntal

Name/nome/name:
Architekten Pardeller+Putzer+Scherer
Walter Pardeller
Geboren/nato/born: 1947 Welschnofen
Studium/studi/education: TU Wien, Diplom 1974
Josef Putzer
Geboren/nato/born: 1946 Vahrn
Studium/studi/education: TU Wien, Diplom 1973
Michael Scherer
Geboren/nato/born: 1962 Heidenheim (D)
Studium/studi/education: FHT Stuttgart, Diplom 1989
Büro/studio professionale/office: Bürogemeinschaft Pardeller+Putzer seit 1980, Bürogemeinschaft Pardeller+Putzer+Scherer seit 1999
Lehrtätigkeit/attività didattica/teaching: –
Hauptwerke/progetti scelti/main projects: Turnhalle der deutschsprachigen Grundschule „A. Rosmini", Bozen-Gries; Erweiterung Berufsfeuerwehr Bozen, Sanierung Sanatorium Brixen; Erweiterung Krankenhaus, Brixen; Altersheim, Meran; verschiedene Häuser, Lokale und Einrichtungen für Kinder und Jugendliche

Name/nome/name:
Wolfgang Piller
Geboren/nato/born: 1949 in Meran
Studium/studi/education: TU Wien und I.U.A.V. in Venedig (Staatsexamen 1977)
Büro/studio professionale/office: 1978–1990 Bürogemeinschaft mit Arnold Gapp; seit 1991 Bürogemeinschaft mit Benno Simma
Lehrtätigkeit/attività didattica/teaching: 1996 Lehrauftrag an der FH Trier
Hauptwerke/progetti scelti/main projects: Straßenmeisterei, Kastelruth; Einfamilienhaus, Nals; Wohnanlage Unterberg, Leifers; Sitz der Investitionsbank Trentino-Südtirol, Bozen; Oberschule für Landwirtschaft, Ansitz Baumgarten, Auer; Umbau Hotel Figl, Bozen; Sozialer Wohnbau, Zone „Firmian", Bozen; Publizistische Tätigkeit, u. a.: Architektur in Südtirol 1900–heute (Chefredaktion und Koordination); „Im Dialog mit überwältigender Architektur – Neue Architektur in Südtirol", Süddeutschen Zeitung, Nr. 116/22.5.1998

Name/nome/name:
Dr. Arch. Peter Plattner
Geboren/nato/born: 1969 in Graz (A)
Studium/studi/education: Universität Innsbruck
Büro/studio professionale/office: seit 1998
Lehrtätigkeit/attività didattica/teaching: –
Hauptwerke/progetti scelti/main projects: Landwirtschaftliches Betriebsgebäude, Ladstätterhof, Sinich bei Meran; Sanierung und Erweiterung Haus Amonn, Bozen; Raiffeisenbar, Bozen; Juwelier Tomasi, Bozen; Juwelier Tomasi-T-side, Trient; Rolex- Tomasi, Trient; Wohnhäuser der Gebrüder Pichler, Montiggl, Kaltern, Villa Lielupe, LV- Jurmala; Sanierung Altstadthaus, LV-Riga

Name/nome/name:
PVC – architects
Wolfram H. Pardatscher
Geboren/nato/born: 1956 Bozen
Studium/studi/education: Universität Innsbruck, Hochschule für Angewandte Kunst Wien, Diplom 1987
Joachim M. Clemens
Geboren/nato/born: 1967 D-Wittlich
Studium/studi/education: Architekturstudium an der Fachhochschule Rheinland Pfalz/Abteilung Trier, Diplom 1994
Alessandro Teti
Geboren/nato/born: 1970 Meran
Studium/studi/education: Istituto Universitario di Architettura di Venezia (IUAV), TU Graz, Diplom 1996
Büro/studio professionale/office: seit 1995 (Pardatscher); Bürogemeinschaft PVC – architects seit 2001
Lehrtätigkeit/attività didattica/teaching: FH Trier 1989–1996
Hauptwerke/progetti scelti/main projects: Haus MK, Meran; Clinique, St. Louis, L-Ettelbruck; Hotel Jagdhof, Marling; Kulturhaus, Kurtatsch; Die Gärten von Schloss Trauttmansdorff, Meran (mit Margit Klammer und Steiner Sarnen Schweiz)

Name/nome/name:
Bruno Rubner
Geboren/nato/born: 1962 Sterzing
Studium/studi/education: Universität Innsbruck, IUAV Venedig, Diplom 1991
Büro/studio professionale/office: seit 1999
Lehrtätigkeit/attività didattica/teaching: –
Hauptwerke/progetti scelti/main projects: Wohnanlage G3D Stegen, Bruneck (mit dkp-architektur pedevilla, dreiplus Architektur); Sanierung Grundschule, Prettau, Dienstleistungszentrum, Kasern;

Dorfplatzgestaltung, Prettau; Gestaltung Sportzone St. Georgen, Bruneck; Passivhaus, Vahrn, div. Ein- und Mehrfamilienhäuser in Niedrigenergiebauweise

Name/nome/name:
Markus Scherer
Geboren/nato/born: 1962 Wien (A)
Studium/studi/education: TU Wien, IAUV Venedig
Büro/studio professionale/office: eigenes Büro und Übernahme des Büros A5 Architekten seit 2001
Lehrtätigkeit/attività didattica/teaching: –
Hauptwerke/progetti scelti/main projects: Projekte, die vor 2001 noch in Zusammenarbeit mit Walter Angonese begonnen wurden: Platzgestaltungen, Kaltern; Weinkellerei St. Michael, Eppan; Anbau Ansitz Barthenau/Hofstätter, Mazzon; <u>Südtiroler Landesmuseum für Kultur- und Landesgeschichte, Schloss Tirol bei Meran (mit Walter Angonese und Klaus Hellweger)</u>. Projekte, die nach 2001 im eigenen Büro entstanden sind: Durchführungsplan für das Gewerbegebiet Wurzer; Beauty Spa Daniela Steiner, Montecarlo und Kairo; Weinkellerei, Klausen; Lagerkeller der Weinkellerei Tiefenbrunner, Margreid; Wohnanlage, Girlan (Projekt); Eventprojekt Musik und Farbe im Kraftwerk Kardaun (mit Dieter Bartenbach); Haus Deetjen, Frangart; Boutique Linas, Bozen; Firmensitz Eurolicht/Hess Italia, Bozen

Name/nome/name:
Christian Schwienbacher
Geboren/nato/born: 1968 Schlanders
Studium/studi/education: Universität Innsbruck, Diplom 1995
Büro/studio professionale/office: seit 1998
Lehrtätigkeit/attività didattica/teaching: Akademie für Design, Bozen, Assistent 2001/2002
Hauptwerke/progetti scelti/main projects: Wohnhaus Preindl, Mösl, Brixen; Wohnhaus Barth, Brixen; Wohnhaus Richter, Brixen; <u>Wohnhaus in Stilfes (Haus Holzer), Freienfeld</u>; Erweiterung Chinarestaurant, Brixen-Milland; Wohnhaus Palfrader, Brixen; Bar Bistro Pitzock, Villnöß (mit Gerd Bergmeister); Projekte in Ausarbeitung: Erweiterung Stadtmuseum, Bozen (mit Stefan Hitthaler); Wohnhaus Leitner, St. Andrae (mit Gerd Bergmeister)

Name/nome/name:
Studio architetto Luigi Scolari
Luigi Scolari
Geboren/nato/born: 1968 Verona
Studium/studi/education: Scuola Politecnica di Design di Milano (Industrial Design), Diplom 1988; Politecnico di Milano (Architektur), Diplom 1994
Büro/studio professionale/office: Bürogemeinschaft mit Walter Dietl 1994–1997, Bürogemeinschaft mit Wolfgang Piller und Benno Simma 1997–1999, eigenes Büro seit 1999
Lehrtätigkeit/attività didattica/teaching: –
Hauptwerke/progetti scelti/main projects: Umbau und Erweiterung der Schlosserei Senn, Oberbozen; Geschäft Matt, Meran; Innenraumgestaltung der Stiftung der Kammer der Architekten, Raumplaner, Landschaftsplaner, Denkmalpfleger der Autonomen Provinz Bozen-Südtirol, Bozen; Innenraumgestaltung des Penthouse B., Bozen; <u>Neubau einer Industriehalle mit Bürotrakt, Firma BEL, Bozen</u>

Name/nome/name:
S.O.F.A. architekten
Andreas Grasser
Geboren/nato/born: 1969 Laas
Studium/studi/education: TU Wien, Diplom 1998
Rita Pirpamer
Geboren/nato/born: 1965 Meran
Studium/studi/education: Universität Innsbruck, TU Wien, Diplom 1997
Kurt Rauch
Geboren/nato/born: 1967 Meran
Studium/studi/education: TU Wien, Diplom 1997
Büro/studio professionale/office: Bürogemeinschaft S.O.F.A. architekten seit 2000
Lehrtätigkeit/attività didattica/teaching: –
Hauptwerke/progetti scelti/main projects: Restaurant in „Die Gärten von Trauttmansdorff" Meran; Wettbewerb „Volksbank Laa an der Thaya" Niederösterreich, 1. Preis (nicht realisiert); Planungsbeginn der Grundschule Ulten, Ulten; Sanierung der Schlossanlage von „Die Gärten von Schloss Trauttmansdorff", Meran; „Cafe am See", Meran; Wettberwerb „Feuerwehr Raasdorf" Marchfeld, 1. Preis (nicht realisiert); Käuterverarbeitungsstelle „Gachhof", Labers; Umbau und Sanierung des Betriebsgebäudes „Putzengütl", Dorf Tirol; Haus Lang, Maria Anzbach; <u>Besucherzentrum „Die Gärten von Schloss Trauttmansdorff", Meran, 1. Preis (mit Georg Mitterhofer)</u>

Name/nome/name:
Karl Spitaler
Geboren/nato/born: 1951 Schlanders (I)
Studium/studi/education: Universität Innsbruck, IAUV Venedig, Diplom 1977
Büro/studio professionale/office: seit 1978
Lehrtätigkeit/attività didattica/teaching: Universität Innsbruck und Institut für Denkmalpflege, Lehrauftrag 1991/92; TU Wien, Institut für Gebäudelehre, Lehrauftrag 2003–2005; Universitá degli studi dell'Aquila, Facolta d'ingegneria 2005
Hauptwerke/progetti scelti/main projects: <u>Fahrradverleih Bahnhof Schlanders</u>; Fachschule für soziale Berufe im Kapuzinerkloster, Bozen; Gestaltung des Kapuzinerklostergartens, Bozen; Abbruch und Wiederaufbau der Musikschule, Naturns; Freizeit- und Volkssportanlage Trattla, Martell; Sanierung und Erweiterung der Zivilschutzzentrale, Martell; Kloster St. Johann, CH-Müstair; Sanierung Schloss Juval, Kastellbel, Tschars

Name/nome/name:
Steiner Sarnen Schweiz
Geboren/nato/born: –
Studium/studi/education: –
Büro/studio professionale/office: Seit 1984
Lehrtätigkeit/attività didattica/teaching: –
Hauptwerke/progetti scelti/main projects: <u>Die Gärten von Schloss Trauttmansdorff (mit PVC – architects und Margit Klammer)</u>; Glasi Hergiswil, CH-Hergiswil; Loisium Weinvisionen, A-Langenlois; Historisches Museum Luzern. CH-Luzern; J. F. Schreiber-Museum, D-Esslingen;

Kunstpalast Düsseldorf, D-Düsseldorf; Fürst-Pückler-Museum im Branitzer Park, D-Cottbus; Zermattlantis, CH-Zermatt

Name/nome/name:
Architekturbüro Studio Matteo Thun
Matteo Thun
Geboren/nato/born: 1952 Bozen
Studium/studi/education: Akademie Salzburg, Universität Florenz, Diplom 1975
Büro/studio professionale/office: Mitbegründer Sottsass Associati und Gruppe Memphis1981; Studio Matteo Thun & Partner seit 1984
Lehrtätigkeit/attività didattica/teaching: Hochschule für angewandte Kunst Wien, Professur 1983–1996
Hauptwerke/progetti scelti/main projects: Side Hotel, Hamburg; Vigilius Mountain Resort, Lana; Pergola Residence, Algund; Thermen Meran, Meran; Radisson SAS Hotel, Frankfurt; Radisson SAS Media Harbour Hotel, Düsseldorf; Hotel Therme Meran, Meran

Name/nome/name:
Werner Tscholl
Geboren/nato/born: 1955 Latsch
Studium/studi/education: Universität Florenz, Diplom 1981
Büro/studio professionale/office: seit 1983
Lehrtätigkeit/attività didattica/teaching: –
Hauptwerke/progetti scelti/main projects: Haus Schöpf, Vezzan, Schlanders; Haus Mumelter, Bozen; Landwirtschaftsschule Fürstenburg, Burgeis; Bürohaus Selimex, Latsch; Haus Rizzi, St. Martin, Latsch; Haus Knoll, Galsaun, Kastelbell-Tschars; Messner Mountain Museum Firmian, Schloss Sigmundskron (Eröffnung 04/2006); Architekturpreis der Stadt Oderzo

Name/nome/name:
Oswald Zoeggeler
Geboren/nato/born: 1944 Meran
Studium/studi/education: TU Wien, IAUV Venedig, Diplom 1969
Büro/studio professionale/office: Bürogemeinschaft mit W. Gutweniger und G. Piarulli 1974, eigenes Büro seit 1975
Lehrtätigkeit/attività didattica/teaching: TU München, Gastdozentur 1981; Universität Florenz, Professur seit 1987, Universität Innsbruck, Gastdozentur 1989–1994
Hauptwerke/progetti scelti/main projects: Roen-Schule, Bozen (mit S. Bassetti und A. Cleva); Schwimmbad, Klausen; Wohnbaugenossenschaft, Klausen; Gestaltung der Schinkel-Ausstellung im Museo Correr, Venedig; Gestaltung der Schinkel-Ausstellung im Museo Capitolino, Rom; Gasteiner-Schule, Bozen (mit S. Bassetti); Umbau des Athesia-Hauses, Sterzing; Ausbau der Schule, Klausen; Gestaltung der Biennale von Venedig; Ausbauarbeiten am Museion für moderne Kunst, Bozen; Golfklub La Contrada, Costermano am Gardasee; Wohnhaus Hoher Weg mit 100 Wohnungen, Rentsch, Bozen; Landhaus 2, Verwaltungsgebäude der Landesregierung; Landhaus 1, Glassaal im Innenhof, Palais Widmann, Bozen; Ausbau des Rathauses, Canazei (mit G. Pettena und A. Negri); 50 Wohneinheiten in der „Semirurali"-Zone in Bozen; Von-Gilm-Schule Obermais, Meran; Sassuolo (Modena); Villa und Kondominium Oberrauch, Bozen; Haus am Fluß, Wohnhaus mit 50 Wohneinheiten, Bozen; Landhaus 3, Verwaltungsgebäude der Landesregierung; Villa Mozart, Meran; Villa Rimbl, Bozen.

Autoren, Fotograf **Autori, fotografo** **Authors, photographer**

Joseph Grima

Nach dem Abschluss der Architectural Association in London, begann der Architekt bei der Zeitschrift „Domus" in Mailand als Architektur-Berater und Redakteur zu arbeiten. Er schreibt regelmäßig für verschiedene Zeitschriften und Zeitungen, darunter „Il Sole – 24 Ore" and „Tank". Darüber hinaus fungiert er als Gastkritiker an der Architectural Association in London und an der Trondheim School of Fine Art in Norwegen.

Robert Fleischanderl

1967 in Brixlegg geboren, lebt und arbeitet als freier Fotograf und Künstler in Innsbruck. Er studierte Chemie an der Universität Innsbruck, machte 1996 in der Folge auf sein Diplom in Chemie ein Praktikum bei Magnum Photos, New York, bzw. assistierte bei Erich Hartmann, ebenfalls Magnum Photos, New York. 1997 Abschluss mit dem Master of Art, Image & Communications, Goldsmiths College, University of London. Ausstellungen, u. a.: 2000: „Fourteen People", Galerie im Taxispalais, Innsbruck; 2001: „WegZiehen", Frauen Museum, Bonn; 2004: „Guschlbauer weiche Kokosbusserl", Alte Schmiede, Wien; 2005: „unrealities", Fotoforum West, Innsbruck. Zahlreiche Publikationen, u. a.: 2000: „Fourteen People", Weidle Verlag, Bonn, Deutschland; 2000: Katalog „Familie Foto Familie", Ethnographisches Museum Schloss Kittsee, Burgenland; 2003: „Guschlbauer weiche Kokosbusserl", Skarabaeus Verlag, Innsbruck.

Roman Hollenstein

Der promovierte Kunst- und Architekturhistoriker war zunächst als wissenschaftlicher Assistent der Sammlungen des Fürsten von Liechtenstein in Vaduz und Wien tätig und arbeitete als freier Ausstellungsmitarbeiter am Kunstmuseum Basel (Monet: die Seerosen). Er unterrichtete an der Hochschule für Gestaltung in Zürich. Als Direktionsmitglied stand er 1987 bis 1990 der Abteilung Kunstgeschichte des Schweizerischen Instituts für Kunstwissenschaft in Zürich vor. Seit 1990 ist er bei der Neuen Zürcher Zeitung in Zürich tätig,

Joseph Grima

Joseph Grima è architetto. Laureato presso l'Architectural Association di Londra, lavora presso Domus, una rivista di architettura, come consulente e redattore. Collabora regolarmente anche con altre riviste e quotidiani, tra cui Il Sole - 24 Ore e Tank. È visiting critic dell'Architectural Association di Londra e per la Trondheim School of Fine Art di Norway.

Robert Fleischanderl

Nasce a Brixlegg nel 1967, vive e lavora come fotografo e artista free lancer a Innsbruck.
Studia chimica all'università di Innsbruck, e svolge, in seguito al diploma in chimica, un tirocinio presso la Magnum Photos di New York, nello specifico è assistente di Erich Hartmann. Nel 1997 conclude il Master in Art, Image & Communications, del Goldsmiths College, presso la University of London.
Mostre - 2000: "Fourteen People", Galerie im Taxispalais, Innsbruck; 2001: "WegZiehen", Frauen Museum, Bonn; 2004: "Guschlbauer weiche Kokosbusserl", Alte Schmiede, Vienna; 2005: "unrealities", Fotoforum West, Innsbruck.
Pubblicazioni - 2000: "Fourteen People", Edizioni Weidle, Bonn, Germania; 2000: Catalogo "Familie Foto Familie", Museo Etnografico Schloss Kittsee, Burgenland; 2003: "Guschlbauer weiche Kokosbusserl", Edizioni Skarabaeus, Innsbruck.

Roman Hollenstein

Laureato in storia dell'arte e dell'architettura ha dapprima lavoravorato come asistente scientifico delle collezioni dei principi del Liechtenstein a Vaduz e Vienna e ha collaborato con il Kunstmuseum di Basilea a diverse mostre (Monet: le Ninfee). Ha insegnato alla Hochschule für Gestaltung, dove come membro del direttivo ha presieduto, dal 1987 al 1990, il Dipartimento di storia dell'arte presso il Schweizerischen Instituts für Kunstwissenschaft di Zurigo Dal 1990 lavora presso il Neuen Zürcher Zeitung a Zurigo scrivendo articoli riguar-

Joseph Grima

Joseph Grima is an architect. After graduating from the Architectural Association in London he joined Domus magazine as architecture consultant and editor. He contributes regularly to various other magazines and papers, including Il Sole – 24 Ore and Tank. He is a visiting critic at the Architectural Association, London, and Trondheim School of Fine Art, Norway.

Robert Fleischanderl

Robert Fleischanderl was born in 1967 in Brixlegg and lives and works as a free-lance photographer and artist in Innsbruck. He studied chemistry at the University of Innsbruck and after graduation there acquired work experience with Magnum Photos, New York and worked as an assistant to Erich Hartmann, also from Magnum Photos, New York. He completed his studies at Goldsmiths College, University of London with a master's degree in art, image & communications. His exhibitions include: 2000: "Fourteen People", Galerie im Taxispalais, Innsbruck; 2001: "WegZiehen", Frauen Museum, Bonn; 2004: "Guschlbauer weiche Kokosbusserl", Alte Schmiede, Vienna; 2005: "unrealities", Fotoforum West, Innsbruck. His numerous publications include: 2000: "Fourteen People", Weidle Verlag, Bonn, Germany; 2000: catalogue "Familie Foto Familie", Ethnographisches Museum Schloss Kittsee, Burgenland; 2003: "Guschlbauer weiche Kokosbusserl", Skarabaeus Verlag, Innsbruck.

Roman Hollenstein

Roman Hollenstein, who holds a doctorate in history of art and architecture, first worked as a research assistant for the Collections of the Prince of Liechtenstein in Vaduz and Vienna. He has also worked as a freelance exhibition organiser at the Kunstmuseum Basel (Monet: The Water Lilies). He taught at the Hochschule für Gestaltung in Zurich. As a member of the board he was head of the department of art history at the Swiss Institute for Art Research in Zurich from 1987 to 1990. Since 1990 he has worked for the Neue Zürcher Zeitung

wo er die Kunsthandelsbeilage aufbaute und die Architekturbeilage erweiterte. Als Feuilleton-Redakteur zeichnet er für die Gebiete Architektur, Denkmalpflege und Design verantwortlich. Neben Aufsätzen und Kritiken in der Neuen Zürcher Zeitung publizierte er zur Kunst um 1800, zur internationalen zeitgenössischen Kunst, zur Schweizer Kunst, zur zeitgenössischen Schweizer Architektur, zur Museumsarchitektur, zum Synagogenbau sowie zur Architektur in Israel.

Bettina Schlorhaufer
Sie war zuletzt als Kuratorin der Ausstellung und des Buches „Gion A. Caminada – Cul zuffel e l'aura dado" („Architektur mit den Winden") im Auftrag von „kunst Meran" tätig, sie studierte Kunstgeschichte und Geschichte an der Universität Innsbruck und absolvierte ein Post-doc-Studium in Kunst-Management am Institut Supérieur de Management Culturel in Paris. Bettina Schlorhaufer ist Verfasserin von Büchern und Artikeln, z. B. in architektur.aktuell (Springer Verlag, Wien-New York) und fungiert als Kuratorin der Galerie im „Rabalderhaus" in Schwaz, Tirol.
Ihre wissenschaftlichen Interessen gelten im Bereich der Baugeschichte Persönlichkeiten wie Franz Baumann, über den sie bereits mehrere Arbeiten veröffentlich hat, sowie dem Bauen in den Alpen, wo sie sich im Besonderen mit der aktuellen bzw. unmittelbar bevorstehenden urbanistischen Entwicklung der Gebirgsregionen und der rasanten Veränderung der Landschaft beschäftigt.

Walter Zschokke
Geboren 1948 in der Schweiz, Architekturstudium an der ETH Zürich (Diplom 1973, Dr.sc.techn. ETH 1986). Seit 1985 in Wien als Architekt, Ausstellungsgestalter, Kritiker und Publizist tätig. Seit 1988 regelmäßige Architekturkritiken, u. a. in: „Spectrum" (Die Presse, Wien).

danti l'arte e l'architettura. Come redattore dell'inserto Feuilleton si occupa di architettura, di conservazione dei beni culturali e di design.
Parallelamente agli articoli per Neuen Zürcher Zeitung ha pubblicato anche articoli e saggi sull' arte dell'800, l'arte contemporanea internazionale, l'arte svizzera, l'architettura contemporanea svizzera, l'architettura museale, l'edificazione delle sinagoghe e anche sull'architettura in Israele.

Bettina Schlorhaufer
Curatrice di recente della mostra e del progetto editoriale "Gion A. Caminada – Cul zuffel e l'aura dado" ("Architettura dei Venti") sempre per Merano arte, ha studiato storia e storia dell'arte all'università di Innsbruck, e ha conseguito un dottorato in management culturale presseo l' Institut Supérieur de Management Culturel a Parigi. È autrice di libri e articoli per la rivista "architektur.aktuell"(edizioni Springer, Vienna-New York) e lavora come curatrice nella "Galerie im Rabalderhaus" a Schwaz, in Tirolo.
I suoi interessi spaziano dalle personalità della storia della costruzioni come Franz Baumann, del quale ha promosso diverse opere, agli edifici nelle Alpi, dove si interessa in particolare dell'attuale sviluppo urbanistico delle regioni dell'arco alpino e dei rapidi cambiamenti che investono il paesaggio.

Walter Zschokke
Nasce in Svizzera nel 1948, si laurea in architettura presso ETH di Zurigo (diploma 1973, Dr.sc.techn.ETH 1986). Dal 1985 lavora e vive a Vienna come architetto, si occupa inoltre di allestimenti di mostre ed è anche critico e pubblicista. Dal 1988 scrive regolarmente critiche di Architettura, in "Spectrum" (die Presse, Vienna).

(daily newspaper) in Zurich, where he has built up the art market supplement and expanded the architecture supplement. As editor of the feature pages he is responsible for the areas architecture, monument conservation and design. In addition to essays and critiques in the Neue Zürcher Zeitung he has published on art around 1800, international contemporary art, Swiss art, contemporary Swiss architecture, museum architecture, synagogue building as well as on architecture in Israel.

Bettina Schlorhaufer
Bettina Schlorhaufer was most recently curator of the exhibition and book "Gion A. Caminada – Cul zuffel e l'aura dado" ("Architecture with the Winds") commissioned by "kunst Meran". She studied art history and history at the University of Innsbruck and completed post-doctorate studies in art management at the Institut Supérieur de Management Culturel in Paris. She is the author of several books and articles, for example in architektur: aktuell (Springer Verlag, Wien-New York) and acts as the curator of the "Galerie im Rabalderhaus" in Schwaz, Tyrol.
Her specialist interest in the field of building history focuses on personalities such as Franz Baumann about whom she has published several works, as well as on the theme of building in the Alps where she examines current and future urban developments in mountainous regions, as well as the rapid changes they cause to the landscape.

Walter Zschokke
Walter Zschokke was born in 1948 in Switzerland. He studied architecture at the ETH in Zurich (degree 1973, Dr.sc.techn. ETH 1986). He has worked since 1985 in Vienna as an architect, exhibition designer, critic and journalist. Since 1988 he has regularly published pieces of architectural criticism, for example in: "Spectrum" (Die Presse, Vienna).

Das Auge denkt

Sehen ist denken

Das Auge erinnert, fügt zusammen, ergänzt, berechnet, verwirft, vergleicht und interpretiert.

Was wir entwerfen, sind Wahrnehmungsvorgänge. Komplexe Botschaften mit Lichtgeschwindigkeit. Licht, dessen kleinste Veränderung wahrgenommen wird, Licht, das immer wirkt, als bewusster und überwiegend unbewusster Eindruck. Wirkungen und Reaktionen, die im Inneren unseres mentalen und physischen Systems ablaufen und die wir verstehen müssen, um den Entwurfsprozess zu ermöglichen.

Die Architektur, das Licht

Nicht dazu, nicht darüber, nicht aufgesetzt, sondern mittels und aus der Architektur heraus wird Licht zum Transmitter. Die Idee, die Botschaften von Material und Textur, der Zweck, die Orientierung, Stimmung und Atmosphäre – integrativ gestaltete Beleuchtung vermittelt selbstverständlich.

Architektur hat eine jahrtausende alte Tradition, Kunstlicht ist erst 100 Jahre jung. Deshalb vielleicht immer noch die fast kindliche Freude, dass wir es erzeugen können, und deshalb auch die fast ausschließliche quantitative Betrachtung. Die Beleuchtung bestimmt im wesentlichen die Atmosphäre, die Stimmung von Außen- und Innenräumen. Architektur und Stadträume immer noch in fast zufälligem, beliebigem Licht? Die Wirkung von ergänzendem Kunstlicht, die Nachtgestalt unserer Außenräume, Atmosphäre, die im Zusammenhang mit der Architekturwirkung gestaltet ist, befreit von beliebigen Lichteinsätzen, Schattenkanten; blendenden und irreführenden Lichtquellen.

Die Wirkung, der Einfluss und überhaupt der ganze Wahrnehmungsprozess sind die Grundlagen der Lichtgestaltung, nicht elektrotechnische Parameter oder abstrakte Beleuchtungsstärkenwerte.

In den letzten Jahren entstandene Südtiroler Architekturprojekte zeigen Wege auf, wie Licht neben Kunst und Bauphysik konzeptionell und integrativ gedacht und entworfen werden kann, kostenneutral und ökonomisch.

In Zukunft gilt es, völlig überzogene normative Empfehlungen zu hinterfragen, um ressourcenschonende Lichtanlagen mit geringen Anschlusswerten und reduzierten Leuchtenstückzahlen zu installieren.

Weniger Licht, bessere Wahrnehmungsbedingungen.

Licht ist sichtbar.
Manfred Draxl

conceptlicht at

a 6068 mils / innsbruck
eschenweg 3
tel +43 5223 53692
fax +43 5223 536925

Costruire il futuro

In Italia e nel mondo, da oltre un secolo costruiamo il futuro.

Nata dal patrimonio di esperienza di due grandi imprese italiane, la Rizzani de Eccher è oggi uno dei principali gruppi italiani nel settore delle costruzioni. Il gruppo si articola in diverse società che operano, in Italia ed all'estero, nel general contracting, nei servizi di ingegneria e nella produzione di attrezzature specialistiche.

Rizzani de Eccher S.p.A.
Via Buttrio - Frazione Cargnacco
33050 Pozzuolo del Friuli (UD) - Italy
Tel. +39 0432 6071
Fax +39 0432 522336
mail@rizzanideeccher.com

www.rizzanideeccher.com

GUFLER
HOLZWERKSTATT

I – 39012 Meran/o
via Kuperion Str. 26
Tel. +39/0473/448259
Fax +39/0473/440777
www.gufler.com
info@gufler.com

einige unserer Referenzen
alcune nostre referenze

Freibad Schenna / Lido di Scena
Meldeamt Meran / Ufficio anagrafe di Merano
Bahnhof Marling / Stazione ferroviaria di Marlengo
Turnhalle Wenter - Meran / Palestra Wenter - Merano
Altes Krankenhaus Meran / Vecchio ospedale di Merano
Kirche Leifers / Parrocchia di Laives
kunst Meran / Merano arte
Sparkasse Meran / Cassa di Risparmio di Merano
Università Bozen / Università di Bolzano
Turnhalle Tramin / Palestra Termeno
Realgymnasium Sterzing / Liceo scientifico Vipiteno
Restaurant Messe Bozen / Ristorante Fiera di Bolzano
Residence Meran 2000 / Residenza Merano 2000
Raiffeisenkasse Meran / Cassa rurale di Merano
Rechtsanwaltskanzlei - / Studio legale - Prof. Dr. Rland Riz
Hotel Vigilius / Albergo Vigilius mountain resort

Offizieller Thoma Holz100 Haus - Partner

Peter Senoner LEM & LUD (2002-05) Installationsansicht - LEM Bronzeguss, Kryolithglas 200 x 50 x 45 cm - LUD Bronzeguss 60 x 25 x 25 cm - Foto: Othmar Prenner

EINE BEGEGNUNG

Wie war das? Wie ist das?
Zusammenarbeit zwischen Architekt und Leuchtenhersteller.
Meist beginnen "die Dinge" ja weit vor dem eigentlichen Beginn. Vielleicht waren es die Leuchtenmuster im Büro meines Vaters - diese verzinkten Blechzylinder wo im Kreuz aufgeschnittene, nach hinten gebogene, Blechdreiecke farbige Gussglasbrocken hielten, die dieses 'Selber' machen von Leuchten initiierte. Jedenfalls war von ersten Bau weg das künstliche Licht ein Anliegen. 25000.- öS kostete damals eine Leuchte im Treibhaus; und diese wurde schon "hinterlistig" aus einem noch teureren - nicht ganz funktionierendem, "einsamen" Prototypen entwickelt, ganz geliebt wurden sie nie - trotzdem - ich mag sie immer noch - ein bisschen primitiv, irgendwie zwischen Werkstattleuchte und Luster, diese komische "Linsenlusterleuchte". Neun Stück - 225000.- öS das war schon verrückt damals - für das Alternative Kulturzentrum. Aber immerhin - für's Licht im Café ....
Mit Halotech begann's dann 10 Jahre später. Eigentlich diesmal mit etwas völlig nebensächlichem. Mit einer

ZIMMERSIGNALNOTLEUCHTE. ICH WUSSTE NACH WETTBEWERBSGEWINN, DASS ICH DIESE DOCH PRÄGENDEN, ÜBLICHEN ALTERSHEIMNOTLEUCHTEN EINFACH NICHT "HABEN WOLLEN WERDE". UND. DIE "NACHBARN" BAUTEN LEUCHTEN; UND DER HERR MIT DEN LANGEN HAAREN SCHIEN SYMPATHISCH. EINE DIESER STANDARD SIEMENSLEUCHTEN ORGANISIERTE ICH MIR, SOGAR SCHON VOR DER EINREICHUNG DES PROJEKTS. DAMIT BESUCHTE ICH DIE NACHBARN. "WAS KANN MAN DA MACHEN". UND ES ENTSTAND ETWAS VÖLLIG NEUES - ZUSAMMEN - AM TISCH.

IM LAUFE DER ZEIT ENTSTANDEN ZAHLREICHE LEUCHTEN ZU EIGENTLICH ALLEN MEINEN PROJEKTEN. ICH VERSTAND DAS LICHT AUS LEIDENSCHAFT, ABER AUCH, DASS EINE GEKANTETE BLECHSCHACHTEL BILLIGER IST, ALS EINE SCHÖNE GEFRÄSTE BOX; BEKAM GEFÜHL FÜR METALLVERARBEITUNG IM KLEINEN UND KONNTE DADURCH BEEINFLUSSEN WOHIN SICH DER PREIS BEWEGT, UNABHÄNGIG VOM EIGENTLICHEN LICHT. MIT LICHT UND MATERIAL JONGLIEREN. ZUSAMMENSITZEN!

UND - DAS WICHTIGSTE: DIE KUNST BESTEHT, WIE ÜBERALL, MIT MÖGLICHST WENIG, HIER MIT LICHT - DEM RAUM STIMMUNG ZU GEBEN. DAS HÖREN LEUCHTENHERSTELLER NICHT GERNE. HALOTECH SCHON!

Rainer Köberl, Architekt
Weihnachten 05

LICHTFABRIK HALOTECH
Ferdinand-Weyrer-Straße 5, 6020 Innsbruck, Tel.: +43-512-269064

maßstab : qualität

regensberger innenausbau
industriezone 7, I-39032 sand in taufers | zona industriale 7, 39032 campo tures
t 0039 0474 678281, f 0039 0474 678872 | e-mail info@regensberger.com, www.regensberger.com

„....Container by Niederstätter"

Hauptdepot Steg
Steg 1 - Atzwang

Depot Vinschgau
Handwerkerzone Vetzan 123
39028 Schlanders

Depot Pustertal
Nordring 13
39031 Bruneck

Niederstätter AG
Achille-Grandi-Straße 1
39100 Bozen
Tel. 0471 061100
Fax 0471 061101
info@niederstaetter.it
www.niederstaetter.it

Niederstätter

Wenn alle so wären wie wir, würden wir uns ändern, um nicht so zu sein, wie alle anderen – diesem Leitfaden haben wir uns mit Herz und Hand verschrieben und einige Ergebnisse sehen Sie auf den Bildern dieser Seite. Weitere Informationen finden Sie auf unserer Homepage und den ganzen Rest bei einem persönlichen Gespräch – wir freuen uns schon darauf...

www.arredis.it

Arredis GmbH
Gewerbezone Kalten Keller 1
I-39040 Barbian (BZ)
Tel. 0471 65 30 11, Fax 0471 65 32 42
E-mail: info@arredis.it

Yosyag – Young syn Age in Meran

Sennibar und Senni-Mila-Shop in Bruneck: schlüsselfertige Ausführung aller Arbeiten

Bund der Genossenschaften Legacoopbund in Bozen

Trias

Leben, wohnen, arbeiten.

Romstrasse 48 A, 39012 Meran
Tel. 0473 237 811

Ein besonderer Dank gilt den Institutionen und Sponsoren, deren finanzielle Unterstützung wesentlich zum Entstehen dieses Buches beigetragen hat. Ihr Engagement ermöglicht ein nachhaltiges und freundschaftliches Zusammenwirken von Kultur, Architektur und Wirtschaft in Südtirol und darüber hinaus.

Un sentito ringraziamento va alle istituzioni e agli sponsor che con il loro contributo e sostegno hanno reso possibile la realizzazione di questa pubblicazione. Il loro impegno culturale è alla base di una fertile e amichevole collaborazione tra la cultura edile architettonica e commerciale che muove dall'Alto Adige.

Particular thanks are also due to the institutions and sponsors whose financial support made a vital contribution to the production of this book. Their commitment has made possible lasting and collegial collaboration between culture, architecture and business in South Tyrol and beyond.

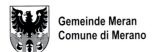

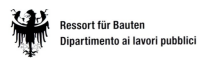